FRAMING THE ISLANDS

POWER AND DIPLOMATIC AGENCY IN PACIFIC REGIONALISM

FRAMING THE ISLANDS

POWER AND DIPLOMATIC AGENCY IN PACIFIC REGIONALISM

GREG FRY

Australian
National
University

PRESS

PACIFIC SERIES

For my mother and father, Dorothy June McCann (1917–1999)
and Ronald Gordon Fry (1916–2016)

ANU PRESS

Published by ANU Press
The Australian National University
Acton ACT 2601, Australia
Email: anupress@anu.edu.au

Available to download for free at press.anu.edu.au

ISBN (print): 9781760463144
ISBN (online): 9781760463151

WorldCat (print): 1124640656
WorldCat (online): 1124640666

DOI: 10.22459/FI.2019

Cover design and layout by ANU Press

Contents

Abbreviations ix

Acknowledgements xi

1.   Introduction: Framing Oceania 1

2.   Rethinking the political meaning of Pacific regionalism 23

3.   The 'South Seas' in the imperial imagination. 43

4.   Colonial regionalism 61

5.   The South Pacific experiment. 77

6.   The decolonisation of regional governance 101

7.   The postcolonial regional polity. 125

8.   Regional self-determination 151

9.   Negotiating regional security in the Cold War 167

10.   Negotiating Pacific island development in the
      post-independence era 191

11.   The neoliberal ascendancy and its critics 217

12.   Reframing regional security in the post–Cold War era 249

13.   The 'new' Pacific diplomacy and the transformation
      of regionalism. 275

14.   Conclusion: Power and diplomatic agency
      in Pacific regionalism 305

Bibliography 327

Index 373

Abbreviations

ADB	Asian Development Bank
ANU	The Australian National University
ANZUS	Australia, New Zealand and United States Security Treaty
AOSIS	Alliance of Small Island States
ATOM	Against Testing on Moruroa
CROP	Council of Regional Organisations of the Pacific
CRPG	Committee of Representatives of Participating Governments
DWFN	Distant Water Fishing Nation
EEC	European Economic Community
EPA	Economic Partnership Agreement
EPG	Eminent Persons' Group
EU	European Union
EWTP	Engaging With the Pacific Leaders
FEMM	Forum Economic Ministers Meeting
FFA	Forum Fisheries Agency
FFMM	Forum Foreign Ministers Meeting
FICs	Forum Island Countries
FLNKS	Front de Libération Nationale Kanak et Socialiste (Kanak and Socialist National Liberation Front)
FRSC	Forum Regional Security Committee
G-77	Group of 77
IMF	International Monetary Fund
MDG	Millennium Development Goal

MSG	Melanesian Spearhead Group
NGO	non-governmental organisation
OCTA	Office of the Chief Trade Adviser
PACER	Pacific Agreement on Closer Economic Relations
PACER Plus	Pacific Agreement on Closer Economic Relations Plus
PACP	Pacific members of the African, Caribbean and Pacific group
PANG	Pacific Network on Globalisation
PIDF	Pacific Islands Development Forum
PIF	Pacific Islands Forum
PIFS	Pacific Islands Forum Secretariat
PIPA	Pacific Islands Producers' Association
PNA	Parties to the Nauru Agreement
PNG	Papua New Guinea
PSIDS	Pacific Small Island Developing States
PTCCC	Pacific Transnational Crime Coordination Centre
RAMSI	Regional Assistance Mission to Solomon Islands
SDG	Sustainable Development Goal
SPARTECA	South Pacific Regional Trade and Economic Co-operation Agreement
SPC	South Pacific Commission
SPEC	South Pacific Bureau for Economic Co-operation
SPF	South Pacific Forum
SPREP	Secretariat of the Pacific Regional Environment Programme
UN	United Nations
UNCTAD	United Nations Conference on Trade and Development
UNDP	United Nations Development Programme
UNFCCC	United Nations Framework Convention on Climate Change
USP	University of the South Pacific
WTO	World Trade Organization
YWCA	Young Women's Christian Association

Acknowledgements

The research for this book began in 1975 as fieldwork for an ANU thesis on the developing indigenous commitment to Pacific regionalism in the early postcolonial period. Over the next 45 years, the politics of regional diplomacy in the Pacific remained a primary focus of my research at The Australian National University and the University of the South Pacific. This book represents an attempt to share the results of this long research journey. I have therefore incurred a very large debt to an enormous number of people across the Pacific island region.

From that first field trip around the Pacific island region in 1975, I particularly want to thank the following for their insights on the early years of indigenous Pacific regionalism: Ahmed Ali, Poseci Bune, Karanita Enari, Kilifoti Eteuati, Teo J. Fuavai, Francis Hong Tiy, Tony Hughes, George Kalkoa, David Kausimae, Sione Kite, Robert Kwaniarara, Ruth Lechte, Falemoti Malietoa, Solomon Mamaloni, James Maraj, Robin Mauala, Spike Padarath, Vainga Palu, Macu Salato, Fred Sevele, Tomasi Simiki, Claire Slatter, Mefi Tauleolo, Fa`amatala Toleafoa, Palauni Tuiasosopo, Mahe Tupouniua, Sione Tupouniua, Sitiveni Vete, Albert Wendt and Felix Wendt.

Over the next three decades, I regularly visited the Pacific island region, including as a visiting fellow and lecturer at the University of the South Pacific and as an observer at the annual conferences of the South Pacific Commission. I owe a debt of gratitude to the many national, regional and international agency officials, as well as academic colleagues and journalists, who assisted me with my research into the politics of a very complex and evolving regional system over this period. They include Ron Crocombe, Graeme Dobell, Sean Dorney, Helen Fraser, Jemima Garrett, Sitiveni Halapua, Epeli Hau`ofa, Tarcisius Kabutaulaka, Robert Kiste, Joji Kotobalavu, Brij Lal, Noel Levi, Vito Lui, Nic Maclellan, Iosefa Maiava, Vijay Naidu, Tess Newton Cain, Patteson Oti, Maureen Penjueli, Ropate

Qalo, Sitiveni Ratuva, Suliana Siwatibau, Claire Slatter, Asofou So`o, Bill Standish, William Sutherland, Larry Thomas, Iulai Toma, Dan Tufui, Morgan Tuimalealiifano, Kampati Uriam and Garry Wiseman.

Between 2011 and 2016, I was fortunate to be working at the University of the South Pacific as coordinator of the Graduate Studies in Diplomacy and International Affairs program. This was a time of extraordinary excitement in the development of a region-wide assertion by Pacific island leaders of a right to 'chart their own course' in regional and global affairs. I wish to acknowledge the many people who helped me understand the significance of these developments. They include Transform Aqorau, Nicola Baker, Collin Beck, Sala George Carter, Peter Folau, Nicolette Goulding, Vili Hereniko, Peter Kenilorea junior, Suzanne Lowe Gallan, Iosefa Maiava, Fulori Manoa, Sovaia Marawa, Wesley Morgan, Litia Mawi, Gordon Nanau, Anna Naupa, Robert Nicole, Raijeli Nicole, Michael O'Keefe, Patteson Otti, Maureen Penjueli, Cristelle Pratt, Claire Slatter, Jope Tarai, Fei Tevi, Sandra Tarte, Kaliopate Tavola and Dame Meg Taylor.

I particularly want to thank my close friends in Fiji who made Suva a home away from home over this long period of research: Nicola Baker, Vijay Naidu, Jen Namgyal, Raijeli Nicole, Robert Nicole, Ropate and Salote Qalo, Claire Slatter, William and Helen Sutherland, Daryl and Jacqui Tarte, Sandra Tarte, Larry Thomas and Morgan and Eileen Tuimaleali'ifano. *Vinaka vakalevu*!

From 2016 to 2018, the Asia-Pacific College of Diplomacy (APCD) at The Australian National University provided the ideal intellectual environment in which to write the last four chapters of the book, which bring together the contemporary story of Pacific regionalism as a series of diplomatic contests over security, development, climate change and the ownership of regional institutions. I would like to acknowledge Pauline Kerr for proposing the attachment and APCD Director Geoffrey Wiseman for his strong support for the project.

I am indebted to the historian Dipesh Chakrabarty, who in the mid 1990s, introduced me to postcolonial theory and, in particular, to the work of Edward Said. The reading of *Orientalism* marked a major turning point in my approach to understanding the politics of Pacific regionalism. I also have an intellectual debt to Epeli Hau`ofa, whose influential essay 'Our Sea of Islands' also led me in the direction of foregrounding the power inherent in the normative policy frames that were projected on to the Pacific island region over time. His influence on the project intensified when I met him at his home at Wanadoi in 1997 while he was working on 'The Ocean in Us'. It is sad that he did not live to see his own counter-regional discourse—of a powerful Oceanic identity, emphasising the power of large ocean states rather than small islands—become the dominant 'Blue Pacific' ideological framing of the region in the second decade of the twenty-first century.

I thank Chris Reus-Smit, my colleague in the Department of International Relations at The Australian National University, for encouraging me to locate the Pacific experience of regionalism in a broader global theoretical debate about the political meaning of regionalism, and Tony Payne of Sheffield University for suggesting an approach that would foreground global epochs and their dominant ideas as the crucial context in which the regional diplomatic contests occur. I also acknowledge the influence of Geoffrey Wiseman's concept of global diplomatic culture as a stimulus in examining the transitions in diplomatic culture at the regional level in the Pacific.

I am very grateful to those at ANU Press who have managed the publication process—to Stewart Firth, Chair of the Pacific Editorial Board, who has been very encouraging and supportive at all stages of the process; to Emily Hazlewood, ANU Press deputy manager; and to Teresa Prowse, who designed the cover. I would also like to thank Jan Borrie for her meticulous copyediting and indexing, and Mary-Lou Hickey for her editorial support and assistance at earlier stages of the process.

I would like to acknowledge Karina Pelling of the College of Asia and the Pacific Cartography, at The Australian National University, for creating the maps; and Tom Foley, ANU Pacific librarian, for helping me locate source materials in the Menzies Library.

Such a long journey also requires strong support from friends and colleagues along the way. I particularly want to thank Nicole George, Paul Keal, Alvaro Marques, Gavin Mount, Jacinta O'Hagan, Heather Rae, Amin Saikal, Peter Van Ness, Terence Wesley-Smith and Geoffrey Wiseman.

Paul D'Arcy, Chris Reus-Smit, Tony Payne, Sandra Tarte and Terence Wesley-Smith gave very strong support to the project over a long period and were kind enough to read parts of the manuscript and provide invaluable feedback. I would particularly like to express my heartfelt gratitude to Tony Payne, who was enormously helpful throughout, providing intellectual engagement with the argument, close reading of the text and personal encouragement. I am not sure the book would have been finished without Tony's strong support in the final months.

Finally, I owe enormous gratitude to my wife, Annie, who has lived with this project all the years we have lived together. It would not have seen the light of day had it not been for her quiet patience and loving support as I worked through countless versions of the chapters over so many years. It has also been a joy to share some of that journey with her in Suva, Honiara, Rarotonga and Port Vila. I would also like to thank my daughter, Nikki, who grew old enough during the life of this project to critically and persuasively engage with the argument and to suggest the title of the book.

Finally, I would like to acknowledge my father, Ron Fry, who constantly provided enthusiastic encouragement for the project for 40 years; at age 100, he decided he could not wait any longer to see it finished, but he had confidence that it would happen.

Greg Fry
Canberra
October 2019

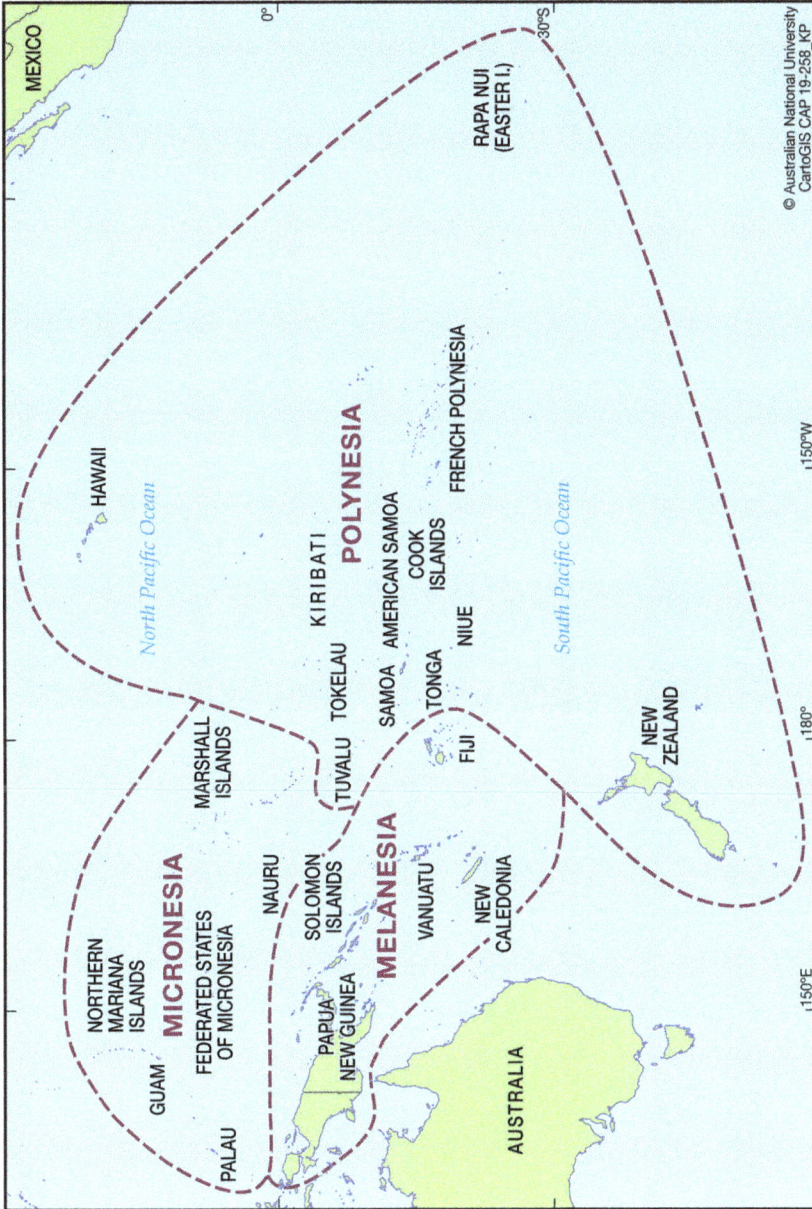

Map 1 Cultural areas of the Pacific

Source: CartoGIS, The Australian National University.

Map 2 200-mile exclusive economic zones of the Pacific

Source: CartoGIS, The Australian National University.

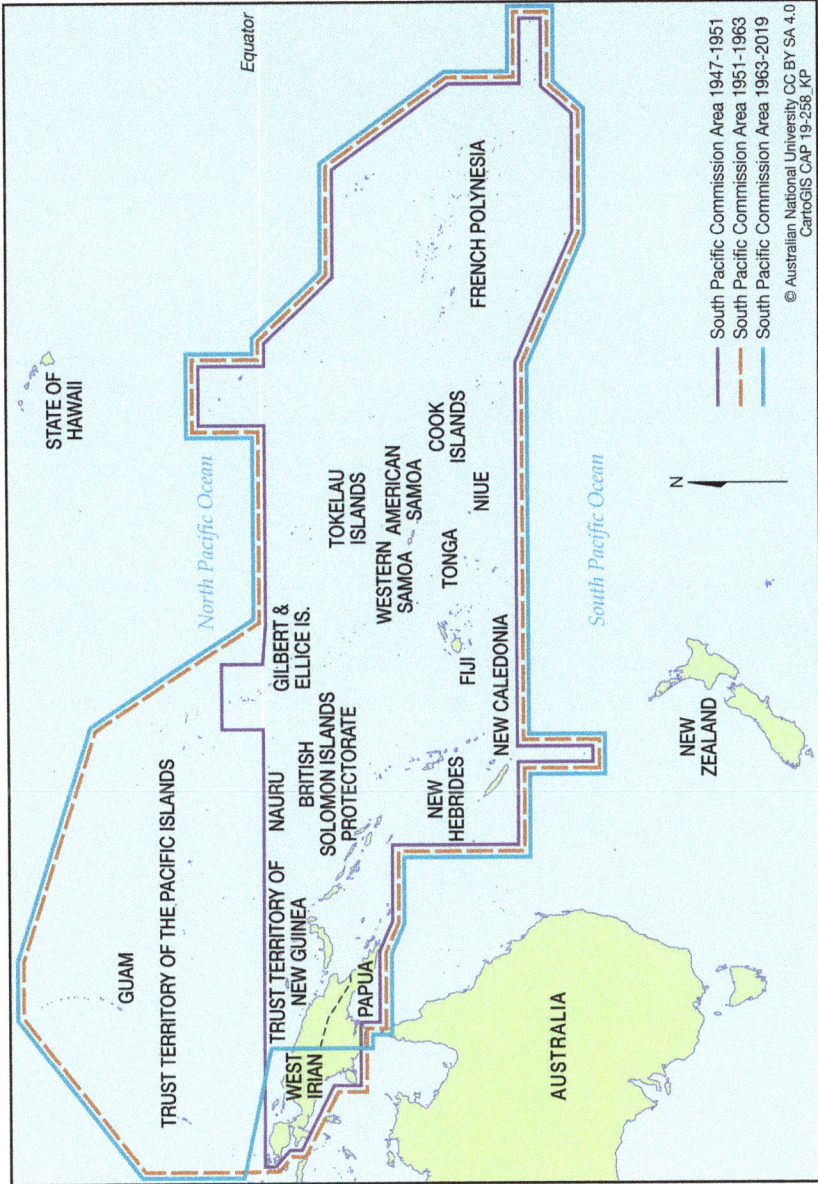

Map 3 South Pacific Commission boundaries

Source: CartoGIS, The Australian National University.

1

Introduction: Framing Oceania

This book tells the story of power and diplomatic agency in Pacific regionalism against the backdrop of a changing global order and a changing political situation within Pacific societies and states. Its purpose is to explore the political significance of this region-building activity for Pacific societies and its political meaning within a broader global politics. It examines the power of the regional site of politics and diplomacy vis-a-vis that of the postcolonial state, on the one hand, and that of the global order, on the other. It asks whether this region-building activity has mattered, why it has mattered and for whom? It also engages with a wider debate concerning the power and authority of regionalism and regional governance in global politics.

The political puzzle

Since its origins in late–eighteenth-century European thought, the idea of placing a regional frame around the Pacific islands and seeing this bounded entity in the context of a wider global system has never been just an exercise in geographical mapping. This imagining of the Pacific— sometimes termed Oceania, the South Seas, the south-west Pacific or the South Pacific—has always been a political exercise. Contending regional projects and visions of the colonial and postcolonial eras— whether promoted by larger powers, administrators, church people, island governments, international agencies, sovereignty movements, non-governmental organisations (NGOs), politicians, artists or social scientists—have been part of a political struggle concerning how 'Pacific islanders', scattered in hundreds of societies over an area of ocean larger than Africa, should live their lives.

As a result of this intensive region-making activity, the region now appears to be an entrenched objective reality. It is a name in a school textbook, a category in the social sciences, a department in the foreign ministries of larger states and an assumed category in global management by international agencies, the United Nations and international NGOs. The idea also has solid expression in the bricks and mortar of a vast array of regional organisations such as the Secretariat of the Pacific Community, the Pacific Islands Forum Secretariat, the University of the South Pacific and the Secretariat of the Pacific Regional Environment Programme. It is reflected in the efforts of hundreds of regional public servants, and it is codified in countless regional treaties.

The political meaning of this region-building activity for postcolonial Pacific societies is nevertheless puzzling. It is clearly much more than a set of formal organisations for interstate cooperation. It goes beyond a set of international agreements and conventions on everything from security, conflict resolution and fishing to shipping, trade, nuclear issues and the environment. The Pacific is invoked sometimes as a regional cultural identity; sometimes as a political community with its own values, norms and practices; sometimes as a collective diplomatic agent; and sometimes as a site of political struggle. Situated between the global arena and local states and societies, it also appears as a mediator of global processes— sometimes as an agent for outside forces and sometimes as a 'shield' for local practices.

Despite the extensive region-building activity in the Pacific during and since the colonial period, there has been a tendency on the part of practitioners and scholars to undervalue its significance. The story of the politics of region-building has been overshadowed by the story of state-building. This is not surprising. In a postcolonial context, the state is where sovereignty sits. It is the site of formal government, lawmaking, taxation and policing. Accordingly, indigenous leaders and international agencies have focused their efforts on the stability and development of states. For the international community and for scholars, state failure—or potential failure—is seen as a key problem. This further encourages state-building as the primary focus of efforts to influence how Pacific islanders should live in modern political communities.

By contrast, the regional political community in the Pacific context appears to be of less political significance. Region-building efforts have not sought to seriously dilute state sovereignty within a new integrated regional entity. The region is not a new 'state-in-the-making' with state-like attributes. Unlike the state, the region has no executive power, and there is no ethical obligation on the part of a 'citizen' to the regional political community. The Pacific region therefore does not appear on the scholarly radar as a powerful political entity or political community, at least in comparison with the emergent Pacific island states.

Ironically, the dismissal of the political significance of Pacific regional politics is most evident in the positions of those scholars and practitioners most concerned with establishing effective Pacific regional governance in the future as a means of dealing with the perceived failure or limitations of the postcolonial state. Seen from this viewpoint, the regional level has the potential to moderate the excesses of national governance through establishing obligations to regional norms about good governance and economic management. It is also seen as having the potential to assist in resolving conflict, to increase the economic viability of the smaller states through the pooling of limited resources and to provide a *cordon sanitaire* against global terrorism. While the position of these commentators endorses the *potential* significance of regional governance, it implicitly dismisses the significance of the region-building of the past century.[1]

Against these positions, this book tells the story of region-building in the Pacific as a politically significant exercise inextricably intertwined with state-building. To do so, it introduces a novel conceptualisation of the power associated with region-building and regional governance. The novelty of the approach adopted here has its main roots in the postcolonial writings of Edward Said and Epeli Hau῾ofa, and in particular

---

1   Satish Chand, ed., *Pacific Islands Regional Integration and Governance*, Canberra: ANU E Press and Asia Pacific Press, 2005; Dave Peebles, *Pacific Regional Order*, Canberra: ANU E Press and Asia Pacific Press, 2005; Kennedy Graham, ed., *Models of Regional Governance for the Pacific: Sovereignty and the Future Architecture of Regionalism*, Christchurch, NZ: Canterbury University Press, 2008; and the various proposals surrounding the emergence of the 'Pacific Plan' under the auspices of the Pacific Islands Forum in 2003–04, as surveyed in G.E. Fry, 'Whose Oceania? Contending Visions of Community in Pacific Region-Building', in Michael Powles, ed., *Pacific Futures*, Canberra: Pandanus Books, 2006, pp. 204–15.

their emphasis on the power of normative regional framing in influencing how policy is determined towards the people within that regional frame.[2] But I depart from Said's assumption of the West as an undifferentiated whole framing a powerless Orient. Instead, I posit the regional framing as a contested space in which various local and global framings of the Pacific compete for influence on how Pacific islanders should live their lives. This approach is developed and explained in Chapter 2.

In relation to the question of which interests prevail in these normative contests, I develop a line of argument that rejects the usual assumptions concerning who has power in regionalism. This includes those theories that emphasise 'the hegemon', the largest state in the regional community, the broader 'West' or 'globalisation' as being the main shaper of the direction of region-building. I also argue against those who emphasise states as the only influential actors in region-building projects. Drawing on positions within debates in Pacific history and anthropology about Western/islander power relations in the nineteenth century, I argue for a much more contingent answer to the question 'who is the region-building enterprise for' than that implied in conventional approaches— and one that assigns a good deal more political agency to local states and societies. I develop this approach in Chapter 2.

The region in world politics

This study seeks to engage with a broader debate about the changing political character of regionalism in world politics. Although not all those involved in this debate would go as far as endorsing W.W. Rostow's claim, made at the beginning of the 1990s, that a 'coming age of regionalism' is *the* metaphor for our times, there is increasing support for the idea that regions have come to matter in world politics in a way that they did not before.[3] From the mid 1990s, academics, policymakers and commentators began to speak not only of a 'new regionalism', to capture a new institutional and policy emphasis on regionalism, but also of a new

2   Edward W. Said, *Orientalism*, New York: Vintage Books, 1979; Epeli Hau`ofa, *We Are the Ocean: Selected Works*, Honolulu: University of Hawai`i Press, 2008.
3   W.W. Rostow, 'The Coming Age of Regionalism: A "Metaphor" for our Time?', *Encounter*, 74(5), 1990: 3–7.

status for regions within the world order.[4] Peter Katzenstein offered the image of 'a world of regions' to capture what he saw as the move towards a new 'political arena' for world politics;[5] and prominent security theorists suggested that global security must now be seen largely as the sum of its regional parts rather than as a product of a global logic.[6] Economists also talked of a new significance for regionalism: Jagdish Bhagwati asserted the emergence of a 'second regionalism' and Wilfred Ethier of a 'new regionalism'.[7] For other scholars, the regional political community offered a possible new site of promotion of world-order values of democracy and human rights, and a possible site of resistance to globalisation.[8]

While the scholars of 'new regionalism' recognise that there is a 50-year history of regional schemes and doctrines of various kinds, they see these previous efforts as ineffective, as having been idealistic non-starters or as derivative of hegemonic power, and therefore not powerful in their own right. This, they imply, is the first time that developments in regionalism are occurring in a form that really matters in world politics. They also come together in seeing this new regionalism as occurring as a response

4   See, for example, Norman D. Palmer, *The New Regionalism in Asia and the Pacific*, Lexington, MA: Lexington Books, 1991, particularly Ch. 1; Louise Fawcett and Andrew Hurrell, eds, *Regionalism in World Politics: Regional Organization and International Order*, Oxford: Oxford University Press, 1995; Björn Hettne and András Inotai, *The New Regionalism: Implications for Global Development and International Security*, Helsinki: United Nations University World Institute for Development Economics Research, 1994; Andrew Gamble and Anthony Payne, eds, *Regionalism and World Order*, Basingstoke, UK: Macmillan, 1996; David A. Lake and Patrick M. Morgan, eds, *Regional Orders: Building Security in a New World*, University Park, PA: Pennsylvania State University Press, 1997; Jean Grugel and Wil Hout, eds, *Regionalism Across the North–South Divide: State Strategies and Globalization*, Abingdon, UK: Routledge, 1999; Peter Robson, 'The New Regionalism and the Developing Countries', *Journal of Common Market Studies*, 31(3), 1993: 329–48.

5   Peter J. Katzenstein, in Atul Kohli, Peter Evans, Peter J. Katzenstein, Adam Przeworski, Susanne Hoeber Rudolph, James C. Scott, and Theda Skocpol, 'The Role of Theory in Comparative Politics: A Symposium', *World Politics*, 48(1), 1995: 14–15.

6   Barry Buzan, *People, States and Fear: The National Security Problem in International Relations*, Brighton, UK: Wheatsheaf, 1983; Barry Buzan, *People, States and Fear: An Agenda for International Security Studies in the Post–Cold War Era*, 2nd edn, London: Harvester Wheatsheaf, 1991; Muthiah Alagappa, 'Regionalism and Conflict Management: A Framework for Analysis', *Review of International Studies*, 21(4), 1995: 359–87; Mohammed Ayoob, 'From Regional System to Regional Society: Exploring Key Variables in the Construction of Regional Order', *Australian Journal of International Affairs*, 53(3), 1999: 247–60.

7   Jagdish Bhagwati, 'Regionalism and Multilateralism: An Overview', in Jaime de Melo and Arvind Panagariya, eds, *New Dimensions in Regional Integration*, Cambridge: Cambridge University Press, 1993, pp. 22–51; Wilfred J. Ethier, 'The New Regionalism', *Economic Journal*, 108(449), 1998: 1149–61.

8   Richard Falk, 'Regionalism and World Order after the Cold War', *Australian Journal of International Affairs*, 49(1), 1995: 1–15.

to a new era of post–Cold War globalisation of markets and associated neoliberal economic ideas, to a new US-led global security order and to unprecedented global governance through the United Nations.

For these scholars, the key question around the power of regionalism concerns how to characterise the politics of the relationship between regions and the global order or globalisation, on the one hand, and— at least for some—the relationship with the state and society, on the other. This is a very different question about the power associated with regionalism to that posed by an earlier generation of regionalism scholars who focused on the regional integration process itself and who asked whether the regional organisation was moving towards the goal set by the integration model underpinning European regionalism. For the scholars of 'new regionalism', the answers regarding the political significance of new developments in regionalism are varied. For some, this constitutes a transformation—a shift in the site of political agency, community and identity away from the state. For others, the region is not displacing the state; it is merely adding another layer of politics—a move that has prompted the image of a 'new medievalism'.[9]

The Pacific may seem to be an odd vantage point from which to reflect on this broader debate about the changing power of regions within world politics. Although encompassing an enormous area of ocean, this is, after all, a region of small island societies, its states marginal to global politics in geographical, economic and cultural terms, and its population relatively small. The argument of this study proceeds, however, on the assumption that the Pacific experience nevertheless has something of real interest to contribute to an exploration of the power of regions and their political role between local societies and global processes, precisely because of this marginality. In fact, it could be argued that just as the claims of empires are often best tested in their remotest outpost, so a peripheral region offers a unique vantage point from which to explore global relevance.

The Pacific also offers an interesting counter to Europe, the region that so often drives general understandings of the political meaning of region. As a postcolonial, non-Western region, the Pacific offers a series of insights derived from being at the receiving end of imperialism. For example, there are issues to do with the transfer of the regional idea from colonial powers

---

9   Andrew Gamble and Anthony Payne, 'Conclusion: The New Regionalism', in Andrew Gamble and Anthony Payne, eds, *Regionalism and World Order*, Basingstoke, UK: Macmillan, 1996, pp. 247–64.

to the new elites, and in the postcolonial period there are issues to do with the struggle over Western ideas and practices that accompany economic assistance, UN interventions or World Bank conditions, or the clash with cultural processes, landownership and customary practices. In this context, Europe is an important source of global processes and influential ideas, whereas the Pacific has typically been subject to them.

The Pacific experience further challenges the impression often given in the academic literature that it is only recently that regionalism has become important in global politics. The reality is that the region has provided a locus of power since the colonial period, and even before. The story does not therefore begin in the late 1980s, when the so-called new regionalism emerged. The idea of region—in the sense of a category, affinity or identity larger than the nation, tribe or state, with a geographical, although often shifting, basis—was a major part of global politics throughout the postcolonial period in particular. Whether as part of Cold War security management, developmental theory and practice, Third World anticolonialism, collective self-reliance strategies or as an expression of cultural identity, region-building was advanced by powerful states, local elites, social movements, anticolonial forces, environmentalists, human rights activists, strategists and global institutional managers.

The Pacific region-building story, then, suggests some interesting questions for understanding the political meaning of 'region' more generally, but particularly in postcolonial areas. The centrality of colonialism, postcolonialism and the Cold War in defining and remaking 'region' in all non-European regions is an important common feature. The region has provided an important site for the contests over the norms and practices of postcolonial societies in relation to security, development, ecology, cultural identity and sovereignty. The Pacific provides a good example of this, but similar stories could be told for South-East Asia, parts of Africa, the Caribbean and Eastern Europe.

The region in Pacific studies

This region-building story is not one that has been told in the general histories of the Pacific island region.[10] These general Pacific histories are interpretations of what happened inside, or across, an assumed geographical category called the Pacific, the Pacific island region or the South Pacific. This study, on the other hand, provides a political history of 'the idea of the Pacific' itself. It is concerned with the political significance of the contest over what this idea should stand for and its expression in forms of regional governing ideas and social institutions that impact on local societies. Even in *The Cambridge History of the Pacific Islanders*, in which Donald Denoon and his co-authors recognise the constructed nature of the subcategories of the Pacific island region—Melanesia, Polynesia and Micronesia—and of the boundaries of states, this reflection is not applied to the regional category itself except in a brief section on Pacific regional identity.[11]

This study nevertheless engages with the central question animating these general Pacific histories: how to characterise the relationship between 'the West' ('Europeans' or 'the global system') and Pacific island societies since the late-eighteenth century. What agency should be assigned to Pacific peoples in this engagement? Whereas these general works bring together narratives of local engagements to build up a larger picture of regionwide experiences, this study is concerned with the regional site of engagement per se—in knowledge systems, diplomacy and institutions. As indicated above, in examining this regional site of politics, I draw on, and adapt, the approaches developed within the historiographical debate underlying Pacific history (together with key interventions from Pacific anthropology) concerning local engagements between Pacific societies and the European world in the precolonial and colonial periods.

---

10   Deryck Scarr, *The History of the Pacific Islands: Kingdoms of the Reefs*, Melbourne: Macmillan, 1990; Donald Denoon, Malama Meleisea, Stewart Firth, Jocelyn Linnekin, and Karen Nero, *The Cambridge History of the Pacific Islanders*, Cambridge: Cambridge University Press, 1997; Ian C. Campbell, *Worlds Apart: A History of the Pacific Islands*, Christchurch, NZ: Canterbury University Press, 2003; Kerry R. Howe, Robert C. Kiste, and Brij V. Lal, eds, *Tides of History: The Pacific Islands in the Twentieth Century*, Sydney: Allen & Unwin, 1994.
11   Denoon et al., *The Cambridge History of the Pacific Islanders*.

As will become evident in Chapter 3, where I explore the South Seas in the imperial imagination, the insights of three historians, in particular, provide an important conceptual entry point for this study. Oskar Spate's magisterial study *The Pacific Since Magellan* is built around the idea of the Pacific as a European construction.[12] Where Spate's approach becomes crucial for this study is his consideration of the importance of the various European ideas about Pacific islanders and Pacific island societies in the late-eighteenth and early-nineteenth centuries. This focus on the European constructions of what Pacific island societies and Pacific islanders were, and could be, and seeing these as a function of particular points in debates about European society, is the beginning of the story I tell here. Art historian Bernard Smith had already made a similar argument in *European Vision and the South Pacific 1768–1850*,[13] and Kerry Howe later developed the theme in *Nature, Culture, and History*.[14]

While these writers' insights are invaluable as an intellectual opening, it is important to note how this study develops these ideas in relation to the politics of regionalism. Where the main concern of these authors is to provide an understanding of shifting European ideas and how these construct competing notions of Pacific 'reality', I am concerned with the political significance of these imaginings and representations in relation to colonial and postcolonial authority over how Pacific societies should be organised. Furthermore, I am concerned not with how the Pacific shapes key ideas in European theory about how European society should be organised, but with how these changing and contesting European representations have impacted on Pacific societies. Whereas these authors are focused on the late-eighteenth and nineteenth centuries, this study focuses mainly on the colonial and postcolonial periods of the twentieth and twenty-first centuries. Furthermore, by dint of the period with which they are concerned, they are focused only on *European* representations of the Pacific, whereas this study is also interested in indigenous representations of the region.

---

12   O.H.K. Spate, *The Pacific Since Magellan. Volume 1: The Spanish Lake*, Canberra: Australian National University Press, 1979.
13   Bernard Smith, *European Vision and the South Pacific 1768–1850: A Study in the History of Art and Ideas*, Oxford: Clarendon Press, 1960.
14   Kerry R. Howe, *Nature, Culture, and History: The 'Knowing' of Oceania*, Honolulu: University of Hawai`i Press, 2000.

Although they asked different questions from this study, the various accounts of regional institution-building in the Pacific each inform part of the story told here. Again, it is curious that this does not form part of the general histories of the Pacific. Richard Herr's chapter, 'Regionalism and Nationalism', in Howe et al.'s *Tides of History* is an important exception.[15] Ron Crocombe's influential early examination of regional identity and Uentabo Neemia's critique of the costs and benefits of regional cooperation until 1980 provide key dimensions of the regionalism question.[16] Other scholars, such as Sandra Tarte, Yoko Ogashiwa and Jeremy Carew-Reid, have provided important sectoral studies of regional cooperation in fisheries management, nuclear issues and environmental issues, respectively.[17] There have also been very useful recollections from key players in regional organisations: W.D. Forsyth and T.R. Smith, former secretaries-general of the South Pacific Commission (SPC), focused on the operations of the commission between the 1940s and the 1960s, and Ratu Sir Kamisese Mara's *The Pacific Way* provides invaluable reflections on his time as a leading participant in the decolonisation of regionalism.[18]

Hau'ofa's influential essay 'Our Sea of Islands'[19] is the Pacific work that is closest to the concerns of this study, and which has been a major influence on the conceptual approach adopted here. Hau'ofa draws our attention to the power associated with unquestioned characterisations of the postcolonial Pacific—and of the typical island society and economy—prevalent in the social sciences. He sees this knowledge reflecting the

15   Richard A. Herr, 'Regionalism and Nationalism' (in Kerry R. Howe, Robert C. Kiste, and Brij V. Lal, eds, *Tides of History: The Pacific Islands in the Twentieth Century*, Sydney: Allen & Unwin, 1994, pp. 283–99); this is a persuasive examination of institutional developments until the late 1980s. His unpublished PhD is the definitive work on the political history of the South Pacific Commission from 1947 to 1974. See R.A. Herr, 'Regionalism in the South Seas: The Impact of the South Pacific Commission 1947–1974', PhD dissertation, Duke University, Durham, NC, 1976.

16   Ron Crocombe, *The Pacific Way: An Emerging Identity*, Suva: Lotu Pasifika Productions, 1976; Uentabo Fakaofo Neemia, *Cooperation and Conflict: Costs, Benefits, and National Interests in Pacific Regional Cooperation*, Suva: Institute of Pacific Studies, University of the South Pacific, 1986.

17   See Sandra Tarte, 'Negotiating a Tuna Management Regime for the Western and Central Pacific: The MHLC Process 1994–1999', *Journal of Pacific History*, 34(3), 1999: 273–80; Yoko S. Ogashiwa, *Microstates and Nuclear Issues: Regional Cooperation in the Pacific*, Suva: Institute of Pacific Studies, University of the South Pacific, 1991; Jeremy Carew-Reid, *Environment, Aid and Regionalism in the South Pacific*, Pacific Research Monograph No. 22, Canberra: National Centre for Development Studies, The Australian National University, 1989.

18   W.D. Forsyth, 'South Pacific: Regional Organisation', *New Guinea and Australia, the Pacific and South-East Asia*, 6(3), 1971: 6–23; T. R. Smith, *South Pacific Commission: An Analysis after Twenty-Five Years*, Wellington: Price Milburn for the New Zealand Institute of International Affairs, 1972; Ratu Sir Kamisese Mara, *The Pacific Way: A Memoir*, Honolulu: University of Hawai'i Press, 1997, Ch. 18.

19   Epeli Hau'ofa, 'Our Sea of Islands', in Eric Waddell, Vijay Naidu, and Epeli Hau'ofa, eds, *A New Oceania: Rediscovering Our Sea of Islands*, Suva: University of the South Pacific, 1993.

dominant mindsets outside the Pacific and not depicting the reality of the experience of ordinary Pacific islanders. Furthermore, he sees these authoritative depictions as consistently belittling and continuing a practice prevalent in the colonial period. In a position reminiscent of Said, he also sees these depictions as powerful. Taught through authoritative institutions, Pacific islanders take these on as self-images. Hau`ofa is speaking here, he says, as a teacher at the regional university where he had taught these 'small is powerless' depictions for many years. They are, he argues, as disempowering as when men were called 'boys' in colonial Melanesia. This study expands on these insights in examining policy-related knowledge contests about how the Pacific island region should be depicted over time.

Hau`ofa's work features in this study not only because of his influential ideas concerning the power of these regional characterisations within knowledge systems and the sources of this power in the authority of knowledge; his ideas are also *part* of the political contest over legitimate political community conducted at the regional level on which this study is focused. Hau`ofa is joined by many other indigenous Pacific scholars who have been engaged in the debate about the decolonisation of Pacific knowledge and who, in so doing, have become part of the political contest over region-building examined in the following chapters.[20] Other scholars become relevant to the study when they enter a debate about how the idealised 'Pacific island society' should be organised. Ideas about how Pacific islanders—thought of collectively—should live have been prominent and powerful throughout the period covered here. Anthropological studies were important in the promotion of native welfare in the Pacific in the 1940s; Pacific geographers were important to the idea of the Pacific island economy, strategic studies analysts to the construction of a Pacific strategic entity and economists to the construction of a neoliberal economic order in the 1990s and 2000s. All of these influences will be considered in the chapters that follow.

---

20 See, for example, Subramani, 'The Oceanic Imaginary', *The Contemporary Pacific*, 13(1), 2001: 149–62; Konai Helu Thaman, 'Decolonizing Pacific Studies: Indigenous Perspectives, Knowledge, and Wisdom in Higher Education', *The Contemporary Pacific*, 15(1), 2003: 1–17; Vilsoni Hereniko, 'Indigenous Knowledge and Academic Imperialism', in Robert Borofsky, ed., *Remembrance of Pacific Pasts: An Invitation to Remake History*, Honolulu: University of Hawai`i Press, 2000, pp. 78–91.

Which regional boundaries?

Before we enter a version of the Pacific region-building narrative that emphasises the above commitments, assumptions and questions, we should note the extent to which the boundaries of the framed region, and the name given to it, have been in continual contest. These boundaries have varied according to time, issues and perspectives on a particular issue. They are indicative of political aspirations and political outcomes. Even the regional institutional arrangements have not succeeded in establishing a fixed idea of regional boundaries.

What we can say, however, is that at the core of the idea of the Pacific are the thousands of islands scattered across the central and southern Pacific Ocean, including to the north of the equator. They stretch from the Micronesian islands just south of Japan and east of the Philippines, south to Papua New Guinea, and south-east along the Melanesian chain to New Caledonia, and then east across the Polynesian Pacific to Tahiti. These societies are organised into nine independent states (Fiji, Kiribati, Nauru, Papua New Guinea, Samoa, Solomon Islands, Tonga, Tuvalu and Vanuatu); five associated states (Cook Islands, Federated States of Micronesia, Niue, Palau and Marshall Islands); and eight dependent territories—of France (New Caledonia, Wallis and Futuna, and French Polynesia), the United Kingdom (Pitcairn Islands), New Zealand (Tokelau) and the United States (American Samoa, Guam and the Commonwealth of the Northern Mariana Islands). It also includes, importantly, the sea around them—extending out to 200 nautical miles for some purposes. This area—which is recognised as constituting the boundaries of the oldest regional organisation, the SPC (renamed the Pacific Community at its fiftieth anniversary conference in October 1997)—covers more than 30 million square kilometres (not including Australia and New Zealand).

In terms of politically weighty decision-making, such as treaty-making and collective diplomacy, the membership is a little smaller because, until 2016, only independent states were recognised in the Pacific Islands Forum (PIF). But, even here, the regional boundaries seen as relevant for political action include the dependent territories, as, for example, when the organisation takes a collective position on decolonisation in New Caledonia or nuclear issues in French Polynesia. For some purposes— and particularly for sovereignty movements and regional NGOs, such as the Pacific Islands Association of Non-Governmental Organisations and the Nuclear-Free and Independent Pacific movement—the cultural and political identities of the Pacific stretch to an extended outer boundary incorporating Hawai`i in the north, New Zealand in the south, Easter Island (a territory of Chile) to the east and West Papua, a province of Indonesia, in the west. Although they are members of the Pacific Community and the PIF, Australia and New Zealand do not always put themselves within the regional boundaries. This in/out behaviour is an important variation in what is seen as constituting 'the region'. Australia, for example, sees itself as part of the South-East Asian and Indian Ocean regions as well as the Pacific. But, despite its significant region-making initiatives in the other two areas, it is the Pacific where it has seen itself as having a leadership and management role.

As we have already noted, the region has also attracted different names—South Pacific, Pacific islands, Pacific, Oceania, South Seas, south-west Pacific—at different times or on different issues, or even by different actors in relation to the same issue. To add to the confusion, some of the names used to refer to this island area have also been used at times to refer to a broader region, which encompasses the Pacific Rim. In this study, there is no attempt made to standardise the naming, but rather, this contest becomes part of the political story. Names can signal ownership, belonging and political purpose. Thus, for example, the move from the use of Pacific or the Southern Ocean or the South Sea (singular) to the South Seas in the nineteenth century depicted a new consciousness of the island region against the broader Pacific Rim. The tension over naming resurfaced in the 1980s when Pacific island countries north of the equator demanded that the regional nomenclature reflect their inclusion. This was generally resolved through the shift from South Pacific to the more general 'Pacific islands', as in the change to Pacific Islands Forum, or 'Pacific', as in the change to Pacific Community. Similarly, naming became part of regional debates about what regional governance should stand for in the 1990s when 'Oceania' began to reemerge as a way of denoting a different position from official regionalism, which employed 'Pacific island region'.

Where to begin?

As in the case of 'the idea of Europe', the chosen starting point for considering 'the idea of the Pacific' has implications for the authority of particular positions in current debates about who belongs to the region, who should speak on its behalf and what the ideas should stand for. The answer to the question of 'where to begin' is also highly dependent on how we conceptualise the authority of regional governance and how we think about the politics of region-building. For those who see regional governance as having significance only when there is the level of integration and the kind of coercion that are present in the European model of regionalism, the story has not yet begun. This, for example, has been the position of the economists and policymakers around the Australian Government's influential attempts to create 'pooled regional governance' in the Pacific since 2003. On the other hand, for those seeing political significance as lying mainly in formal institutional development, the story typically began in 1944–47 with the formation of the SPC, but with acknowledgement of forerunners in colonial institutions such as the Central Medical School and the Western Pacific High Commission.

For some prominent Pacific islanders involved in this debate, the political legitimacy of the regional idea hinges particularly on who is promoting it and on the degree to which there is indigenous control or participation in these regional visions. Even within this position, however, there is wide variation on the suggested starting point for telling the region-building story. Macu Salato, Fijian secretary-general of the SPC from 1975 to 1979, claimed that South Pacific regionalism had its 'first appearance in the world … at the Sixth South Pacific Conference' in 1965 of the SPC[21]—a reference to the 'Lae Rebellion' (the conference was held in Lae, Papua New Guinea) in which Pacific island leaders first challenged the right of colonial powers to direct the regional organisation without indigenous participation. Rather than seeing the 'rebellion' as the next stage in an already long history of regional thinking, it was important for Dr Salato that earlier regional thinking, in which Pacific islanders had no voice, be delegitimated.[22]

Working from the same principle, Ratu Mara, then prime minister of Fiji, and the leading figure in the indigenous regional movement of the 1970s, asserted a more distant origin for the idea of the Pacific. He argued that contemporary indigenous regional identity had its roots not in the rebellion associated with decolonisation in the 1960s or the coming together of Pacific island representatives in the South Pacific

---

21   E. Macu Salato, 'South Pacific Regionalism: "Unity in Diversity"', *South Pacific Bulletin*, 26(Fourth Quarter), 1976: 30–5, at p. 35.
22   ibid., p. 31.

Conference from 1950, but in ancient connections among Pacific island peoples. He further asserted that indigenous regional connections were interrupted by colonialism (rather than being a product of colonialism).[23] Hau`ofa developed this position in the 1990s as part of his advocacy of a new kind of regional thinking during his tenure as director of the Oceanic Centre for Arts and Culture at the University of the South Pacific (USP). He argued that, for thousands of years, there had been a network of connections across the Pacific, which was interrupted by colonialism. For Hau`ofa, the 'new Oceania' needed to draw on these unifying links of the past—the epic ocean voyages, the exchange relationships and the unifying Pacific Ocean that made Oceania a connected 'sea of islands' rather than remote 'islands in the sea'.[24]

In this study, I have chosen to begin the region-building story with the emergence of European imaginings of the Pacific around the time of the voyages of James Cook and Louis Antoine de Bougainville in the late eighteenth century. This choice follows from the conceptualisation of region-building and regional governance that I outlined earlier. I asserted that the idea of a Pacific island region emerged as a result of European imperialistic processes and that Pacific islanders later embraced the idea as a vehicle for negotiating these global ideas and processes. This is so whether 'region' is employed as a category, an identity, a community, as a shield against global forces or as an agent of them. Following this conceptual approach, the Pacific as a region of a larger global system is, at first, a construct of the European imagination and of European power. In the felicitous phrase of Spate, speaking of a broader geopolitical notion of the Pacific (and not of the peoples and societies within it, which are the subject of this study), it is to be seen as a 'European artefact'.[25] The story

---

23   Ratu Sir Kamisese Mara, 'Twenty-Fifth Anniversary Messages: South Pacific Commission', *South Pacific Bulletin*, 21(Second Quarter), 1972: 15–19, at p. 15; S.K. Sikivou, 'Statement to the Twenty-Eighth Regular Session of the UN General Assembly: 1973', in Ratu Sir Kamisese Mara, *Report on Foreign Affairs for the Period 10th October 1970 – 31st December 1973*, Parliamentary Paper No. 19, Suva: Parliament of Fiji, 1974, Appendix 111(d), p. 32; Ratu Sir Kamisese Mara, 'Regional Co-operation in the South Pacific', Address at the University of Papua New Guinea, Port Moresby, 27 May 1974, pp. 1–2; Ratu Sir Kamisese Mara and Michael Somare, 'Joint Communiqué', Port Moresby, 27 May 1974; South Pacific Forum Secretariat, 'Summary Record and Final Press Communiqué', in *Leaders' Communiqué: Fifth South Pacific Forum, Rarotonga, Cook Islands, 20–22 March 1974*, Suva: South Pacific Forum Secretariat, 1974, p. 10.
24   Epeli Hau`ofa, 'Our Sea of Islands', *The Contemporary Pacific*, 6(1), 1994: 148–61.
25   O.H.K. Spate, 'The Pacific as an Artefact', in Niel Gunson, ed., *The Changing Pacific: Essays in Honour of H. E. Maude*, Melbourne: Oxford University Press, 1978, pp. 32–45.

therefore begins when global actors start to place a conceptual frame around the Pacific islands and want to influence how people within that frame should live.

This approach may appear to deny a previous long and rich history of Pacific island societies, and therefore to reinforce the tendency to see Pacific history as only beginning with European imperialism.[26] This study should not be interpreted as a denial of the idea of precolonial connectedness and affinity between various Pacific island societies as put forward by Ratu Mara and Hau`ofa. In the approach I adopt here, I fully acknowledge the importance of the long history of interisland voyaging, of the existence of kingdoms (such as the Manono-based Kanokupolu kingdom), 'empires' (such as the Yap empire) and tributary systems (such as in Ponape and the Caroline Islands) all spread over large areas of the Pacific Ocean. I also acknowledge the extensive trading and exchange networks (such as the *kula* trading ring around the eastern end of New Guinea) and the longstanding intermarriage among the royal families of Fiji, Tonga and Samoa.[27] In terms of the concerns of this study, this history of island connectedness becomes germane to the story when postcolonial indigenous actors draw on this rich history to engage in contemporary debates about how Pacific islanders should engage in regional politics within a global context. But these ancient connections, while sometimes conducted over vast areas of ocean, were not 'framing Oceania' in a global context; Oceania was their vast known world.

There is an important exception: the Hawaiian kingdom's nineteenth-century vision of a Polynesian confederation, encompassing Fiji, Tahiti, Samoa and Tonga.[28] This was a political project to create a Hawaiian-led Oceanic entity that could both defend the kingdoms of Polynesia from

---

26   Epeli Hau`ofa, 'Epilogue: Pasts to Remember', in Robert Borofsky, ed., *Remembrance of Pacific Pasts: An Invitation to Remake History*, Honolulu: University of Hawai`i Press, 2000, pp. 453–71.

27   See, for example, Paul D'Arcy, *The People of the Sea: Environment, Identity, and History in Oceania*, Honolulu: University of Hawai`i Press, 2006, Chs 1, 5; Niel Gunson, 'Early Society and Authority Systems', in Brij V. Lal and Kate Fortune, eds, *The Pacific Islands: An Encyclopedia*, Honolulu: University of Hawai`i Press, 2000, pp. 132–9; Bronislaw Malinowski, *Argonauts of the Western Pacific*, London: George Routledge & Sons, 1922; Patrick Kirch, *On the Road of the Winds: An Archaeological History of the Pacific Islands before European Contact*, Berkeley, CA: University of California Press, 2000, pp. 191–3.

28   The case for seeing Hawai`i's Polynesian confederation diplomacy project as the first assertion of an indigenous attempt to build a regional Oceanic identity in relation to an impinging world system is persuasively made by Lorenz Gonschor, *A Power in the World: The Hawaiian Kingdom in Oceania*, Honolulu: University of Hawai`i Press, 2019. He provides a comprehensive and definitive examination of the Hawaiian diplomatic project over several decades.

imperial control and be recognised as a 'power in the world', much like the Hawaiian kingdom had already achieved for itself. The vision was strongly supported by Kings Kamehameha III and IV, but was largely devised by Charles St Julian, their *haole* (white) adviser. The vision was promoted actively as a diplomatic project from the 1880s. Under King Kalākaua, extensive relations were pursued with the Polynesian kingdoms: King Pomare V of Tahiti, King George Tupou I of Tonga and Malietoa Laupepa of Samoa. The project was, however, severely constrained by the growing impact of imperial powers on the sovereignty of these kingdoms. Ultimately, it was the Missionary Party's 'Bayonet Coup' of 1887, followed by the American invasion and occupation of Hawai`i, which abruptly stopped any further development of the idea of a Polynesian confederation. The confederation nevertheless has its historical significance in being the first indigenous project to create an Oceanic regional grouping to control the pressures of an impinging global system. It also has contemporary importance as a source of inspiration for attempts to forge subregional links among Polynesian leaders in the Polynesian Leaders' Group.[29]

Structure of the book

Before entering the story of Pacific region-building, Chapter 2 first explains why conventional conceptual approaches to regionalism make it difficult to see the political significance of the long history of Pacific regionalism. It then develops an alternative approach, focused on the power of normative framing, which, it is argued, provides a more useful way of examining the political meaning of the region-building experience in the Pacific. This chapter also explains the conceptual approach employed to examine the authority of Pacific regional governance and posits a novel approach to the question of whom the regionalism project serves at different points in its history.

Chapter 3 focuses on the emergence of the idea of the Pacific in the European imagination and its gradual incorporation into colonial and other European practices of the imperial era. The chapter examines the application of powerful European normative frames associated with the imperial era—such as trusteeship, native welfare and self-determination—

---

29   See, for example, Tupuola Terry Tavita, 'Samoa PM Talks about the Polynesian Leaders Group', *Savali*, 28 November 2011, available from: www.pireport.org/articles/2011/12/01/samoa-pm-talks-about-polynesian-leaders-group.

through the content given to an idealised 'Pacific islander', such as a 'dying race', inferior and civilisable, and to the policies these characterisations informed. It argues that the idea of the Pacific region was one that arose in relation to contending global discourses promoted by the imperial powers and other European agents, such as missionaries—some concerned with welfare, others with self-determination and others with the maintenance of colonial control. These normative contests were contests among Europeans and were mainly about the agency—or potential agency—of Pacific islanders. Ultimately, they had a significant influence on Pacific island societies given the relationship to colonial policies.

These same contests over the appropriate political agency of Pacific islanders can be clearly seen in the formal colonial region-building examined in Chapter 4. The chapter examines the establishment of the main regional organisation, the SPC, and the tensions it set up between the colonial powers and the emergent indigenous elite experiencing decolonisation in their own territories. These tensions would not finally be resolved in favour of indigenous agency until the late 1970s. The chapter emphasises the impact of World War II as a major influence on the ideas and interests that coalesced to promote the modern idea of the Pacific island region and its regional governance.

In contrast to the ambitious sweep of Chapters 3 and 4, which range over the long period from the late eighteenth century to the end of the Pacific War in the early 1940s, Chapter 5 focuses on one event that took place over four days in November 1950 at the assembly hall of the Nasinu Teachers' College in Suva. This was the first regional meeting of Pacific islander representatives drawn from 20 territories across the broad region from West Papua in the west to Tahiti in the east. The South Pacific Conference was widely represented in the colonial press and policy papers as an 'experiment' in creating a regional identity among Pacific island leaders. The idea of creating a sense of affinity among these diverse peoples was seen as working 'against the odds', but in the end was proclaimed a success. It was also an experiment in whether Pacific islanders could be seen as ready to begin the process of political development and to participate in the decisions affecting Pacific communities. In the view of these observers, the values of the idealised Pacific community were assumed to be those associated with the modernisation trajectory. It is also here that we first hear the voices of Pacific islanders in the region-building story. Polynesian chiefly leaders and Melanesian 'high achievers' saw the experiment as novel and embraced the idea of a regional identity.

Chapter 6 is concerned with the impact of the political change associated with decolonisation in the 1960s and 1970s on the development of regional identity among the emergent political elites in the so-called New South Pacific. It first examines the regional norms concerning decolonisation and legitimate statehood; moves to an exploration of the link between ideas of national self-determination and regional identity; and then examines the institutional expression of a commitment to self-determination in the efforts to take control of the colonial regional structures and to create new organisations, particularly the South Pacific Forum (SPF). It ends with an examination of the 'Pacific way' ideology, developed at this time, and asks what it said about region-level community, identity and agency.

Chapter 7 explores various dimensions of the new postcolonial regional polity of the 1970s—its founding ideas and normative framework, and its participants and organisational expressions. We first explore the emergent regional 'society of states' and its founding principles and procedural norms. We then examine the influence of global norms on the rituals of this emergent diplomatic culture. I argue that a broader regional polity—a regional political community—emerged at this time, which included regional and international NGOs, international agencies and academics, as well as state leaders and officials. I further argue that the tensions around agency arose not only between independent countries and the leaders of dependent territories and between small states and Fiji, but also between Australia and New Zealand and the island countries. The regional discourse of Pacific and international NGOs raised alternative versions of the boundaries of Pacific identity to those that were accepted by the 'society of states' and offered another view on how societies should be organised and developed.

In Chapter 8, I examine the development of regional governance over the first two decades of the postcolonial era, set against the backdrop of a changing global order dominated by the Cold War. Here the focus is on the region as a site of politics over self-determination and in relation to three key aspects of regional governance: environmental protection, anticolonialism and political agency within regional decision-making.

Chapter 9 deals with how the region mediated the impact of the changing global strategic order in the 1970s and 1980s. In the postcolonial period, the Cold War was the dominant global strategic order within which island societies had to work. It was a major part of the region-building story because of the efforts of Western powers to encourage an idea of 'regional security' as a way of countering possible Soviet influence in the island region from the mid 1970s. From that time, various interests promoted distinct meanings of 'regional security', each with very significant implications for Pacific societies. The nuclear issue was central to this debate. It was the global issue of highest concern for all parties and the ultimate case of a contest over Pacific community, identity and agency. The chapter considers the quite different conceptualisations of the United States, Australia, New Zealand, the island states and antinuclear groups, and again includes the central role of social science (security studies) in defining a regional strategic entity, giving content to the idea of regional security and creating a security personality for the typical island state.

Chapter 10 is concerned with the efforts of Pacific islanders to collectively influence their relationship with the global economic order and promote development, and the efforts of outside economic partners and UN agencies to influence regional development norms and practices through a regional approach. The chapter also considers the regionally organised critique of these ideas. I characterise the period as a shift from the regional integration ideas of the 1970s to the collective diplomacy ideas of the 1980s. Again, the social sciences are seen as part of this story, and particularly in the set of assumptions created about 'Pacific economic man', the Pacific entrepreneur, the 'smallness' assumption and in relation to modernisation and integration theory. This chapter is particularly concerned with the power of ideas transmitted at the regional level to establish norms about the concept of development and appropriate development policies.

Chapter 11 deals with the post–Cold War period from the 1990s into the twenty-first century, focusing on the dominant global pressure on the Pacific community: the attempt to impose a regional economic order based on neoliberal principles and a related discourse of 'good governance'. It focuses on attempts by donor countries, particularly Australia, to introduce institutions of regional governance in finance, investment and trade and instil regional norms of accountability and transparency. As part of this, it examines the ideas of development studies and their influence on policy, and the response of the Pacific leaders and NGOs. It includes the debate over the regional free-trade area, which has continued as a key issue in the second decade of the twenty-first century.

Chapter 12 explores the attempt by Australia and New Zealand in the post–Cold War era to reconceptualise the regional security 'problem' in the Pacific, and to rethink the regional approaches to its solution. Australia and New Zealand now saw threats as emanating not from foreign powers, but rather from transnational forces interacting with the internal fragility and vulnerability of Pacific island states. Spurred initially in the early 1990s by global developments in transnational crime, then from 2000 by political crises in some Pacific island states, and then from 2001 by the global war on terror, Australia and New Zealand proposed ever deepening levels of regional integration to activate regional intervention both preemptively and at times of crisis. An attempt by Australia and New Zealand in 2018 to promote a geopolitical conceptualisation of Pacific regional security aimed at countering a perceived threat from China came up against a very different policy framing promoted by the Pacific island leaders—that of broader human security and climate change. This chapter examines this contest over the reframing of regional security and assesses its influence on regional security governance.

Chapter 13 examines a third key contest over region-building in the contemporary period: the emergence of a 'new' Pacific diplomacy and its challenge to the existing diplomatic culture, especially the question of who should control the regional institutions and the regional agenda. Primarily a contest over political agency, this brings the regional story back to the issues of the immediate post-independence period when Pacific island leaders asserted a Pacific right to regional self-determination. This chapter examines the implications of this contest for the framing of the regional architecture and for key areas of regional concern, particularly climate policy.

The concluding chapter returns to the question of the political meaning of Pacific regionalism as viewed through the unpacking of two key puzzles: first, what is the political significance of Pacific regionalism? And second, whom has this region-building project served? Who has power? In relation to the first puzzle, it makes an argument for viewing political significance not through the lens of the European model with its emphasis on integration and coercion, but rather through its political roles: as a regional arena for negotiating globalisation, as a source of regional governance through agreed norms, as a regional political community and as a diplomatic bloc. On the second puzzle, it considers conventional explanations of who has power in Pacific regionalism, focused on hegemonic states, globalisation and Pacific island states, before making an argument for a more complex amalgam of these explanations. It argues that how these complex power relations are resolved within Pacific regionalism at any given time is highly contingent. It suggests what the key contingent factors are based on this long history of Pacific regionalism.

2

Rethinking the political meaning of Pacific regionalism

The premise for this study is that existing conceptual approaches to regionalism make it difficult to 'see' the political significance of the long history of region-building in the Pacific and the political authority of the forms of regional governance that have eventuated at various points in that history. The first section of this chapter seeks to explain why this is the case. I then consider the openings provided by some theorists who go beyond the dominant 'new regionalism' approaches towards developing a more useful reading of the political meaning of regionalism outside Europe. In the third section, I build on these openings to develop a conceptual approach to thinking about the politics of region-building in Oceania. The fourth section develops a new approach to understanding the political authority of regional governance in the absence of coercion. Finally, I develop a novel approach to thinking about the ultimate political question: for whom has the region-building project been intended?

The limitations of conventional approaches

Early regionalist theory, which dominated the study of regions as political entities from the 1950s until the 1970s, associated the political significance to be attached to region-building with the degree of success in moving along a continuum towards full integration. Underpinning this approach was a commitment to the desirability of achieving integration for security and development purposes. The model was Western Europe. The European developments, which involved the prospect of the voluntary creation of a political unit larger than the nation-state, attracted the interest of political scientists. Prominent scholars such as Ernst Haas and Karl Deutsch saw this as a very significant development in international relations, which could be applied elsewhere, with benefits for the global order.[1] The approach they adopted is termed 'analytical neofunctionalism' because of its relationship to the neofunctionalist strategy for achieving political integration that underlay European regionalism.

The neofunctionalist strategy is a suggested means of moving from fully independent nation-states, through a stage of economic integration, and then on to full political unification. The approach adopted by Haas and other analytical neofunctionalists to the study of regionalism in Europe, and later in Africa and Latin America, reflected their concern with this strategy and with its proposed outcome—political integration or unification. They wanted to establish the structural conditions required for the neofunctionalist strategy to work.[2] The general theoretical question that governed their approach to the study of regionalism was: are there certain conditions under which economic integration of a group of nations automatically triggers political unity?[3] For them, the political significance of regionalism started when states began to surrender sovereignty in achieving a high level of regional integration such as a customs union. Regional schemes that had not achieved this stage of integration were seen as politically insignificant.

This conceptual approach implicitly employed the analogy of the state as a basis for judgement about the political significance of the regional entity. Seen through this lens, regions begin to matter when they start to look like states—with centralised authority, policy instruments that bite, coercive sanctions if required and fixed and acknowledged boundaries

1   The pioneering works in the field were E.B. Haas, *The Uniting of Europe: Political, Social and Economic Forces, 1950–57*, Stanford, CA: Stanford University Press, 1958; and K.W. Deutsch, *Political Community and the North Atlantic Area: International Organization in the Light of Historical Experience*, Princeton, NJ: Princeton University Press, 1957.

2   Robert Keohane and Joe Nye, 'International Interdependence and Integration', in F.I. Greenstein and N.W. Polsby, eds, *International Politics*, Reading, MA: Addison-Wesley Publishing, 1975, pp. 363–414, at pp. 379–81.

3   Joseph S. Nye, 'Patterns and Catalysts in Regional Integration', in Joseph S. Nye, ed., *International Regionalism: Readings*, Boston: Little, Brown & Co., 1968, pp. 333–49.

around given territory. With the failure of regional integration attempts outside Europe by the end of the 1970s, the political significance of this more restricted form of regionalism was generally dismissed.

To tell the Pacific story as a quest for the achievement of regional integration would require that we begin in the early 1970s with the stated goals and efforts of the postcolonial states to integrate their economies. We would focus only on regional institutions and cooperative schemes and see whether they were moving the region towards a new integrated entity. We would be particularly interested in the establishment of the South Pacific Bureau for Economic Co-operation (SPEC), the early commitment to promoting a regional free-trade area and the founding of a regional airline and a regional shipping line. With the failure of these integration attempts by the early 1980s, the story would trail off and the conclusion would be drawn that regionalism did not yet matter politically in the Pacific. In this formulation, power is associated with coercion and the focus remains firmly institutional.

The 'new regionalism' theorists who emerged during the mid 1990s were responding to what they saw as a substantial strengthening of existing regional institutions and the creation of a significant number of new regional associations among states since the mid 1980s.[4] The so-called new regionalism is usually taken to have its roots in the *Single European Act* of 1986 and the move by the Ronald Reagan administration to negotiate 'regional' preferential trade agreements with Canada and Israel. The subsequent profound deepening and widening of European integration in the 1990s—culminating in the Maastricht Treaty, together with the creation of the North American Free Trade Agreement in 1992—are cited as the most impressive institutional developments. However, more tentative developments in the economic arena in East Asia around the Asia-Pacific Economic Cooperation and Association of Southeast Asian Nations, and the dramatic increase in the number of new regional preferential trade agreements elsewhere in the world, were also seen as very important. The developments in Europe, Asia and North America, in particular, had by the mid 1990s suggested for many that the fundamentals of future world politics were to be found in the interaction

---

4   See Louise Fawcett and Andrew Hurrell, 'Introduction', in Louise Fawcett and Andrew Hurrell, eds, *Regionalism in World Politics: Regional Organization and International Order*, Oxford: Oxford University Press, 1995.

of these three powerful economic blocs.[5] Supporters of the notion of a new regionalism also point to the creation of new regional institutions and the reinvigoration of established ones in Latin America, the Middle East and Africa.[6]

While heralding the significance of a new wave of regionalism, these theorists at the same time implicitly denied the political significance of what went before. Despite the move away from the focus on regional integration and the shift to a central interest in the worldwide development of 'open regionalism', and its link to the globalisation of neoliberal ideas, the 'new regionalism' scholars also implicitly maintained the state analogy as their benchmark for judging political significance. The new regionalism was sparked first and foremost by new developments in European regionalism. Europe was therefore still seen implicitly as a model against which to view the global revival of regional associations. There was still a tendency to judge the power of new forms of regionalism elsewhere in terms of the degree of institutionalisation and formal organisation of governance.

Employing this lens, the Pacific would appear as part of Anthony Payne's 'pre-regionalist' governance category, which he uses to describe Asian regionalism compared with the more developed European regional governance model.[7] The assumption here is that governance is associated with a level of political authority indicated by formal institutional development and the surrendering of sovereignty. This misses the political significance of the Pacific experience with its very different forms of regional governance. As we have seen, this is a lens shared by a number of scholars and practitioners who view regional governance as a desired good in the Pacific case rather than as having already formed an important part of the region-building story since the colonial period.

---

5   The developments in economic regionalism are well surveyed in Andrew Wyatt-Walter, 'Regionalism, Globalization, and World Economic Order', in Fawcett and Hurrell, *Regionalism in World Politics*.

6   These new developments in regionalism in Asia, Latin America and Africa are surveyed in Gamble and Payne, *Regionalism and World Order*; W. Andrew Axline, ed., *The Political Economy of Regional Cooperation: Comparative Case Studies*, London: Pinter Press, 1994; and Grugel and Hout, *Regionalism Across the North–South Divide*.

7   Anthony Payne, 'Globalization and Modes of Regionalist Governance', in Jon Pierre, ed., *Debating Governance: Authority, Steering, and Democracy*, Oxford: Oxford University Press, 2000.

Openings to an alternative approach

How, then, should we think beyond the assumptions that regions must be significantly integrated and that formal regional governance is the key test of whether region-building should be seen as politically significant? How do we 'see' the political significance of forms of regionalism that fall below this threshold?

A first, important opening to this possibility is provided by Mohammed Ayoob's idea of adapting Hedley Bull's notion of 'international society' to regional international systems.[8] In this view, the regional 'society of states' is a minimal society in which certain limited rules are acknowledged by the constituent states based on mutual interest. Implicit in this position is that regions can matter, if only minimally, even where states are not integrating into a regional whole and where state sovereignty is not surrendered to a regional authority.

Told as the development of a 'society of states', the region-building story in the Pacific, for example, would begin in 1971 and would explore the gradual development of the rules and norms governing the emergent society of states, such as non-intervention, equality and cooperation. While Ayoob sees many Third World regions as not yet having achieved the status of a 'society of states'—and implicitly therefore as not having political significance—he would most likely see the Pacific as fitting his definition of such a society. This tells us some important things about the political role of regionalism in the Pacific that would be missed by those concerned only with integration or the surrendering of sovereignty entailed in free-trade areas, for example. But this is still a political significance derived from the power of the constituent states and their mutual interests. Its minimal social attributes do not really begin to get at the full political meaning of the regional site of politics in postcolonial contexts. It nevertheless provides a good starting point for thinking about this puzzle (the way in which a Pacific 'society of states' appears in the Pacific regional story is developed in some detail in Chapter 7).

Second, there are also important openings for an alternative understanding of the political significance of region-building in postcolonial regions among those theorists who see themselves as explicitly going beyond

---

8   Ayoob, 'From Regional System to Regional Society'.

the Eurocentric assumptions of the 'new regionalism' theorists. Such theorists have attempted to lessen the emphasis on formal organisation and to elevate instead the political significance of social institutions and norms in regional practice. Promoted mainly by those who study Asian regionalism, this perspective has created an awareness that regions matter in different ways in different parts of the world and, in particular, that Asian regionalism is significant even while it lacks the formal institutionalisation of Europe.[9] Fredrik Söderbaum makes a similar general point in relation to African regionalism—that the political purposes of state participants are very different from those assumed, and sometimes desired, by the 'new regionalism' theorists employing Europe as a model.[10]

Third, Peter Katzenstein's characterisation of 'the region' as a political *arena* provides an important starting point for 'seeing' the politics of region-building in the Pacific. Rather than being caught up in seeing regionalism as static, fixed formal institutional structures, or as an integrative process, this conceptualisation creates the basis for thinking about regionalism as a site of politics.[11]

Fourth, there are also potential theoretical openings in the efforts of some scholars to employ the analogy of 'the nation' to help in understanding the political meaning of 'region'. Here the focus is on identity and region-building by states for particular political/cultural purposes, and the power of region-building is implicitly tied up with the region's symbolic value as an 'imagined community'. Employed most prominently by Iver Neumann in relation to Europe and Amitav Acharya in relation to South-East Asia, this approach is very useful in introducing identity into the discussion of the political significance of region-building.[12] These analysts also usefully remind us that regions are political constructions. Rather than having an objective reality, they are therefore to be seen as *for* someone and *for* some purpose. The politics of construction therefore becomes important in understanding what the region stands for, politically speaking.

---

9   See, in particular, Kanishka Jayasuriya, ed., *Governing the Asia Pacific: Beyond the 'New Regionalism'*, New York: Palgrave Macmillan, 2004.

10   Fredrik Söderbaum, 'Modes of Regional Governance in Africa: Neoliberalism, Sovereignty Boosting, and Shadow Networks', *Global Governance*, 10(4), 2004: 419–36.

11   Peter J. Katzenstein, in Kohli et al., 'The Role of Theory in Comparative Politics'.

12   Iver Neumann, *Uses of the Other: 'The East' in European Identity Formation*, Minneapolis: University of Minnesota Press, 1999, pp. 113–15; Amitav Acharya, *The Quest for Identity: International Relations of Southeast Asia*, Singapore: Oxford University Press, 2000.

However, Neumann's and Acharya's positions are limited by their use of the Andersonian concept of 'imagined community' to explore the analogy of the nation.[13] Where Benedict Anderson was seeking to understand the deep cultural roots that create a 'life and death' attachment on the part of ordinary people to an imagined national community, these scholars are attempting to understand a community of states, with a much shallower level of affectation. To adapt Anderson's test for the existence of a national identity, Europeans are not about to die for the idea of Europe. This elite-driven quest for a collective regional identity of states is, of course, an important part of the story. But, while drawing attention to the importance of the contest among these elites, this perspective leaves out the normative contest among those outside the region who wish to influence the content to be given to the idea of 'Europe' or 'South-East Asia'. This state-centric approach also leaves out nonstate actors and knowledge-makers in policy circles and in international and regional agencies, academia and the media.

A fifth opening for a more useful approach is therefore provided by those who recognise this gap in the state-centric 'new regionalism' literature. Söderbaum and Timothy Shaw, for example, have called for more attention to civil society and transnational actors in the theorising of 'new regionalism'.[14] In relation to the Pacific case, Nicole George has made a persuasive case for the lack of attention to more informal modes of Pacific island regional integration, which she terms 'bottom-up' regionalism. She illustrates her case by showing the importance of Pacific women's regional peacebuilding collaborations since the 1960s and 1970s.[15]

Sixth, Andrew Gamble and Anthony Payne introduce the 'neo-medievalist' image to describe the overlapping authorities, identities and jurisdictions involved in the relationship between the regional level and the state and global levels of governance, thereby introducing the possibility of moving the debate away from a fixation on separate authority spheres with a zero-sum power relationship between them.[16] Typically, theories of regionalism previously assumed that an increase in regional integration necessarily

---

13   Benedict Anderson, *Imagined Communities: Reflections on the Origin and Spread of Nationalism*, London: Verso, 1983.
14   Fredrik Söderbaum and Timothy M. Shaw, 'Conclusion: What Futures for New Regionalism?', in Fredrik Söderbaum and Timothy M. Shaw, eds, *Theories of New Regionalism: A Palgrave Reader*, Basingstoke, UK: Palgrave Macmillan, 2003, pp. 211–25, at pp. 220–2.
15   Nicole George, 'Pacific Women Building Peace: A Regional Perspective', *The Contemporary Pacific*, 23(1), 2011: 37–71.
16   Gamble and Payne, 'Conclusion', p. 263.

meant a surrendering of state sovereignty. Gamble and Payne's point provides the basis for seeing a much more complex relationship between the global, regional and national levels of authority.

Taken together, all of these seemingly disparate ideas provide a foundation for developing a novel approach to the political meaning of region-building that can help us 'see' the otherwise obscured political significance of the regional level of politics in the Pacific. Of particular interest for the approach developed here are the insights that the region is a site of political contest; that the regional polity should be broadly conceived to include 'bottom-up' regionalism; that there is an intertwining of power at the national, regional and global levels; and that region-building should be seen as a political contest that matters even in the absence of formal regional governance or high levels of regional integration.

Characterising the politics of regionalism

The starting point in developing an alternative conceptual approach that is better able to capture the political significance of the Pacific case, and perhaps other cases, is the proposition that the political meaning of regionalism is best understood as a site of contest over how people in a region should live their lives in the context of an impinging, but changing global order.[17] I argue that this is seen most usefully as a battle of big ideas about what constitutes a legitimate political community, whether at regional, national or substate levels. These contests can then be seen as legitimacy contests over rightful rule and, at a fundamental level, as a contest between different legitimating principles of regional governance.

These contests can usefully be broken down further, to being over three key aspects of legitimate political community: purpose, identity and agency. The contest over purpose includes such questions as how should the community be developed, secured and governed, and how should disputes be resolved? The contest over identity includes the questions not only of 'who belongs', but also of 'on what basis'. Should it be, for example, on the basis of race, appearance, residence, normative commitment or territorial attachment? This may take the form of struggles over formal membership of regional organisations, cartographic decisions about inclusion on a map or declarations about the basis of identity or implied in the use of 'us'

---

17   I am defining politics as 'the contest over how we live'.

and 'them' when referring to regional labels such as the Pacific or Oceania. The struggle over the third aspect of legitimate political community not only includes the question of who is regarded as legitimate to speak on behalf of the region; it also includes the issue of who has the right to represent the region and create knowledge about it and on what basis.

A key aspect of this normative contest over a legitimate regional political community is that it always occurs in the context of reacting or adapting to, invoking, resisting or moderating global processes and ideas. This is to argue that the ideas and processes associated with a changing global order set the *agenda* and *terms* of debate, but not the *outcome*. In the case of the Pacific, for example, it is contended that the normative contest over region-building has to be seen against a backdrop of imperialism, colonialism, decolonisation, the Cold War, the post–Cold War changes in the global economy and global governance. It is just as importantly to be seen against changing influential Western or global ideas such as imperialism, Darwinism, 'native welfare', self-determination, neoliberalism, biodiversity, gender equality, 'good governance', human rights and sustainable development.

This conceptualisation of the politics of region-building that sees it both as a site of contest over legitimate purpose, identity and political agency *and* as a mediator of global ideas and processes opens up the region-building story in several important ways. It focuses our attention on the actual political role of region-building at a particular time, rather than only those aspects of the regional experience that are seen as contributing to, or obstructing, the achievement of a supposed goal of regional integration, formal organisation or a surrendering of sovereignty. It also suggests the importance of viewing the political significance of region-building over the *longue durée* and, for colonised regions, at least back to the global order of colonialism. The attempts to influence how people live in a particular region began in the colonial period, if not before. Global influences on the framing of regions did not start with the neoliberal globalisation of the 1980s and the advent of new regionalism.

This conceptualisation also suggests a broader regional political arena. The contest over purpose, identity and agency is likely to be found as much in textbooks and international agency reports as it is in diplomatic gatherings; in battles over organisational membership as much as it is in substantive debate about development programs; and in the deployment of concepts such as 'regional security' as much as it is in relation to positions taken in treaty negotiations. It follows that this conceptualisation of region-building also includes a much broader range of protagonists than is usual in studies of regionalism, in which, even among critical regionalism scholars, the analysis can be surprisingly state-centric.[18] States are not the only actors in this arena. Civil society organisations, knowledge-makers, artists, scholars, sovereignty and independence movements and international agencies are also very much part of this political story.

The political authority of regional governance

While there is an ongoing normative contest in the regional arena over what the regional political community should stand for as a set of ideas, there is at any one period in this history a dominant set of norms that contributes to the shaping of how society is organised and how individuals live their lives. These dominant framing ideas and guiding principles may find expression in law and formal organisations or in less formalised norms of conduct. This conceptualisation of regional governance is broader than that commonly used in the new regionalism debate, where it is seen either as formal institutionalisation or as diffuse regional networks based on economic interdependence. The existence of significant governance of the kind I am positing here crucially depends on the authority of normative framing.

In thinking about the sources of the authority of this regional governance, my starting point is Edward Said's *Orientalism*.[19] Although he focused on British, French and American representations of the Middle and Far East, Said's ideas are relevant to other contexts in which peoples are grouped together and represented by outsiders who wish at the same time to manage, control or prescribe for the peoples they are depicting. Said's central thesis is that, in the case of Europeans and Americans depicting the Orient, this has never just been a harmless imagining of far-off places: it contributed to, and became part of, the structure of power. He argues that this knowledge has an impact on the people so depicted, not just because it informs and justifies colonial and neocolonial practices by providing the lenses through which Europeans see the Orient and make policies for it, but also because it begins to be taken on as a self-image by those so depicted.

---

18   See, for example, Neumann, *Uses of the Other*.
19   Said, *Orientalism*.

The full authoritative significance of this regional framing in colonial and postcolonial contexts can only be understood if we are aware that the community being shaped is not only the *regional* community; the making of 'region' is also accompanied by the making of an idealised *local* society. Said famously drew attention to this 'double move'—of affecting *the regional* and *the local* at the same time—as part of Orientalism. He claims that the framing of a vast region called the Orient—and the generalised depiction of an idealised regional identity—was at once to create an idealised Oriental person and an idealised local Oriental society. And because of its authority as knowledge and its attachment to the power of imperialism, this depiction was powerful.[20]

In relation to the Pacific island region, Epeli Hau`ofa has argued that such authoritative depictions not only influence the behaviour of the powerful; they also have in the past affected the self-image of 'subordinates', whether images of darkness prior to Christianity being brought by the missionaries or images of inferiority captured, for example, in the term 'boy' to refer to an adult man. Although Hau`ofa was concerned about the influence of previous Western conceptions on the self-image of Pacific islanders, his main concern was with the representation of Pacific island states as small and powerless, as promoted by social scientists, consultants, international agencies and metropolitan governments in their framings of the region in the postcolonial period.[21] What distressed him was the disempowering effect of this conception; its determinism, he contended, perpetuated dependency and subordination.

Although seemingly lacking the intimacy of face-to-face communities, Pacific regional governance has an intimacy in its influence that operates through this double move. In such a case the individual may know nothing about their membership of the Pacific regional community but could still be affected intimately because of the regional contest over the norms governing the idealised local Pacific society and 'Pacific islander' and the link between these dominant conceptions and policy, whether that policy be that of the transnational church, the colonial or postcolonial state, international agencies or aid donors.

---

20   ibid., pp. 26–7.
21   Hau`ofa, 'Our Sea of Islands' (1994), p. 149.

I propose to develop the argument that the authority of regional governance in postcolonial situations in particular is derived from the strategic location of the regional site of politics in a globalising world. It sits between global management, global norms and knowledge-making, on the one hand, and local aspirations for development, security and sovereignty, on the other. The region has had a key role as a knowledge and management category and therefore as a site for the determination of authoritative conceptions of what the idealised political community is and ought to be. The region takes a special role as a knowledge and policy category in global management, and in local resistance to it. For those seeking to have global reach in influencing how society is organised, the idea of dividing the world into regions is compelling as a management strategy. It is a strategy adopted by foreign offices, the United Nations, international agencies, aid bureaus and international NGOs such as Amnesty International and Greenpeace. This tendency is not new, although it is now more widespread. It was, for example, natural for imperial powers to map and categorise far-off places and group and name them.

Another source of authority for regional governance in postcolonial contexts is its role in granting legal personality and bestowing legitimacy on would-be sovereignties, whether aspiring states or nations. It is not that we are seeing a transfer of authority and sovereignty from the state to the region, rather that each is mutually constitutive. This is to argue that the region has both strengthened the authority of other levels of governance and been strengthened by this process. This authoritative role for regional governance is seen in its control over who is accepted as a member of the regional society of states or as sharing a regional cultural identity. Regional governance can have a legitimating function for states, social movements and peoples in the granting of legal personality, the recognition of sovereignty and the conferring of legitimacy. As a political community, it can bestow regional citizenship and a right to belong and participate—a right that has been valued and, in some cases, hard-fought.

In conceptualising the sources of power for regional governance, the emphasis here is on the authority of policy-related knowledge systems situated at the strategic location of the regional site, together with the legitimating functions associated with sovereignty. This is not to deny the importance of other sources of power associated with regional governance. Collective diplomacy, for example, based on more traditional sources of power such as a pooling of bargaining power and voting power in international forums, is a major part of the regional governance story. Nor is this an argument for the absolute authority of regional governance in Pacific life. In this regard, this study endorses Gamble and Payne's characterisation of regional governance as one of several intersecting layers of authority in world politics.[22] In the Pacific case, I propose to demonstrate how the regional layer of authority interacts with nation-building, as well as with global governance, to shape how Pacific societies are organised.

Who is regional governance for?

Telling the regional politics story as a contest over the nature of legitimate political community in a context of global change reveals much about the source and nature of the authority of regional governance, and the political significance of regional diplomacy. However, it still leaves hanging the question: Who exercises this power? Who has the regional enterprise been for? In contemporary studies of regionalism, this question takes the form of asking: to what extent is regionalism or regional governance to be seen as serving global or local interests? The new regionalism literature was spurred by the advent of new forms of regional association emerging from the late 1980s in response to the regionalist policies of the United Nations and the United States and the global spread of neoliberal economic discourse. The approach of those focusing on the political significance of regions in the security realm assumed that regions were working for the purposes of global or regional hegemonic states. Seen from this realist perspective, regional organisations reflect geopolitical management of regional security. For many of those coming at the new regionalism from the angle of an international political economy or economics, new regionalism represented the dominance of global economic ideas promoted through UN institutions, the West and global economic managers.

An interesting bridging of these two spheres is contained in Katzenstein's argument that global politics needs to be seen as a 'world of regions' in an American imperium. This bridges the international political economy and security aspects of regionalism. It also links the global hegemon, the American imperium, to regional hegemons—Germany in Europe

---

22 Gamble and Payne, 'Conclusion'.

and Japan in Asia. This approach sees regional governance as ultimately determined by American power but with the proviso that the US Government may be constrained by the system of regions it has set up.

Katzenstein's approach provides an important entry point into the question of 'who is it for?'. This answer to the question of who exercises power in the regional arena appears at first glance to be a highly relevant approach to the Pacific case.[23] Like Germany and Japan, Australia is both a pro-American ally and a regional power in the postcolonial Pacific region, and has actively sought to give leadership to region-building. There is open talk of Australia having responsibility on behalf of the United States, or more broadly on behalf of the West, for managing this area in security and diplomatic terms. However, Australia also has its own hegemonic agenda, with its very long history, in relation to the control of the region. In the late nineteenth century, Otto von Bismarck called it the 'Australasian Monroe doctrine'.[24] In 1883, concern about building capacity to flex muscle in managing security in the Pacific island region was the prime motive for organising the intercolonial convention to talk about creating the Australian nation.[25] The Australian attempt to exert hegemonic power over regional governance in the Pacific on its own behalf therefore assumes a prime focus in this inquiry. Although the general realist argument about regional governance serving the interests of the regional hegemon, and Katzenstein's more nuanced argument about a world of regions in service of American power, opens up key areas of understanding in the Pacific case, I propose to argue that we nevertheless need to explore a more complex and contingent characterisation of who is served by regional governance.

A second entry point into the issue of 'who is it for?' is to consider Richard Falk's question: Does 'the region' act as a new defender of local interests against undesirable global processes and ideas? Or, conversely, does it act as an agent of global forces?[26] This focus on globalisation fits well with the characterisation of the politics of regional governance presented above, as being about a normative contest, which mediates and negotiates large

---

23   Peter J. Katzenstein, *A World of Regions: Asia and Europe in the American Imperium*, Ithaca, NY: Cornell University Press, 2005.

24   Merze Tate, 'The Australasian Monroe Doctrine: Genesis of the Doctrine', *Political Science Quarterly*, 76(2), 1961: 264–84, at p. 281.

25   Alfred Deakin, *The Federal Story: The Inner History of the Federal Cause, 1880–1900*, Melbourne: Robertson & Mullins, 1944.

26   Falk, 'Regionalism and World Order after the Cold War'.

global framing ideas and interventions. Falk's general argument is that 'the region' is not acting as a shield for local societies against the onslaught of neoliberal processes and ideas, but is instead becoming an agent of this form of globalisation.

This book offers a different answer for the Pacific. While Falk's 'shield' analogy creates an opening for thinking about the power of region vis-a-vis global processes, I depart from his approach on a number of key points: first, in seeing this mediating role as crucial in understanding the power of regional governance and certainly not to be dismissed; second, in seeing this role as longstanding rather than emerging with potential in the 1990s; third, in not limiting globalisation to economic processes of neoliberalism but in broadening it to include all global processes; fourth, in rejecting the simple 'global versus local' dichotomy inherent in Falk's approach; and, finally, in seeing local agency as always present, although contingent.

Amitav Acharya provides a third entry point. He introduces the local agency of Asian elites in explaining regional organisational outcomes. He seeks to establish the power of norm-takers in the face of global norm diffusion. With his focus on the ideas that frame regional outcomes and its emphasis on the power of 'Asia's cognitive prior', Acharya opens up the possibility of local agency and a more contingent view of whose interests—global or local—particular regional outcomes might represent.[27] His position has the limitation, however, of seeing a homogeneous 'global' and 'local' and a preordained 'Asian cognitive prior'. I propose an approach to understanding the question 'who is regional governance for' that both expands on the contingent nature of the outcomes of this contest and problematises the categories of 'the local' and 'the global' in these power exchanges over the ideas that influence region-building and regional governance.

---

27   Amitav Acharya, *Whose Ideas Matter? Agency and Power in Asian Regionalism*, Ithaca, NY: Cornell University Press, 2009.

To achieve this, I draw on the rich debate concerning the relationship between European material and normative power and indigenous island societies that has appeared in Pacific history and Pacific anthropology.[28] The debate has focused particularly on the impact of imperialism on Pacific island society in the nineteenth and early twentieth centuries. The approaches that were put forward as part of that debate can be usefully adapted to the concerns of this book, especially on the question of who exercises power in the interaction of global processes and ideas and local practices in the regional arena of politics.

One position in this debate—associated particularly with early scholars of the Western influence on Pacific island societies—sees Pacific island contact with the global forces of imperialism, colonialism and capitalism as constituting a 'fatal impact'.[29] European ideas and practices are seen as displacing and destroying local ways; Pacific islanders are seen only as passive recipients or victims as their societies changed inevitably towards the Western mode.

A second approach has stressed the importance of an island-centred history, island resistance to or mediation of global influences and the differences in experience of different island groups thus moving away from the dramatic regionwide generalisations associated with the 'fatal impact' histories.[30] This alternative position represents the interface as a more complex interaction, involving islander agendas and influences.

A third approach, coming from a more structuralist position, begins with a critique of the celebration of Pacific islander agency that had been prevalent in Pacific history and seeks to reinsert the island world into

---

28 Robert Borofsky, ed., *Remembrance of Pacific Pasts: An Invitation to Remake History*, Honolulu: University of Hawai`i Press, 2000; Nicholas Thomas, *Entangled Objects: Exchange, Material Culture, and Colonialism in the Pacific*, Cambridge, MA: Harvard University Press, 1991; Nicholas Thomas, *In Oceania: Visions, Artifacts, Histories*, Durham, NC: Duke University Press, 1997; Kerry R. Howe, *Where the Waves Fall: A New South Sea Islands History from First Settlement to Colonial Rule*, Sydney: Allen & Unwin, 1984, pp. 347–52.

29 The definitive portrait of this school of thought is provided in Kerry R. Howe, 'The Fate of the "Savage" in Pacific Historiography', *New Zealand Journal of History*, 11(2), 1977: 137–54. For oft-cited examples of this school, see Alan Moorehead, *The Fatal Impact: An Account of the Invasion of the South Pacific, 1767–1840*, Harmondsworth, UK: Penguin, 1968; Douglas L. Oliver, *The Pacific Islands*, Cambridge, MA: Harvard University Press, 1961; and J.C. Furnas, *Anatomy of Paradise: Hawaii and the Islands of the South Seas*, London: Victor Gollancz, 1950.

30 This is associated with the modern school of Pacific history under the leadership of J.W. Davidson at The Australian National University. See J.W. Davidson, 'Problems of Pacific History', *Journal of Pacific History*, 1(1), 1966: 5–21; Howe, *Where the Waves Fall*, pp. 347–52.

a larger global system that has often suppressed local societies.[31] Brij Lal, for example, while being careful not to embrace the extremes of the 'fatal impact' position, and after recognising the vast range of experiences where islander agency was exercised, nevertheless asserts that in thinking about the impact of colonial rule we need to move the emphasis away from an unthinking celebration of Pacific islander agency (which, he argues, is in danger of becoming a new orthodoxy) in contexts where outside forces clearly have set the agenda. After all, he argues, 'the ultimate aim' of the colonial administrators was 'the subversion of the indigenous cultural and moral order'.[32]

This study broadly supports the characterisation of the power engagement developed by Howe and Lal—a position that recognises local agency but also acknowledges that such agency acts within a very powerful structure of the global system, whether colonial or postcolonial.[33] However, it also adapts the insights of those who write from a more postcolonial and poststructural perspective pointing out messy entanglements between the West and Pacific islanders. Nicholas Thomas's approach, developed in his work mainly in relation to the colonial period, is of particular relevance. His characterisation of 'colonialism's culture' is very useful in contemplating the very different, often conflicting, discourses that fall under the label 'global' in the postcolonial period.[34] Local agency is also differentiated. My starting point is that there are 'complex entanglements' between particular local agents and particular global discourses at work in the regional site of politics in the twentieth and twenty-first centuries, just as in the engagements in the nineteenth-century cases that Thomas analysed.

Telling the Pacific region-building story

Reflecting the conceptual approach developed above, the following chapters are snapshots of region-building against the backdrop of a changing global order from the colonial period through to the present day. Each chapter is set in the context of a changing global structure of power—from imperial, to Cold War, to post–Cold War, to the war on

---

31 Howe et al., *Tides of History*.
32 Brij V. Lal, 'The Passage Out', in Howe et al., *Tides of History*.
33 Kerry Howe, 'Preface', in Howe et al., *Tides of History*; and Lal, in ibid., p. 444.
34 Nicholas Thomas, *Colonialism's Culture: Anthropology, Travel and Government*, Princeton, NJ: Princeton University Press, 1994.

terror and to the rise of Asia—and the pressures this imposes on Pacific societies, such as colonial expansion, resource exploitation, nuclear testing, war and trade and investment. This is accompanied by a change in the large global framing ideas: imperialism, Darwinism, ideas of native welfare and trusteeship, self-determination, modernisation, neoliberalism, democracy and 'good governance'. The chapters are also set against a changing political situation within Pacific societies and states—from colonised societies to emergent new state politics associated with state-building and negotiating global relationships, to state disruption, civil conflict and coups.

The chronological snapshot approach to telling the story further reveals the changing nature of the regional polity. At the outset, the political players contesting how the idealised Pacific island society should be organised are all European colonial administrators, missionaries, writers and social scientists. From the late colonial period, an emergent indigenous elite then introduces itself as a set of actors in this regional story—some as scholars and others as national leaders and civil society advocates. After 1970, a wider set of global actors also joins this broadening array of indigenous participants in a more complex regional polity. These include former colonial powers and new interests from China, the European Union, Indonesia, Japan, Russia, South Korea and Taiwan, and various nonstate actors—international NGOs such as Greenpeace and Amnesty International, international agencies and private sector associations.

The focus of each chapter is the political contest over legitimate regional political community in the Pacific set against the backdrop of a changing world order and its framing ideas. For example, the story begins as a contest between various global actors over the agency of Pacific peoples. This normative contest was intimately linked to the power of colonialism and imperialism and centred on a tension between the right of self-determination and the possibility of political agency for Pacific islanders. This normative contest remained centre-stage in the political contests between the 1940s and the 1970s. In subsequent periods, the self-determination debates continued but were matched by a series of regional contests over how independent Pacific states should be organised around questions of development, security, sovereignty, ecology and national governance, in the face of global pressures.

Shadowing—or often foreshadowing—policy contests over how to manage Oceanic societies has been an academic debate over the content of the idea of the Pacific. These academic representations of Oceania have been important because they have often provided the presuppositions on which policy is built. While for some scholars, the region has provided a comparative frame, for others it has become a unitary category such as 'state' or 'society' that is portrayed as having its own economy, culture or ecosystem. The latter approach has encouraged regional generalisations and the creation of an idealised Pacific island state, society or person. These conceptualisations have often taken the form of powerful images—'the fragile region', 'the nuclear playground', 'earth's empty quarter', the Pacific 'doomsday scenario', 'the hole in the Asia-Pacific doughnut', the 'vulnerable' region, the 'nonviable' region, the 'failed' region, 'the Pacific paradox'—that have become preconceptions in policy debates.

Thus, in this story of Pacific regional governance, 'Pacific studies' is seen as an important part of the politics of region-building and of the normative contests over how people should live in postcolonial Pacific states. The role of anthropology in the 1920s and 1930s is examined in supporting ideas of native welfare and trusteeship as a regionwide policy. In the 1960s and 1970s, economists and geographers played an important role in shaping the regional narrative concerning the problem and the solution for Pacific island states. In the 1980s and beyond, strategic studies, political science, environmental studies and economics came to the fore. In the first decade of the twenty-first century, Pacific academics promoted Pacific epistemology and the decolonisation of Pacific studies. Each of these interventions has influenced the regional policy debate about how Pacific societies should be organised.

As well as characterising these normative contests over regional governance and the legitimating principles at stake in these struggles, the task of each chapter is to reflect on what eventuates as a form of regional governance. What does regional governance stand for at various points and whose interests and ideas are represented? What legitimating principles does it represent? As a crucial part of tracing the nature of regional governance, the book depicts the changing nature of the governing ideas and the influence of knowledge-making on them. The story shows the strong involvement of key academic disciplines but also of the major agencies—the World Bank, AusAID, Amnesty International, Greenpeace and the United Nations Development Programme (UNDP)—in defining 'the Pacific problem' and proposing 'the Pacific answer'. This policy-related knowledge provides a significant basis for the authority of regional governance.

3

The 'South Seas' in the imperial imagination

From the time of the Pacific voyages of Louis Antoine de Bougainville and Captain James Cook in the late eighteenth century, Europeans began to discern significant diversity in language, culture and attitude among the island societies across the Pacific Ocean; yet at the same time, they saw this diversity as existing within a broader regional unity. For the European cartographer, voyager, natural scientist and 'man of letters' of the eighteenth and nineteenth centuries, the creation of this new unifying frame—referred to variously as 'the Pacific', 'Oceania', the 'South Seas' or the 'Pacific islands'—was an important part of mapping, cataloguing and creating knowledge about this last part of the 'unknown' world in relation to what was known. The accompanying ideas about the nature, or desired nature, of an idealised 'Pacific islander' and 'island society' were constant reminders of the existence of this underlying regional frame in the European imagination.[1] This conceptual framing of the Pacific island region created the context in which the establishment of imperial control of these societies was thought possible, and indeed became part of the imposition and management of empire. It was also an important influence on the successful efforts of evangelical Christians to spread their religious ideas across all Pacific island societies in the nineteenth century.

---

1   Smith, *European Vision and the South Pacific 1768–1850*, Ch. 1; Howe, *Nature, Culture and History*, Ch. 1.

While Europeans shared the idea of the existence of a regional unity within which particularities might be approached, they differed on the content they gave to the idea. To adapt Nicholas Thomas's insight, 'colonialism's culture' was complex: it was never 'a coherent imposition'.[2] Within the European imagination there were contending ideas about how to represent the idealised Pacific society and how that society should be changed. There were also contending ideas about the question of whether it was possible or desirable for Pacific islanders to have political agency, and indeed on the question of who belonged to the region, and on what basis. These differences varied over time depending on the changing self-image of Europeans, on geopolitical developments and on the rise and fall of grand ideas such as neoclassicism, racial hierarchy, Darwinism, imperialism, evangelism and self-determination.

These differences also varied according to which colonial power was involved and which particular interests within a colonial empire were representing Pacific island life and its possibilities. There were, for example, vast differences between the attitudes of planters, traders, anthropologists, missionaries, artists and colonial officials. There was also variation depending on which part of the island region was influencing the image of the idealised Pacific society. A Tahitian-driven regional image of 'the noble savage' was, for example, very different from one drawn from Tanna or Malekula in current-day Vanuatu.[3]

The contest within the European imagination about how '*the* Pacific society' should be characterised and changed occurred in three key intersecting arenas: the world of official policymaking, the world of the representatives of religion and commerce and the world of the creators of knowledge—the *philosophes* and the natural and social scientists. As we have seen, the official 'framing of the islands' began as an idea associated with exploration, cartography and science and, later, with imperialism. Colonial management also encouraged regional thinking as a practical way of rationalising administration over a number of territories, institutionalised in the British Western Pacific High Commission, and later the Central Medical School and the Makogai Leper Colony.

---

2   Thomas, *Colonialism's Culture*, p. 3.
3   O.H.K. Spate, *The Pacific Since Magellan. Volume 3: Paradise Found and Lost*, Sydney: Australian National University Press, 1988, pp. 200–1.

In examining these political contests among Europeans concerning the nature of the ideas that should govern the peoples of this region from the late eighteenth century to the 1930s, this chapter focuses on five particular aspects of this story. The first is the debate concerning the characterisation of Pacific islanders and Pacific island societies that underpinned the establishment of the imperial practices and Christian evangelism of the nineteenth century. The second is the emergence and development of the so-called Australasian Monroe doctrine of the late nineteenth century—a set of ideas that has continued to influence Australian and New Zealand hegemonic approaches to framing the Pacific island region. Third are the shared imperial norms concerned with establishing legitimate colonial forms in the Pacific. The fourth is the way in which the formal colonisation of the Pacific encouraged *regional* and subregional governance. Fifth are some of the proposals for regional confederation put forward by European planters and traders in the late colonial period.

Noble, ignoble and romantic savages

Following the publication of Bougainville's *A Voyage Round the World* in 1772 and, in the following year, John Hawkesworth's account of Cook's first Pacific voyage, the idealised Pacific islander and the idealised island society became influential in philosophical debates within Europe. They provided various 'state of nature' assumptions in normative debates about political and social organisation.[4] In his magisterial account of the interplay between European conceptions and the Pacific world between 1768 and 1850, Bernard Smith argues that Bougainville's description of his visit to Tahiti in particular 'stamped itself permanently upon the imagination of Europe'.[5] Bougainville's description of Tahiti as the Garden of Eden, and elsewhere as the Elysian fields and *la Nouvelle Cythère*, seemed to confirm for many the existence of a 'golden age' and a state of nature in which the 'savage' was 'noble' or, in the case of the French, *bon* or *beau*.

---

4   Louis Antoine de Bougainville, *A Voyage Round the World*, trans. J.R. Forster, London, 1772; John Hawkesworth, *An Account of the Voyages Undertaken by the Order of His Present Majesty for Making Discoveries in the Southern Hemisphere*, London, 1773; Denis Diderot, *Supplement au Voyage de Bougainville*, 1796.

5   Smith, *European Vision*, p. 25.

This was reinforced by Hawkesworth's interpretation of the journals of Cook and Joseph Banks and his provocative observation that, based on these accounts, the Tahitians were perhaps 'happier than we are'.[6]

While the impact of these Arcadian images on European thought was particularly marked at the end of the eighteenth century, this was not the first time European voyagers had created such pictures of the islands of the South Sea—or Mar del Sur, as it was called before the nineteenth century. Over the previous 200 years, this had in fact been a dominant conception in the observations of Portuguese, Spanish and Dutch navigators as they explored the Pacific and came in touch with local inhabitants.[7] As Smith so persuasively argues for the Cook and Bougainville voyages, this Arcadian imagery was as much a product of preexisting currents in European thought as it was of what these navigators experienced in the Pacific itself.[8] Smith prefigures Edward Said in seeing these early European conceptions of the Pacific as saying as much about the idea of Europe as about the idea of the Pacific. He graphically illustrates this point by reference to the paintings made on these voyages and the influence of neoclassical themes on the representation of people and the landscape.

Other protagonists in the debate over the nature of man and society at this crucial juncture in European history read the reports of the Cook and Bougainville voyages very differently. Instead of drawing an image of a noble savage living in Arcadia, they drew from the social practices reported in the manuscripts by Bougainville and Hawkesworth another idealised and exaggerated creation: an ignoble savage living in an amoral society.[9] Kerry Howe is very persuasive in painting a nineteenth century in which the 'ignoble savage' image comes to predominate, encouraged by the experiences of 'death and fear' in the Pacific—particularly Cook's murder in Hawai`i in 1779 and the disappearance of Jean-François de La Pérouse in Melanesia in 1788—and how that was reported; and later by evangelism and scientific views of racial hierarchy.[10] The evangelical mindset required a wild and fallen 'other'.

---

6   Cited in ibid., p. 27, as drawn from Hawkesworth's account of the first voyage.
7   ibid.; Spate, *The Pacific Since Magellan*, Vol. 3; and particularly Howe, *Nature, Culture and History*.
8   Smith, *European Vision*, Ch. 2.
9   Howe, 'The Fate of the "Savage" in Pacific Historiography'.
10   Howe, *Nature, Culture and History*, Ch. 1.

Howe argues that this image of the Pacific islander continued through the nineteenth century, encouraged by evolutionist thinking, and in the early twentieth century by the decline in island populations and the rise of the perception that these 'races' were dying out. His portrayal is of a shift in European thought from one in which culture prevails over nature to one in which nature prevails over culture (for example, in environmental determinism or racial hierarchy).[11] Smith paints a slightly more complex picture. He argues that not only do we see the emergence of an ignoble savage in European thought that becomes influential in the nineteenth century, but also we see the offspring of the noble *and* ignoble savage—the Romantic savage.[12]

Of importance for the story of the idea of region-building told here is that these images, generated by a particular place in the Pacific, become a generalised image of a South Sea islander in terms of European scientific and philosophical debates. There is constant slippage between the particular and the general. An idealised Pacific island society and Pacific islander are born. They become the site of a European debate about how all Pacific islanders live and should live.

The crucial move is the shift in the dominance of the longstanding 'noble savage' idealisation to the 'ignoble' and 'romantic' savage of the nineteenth century. The initial noble savage framing led to ideas of treating Pacific islanders equally and even to the idea that contact with an impure Europe was to be discouraged and the innocence of such societies protected. But the shift in the nineteenth century to conceptions of the ignoble savage and the romantic savage had implications for what was thinkable for Europeans to do in relation to Pacific islanders. This framing licensed and even compelled Europeans to have power over Pacific islanders, either to bring civilisation and protection or to save their souls. In particular, it allowed and encouraged imperialism and evangelism. Following the logic of their conceptual starting point, pagans needed Christianity and to be civilised; the 'child races' needed protection, the wild needed to be tamed and, as science had established that Pacific islanders were lower on the racial hierarchy, they required European rule.[13]

---

11   ibid., Ch. 2.

12   Smith, *European Vision*, Ch. 11.

13   On the link between the ignoble savage conception and the 'evangelical mind' and its application in the Pacific, see Howe, *Where the Waves Fall*, Ch. 6.

Smith, Howe and Spate all provide some openings to understanding how we might consider the political implications of these European framings of the Pacific in the late eighteenth and nineteenth centuries. For example, with regard to the ignoble savage idealisation of the Pacific native promoted by the evangelicals, Smith says:

> Evangelism in a greater or lesser degree permeated all phases of British life and thought during the first half of the century and the graphic portrayal of Pacific islanders in general took on an evangelical purpose and direction.[14]

The evangelicals needed an ignoble 'other' to justify their actions. This set the context in which missionary activity was seen as not only justified, but also required. The 'noble savage' imagery, on the other hand, informed a very different policy attitude. After stating that the Tahitians are perhaps happier than we are, Hawkesworth's moral judgement is 'why then should we stand in judgement upon them!'.[15] The 'noble savage' idea could later be seen as inherent in indirect rule and protection strategies, whereas the 'ignoble savage' depiction underpinned missionary activity, imperialism and the civilising mission.

While there were significant differences in these European representations of Pacific peoples, they came together in seeing Pacific islanders as childlike or as 'child races', particularly once Darwinian theories of racial hierarchy were influential from the mid nineteenth century. These conceptions made it possible for Europeans to think they had the right, and even the responsibility, to colonise this part of the world. French, British and German annexation of nearly all of the island territories of the Pacific in the nineteenth century, followed by Australian and New Zealand colonisation in the twentieth century, was enabled by a characterisation of Pacific islanders as 'child races', savages (whether noble or ignoble) and, later, seen through Darwinian lenses, as 'dying out'.[16]

This general image of Pacific islanders was moderated, in policy terms, by perceptions of difference within the Pacific. Those Europeans who spent time in the South Seas saw considerable differences within the Pacific. From his first voyage, Cook was differentiating the Polynesians in the east

---

14   Smith, *European Vision*, p. 244.
15   ibid., p. 27.
16   See, for example, Howe, *Nature, Culture and History*, pp. 31–57; and J.W. Burton, *The Call of the Pacific*, London: Charles H. Kelly, Every Age Library, 1912, p. 5.

of the region from 'races' in the west. From the 1830s, it became common to divide Oceania into three cultural areas: Polynesia, Micronesia and Melanesia (indeed, there was also a fourth, covering present-day island South-East Asia). While it was common to see the South Seas peoples as belonging to 'races' located at different levels on a perceived hierarchy of races (whether as fixed for all time or part of an evolutionary scale), with the Tahitians and their 'noble savage' status at the high end, all Pacific islanders were seen as below 'the European'.[17] They were seen as being in need of protection or civilisation, and as not qualifying for the rights of the liberal individual.

The Australasian Monroe doctrine

Although Britain did not begin to acquire an island empire until 1874, it nevertheless enjoyed 'primacy of influence' in the area in the preceding century. According to W.P. Morrell:

> [T]he advent of a Power which was mistress of the sea and hence of the means of communication between the island groups gave the history of the Pacific islands a unity it never previously had.[18]

The flow of British settlers to the South Pacific in the nineteenth century made the emergence of regional thinking inevitable. Those who came to the Australian and New Zealand colonies were quick to see the need for a secure region under one flag; the lawlessness of British labour recruiters and traders was to impel the British Government to attempt a regional solution; British administrators had to coordinate policy towards the territories of a newly acquired Pacific island empire; and British planters and other settlers in the islands were later to see the economic advantages of regional cooperation. Despite the penetration of the South Pacific by other European powers, it was the more extensive British settlement that led to the most significant developments in regional thinking.

British reluctance to formalise its dominant position in the region was of concern to the settlers in the new colonies of Australia and New Zealand who called throughout the latter half of the nineteenth century for British

---

17   Thomas, *In Oceania*, Ch. 5.
18   W.P. Morrell, *Britain in the Pacific Islands*, London: Oxford University Press, 1960, p. 1.

annexation of the Western Pacific region.[19] They wanted a united region under a British flag: 'Oceania for the Anglo-Saxons', as the demand was later to be described.[20] Imperialistic in design and motive, the Australasian proposals were expressions of the first official regional thinking in the South Pacific.[21]

The Australasian position was most forcefully put at an intercolonial convention held in Sydney in 1883. It was resolved that

> further acquisition of dominion in the Pacific, south of the Equator, by any Foreign Power, would be highly detrimental to the safety and well-being of the British possessions in Australasia, and injurious to the interests of the Empire.[22]

A second resolution urged the British Government to 'promptly adopt the wisest and most effectual measures for securing the safety and contentment of this portion of Her Majesty's dominions'.[23] This stance immediately became known as the 'Australasian Monroe doctrine' because it was seen as proclaiming that the South Pacific was an Anglo-Saxon preserve in which other 'powers' should not trespass. This is certainly how the resolutions were interpreted by other powers, particularly France and Germany, and by the British Colonial Secretary, who, in a letter to the British prime minister, described the idea of a 'Monroe Doctrine laid down for the whole South Pacific' as 'mere raving'. The prime minister regarded the extreme demands of the convention as 'preposterous'.[24]

The various proposals of a similar vein that had been put forward by the Australian and New Zealand colonies in the 30 years preceding the intercolonial convention had received a similar reception in London. The British Government did not agree with the colonists' assessment of the territorial intentions of other powers. And, in view of the presence

---

19   Even to the point of angering Otto von Bismarck, who found the '"grasping policy" of the English colonists as offensive and irritating as the original "insolent" Monroe "dogma"'. Tate, 'The Australasian Monroe Doctrine', p. 281.
20   A phrase used by Andre Siegfried in the early twentieth century, cited in C. Hartley Grattan, *The Southwest Pacific to 1900: A Modern History*, Ann Arbor: University of Michigan Press, 1963, p. 179.
21   These proposals—variously termed 'Australasian subimperialism', 'the Australasian Monroe doctrine' or 'colonial imperialism'—are examined in John M. Ward, *British Policy in the South Pacific*, Sydney: Australasian Publishing Co., 1948, pp. 197–204; Neville Meaney, *A History of Australian Defence and Foreign Policy, 1901–23. Volume 1: The Search for Security in the Pacific, 1901–1914*, Sydney: Sydney University Press, 1976, pp. 9, 16–22; and Tate, 'The Australasian Monroe Doctrine'.
22   Tate, 'The Australasian Monroe Doctrine', p. 275.
23   ibid.
24   ibid., pp. 277–8.

of German and French interests in the region, they did not think it would be as simple as the colonists claimed to declare British sovereignty over the region, even if there was sufficient reason to attempt to do so.[25]

The Australian and New Zealand colonies wanted a British South Pacific. They were concerned lest other powers gained control of the Pacific islands. They each saw a regional solution as desirable, but beyond this general level of agreement there were important distinctions to be drawn with regard to their respective motives, and to the specific nature of their proposals. The New Zealand schemes invariably involved the idea of a 'confederation'; they centred on the Polynesian groups of Fiji, Tonga and Samoa and, most significantly, they were concerned with gaining more territory for New Zealand.[26] The Australian colonies were less concerned with extending their territorial boundaries. Their schemes did not as a rule involve direct Australian control of the islands.[27] They were concerned, however, to persuade the British Government that it should declare a protectorate over the islands of the Western Pacific.[28] They were motivated in this by commercial interests both extant and potential, by the need for protection of Australian settlers in the region, especially after the 1850s, and by strategic considerations.[29] The last reason was particularly important, and was most evident in the colonists' concern about the future of Fiji, New Guinea and the New Hebrides.

Thus, in contrast to the New Zealand schemes, the Australian proposals tended to place less emphasis on territorial gain; they were not concerned with 'confederation' and they centred more on the Melanesian area of the South Pacific. Already Australia and New Zealand had begun to see different parts of the South Pacific as their concern—a tendency that continued in their later foreign policies. Although the Australasian entreaties to the British Government were unsuccessful, they were

---

25   ibid.

26   For details of the various New Zealand schemes, including governor George Grey's annexation proposals of the 1850s, premier Julius Vogel's proposal for a 'grand island dominion' of the 1870s and premier Richard Seddon's imperialistic designs of the 1890s, see Angus Ross, *New Zealand Aspirations in the Pacific in the Nineteenth Century*, Oxford: Clarendon Press, 1964.

27   The Victorian Government did, however, suggest to the British Government that it annex Samoa after the civil war of 1893–94 because of 'the manifest destiny of Australasia to be the controlling Power in the Southern Pacific'. Meaney, *A History of Australian Defence and Foreign Policy*, p. 22.

28   ibid., pp. 9, 16–21.

29   The importance of Australian trade with its 'Pacific frontier' and the movement of Australians into the islands as traders, missionaries and planters in the nineteenth century are examined in John M.R. Young, ed., *Australia's Pacific Frontier: Economic and Cultural Expansion into the Pacific, 1795–1885*, Melbourne: Cassell Australia, 1967.

nevertheless very important developments in the evolution of regionalist thought. They represented the genesis of an attitude that has, at least in part, been behind all subsequent Australasian efforts to promote region-building in the Pacific.

Imperial norms

The 'messy entanglement' between the imperial ideas of Europe, the United States and the Australasians, on the one hand, and Pacific societies, on the other, began in the nineteenth century and particularly in the 1840s, when the period of annexation and European missionary and trader activity began. The impact varied enormously across the region. The colonial powers had different approaches (contrast the indirect rule of Britain with the assimilationist approach of France), and some island groups experienced several waves of colonial rule (some Micronesian islands experienced Spanish, German, Japanese and American rule, for example). Furthermore, a particular colonial power could adopt different approaches to different Pacific island territories (for example, the significant difference between French colonial rule in New Caledonia and that in French Polynesia).[30]

Although the imperial powers were in strong competition with each other, and while each imparted distinctive forms of colonial rule, there were also shared dominant European norms concerning legitimate statehood and appropriate social organisation, which could be said at a very general level to dramatically influence the political change in the Pacific island region over the following century. While imperial norms could be seen as being diffused by one imperial power in one particular island society, they could also be seen as 'international' norms in the sense that they were accepted shared norms of the European system of states. The rights and responsibilities associated with imperialism itself could be seen as norms of the interstate system of Europe. There was a general acceptance of the idea that the norms concerning sovereign equality did not apply to those who were 'child races' or who were not organised politically in such a way to meet the 'standard of civilisation'.

---

30 Stephen Henningham, 'France in Melanesia and Polynesia', in Howe et al., *Tides of History*, pp. 119–46.

The Kingdom of Tonga was the only Pacific island society that was accepted as conforming to the norms of legitimate statehood. King Taufa'ahau Tupou I worked hard to adopt all the trappings of a modern European state. He unified the Tongan chieftaincies through warfare, converted to Christianity, abolished slavery, set up a new titled nobility, promulgated a constitution that among other things established a Christian state and the rule of law and even changed his name and that of his wife to that of the reigning King and Queen of England, George and Charlotte (Tonganised to Siaosi and Salote).[31]

The annexation of all other island societies by France, Spain, Britain, Germany, the Netherlands, the United States and, later, by Japan, Australia and New Zealand, created revolutionary political change. It created new political boundaries, the idea of a centralised state, 'perpetual peace' between warring tribes (for example, in Fiji, the New Guinea Highlands and Solomon Islands) and new ways of resolving conflict over the larger area of the colonial state through conferencing and council consensus. Although Britain attempted indirect rule, new norms inevitably governed political interactions and processes at the national level. For example, a Fiji-wide Council of Chiefs was set up by the British to introduce a peaceful way of resolving intersociety disputes. The church was also a new source of power, and the changing cosmology associated with conversion impacted on island society.

Colonial regional management

In 1877, in what was the first institutional expression of colonial regional thinking in relation to the South Pacific area, Britain attempted a coordinated approach to controlling its subjects in the then unclaimed islands of the South Pacific through the establishment of the Western Pacific High Commission. The High Commission's territorial jurisdiction was much larger than was suggested by its name. It included Tonga, Samoa, the Union, Phoenix, Ellice, Gilbert, Marshall, Caroline, Solomon and Santa Cruz islands, and Rotuma, New Guinea, New Britain, New Ireland, the Louisiade Archipelago and 'all other islands in the Western Pacific Ocean not being within the limits of Fiji, Queensland or New South Wales and not being within the jurisdiction of any civilised

---

31   Howe, *Where the Waves Fall*, Ch. 9, especially pp. 188–94.

Power'.[32] The High Commission was established partly to obviate the necessity for further annexation in the South Pacific. It was thought that if the high commissioner could use his judicial powers to check lawlessness perpetrated by British subjects then further, and more expensive, involvement in the region could be avoided.[33] It was also seen as a means of satisfying Australasian demands for an official British presence in the area. The high commissioner was given the power to make

> such regulations as to him seem fit for the government of British subjects, by enforcing the observance by them of ... any treaty between Her Majesty and any King, Chief, or other authority in the Western Pacific Islands and for securing the maintenance ... of friendly relations between British subjects and those authorities and persons subject to them.[34]

The High Commission was not successful in checking the problems associated with the labour trade. This failure can be largely attributed to a small budget, poor access to transport, inadequate staff and a high commissioner who also had the demanding job of Governor of Fiji. Also the High Commission could only act after the event in a judicial role; it could not prevent the infringement occurring.[35] With the failure of the High Commission's attempts to cope with the problem, the British Government realised it would have to declare protectorates over some of these territories if it was to handle the problem more effectively.

Despite Britain's initial reluctance to acquire political responsibilities in the South Pacific, the circumstances of the late nineteenth century eventually impelled it to do so. It was by then clear that a political presence was required to check the lawlessness of British subjects involved in labour recruitment and protect the British settlers clustered in trading settlements throughout the region. There was also the impetus provided by the intentions of rival powers, particularly Germany. Apart from moves by France earlier in the century to declare a protectorate in the Marquesas in 1842 and to annex New Caledonia in 1853, and by Britain to accept an offer of cession from the Fijian chief Ratu Seru Epenisa Cakobau in 1874, no substantial annexation of territory took place until 1884. From

---

32   Ward, *British Policy in the South Pacific*, p. 267.
33   Deryck Scarr, *Fragments of Empire: A History of the Western Pacific High Commission 1877–1914*, Canberra: Australian National University Press, 1967, pp. xvi, 21–3.
34   ibid., p. 30.
35   ibid.

that date, Germany and Britain moved quickly to secure territories in which they already enjoyed a predominant influence. By 1900, each island group in Oceania was part of one of four Western empires: British, French, German or American.[36]

The partition of Oceania was an important step in the development of regional governance, in terms of both its immediate effects and its long-term implications. It meant that almost immediately a degree of subregional unity was achieved. Scattered island groups as far apart as the Cook Islands and Solomon Islands now came under the one flag. A degree of subregional unity was promoted not only by the fact that general policy for all of the Pacific islands was now decided in four metropolitan capitals, but also by the efforts of France, Germany and Britain to achieve some form of administrative coordination within their Pacific empires. The great distance separating the American possessions of Guam and American Samoa discouraged the adoption of a coordinated approach to their administration until they were joined, after the Pacific War, by the Trust Territory of the Pacific Islands in Micronesia.[37]

In the French Pacific, although great distances separated possessions in the west from those in the east, a coordinated approach to administration was taken within each group. In the west, the governing of New Caledonia, New Hebrides and the Wallis and Futuna Islands was coordinated by the creation in 1900 of the office of Commissaire Général de la République dans l'Océan Pacifique, which was held by the Governor of New Caledonia. Completing the centralisation of power, the office of Haut-Commissaire de France dans l'archipel des Nouvelles-Hébrides, established in 1907, was also assigned to the Governor of New Caledonia.[38] In the eastern Pacific, the administrative integration of the hundreds of scattered Polynesian islands was achieved by the creation of the Etablissements Français de l'Océanie, which equates with present-day French Polynesia.[39] The German Government also divided its Pacific empire into two segments. The possessions in the western Pacific—Micronesia (including Nauru) and New Guinea—were, after 1906, administered jointly from government headquarters in New Britain.[40] Samoa came under a separate

---

36 For a detailed examination of the partition of Oceania, see Morrell, *Britain in the Pacific Islands*; and Grattan, *The Southwest Pacific*, Chs 22–3.

37 See David Hanlon, 'Patterns of Colonial Rule in Micronesia', in Howe et al., *Tides of History*.

38 Grattan, *The Southwest Pacific*, p. 403.

39 ibid., p. 411.

40 ibid., p. 346.

administration; however, this arrangement was short-lived. The German territories were taken over by Australia, New Zealand and Japan during World War I.

Administrative coordination in the British Pacific was achieved through a reconstituted Western Pacific High Commission. Under the *British Settlements Act* of 1887, which was applied to the South Pacific by the Pacific Order in Council of 1893, the High Commission was to provide a centralised administration for the new British protectorates—Solomon Islands and the Gilbert and Ellice Islands—and continue its old functions in relation to unacquired territories and islands with which Britain had a special treaty relationship.[41] The High Commission did not fare much better in its new task. Suva was too far removed from the territories—a fact aggravated by poor transport and communications—and the old problems of a tight budget and few staff continued. Conflicts arose between resident commissioners and the high commissioner. This arrangement of centralised control continued despite the unsuitability of the High Commission structure to its new responsibilities.[42]

One of the most significant aspects of the High Commission's operations until the 1890s was the emphasis on 'native welfare' or 'trusteeship'. The High Commission was there to protect islanders against the actions of British labour recruiters and settlers. This was reinforced by the personal attitudes of the high commissioners, who were accused by the British settlers of being one-sided. This emphasis, however, was to change around the turn of the century. The interests of the islanders now took second place to those of the European settlers. The high commissioners began to act on the assumption that the 'native races' were dying out and that there was a 'sacred imperial duty' to develop the resources of the region.[43]

The creation of the Central Medical School in 1928 signalled a return to 'native welfare' considerations.[44] The school was an extension of training facilities that already existed for Fijian 'native practitioners'. Its establishment owed much to the inspiration of Dr S. Lambert and

41 Ward, *British Policy in the South Pacific*, pp. 326–30.
42 Scarr, *Fragments of Empire*, pp. 283–5.
43 ibid., pp. 293–4.
44 For a brief discussion of the work of the Central Medical School, see Linden A. Mander, *Some Dependent Peoples of the South Pacific*, Leiden: E.J. Brill for Institute of Pacific Relations, 1954, pp. 495–7; and Felix M. Keesing, *The South Seas in the Modern World*, New York: John Day Co., 1946, pp. 214–16.

to the financial support of the organisation for which he worked, the Rockefeller Foundation. The four-year medical courses were attended by students from Fiji, Tonga, Western Samoa, the Cook Islands, the Gilbert and Ellice Islands, New Hebrides, Solomon Islands and American Samoa after 1933.[45]

Regional confederation proposals

In the 1920s, the British settlers in Fiji and Western Samoa put forward various proposals for regional confederation that were aimed at benefiting the European settler, not the indigenous inhabitant. In 1921, Henry Scott, a member of the Fijian Legislative Council and Mayor of Suva, proposed a confederation of British territories centred on Suva. Although ostensibly aiming at administrative efficiency and the benefits of a coordinated approach, Scott had other things in mind. Richard Herr and Doug Munro argue that the real motive underlying Scott's initiative was the possibility of gaining 'for British subjects in Fiji and other islands a greater measure of political control of "popular representation"', and further, that this was a 'frantic attempt to ensure that Indians and Fijians remained in their state of subservience'.[46] Although enthusiastically supported by the other members of the legislative council, the proposal received only a lukewarm reception from local officials and was not entertained seriously by the Colonial Office. It was the fear of being 'swallowed up' by Australia or New Zealand that motivated another British settler in Fiji, Henry Stead, to advocate some months later another confederation proposal. Stead's idea was intended to benefit the planter who, he thought, faced similar problems throughout the region.[47]

The cause of the planters and traders was taken up in the 1930s by an Australian, Robert W. Robson, who was editor of the magazine *Pacific Islands Monthly*. The establishment of this monthly magazine in Sydney in 1930, and its circulation to the settlers in most islands of the South Pacific, created an awareness of a common situation faced by European settlers throughout the region. It was an important contributor to, as well as a reflection of, the developing regional consciousness of the

---

45   At the same time, there was a considerable saving in cost to the participating governments through the sharing of training facilities and by the use of native practitioners.
46   Doug Munro and Richard A. Herr, 'Island Confederation and George Westbrook', *ANU Historical Journal*, 9(December), 1972: 10–18, at p. 12.
47   ibid., p. 12.

European settlers. In January 1931, a *Pacific Islands Monthly* editorial by Robson advocated the establishment of a Pacific island association 'for the purpose of consultation, so as to secure united action regarding many vital matters of common interest'.[48] The territories Robson had in mind were the 11 British, Australian and New Zealand territories, plus New Caledonia and American Samoa.

His idea was to have a periodic conference, at first initiated among the British administrations, but later to include France, America and even Japan if they were interested.[49] He thought the following interests should be represented at the conferences: administrators, planters and producers, merchants and traders, 'educated natives', missions and those responsible for communications. The main objective of such an association would be 'the consideration and discussion of all matters of common interests to the islands communities, and the dissemination of information relating thereto'. All of the examples Robson gave of items of common interest that could be discussed related to the interests of the planter: copra prices, wages and pests and diseases affecting crops.[50]

Robson continued his campaign later in the decade. In a radio broadcast in Suva on 24 July 1936, subsequently reported in the *Pacific Islands Monthly*, he once again called for the formation of a regional organisation. Although he saw the ideal as cooperation by all of the colonial powers, he asked that the 'British communities' make a practical start. He regarded as particularly urgent the need for a 'central bureau of economics' to advise planters throughout the region.[51]

Robson's proposals were more influential than previous ones because of their regionwide publicity in the *Pacific Islands Monthly*, and because of his constant travels throughout the islands. In his proposals there is a continuation of some of the main themes in regional thinking of the previous decade. Most importantly, his proposals were aimed mainly at benefiting the European settler in the Pacific islands. Regional cooperation was viewed as a means of sharing information and taking united action in relation to crop production, trade and commerce.

---

48   Robert W. Robson, 'Need for a Closer Relationship between Territories', *Pacific Islands Monthly*, 17 January 1931: 1–2.
49   Robson used the term 'British' to refer also to the Australian and New Zealand territories.
50   Robson, 'Need for a Closer Relationship', pp. 1–2.
51   Robert W. Robson, 'Plea for Co-operation in Pacific Affairs', *Pacific Islands Monthly*, 24 September 1936: 53–4.

But Robson also introduced some new dimensions to regional thought. Unlike his predecessors, he was not advocating a solely British regionalism. He wanted, ultimately, to see French, American and Dutch involvement.

His cry was not that of 'Oceania for the Anglo-Saxons', but rather 'Oceania for the white race'. Regional cooperation was seen not only as a means of preparing 'the way for a much bigger settlement of white folks', but also as a defence against the 'countless swarming millions of Asia'.[52] In desiring to see cooperation among all colonial powers in the South Pacific, Robson consequently envisaged a much more extensive region than did his predecessors. It in fact was slightly more extensive than what is today generally acknowledged as constituting the official Pacific island region. Although the various confederation proposals put forward by the British planters and traders were overtaken by the impact of the Pacific War, they nevertheless formed an important stage in the development of regional thinking.

The proponents and initiators of a regional idea in the period from European settlement in the South Pacific until the outbreak of World War II were mainly British. Within the British camp there were, as we have seen, a number of different groups involved, with varying motives and proposals. In particular, the distinction between the role of the British Government, on the one hand, and that of the various groups of British settlers in the region (especially those in Australia and New Zealand), on the other, should be emphasised. The British Government entered into commitments in the Pacific islands reluctantly, drawn in by the activities of its subjects who, by contrast, were eager to become involved in the region.

While the British Government's regional initiatives were concerned with the protection of the indigenous inhabitants and with administrative and judicial rationalisation, British settlers supported the concept of regional cooperation, and a united region under a British flag, for different reasons. They were concerned with the benefits that such an arrangement could bring to them, in the form of security and territorial gain (in the case of the Australasian colonies), profit (in the case of British traders and planters) or prestige. Apart from the spread of the British Pacific empire, which was

---

52   ibid.

a form of regionalism that the Australasian colonies had proposed, the main substantive expressions of regionalism were the regional institutions created within the British Pacific.

By the outbreak of World War II, then, there had already been a long history of regional thinking. Institutions had been established and there was evidence of a regional consciousness among the Europeans living in the islands and recognition of a shared situation in territories thousands of kilometres apart. This regional thinking had already extended to the non-British Pacific in Robson's proposals and already incorporated all of the territories included in the postwar boundaries. Absent, however, from prewar developments was the inclusion of the indigenous inhabitants of the region, the Pacific islanders. Also absent was cooperation among the various colonial governments with territories in the region. This was soon to change. The Pacific War of 1941–45 spurred the social democratic governments of Australia and New Zealand to impose a new regional frame on the Pacific island region.

4

Colonial regionalism

From the mid twentieth century, changing European ideas about the 'Pacific islander', as well as changing ideas Europeans had about themselves, led to a dramatic shift in the moral purpose of 'framing the islands', or at least in some influential quarters. Influenced by ideas of the right to self-determination and 'native welfare', but also by nationalism and geopolitical considerations, the Labor/Labour governments in Australia and New Zealand promoted, between 1943 and 1947, the establishment of a formal intercolonial regional organisation. This marking out of what was then termed the South Pacific (including the islands of the North Pacific from 1951) from a newly formed South-East Asia was accompanied by an effort to create an identity among the diverse peoples of the 20 Pacific colonies from Netherlands New Guinea to French Oceania. Referred to as an experiment by those attempting to create such a regional identity at the time, this colonial construction of a formal region influenced the shape of subsequent indigenous regional thinking and set up the boundaries within which postcolonial questions of Pacific identity, agency and community were later played out.

Formation of the South Pacific Commission

Meeting as the South Seas Conference in a Canberra grammar school in 1947, representatives of six colonial powers—the United States, Britain, the Netherlands, France, Australia and New Zealand—created a formal region with etched-in boundaries to replace the hazier notions of the

'South Seas' or 'the islands'.[1] After some debate over its naming, they decided to call this region 'the South Pacific', and established a regional institution, the South Pacific Commission (SPC), to 'encourage and strengthen international co-operation in promoting the economic and social welfare and advancement of the peoples of the non-self-governing territories in the South Pacific'.[2]

Australia and New Zealand initiated the 1947 conference at which the Canberra Agreement was signed.[3] They had been proposing the establishment of such an organisation since January 1944, when a decision to promote the creation of a South Seas regional commission had formed part of the agreement between Australia and New Zealand (the Anzac Pact).[4] They were delayed in taking their proposal further, first by the war and then by the creation of the United Nations. It is evident that the SPC would not have been formed without the initiative of the Australasian governments. The other colonial powers initially played a passive role and were less than enthusiastic about the proposal.[5]

The membership of the SPC was limited to the six governments which signed the Canberra Agreement. They are referred to in the agreement as 'participating governments'. The financial arrangements reflected the predominant role of Australia. The agreement provided for the following shares of the commission's annual budget to be contributed by participating governments: Australia, 30 per cent; the Netherlands, 15 per cent; New Zealand, 15 per cent; the United Kingdom, 15 per cent; France, 12.5 per cent; and the United States, 12.5 per cent.[6] The only

---

1   Not to be confused with 'the South Sea' (singular), which, following Vasco Núñez de Balboa's sighting of what was later called the Pacific Ocean (and which he called Mar del Sur), was used until the beginning of the nineteenth century to refer to the Pacific Ocean as a whole. From the nineteenth century, when the broader ocean had begun to be generally referred to as the Pacific, 'the South Seas' (plural) suggested a more restricted geographical area covering the islands in the southern and central Pacific and the waters around them. See Spate, 'The Pacific as an Artefact', pp. 34–5.
2   *Agreement Establishing the South Pacific Commission*, Canberra, 6 February 1947, Preamble.
3   The South Seas Commission Conference, 28 January – 6 February 1947. For a full account of the conference, see New Zealand Department of External Affairs, *Report of the New Zealand Delegation on the Conference Held at Canberra, 28 January – 6 February, 1947, for the Purpose of Establishing an Advisory Commission for the South Pacific*, Publication No. 26, Wellington: Government Printer, 1947.
4   Australian Department of External Affairs, 'Australian–New Zealand Agreement', *Current Notes on International Affairs*, [Canberra], 15(1)(January), 1944: 2–9, Clause 31.
5   See Harry E. Maude, 'The South Pacific Commission', *Australia's Neighbours*, Series 4, No. 5, Melbourne: Australian Institute of International Affairs, June 1963, p. l; and Australia, 'South Pacific Commission', *The Round Table: The Commonwealth Journal of International Affairs*, 48(189), 1957: 87–93, at p. 88.
6   *Agreement Establishing the South Pacific Commission*, Art. XIV, S. 49.

changes in membership in the period under study occurred in 1962, when the Netherlands withdrew, and in 1964, when the membership rules were amended to allow the admission of a newly independent Pacific state, Western Samoa.[7]

The area to be covered by the SPC was originally limited to territories 'south of the Equator and east from and including Netherlands New Guinea'.[8] The boundary line was adjusted twice over the next 15 years— first in 1951, when the American territories north of the equator were included,[9] and second in 1962, when West New Guinea was excluded after becoming part of Indonesia.[10] After these changes, there were 19 territories within the commission's scope.

The broad embrace of these new boundaries was not suggested by the scope of any existing regional arrangement. The most inclusive of such arrangements, the Central Medical School in Suva, drew students from as far as Papua in the west and Western Samoa in the east, but did not include the American, French or Dutch Pacific.[11] To those determining postwar arrangements, it was the experience of the Pacific War that suggested a regional vision stretching over a much larger canvas. The prosecution of the war had required a conceptual linking of all the islands in a 'Pacific theatre'. It also necessitated intercolonial collaboration among the Dutch, British, Australian, New Zealand, French and American governments. The war also encouraged, at least in Australia, a breaking down of the conceptual barrier between 'Asia' and 'the Pacific'. In his wartime speeches, Australian external affairs minister Dr Herbert Evatt linked the area stretching from Timor to Fiji and New Caledonia in an 'arc of islands' concept that would underlie the Australian push for the creation of a South Seas region.[12]

---

7 *Agreement Amending the Agreement Establishing the South Pacific Commission of 6 February 1947*, London, 6 October 1964, Art. VII(b).
8 *Agreement Establishing the South Pacific Commission*, Art. II, S. 2.
9 *Agreement Extending the Territorial Scope of the South Pacific Commission*, Nouméa, 7 November 1951.
10 By way of Articles II and XIX of the Canberra Agreement.
11 The leprosy colony at Makogai in Fiji also drew its patients from various British, Australian and New Zealand territories. A more limited region was suggested by the most prominent of existing administrative arrangements, the Western Pacific High Commission, which only covered the British territories, and by the Nasinu Teachers' Training College, which drew its students from Western Samoa, Tonga and Fiji by the time of the 1950 conference.
12 See H.V. Evatt, *Foreign Policy of Australia: Speeches by H.V. Evatt*, Sydney: Angus & Robertson, 1945, pp. 116, 132; and Australian Department of External Affairs, 'Australian–New Zealand Agreement', Clause 31.

By 1947, political developments in South-East Asia suggested a western boundary for the South Pacific that included Dutch New Guinea. The moves towards independence in Indonesia and the Philippines and the creation of a region called South-East Asia confirmed that the South Pacific boundary would include all the remaining island dependencies scattered across the Pacific Ocean.[13] Despite the name 'South Pacific', and the acceptance of the equator as a rough northern border for the time being, it was clearly intended that the American islands north of the equator be included once their administrative arrangements had been settled.[14]

The SPC's role was limited by the inclusion in the Canberra Agreement of a 'saving clause', which ensured there would be no interference by the commission in the relationships between metropolitan powers and their island territories.[15] In accordance with this principle, the role of the commission was restricted to a 'consultative and advisory' one. Its advice was to be given to the metropolitan governments and not to the territorial administrations.[16] The powers and functions of the commission were also limited specifically to economic and social development fields to ensure that political matters were not discussed.[17] This 'no politics' rule was later to have an important effect on indigenous participants in South Pacific conferences.

The organisational structure proposed in the agreement consisted of a 12-person commission (two members representing each participating government) and two 'auxiliary bodies'—a research council to recommend and undertake research and a triennial South Pacific Conference to give the local inhabitants of the region an opportunity to discuss, and make recommendations concerning, matters that came within the commission's jurisdiction. To serve all three bodies, a secretariat was to be established.[18] Control of the organisation's activities rested firmly with the 12 commissioners, who were representatives of the metropolitan governments. They were to be the final authority on all matters. The other bodies established by the agreement were merely advisory

---

13   See Donald K. Emmerson, '"Southeast Asia": What's in a Name?', *Journal of Southeast Asian Studies*, 15(1), 1984: 1–21, at pp. 7–9.
14   Indeed, the boundaries of the South Pacific were redrawn to include the American islands north of the equator in 1951. See *Agreement Extending the Territorial Scope of the South Pacific Commission*.
15   *Agreement Establishing the South Pacific Commission*, Art. XVII (Saving Clause).
16   ibid., Art. IV, S. 6.
17   ibid., Art. IV.
18   ibid., Arts III, V, VI, IX, XIII.

to the central executive body. This arrangement, which ensured the dominance of colonial power in the organisation, became an important source of frustration for Pacific islanders in later years. There had been, however, a special effort made to encourage indigenous involvement in the work of the commission through participation in the South Pacific Conference—a crucial decision for the development of a regional consciousness among island leaders.

Trusteeship and self-determination

When they proposed the establishment of such a regional commission in 1944, the Australian and New Zealand governments were at least partly motivated by concern about promoting a regional community based on trusteeship principles. This owed much to the fact that there were Labor/ Labour parties in government in both countries, and to the personal attitudes of Australian external affairs minister Herbert Evatt and New Zealand prime minister Peter Fraser.[19] Missionaries and anthropologists were also promoting the concept publicly in Australia just prior to the government's decision to initiate the establishment of a regional commission based on these principles. In 1940, the Reverend M. Frater had called for the formation of a 'South Pacific confederation', which would have as its purpose the promotion of security and 'the conservation and development of the native races'.[20] The Reverend John Wear Burton, head of the Methodist Overseas Mission, put forward a similar proposal.[21] In 1943, Adolphus Peter 'A.P.' Elkin, Professor of Anthropology at the University of Sydney—drawing specifically on the principles of the Atlantic Charter—advocated a 'Charter for the Native Peoples of the South Pacific'. It included a provision for a 'Pacific Regional Council' to administer the promotion of native interests.[22]

Ideas about 'native welfare' had been around in different forms since the beginning of colonial rule. But at the end of World War II, these ideas took on new force in world politics. The UN charter spelt out the trusteeship obligations for powers with mandated territories, which included a duty

---

19 Evatt's central role in these developments is described in Paul Hasluck, *The Government and the People*, Canberra: Australian War Memorial, 1970, pp. 478–88. See also Forsyth, 'South Pacific', p. 7.

20 M. Frater, 'Why Not a South Pacific Confederation?', *Pacific Islands Monthly*, 15 May 1940, p. 22.

21 J.W. Burton, *Brown and White in the South Pacific: A Study in Culture Conflict*, Sydney: Australian Institute of International Affairs, 1944, pp. 62–3.

22 A.P. Elkin, *Wanted: A Charter for the Native Peoples of the South-West Pacific*, Sydney: Australasian Publishing Co., 1943, pp. 7–9.

to promote the welfare and political advancement of dependent peoples. But trusteeship ideas were also applied in a more general sense to all dependent territories whether or not they were mandated by the United Nations. In this more general usage, trusteeship was seen as marking 'a formal recognition of the moral obligation to administer dependent territories with justice and a sense of responsibility towards the inhabitants themselves and the world at large'.[23] 'Trusteeship', in the postwar era, took the older 'native welfare' ideas and added legal and moral obligations as well as more explicitly suggesting, in its advocacy of political development, a move towards self-government. It became a strengthened norm of the international community.

These ideas were particularly influential in Canberra and Wellington, where Labor/Labour governments committed to democratic socialist principles were intent on applying the most progressive interpretation of the approach at the United Nations in relation to their own colonies. In July 1945, the Australian Minister for External Territories, Eddie Ward, made a controversial statement to the Australian Parliament outlining the commitment of the Labor Government to promoting native welfare in Papua and New Guinea. Indenture was to be abolished, there was to be a new emphasis on education and health and settlers' rights were for the first time to be constrained by 'native welfare' considerations.[24] According to the historian J.D. Legge, the parliamentary opponents of the new approach saw in 'all talk of improving the material welfare of native peoples in New Guinea merely the sentimental influence of starry-eyed theorists and long-haired anthropologists'.[25] In 1949, the *Papua New Guinea Act* began political development in providing for limited participation by local inhabitants in the new legislative council. The New Zealand Government was much further down this track. It moved quickly to put in place very significant political reforms in Western Samoa. In 1948, it established a ministerial council, comprising the high commissioner and the three *fautua* ('royal sons'), and a legislative council with Samoan members.[26]

---

23   A.H. McDonald, ed., *Trusteeship in the Pacific*, Sydney: Angus & Robertson, published under the auspices of the Australian Institute of International Affairs and the Institute of Pacific Relations, 1949, p. vii.
24   J.D. Legge, *Australian Colonial Policy: A Survey of Native Administration and European Development in Papua*, Sydney: Angus & Robertson under the auspices of the Australian Institute of International Affairs, 1956, pp. 192–5.
25   ibid., p. 194.
26   These developments are described in detail in J.W. Davidson, *Samoa mo Samoa: The Emergence of the Independent State of Western Samoa*, Melbourne: Oxford University Press, 1967, pp. 163–87.

The Australian and New Zealand governments were also intent on promoting native welfare and self-determination principles across the wider region. As early as 1944 these two governments made their intentions known in the Anzac Pact, in which they proposed the application of Atlantic Charter principles to the subject peoples of the Pacific.[27] To promote these principles, including 'political development', they proposed a regional organisation comprising the colonial powers with Pacific territories. The proposed regional commission was to be given the function of recommending

> arrangements for the participation of natives in administration in increasing measure with a view to promoting the ultimate attainment of self-government in the form most suited to the circumstances of the native peoples concerned.[28]

And it was to be given the function of publishing 'periodical reviews of progress towards the development of self-governing institutions in the islands of the Pacific'.[29]

However, the attitudes held by the Australian and New Zealand leaders were not shared by the other colonial powers with territories in the Pacific. These other powers were not motivated to the same extent by a belief in the rights of subject peoples to move towards self-government. While these powers had engaged in what might be described as 'native welfare' policies in the prewar era—even extending to significant political development in some cases—they did not want to encourage self-government as an endpoint, nor did they want any regional institution calling them to task on progress in this area. Their purpose was not to dismantle empire.[30] By January 1947, when the six powers met to establish the SPC, the political development aspects of the Australian–New Zealand proposal had been dropped so that agreement might be reached.[31] In his authoritative history of the formation of the SPC, T.R. Smith argues that, by 1947, 'neither France nor Britain nor the United States was willing to give away any of her rights to decide the political future of her dependent territories'.[32]

---

27 Australian Department of External Affairs, 'Australia–New Zealand Agreement', Clauses 28–31.
28 ibid., Clauses 31(a), 31(f).
29 ibid., Clauses 31(a), 31(f).
30 In the case of the Dutch Government, the aim was to retain West New Guinea against pressure from the new Indonesian Government, which was keen to complete the decolonisation of the Netherlands East Indies.
31 Forsyth, 'South Pacific', p. 7.
32 Smith, *South Pacific Commission*, p. 12.

The colonial rulers did, however, see advantage in promoting regional trusteeship to counter the anticolonial forces at the United Nations. That is, they saw the embrace of the internationalisation of trusteeship as necessary to preclude intrusion by the United Nations. It was ultimately about maintaining empire in the face of the new emphasis on anticolonial norms in the international community. The result was a watered-down form of regional trusteeship, which disallowed the discussion of political development. The US, Australian and New Zealand governments had to bow to this more conservative interpretation of trusteeship to establish an intercolonial organisation concerned with native welfare.

While their main objective was to create a sense of region among themselves, and to be seen to be doing so by an international audience, these colonial powers also decided to encourage the participation of Pacific islanders in this regional project. This was to be done through a regular South Pacific Conference of territorial representatives whose recommendations would be tendered as advice to the new commission.[33] For those concerned with a more progressive interpretation of trusteeship, this was the potential sting in the tail. The United States, New Zealand and Australia promoted the idea of islander participation at the South Seas Conference of 1947. They departed from the recently established Caribbean model in attempting to ensure that the delegates to the conference were as far as possible Pacific islanders, to encourage both indigenous representation and local participatory processes.

Although not heralded as such, this was where their hopes for a broader notion of trusteeship resided. While the SPC was constitutionally forbidden to talk about political development, William D. Forsyth reported that Evatt, the then Australian external affairs minister, for example, was 'not blind' to the 'political potential' inherent in the conference.[34] This proposal was reluctantly accepted by those keen to maintain empire but only on condition that political development issues be prohibited in conference discussions. For those holding this view, there was even an advantage in this experiment because it would strengthen the image of regional trusteeship without giving away anything substantive to the anticolonial position. That is, it could be a showcase for a well-intentioned colonialism, which included Pacific islander participation.

---

33 *Agreement Establishing the South Pacific Commission.*
34 Forsyth, 'South Pacific', p. 7.

Geopolitics and nationalism

While 'native welfare' and trusteeship considerations influenced the decision of the Australasian leaders to promote the establishment of a regional commission, it is evident they were at the same time pursuing other motives of greater significance to them. When Fraser and Evatt met in Canberra in January 1944 and agreed, inter alia, to the establishment of a South Seas regional commission, the war against Japan in the Pacific was still in progress; Japanese troops were still in New Britain, New Guinea and Solomon Islands. Although the function of the proposed regional commission was stated as being 'to secure a common policy on social, economic and political development directed towards the advancement and well-being of the native peoples themselves',[35] the more pressing motive underlying this proposal is reflected elsewhere in the Anzac Pact:

> Within the framework of a general system of world security, a regional zone of defence comprising the South West and South Pacific areas shall be established and that this zone should be based on Australia and New Zealand, stretching through the arc of islands North and North East of Australia, to Western Samoa and the Cook Islands.[36]

In his speeches and writings on foreign policy in 1943 and 1944, Evatt repeatedly stressed the importance of the islands to Australia's security and the desirability of establishing a regional zone of defence. For example, in an address at the Overseas Press Club in New York in April 1943, Evatt said: 'Australia will naturally regard as of crucial importance to its own security the arc of islands lying to the north and north-east of our continent'.[37] He developed this theme further in an article in the Sydney *Daily Telegraph* in August of that year:

> Of crucial importance to Australia's own security will be such Islands as Timor, New Guinea, the Solomons, the New Hebrides, Fiji, and New Caledonia ... I therefore visualize the formation of a great South-west Pacific zone of security against aggression, and in its establishment, Australia must act with such colonial powers as Holland, France and Portugal, as well as with the United States and Great Britain.[38]

---

35 Australian Department of External Affairs, 'Australian–New Zealand Agreement', Clause 31.
36 ibid., Clause 13.
37 Evatt, *Foreign Policy of Australia*, p. 116.
38 ibid., p. 132.

This concern with regional defence does not appear at first to bear any relation to the formation of the SPC, a body concerned with the economic development of the territories and the welfare of Pacific islanders; but it is in fact directly related. It is evident from speeches and writings of the time that Australia saw the welfare of the islanders and the development of their countries as important aspects of the future security of Australia and New Zealand. For example, in a statement to the House of Representatives on 14 October 1943, Evatt said:

> As a result of the war Australia must show a particular interest in the welfare and system of control of those islands and territories which lie close to our shores … We have a definite interest in seeing that, after the war, these islands should maintain sufficient bases and be developed along lines that will make them not a liability but an asset in the defence of the South-west and South Pacific.[39]

And, earlier in the same year, he was reported as saying that no 'regional system of security, however, can be permanent unless it has an adequate basis in economic justice'.[40]

There are two ways, then, in which promotion of economic development in the South Pacific was seen as advantageous to Australia from a defence point of view: first, as a means of developing the infrastructure of island economies so that in the event of war they would prove more useful as bases than they had in World War II, and second, as a means of increasing the welfare of the islanders so they would remain friendly to the powers which made this possible. The Australian and New Zealand governments thought the most effective way to promote the economic, social and political development they wished to see in the islands would be through a regional organisation. In view of the fact that they had control of only a few of the island territories in the region, a cooperative approach initiated and shaped by them was the obvious course to achieve some control over future developments in the region. In the Anzac Pact, the two governments agreed that

> the future of the various territories of the Pacific and the welfare of their inhabitants cannot be successfully promoted without a greater measure of collaboration between the numerous authorities concerned in their control.[41]

---

39 ibid., p. 142.
40 ibid., p. 116.
41 Australian Department of External Affairs, 'Australian–New Zealand Agreement', Clause 29.

To facilitate this collaboration, they proposed the South Seas regional commission. There were, however, additional factors influencing the Australian and New Zealand initiative. Disturbed by the fact that the United States, the United Kingdom and China had taken decisions at the Cairo Conference (in November 1943) regarding the future of the wider Pacific region without consulting them, and conscious of the decrease in British influence in the Pacific island region as a result of World War II, the Australian and New Zealand governments were anxious to devise their own plan for the South Pacific.[42] On 30 March 1944, in a statement to the House of Representatives, Evatt said 'we must have a primary and principal responsibility in determining the future of the particular region in which we live',[43] and, further, that

> Australia and New Zealand have a duty to make a positive contribution to the future of the Pacific. They are the two British Pacific Dominions which must uphold Western civilisation in this part of the world.[44]

Australia and New Zealand had desired such a role since the nineteenth century. However, in view of their ties with Britain and their own low stature on the international stage, their actions had in the past been more of encouraging British involvement rather than taking an active role themselves.[45]

The Australasian initiative can be seen, then, as being motivated primarily by strategic and nationalistic factors. While trusteeship or 'native welfare' considerations were also a significant influence, the evidence suggests that such considerations can be regarded as of secondary importance.[46] They influenced the form and intended preoccupations of the proposed regional commission, and provided the public justification for its establishment, but they were not the determining factors. Australia and New Zealand took the initiative while World War II was still in progress and in the knowledge that larger powers were taking decisions about postwar international

---

42   For the important influence the Cairo Conference had on Evatt's decision to take a regional initiative, see Alan Watt, *The Evolution of Australian Foreign Policy 1938–1965*, Cambridge: Cambridge University Press, 1968, p. 73; and Hasluck, *The Government and the People*, pp. 482, 487.

43   Evatt, *Foreign Policy of Australia*, p. 176. See also C. Hartley Grattan, 'Australia and New Zealand and Pacific-Asia', in F.P. King, ed., *Oceania and Beyond: Essays on the Pacific Since 1945*, Westport, CT: Greenwood Press, 1976, pp. 79–116, at pp. 98–9.

44   Evatt, *Foreign Policy of Australia*, p. 172.

45   Australia and New Zealand had, however, entered the region very eagerly as administering powers during World War I. See Grattan, 'Australia and New Zealand and Pacific-Asia', p. 86.

46   For a view of the motives of the Australasian governments that emphasises trusteeship or 'native welfare' considerations, see Smith, *South Pacific Commission*, Chs 1, 3.

organisation. The Australasian governments held the view that they should have primary responsibility for determining postwar arrangements for the South Pacific region. They wanted those arrangements to be such that they would minimise the opportunity for outside interests to gain a foothold in the region and so be in a position to threaten their security. They saw a regional solution, in the form of a regional commission comprising friendly Western powers responsible for all the territories in the region, as the appropriate organisational arrangement. These attitudes can be seen as an extension of the Australasian Monroe doctrine of the nineteenth century, only this time Australia and New Zealand were in a position to assert foreign policies independently of Britain.

The other colonial powers—the United Kingdom, the United States, the Netherlands and France—were not motivated by the same strategic considerations. Their removed geographical position and other commitments made the security of the South Pacific a low priority. If the stated purpose and subsequent activities of the SPC tell the observer anything about their motives, it is likely that they were at least partly motivated by the desire to promote 'native welfare' in their territories and saw regional cooperation as an effective way of approaching this task. However, as in the Australian and New Zealand case, more important considerations can be shown to underlie their support. In view of the attitude of these powers to the political development of their territories, as revealed in their refusal to have that subject come under the purview of the proposed regional commission, it could be argued that they viewed the establishment of the SPC as a means of keeping UN activity to a minimum in this area. In other words, it is possible to see the involvement of the colonial powers other than Australia and New Zealand as an exercise in tokenism—an effort to comply with the mood of global opinion by setting up an organisation seemingly taking care of the problems of the South Pacific, and consequently forestalling international examination of constitutional development in their territories.

Contending ideas on political agency, 1948–65

The first two decades of the SPC's operation reflected the tension between the two conceptual framings concerning the political agency of Pacific islanders present at the establishment of the organisation. On the one hand, the organisation was governed by the colonial powers for the colonial powers, and the 'no politics' rule was enforced. The commission promoted native welfare programs across areas such as health, education and agriculture, consistent with the framing of Pacific islanders as deserving of development but not capable or deserving of political agency. In this sense, it was a continuation of a regional framing that had been dominant since the nineteenth century.

On the other hand, there were several subtle developments in the operations of the commission that were more representative of the principle of trusteeship: the depiction of an idealised Pacific islander who had the capability and right to exercise political agency, and of an idealised Pacific island society that had the capacity and right to self-determination. The first trend to note is that concerning the direction of the commission's advice. The agreement had stipulated that this should flow directly to the metropolitan governments. By 1957, however, the secretariat and technical officers had established relations with the territorial administrations and 'advice' flowed to them rather than to the participating governments.[47] This change in direction was formalised by the decisions of the review conference held in 1957.[48] By the early 1960s, the practice changed again. The commission began to establish direct relationships with Pacific island leaders. Harry Maude, who had been a member of the commission's research council in its early years, comments that it was here that the commission 'had achieved its most conspicuous success'.[49]

Running parallel with this change in orientation, and related to it, was a change in the work program. Smith distinguishes three stages in this development: the first was one in which the commission concentrated on research and advice; in the second, it emphasised technical aid; and in the third, it became concerned with education and training.[50] The earliest projects consisted largely of exploratory surveys. This gave way to a more applied research stage by about 1953. The 1957 review conference decided that 'the work programme should emphasise projects of applied research, technical assistance, and the dissemination of technical and other information adapted to the practical needs of the local administrations'.[51] In response to this decision, the commission session of that year directed

---

47 Maude, 'The South Pacific Commission', p. 3.
48 Smith, *South Pacific Commission*, p. 101.
49 Maude, 'The South Pacific Commission', p. 3.
50 Smith, *South Pacific Commission*, p. 99.
51 South Pacific Commission, *Seventh Session: Proceedings*, Nouméa: South Pacific Commission, 1957, App. 1, pp. 23–6.

the organisation to concentrate on a priority list of 10 subjects: fisheries, health education, nutrition, mosquito-borne diseases, public health, pests and diseases, plant introduction, literature promotion, education and aided self-help.[52] As the program became more directly related to Pacific islanders in the early 1960s, an increasing emphasis was placed on technical assistance and training courses.

In this period, the SPC was also responsible for establishing other regional institutions in which Pacific islanders could forge links with each other. These included the commission's Community Education Centre and the South Pacific Games. The former, set up in Suva in 1962, was established to train Pacific islander teachers and social workers in domestic science and community work. The idea for the South Pacific Games was first mooted by Pacific islander delegates to the fourth South Pacific Conference in 1959. The commission called the first organising committee, assisted in the formation of the games council and helped Fiji to organise the first South Pacific Games in 1963.

The most important policy expression of the principle of Pacific islander agency was the South Pacific Conference. As we saw above, this was intended as such by the Australian and New Zealand drafters of the Canberra Agreement. The conference provided the first opportunity for Melanesian, Polynesian and Micronesian leaders to get together and exchange views. Beginning in 1950, the conference met every three years until 1965, and annually from 1967. It stands out as the key aspect of the SPC influencing the development of Pacific islander awareness of the region, and of other societies within it. Maude commented that the conference

> has served to create for the first time in Pacific history what may be described as a regional outlook: a sense of common interests and problems and indeed, of common destiny.[53]

The role of the conference in fostering a shared regional consciousness among Pacific island leaders, and ultimately as the arena for a 'rebellion' against the hegemony of colonial regionalism, is developed in the next two chapters.

---

52   ibid.
53   Maude, 'The South Pacific Commission', p. 3.

Conclusion

As a result of the Pacific War, the 'idea of the Pacific' became an intercolonial project expressed in the establishment of the SPC and the creation of formal regional boundaries. While France, the Netherlands, the United Kingdom and the United States were important players in these developments, Australia and New Zealand were the strongest promoters of the new regional commission. This regional project was part of their own nation-building, not only in relation to establishing their security, but also as part of an ideology of a 'civilising mission' and imperial ambition. The 'Australasian Monroe doctrine', as Bismarck called it in the 1880s, thus continued to be a key aspect of this story of the formal 'framing of the islands' in the 1940s.

The contest over the political agency of Pacific islanders began in earnest in the 1940s when the impacts of the Pacific War, Pacific anthropology and changing ideas within the Christian churches created a new idea about the potentiality of 'native peoples'. Rather than the negative images of political agency contained in the images of 'dying races' and 'child races' of earlier decades, there was recognition of the possibility of the capacity for future political agency in the doctrines of trusteeship, 'native welfare' and 'self-determination'. These became the basis of the regional project pursued by Labor/Labour governments in Australia and New Zealand in the period 1943–44. Other powers, however, saw the regional idea as a way of containing the self-determination ideas associated with the UN system of regionalism.

This was the culmination of 100 years of normative contest within the European imagination over whether Pacific islanders had the capacity for political agency and whether they should be encouraged to act on it. It was also the beginning of a three-decade regional contest over political agency within the new regional structure, with France in particular on one side, and Australia, New Zealand and Pacific island leaders on the other.

The boundaries of the Pacific island region began as a hazy notion. 'Oceania', as first conceived in France in the 1830s, included much of what we would now call island South-East Asia. The South Seas generally referred to the island world of the Pacific including the islands north of the equator. But it was in 1947 that the official boundaries of the South Pacific were first drawn. They reflected a division between the new

South-East Asia and the Pacific island region with a boundary west of the island of New Guinea. At first, it included only islands south of the equator, but from 1950 the region expanded to include the American Pacific north of the equator. In 1962, the boundaries of the South Pacific were again redrawn, this time to exclude West New Guinea after it was taken over by Indonesia.[54]

54　West New Guinea remained part of the Pacific as defined by some NGOs and some Pacific island governments.

5

The South Pacific experiment[1]

Whatever the reach and depth of ancient ties among Pacific islanders, the postwar attempt to create a regional identity among the emergent elite of the territories stretching from Dutch New Guinea to Tahiti was regarded as novel by those involved. The novelty is captured in the official photograph of the first South Pacific Conference, which met in the assembly hall of the Nasinu Teachers' Training College in Suva in April–May 1950.[2] In stark contrast to the photographs of the South Seas Conference of 1947, at which no islanders were present, the 1950 photograph shows only one European delegate, the representative of French Oceania. In his opening address as chairman, Sir Brian Freeston, Governor of Fiji and Western Pacific High Commissioner, described the gathering as a 'Parliament of the South Pacific Peoples' and observed:

> Never before in the history of the world have the peoples of the South Pacific met together under one roof … never before has an opportunity been afforded for spokesmen from all the islands, spread over many millions of square miles of ocean, to meet each

1   This chapter was first published as 'The South Pacific Experiment: Reflections on the Origins of Regional Identity', in the *Journal of Pacific History* (32[2], 1997: 180–202). I am grateful to the publishers for permission to reproduce this work.
2   The conference, held from 25 April to 5 May 1950, was attended by 43 representatives of 14 Pacific island territories: American Samoa, British Solomon Islands Protectorate, Cook Islands (including Niue), Ellice Islands, Fiji, French Oceania, Gilbert Islands, Nauru, Netherlands New Guinea, New Caledonia, New Hebrides, Papua, New Guinea and Western Samoa. Representatives of the Tongan Government also participated. Tokelau Islands, although entitled to representation, did not have a delegate present.

> other on common ground, united by a community of interest, and animated by a common purpose … during the next ten days, you will be making history; and that throughout the length and breadth of the Pacific, the generations to come will look back on this conference as an outstanding landmark in their progress … Let us remember that we are embarking together on a momentous experiment.[3]

Other observers echoed these sentiments. Editorials in newspapers in Fiji, New Zealand, Australia and even as far afield as *The Times* and *The New York Times* commented on the significance of the occasion. A *Sydney Morning Herald* editorial, for example, asserted:

> To-morrow a new chapter will be opened in the history of the South Pacific. For the first time, representatives of all the races of the South Seas—Polynesian, Melanesian and Micronesian, together with the more recent immigrant races such as the Indian community in Fiji—will meet to discuss common problems.[4]

Island delegates seemed to share this view. Mariota Tuiasosopo, Speaker of the House of Representatives in American Samoa, for example, commented at the conclusion of the meeting:

> [F]or the first time in history we are gathered here as one people desiring the welfare of our communities. I pray that we, the hereditary leaders will realise that it is now our turn to do our best for our people.[5]

Crown Prince Tungi, the premier of Tonga, was reported as saying 'the conference was a milestone in Pacific relations and could mean a new dawn for the peoples of the South Seas'.[6] Tupua Tamasese Mea'ole, a member of the Council of Ministers of Western Samoa, commented more cryptically (but possibly in reference to the successful struggle of the *Mau* against New Zealand rule) that the conference marked 'the end of the beginning' for the peoples of the South Seas.[7]

---

3   As reported in 'Pacific History Made Today', *Fiji Times and Herald*, 25 April 1950.
4   'South Seas Experiment in Co-operation', *Sydney Morning Herald*, 24 April 1950, p. 2.
5   'Talks End on S. Pacific: Results Pleasing to Delegates', *The Age*, [Melbourne], 6 May 1950.
6   ibid.
7   'New Era for South Seas: Success at Suva', *Sydney Morning Herald*, 6 May 1950.

More intriguing, perhaps, than this image of the Nasinu meeting as a point of departure for a sense of region among islanders is its widespread representation among European officials, observers and media commentators as an 'experiment'—whether 'courageous', 'great', 'historic', 'remarkable' or 'momentous'.[8] In their widely reported comments and confidential reports, they made it clear that, by 'experiment', they meant more than mere novelty. The impression was given of uncertain and even risky outcomes. The Australian observer Reverend Dr J.W. Burton,[9] in his report to the Australian Minister for External Affairs, referred to the 'forebodings' and 'fears' among 'some of us' prior to the conference;[10] Nancy Robson (a French–English interpreter at early South Pacific conferences and author of the only commentary on the conference outside newspaper reports) mentioned 'the misgivings of the uneasy';[11] and governor Freeston, in his concluding statement, was reported as saying that 'when the conference began he had feared that it might be a complete failure'.[12]

Rather than a sense of tapping into a preexisting affinity, of building on ancient ties, the observers gave a strong impression that what was being attempted was social engineering on a grand scale. The sense of attempting something 'against the odds' is also suggested by the widespread surprise among observers when the conference seemed to be successful. Freeston declared that 'never in his life had he been so happy to find out, how wrong he was' (in predicting 'complete failure').[13] And for Nancy Robson, 'the notion of a South Pacific synthesis seem[ed] more for the moment than a mere visionary dream'. She concluded:

---

8   See, for example, 'Pacific Native Chiefs Gather at Suva', *The Age*, [Melbourne], 24 April 1950; 'South Seas Experiment in Co-operation', *Sydney Morning Herald*; 'NZ Observer Reviews Aims and Results of Conference', *Fiji Times and Herald*, 9 May 1950.

9   J.W. Burton had only recently retired as the General Secretary of the Methodist Church of Australasia and had also been General Secretary of the Methodist Overseas Mission for about 20 years. His missionary work had focused on the South Pacific and he had published extensively on the Pacific islands. See, for example, Burton, *Brown and White in the South Pacific*. Burton's son was the head of the Department of External Affairs at the time of the Nasinu conference.

10   J.W. Burton, 'The South Pacific Conference, held at Nasinu, Fiji, May 1950: Report by the Australian Observer, Rev. J. W. Burton (for the Minister of State for External Affairs and External Territories)', Sydney, June 1950, Department of External Affairs, Series A1838/1, file 347/2/6, 1950, folio 79, National Archives of Australia, Canberra.

11   Nancy Robson, 'The Suva Conference of South Pacific Peoples', *Australian Outlook*, 4(3), 1950: 179–85, at p. 179.

12   'South Pacific Peoples' Conference: Successful Experiment', *The Times*, [London], 6 May 1950.

13   ibid.

> [P]erhaps the day will not seem impossibly remote when the vast scattering of disparate islands may achieve a sense of unity, and when there may at last take form some common will of South Pacific peoples.[14]

The idea that the creation of a sense of region among Pacific islanders was difficult and unnatural appears to fly in the face of a longstanding tendency for the Pacific islands to be thought of collectively in the European imagination, and sits oddly with claims by prominent Pacific islanders about ancient affinities and connections.[15] It also runs up against the naturalness of regionalism in the postcolonial setting, where, as a social science category, institution, political site or basis of organisation, it has taken on an unquestioned status. This chapter therefore explores in what sense, and why, this first gathering of island representatives was characterised as an experiment.[16] This in turn suggests a way of thinking about the origins of postcolonial regional identity. Accordingly, this discussion focuses on the way in which the Nasinu conference was represented by those organising, participating in and observing it, rather than on the substance of the discussions and outcomes on the key agenda items concerning mosquito control, village health, village education, vocational training, cooperative societies, fisheries methods, food and export crops.[17]

This exploration proceeds on the premise that several experiments were invested in this attempt to foster a sense of region, operating at different levels and sometimes pulling in different directions. Two 'experiments'

---

14   Robson, 'The Suva Conference of South Pacific Peoples', pp. 179, 185.

15   See, for example, Mara, 'Twenty-Fifth Anniversary Messages'; Sikivou, 'Statement to the Twenty-Eighth Regular Session of the UN General Assembly'; Mara and Somare, 'Joint Communiqué'; and Hau`ofa, 'Our Sea of Islands' (1994).

16   The main scholarly accounts, and accounts by former SPC officials, of the origins and development of the commission either do not mention or mention only in passing this first meeting of Pacific island representatives. See Herr, 'Regionalism in the South Seas'; Smith, *South Pacific Commission*; Forsyth, 'South Pacific'; and Maude, 'The South Pacific Commission'. My earlier accounts of South Pacific regionalism also skate over this important meeting. See, for example, Gregory E. Fry, 'South Pacific Regionalism: The Development of an Indigenous Commitment', MA thesis, Department of Political Science, The Australian National University, Canberra, 1979; and Gregory E. Fry, 'Regionalism and International Politics of the South Pacific', *Pacific Affairs*, 54(3), 1981: 455–84.

17   For the official account of the conference, see South Pacific Commission [hereinafter SPC], *Report of the Secretary-General of the South Pacific Commission on the First South Pacific Conference, 25 April – 5 May 1950, Suva*, Wellington: Government Printer for the South Pacific Commission, 1950. There is no verbatim record of proceedings. The main points of debate were covered in newspaper commentaries, the most complete being those of the *Fiji Times and Herald* and *Pacific Islands Monthly*. The only account in an academic journal, that of Nancy Robson ('The Suva Conference'), was brief and kept mainly to the broad significance of the event.

predominated in the leadup to the conference and during its deliberations: one was an experiment in overcoming what was seen as cultural diversity and different levels of development (which were usually distilled to a concern with whether Melanesians and Polynesians could work together in one entity); the other was captured in the question that David McNicoll, a Sydney journalist, reported being asked by 'nearly everyone' on his return to Sydney: 'How were they?' He goes on to explain:

> 'They' of course, means the native delegates. Obviously, my interrogators expect to hear amusing stories about the delegates spitting out betel nut during the proceedings, jangling outlandish earrings, thumping the floor with their war-clubs and dipping down behind their desks to scoop up an occasional bowl of kava.[18]

This was an experiment in whether island delegates were capable of the necessary standards of Western civilisation for the ideal of potential equality to be recognised. Indeed, in the day-to-day reporting from Suva, the conference represented an experiment in manners—an exotic spectacle for the European observers.

But these were 'experiments' within broader experiments. The Nasinu conference would not have occurred without a more fundamental concern about attempting a regional approach to the implementation of 'trusteeship' principles or 'native welfare' ideas. There were, however, different ideas among officials about what a regional approach to trusteeship might and should achieve; some believed it offered the best, if risky, chance of minimising UN interference in the continuation of colonial control; others saw it as a way of ensuring the ultimate demise of empire. The Nasinu conference, then, was for some an experiment in sowing the seeds of political development and self-determination while minimising international interference in the continued control of empire. Finally, the Nasinu conference has to be seen within a broader experiment in strategic planning and regional order-making in a postwar world. As early as 1950 the promotion of a sense of region among Pacific islanders was seen by some colonial powers as part of an experiment in keeping the region free from communist influence in particular.

---

18 David McNicoll, 'Better Days Ahead for the Natives of South Pacific', *Daily Telegraph*, [Sydney], 12 May 1950: 6.

Which islands? Which islanders?

Just which island peoples would be represented in this experiment derived from a prior decision concerning the boundaries of the region made by the colonial powers at the South Seas Conference of 1947. As we saw in Chapter 4, this initially included all Pacific territories south of the equator—those of France, the United Kingdom, the Netherlands, the United States, Australia and New Zealand. American Pacific territories north of the equator were to join as soon as political settlements were concluded. The individuals who would take part in this experiment, and in what sense they could be said to represent their respective peoples, were rather randomly determined. It was left to territorial administrations to select delegates in whatever manner they chose. The only agreed constraint was that the delegates should be best able to represent the peoples of the territory. Only one administration, that of French Oceania, sent a European to represent the native people; all others honoured the intention of the 1947 conference to involve Pacific islanders in the process. The backgrounds of those chosen in terms of education, occupation and traditional standing, and experience of political affairs, varied dramatically, largely reflecting the very different levels of political development, educational opportunities and social organisation across the territories. But a major criterion affecting the choice of nearly all participants was proficiency in English or French, the official languages of the conference.[19]

At one extreme were American Samoa, Western Samoa, Cook Islands, Fiji and Tonga, whose delegates represented not only the highest traditional authority, but also those highly placed in the political institutions of their territories. Tonga was invited as a special guest in view of its self-governing status. Its principal delegate, Prince Tungi, was already premier of the kingdom; his brother Prince Tu`ipelehake was Governor of Vava`u.

---

19   The list of participants with a very brief description of occupation is contained in SPC, *Report of the Secretary-General*, pp. 10–15. More detailed sketches are provided in contemporary newspaper accounts. See, for example, 'Pacific Talks', *Sydney Morning Herald*, 20 April 1950; Eric Ramsden, 'The Pacific is on the Move: Personalities at First Peoples' Conference', *Auckland Star*, 20 April 1950; 'Pidgin Editors for Suva Talks', *Daily Telegraph*, [Sydney], 21 April 1950; 'More Delegates to Conference at Nasinu', *Fiji Times and Herald*, 22 April 1950; 'Kokoda Trail Carrier is Now Leader-Envoy for his People', *Sunday Telegraph*, [Sydney], 23 April 1950; 'Delegates Gather in Fiji for South Pacific Talks', *Daily Mirror*, [Sydney], 24 April 1950; 'Historic Gathering: First "Parliament of the South Pacific"', *The Age*, [Melbourne], 26 April 1950; Eric Ramsden, 'Sons of Stone Age Peoples Delegates to Fiji Conference', *Auckland Star*, 27 April 1950.

Each of the American Samoan representatives—Tufele, Tuitele and Tuiasosopo—was a high chief and experienced member of the territorial legislature. Tufele was also a member of the governor's Advisory Council and Tuiasosopo was Speaker of the House of Representatives. Western Samoa was represented by two of the three *fautua* (paramount chiefs), Malietoa Tanumafili II and Tupua Tamasese Mea`ole. Along with the high commissioner, they also constituted the newly created Samoan Council of State. In addition, Tupua Tamasese had previously been president of the *Mau* (Samoan independence movement). They were accompanied by Faipule Anapu, chairman of the Fono of Faipule (advisory council) and one of a handful of chiefs providing leadership in the constitutional changes taking place at this time.[20] The representatives of the Fijian community— Joeli Ravai, Roko Tui Tailevu and Ratu Edward Cakobau, a district officer (and son of Tonga's King George Tupou II)—were members of Fiji's Legislative Council. The delegates representing the Indian community, Pandit Vishnu Deo and Mirza Salim Buksh, were very prominent political leaders as well as members of the Legislative Council.

The Cook Islands was also represented by members of the local legislature: Makea Nui Teremoana Ariki, a chief of Rarotonga (and the only female delegate), and Rongomatane Ariki, a chief of Atiu island. Their alternate was Albert Henry, who was then chairman of the Cook Islands Producers' Association. Dr Tom Davis from Rarotonga, who was at that time a medical officer, was part of the New Zealand observer group. Giving some sense of the status and trajectory of those chosen from Tonga, Western Samoa, Cook Islands and Niue (whose delegate was Robert Rex, a clerk in the Niue administration), among the delegates from these eastern territories were three who would become heads of state (Prince Tungi, Malietoa and Tupua Tamasese) and four who would later become prime ministers or premiers (Prince Tu`ipelehake, Davis, Henry and Rex).

In the absence of a local assembly in the Gilbert and Ellice Islands, the Ellice Islands representatives were presumably selected on the basis of their professional achievement. Penitala Teo was one of only two local administrative officers in the colony. He had been captured and starved by the Japanese forces on Ocean Island,[21] while Iosefa Lameko was acting headmaster of King George V School at Tarawa and had recently been awarded the British Empire Medal for his 'exceptional devotion to duty'

20   See Davidson, *Samoa Mo Samoa*, Ch. 6.
21   Penitala Teo later became the first Governor-General of Tuvalu.

during the Japanese occupation. The Gilbert Islands delegate, Tutu Tekanene, was a senior assistant medical practitioner (the highest medical office then available to Pacific islanders) who had studied at the Central Medical School in Suva. The recently restored Australian administration on Nauru selected Jacob Dagabwinare, a community leader and radio operator, and Raymond Gadabu, a government clerk. As senior radio operator on the island after the Australians withdrew in February 1942, Dagabwinare had been hit by machine-gun fire from strafing Japanese planes, and during the Japanese occupation was regularly tortured and imprisoned when Allied planes bombed Nauru.[22]

Of the Melanesian countries, only Dutch New Guinea had any form of political development. The two delegates, Nicolaas Jouwe and Markus Kasiepo, were members of an advisory council elected by Melanesians and were also working in the Dutch administration. They had been in the Netherlands for 'political future' talks the previous year.[23] On the other hand, the representatives of Papua, New Guinea, Solomon Islands and New Hebrides were selected by their administrations on the basis of language ability. Two of the New Guinea delegates, Eluida Ahnon and Aisolf Salin, were clerks in the Department of Education and edited pidgin newspapers (the *Rabaul News* and the *Kavieng Messenger*). They were accompanied by Kamono Walo, a master at Sogeri education centre, and George Kassi, a clerk in the administration at Rabaul.

The Papuan delegates were Miria Gavera, part-time manager of the Poreporena and Hohodae Co-operative Society and former carrier on the Kokoda Track; Willie Gavera, a clerical assistant; Aisa Gu'u, an agricultural assistant; Frank Aisi, who had been at the Central Medical School in Suva; and Bondai Pita, an assistant teacher. The British Solomon Islands Protectorate was represented by Michael Belade, a medical dresser, and Reverend Belshazzar Gina, a New Zealand–educated missionary; while the New Hebrides delegates were John Kalsakau, an assistant medical practitioner who had recently completed a refresher course at the Central Medical School, and Petero, a catechist at the Marist mission on Tanna. New Caledonia's delegates were Maou Djoel, a teacher from

22   See Jemima Garrett, *Island Exiles*, Sydney: ABC Books, 1996, pp. 23, 43.

23   They later became important leaders in the organised opposition to Indonesian rule. See Robin Osborne, *Indonesia's Secret War: The Guerilla Struggle in Irian Jaya*, Sydney: Allen & Unwin, 1985, pp. 32, 35.

the Loyalty Islands, and Raphael Bouanaoue, a medical assistant at the Nouméa hospital who had served in World War I in France as part of the Mixed Pacific Battalion.

Perhaps the most revealing aspect of the experiment was the inclusion of representatives of the Indian community in the Fiji delegation. Although they represented the largest cultural and language group in the South Pacific at that time, the ambivalence which subsequently attended Indian participation in national or regional identity was present at the creation of this modern sense of the 'South Pacific'. At issue was the subtext of authenticity and the right to be regarded as a Pacific islander. This was evident during the selection process in the Fiji Legislative Council. Some European and Fijian representatives opposed the inclusion of Indian delegates.[24] Ratu Edward Cakobau reportedly argued that 'one Indian delegate could not be of help to the South Pacific Islands representatives'[25]—the implication from the context being that, despite the heterogeneity of the region, there was already a concept of 'South Pacific islander' defined in relation to Asian (and presumably European) identity. Australian officials were nervous about the inclusion of Indians because of their reputation for raising anticolonial questions.[26] One commentator described the representatives of the Indian community as 'a lonely group, keeping themselves to themselves'.[27]

Europeans were also present as advisers and observers. They included the representatives of the six colonial powers that made up the SPC. The Australian delegation was led by Dr Burton, and it was cause for comment that Australia, given its prominent role in promoting the regional idea through the commission, had chosen not to send a senior official.[28] Other colonial powers sent higher-ranking representatives (although the United States also included a well-known anthropologist, Felix Keesing). The Nouméa-based commission officials who had organised the conference included William Forsyth, the secretary-general and author of the first proposal for a South Seas commission in 1943–44 when he worked in the

---

24 See 'Fijians and Indians: How Should they be Represented at South Pacific Conference?', *Pacific Islands Monthly*, January 1950 [from a correspondent in Suva, 19 December 1949]; and 'Indian Problem Worries Fiji's Administrators', *The Age*, [Melbourne], 3 May 1950.
25 'Fijians and Indians', *Pacific Islands Monthly*.
26 Burton, 'The South Pacific Conference'.
27 'Historic Gathering', *The Age*.
28 'Leadership in South Seas: Australian Failure', *Sydney Morning Herald*, 8 May 1950; and 'Our Opportunity in South Pacific', [Editorial], *Sydney Morning Herald*, 13 May 1950.

Australian Department of External Affairs, and Harry Maude, director of
social development and a former British colonial official known for his
progressive views on localisation and self-determination.[29] Representing
the Protestant churches was Reverend C.F. Gribble, General Secretary of
the Methodist Overseas Missions of Australasia and former principal of
Tupou College in Nuku`alofa. The media representatives included Robert
W. Robson, the foundation editor of the *Pacific Islands Monthly* and, as
we have seen, an early advocate of regional arrangements to serve the
European settlers in the islands.[30]

A cultural experiment

Much of the reported uneasiness in the leadup to the Nasinu conference
related to the view—widely held among European observers—that this
regional project was working against cultural heterogeneity. This, for
example, underlay the governor's fear that the conference would fail
('because of the wide variety of races, national allegiance, language, and
traditions involved').[31] Surprisingly perhaps—given the longstanding
propensity of some Europeans to generalise about 'the native', 'the child
races', 'the noble savage', 'the savage' or 'the islander'—there was clearly
a dominant view among European observers at this time that this was
an extremely diverse area culturally[32] so that no natural cultural affinity
among 'the races' could be assumed. The task was seen as a battle to forge
unity out of diversity. According to some observers, this task was made
more difficult by the lack of any previous opportunity for representatives
of these cultures to come into contact. One observer claimed that
'this was the first time that natives of the various territories had met
one another';[33] and another claimed that 'Papuans for instance, are as

---

29   See Robert Langdon, 'Harry Maude: Shy Proconsul, Dedicated Pacific Historian', in Niel
Gunson, ed., *The Changing Pacific: Essays in Honour of H.E. Maude*, Melbourne: Oxford University
Press, 1978, pp. 1–21, at pp. 11–12, 16.
30   See Robson, 'Need for a Closer Relationship between Territories'; and Robson, 'Plea for Co-
operation in Pacific Affairs'.
31   'South Pacific Peoples' Conference', *The Times*.
32   This recognition of heterogeneity was a central theme in several prominent regionwide
academic surveys of the Pacific islands that appeared around this time. For example, W.E.H. Stanner,
*The South Seas in Transition: A Study of Post-War Rehabilitation and Reconstruction in Three British
Pacific Dependencies*, Sydney: Australasian Publishing Company, 1953, especially p. 418; Oliver,
The Pacific Islands, pp. 20–1; and Keesing, *The South Seas in the Modern World*, p. 293.
33   McNicoll, 'Better Days Ahead for the Natives of South Pacific'. See also 'Delegates Meet in Suva
to Discuss Broad Programmes for Native Welfare', *The Evening Post*, [Wellington], 21 April 1950.

complete strangers to Tongans as would [be] a delegation from Nigeria or the French Cameroons'.[34] This image of diversity and apartness suggested unnaturalness in the regional project as seen by at least some observers.[35]

There was only one departure from this image. This was the view put by Albert Norman, writing from Sydney for the *Christian Science Monitor*, in June 1949. While addressing the SPC more generally, his comments have relevance to the cultural meaning of the attempt to involve Pacific islanders in this region-building project:

> Southern Oceania, that Pacific 'continent' which mainly is under water, is unique as a 'reclamation' project. Not an inch of soil will be reclaimed. The task is to reclaim something quite different, something that has been submerged by the chauvinistic policies of Europe. And the major item of equipment on the project is the new sense of international moral responsibility which has launched this vast social enterprise … Separating each 'island' group are the waters of the South Pacific which tend to create the impression that this society is broken up and hopelessly separated from its essential parts.
>
> This geographical illusion has been heightened by the occupying European nations who, over the centuries, have 'claimed' for their own the visible peaks of the land. It was thus that the political and meaningless divisions of Europe became arbitrarily superimposed on Oceania. The first step in 'reclamation' has been to free the land of these bonds, to restore the essential regional viewpoint and unity, to overlook the dividing waters, to see the land and its people as united … It will be the task of the South Pacific Commission to … promote the social reclamation of the world's seventh 'continent' and its people.[36]

---

34 'Historic Gathering', *The Age*.

35 Although opportunities for contact between island groups were severely restricted in the colonial period, actual contacts between particular representatives of island cultures suggest that this extreme view was unfounded. Fijian soldiers, including Ratu Edward Cakobau, had served in British Solomon Islands during the recent war; relationships between Tongan and Fijian chiefly lines were very close (Prince Tungi was in fact the nephew of the Fijan representative, Ratu Edward Cakobau); the Central Medical School in Suva had brought many Pacific islanders from the British Pacific together, including two delegates at Nasinu—Aisi from Papua and Kalsakau from New Hebrides; and many Polynesian missionaries had spent time in Melanesian cultures. This extreme view also ignored the language and cultural links among Polynesians.

36 Albert Norman, 'The Reclamation of Oceania', *Christian Science Monitor*, 4 June 1949.

But the island delegates at Nasinu, at least in their reported statements, did not employ a rhetoric of reclamation, seemingly confirming the perception of the European observers that this was a novel development.

The cultural experiment was more particularly represented as whether 'Melanesians' and 'Polynesians' could bridge the gulf. This dichotomy was encouraged by the temporary exclusion of the islands north of the equator, which meant that the only Micronesians at Nasinu were Nauruans and Gilbertese. The Melanesia–Polynesia divide was seen as a question not just of cultural and linguistic difference, but also of different levels of development, reflecting substantial differences in opportunity for 'Westernisation'. In a view owing more to the idea of 'stages of development' than that of innate difference, the Polynesians (or 'the east') were identified as 'the advanced' peoples, while Melanesians (or 'the west') were characterised as 'the backward' peoples. Interestingly, Fiji—usually classified by ethnographers as Melanesian—was in this context seen as part of the east and of Polynesia, based on social organisation, sophistication, level of education, political development and social links with Samoa and Tonga.[37]

Those reporting on the experiment at Nasinu appeared to find the Melanesian delegates more capable than expected. McNicoll, for example, reported that 'the boys from Australian New Guinea and Papua acquitted themselves very well'.[38] Author and journalist Eric Ramsden went further. Reporting from Sydney, where he met the Papuan and New Guinean delegates en route to Suva, he claimed:

> Those who expected these sons of Stone Age men to exhibit an educational standard that would perhaps not compare with Pacific Islands natives with a century and more of association with Europeans, were to be disappointed ... The visitors were, of course, hand-picked men. But all spoke English perfectly ... Intellectually, these young men from the jungles and mountain slopes of wild New Guinea, will compare quite favourably with the other delegates.[39]

---

37   Although the labels 'Melanesian' and 'Polynesian' were used, it was clear that the island delegates being referred to as evidence for these generalisations were more specifically from Papua and New Guinea on the Melanesian side, and Fiji, Tonga, American Samoa and Western Samoa on the Polynesian side. This characterisation left out French Oceania, French and Dutch-speaking Melanesia, the Ellice Islands, the Gilbert Islands and Nauru.

38   David McNicoll, 'Better days ahead for the natives of the South Pacific', *Daily Telegraph*, 12 May 1950.

39   Ramsden, 'Sons of Stone Age Peoples Delegates to Fiji Conference'.

Nevertheless, the observers were clear about the gulf they expected between the Melanesian and Polynesian delegates. Nancy Robson, for example, commented:

> Most striking feature of the native representation was the vast gap separating eastern and western Pacific. Between the fluency and mental independence displayed in discussions by the hereditary princes of Polynesia, and the contributions, by comparison infinitely laboured and derivative, of Melanesians only just emerging from the horizon-bounded village community, yawned a gulf which the Melanesians themselves recognised with an emphatic and disarming humility.[40]

The *Fiji Times and Herald* asserted:

> The conference has also emphasised the fact that the people of Samoa, Tonga and Fiji are much more advanced in many ways than the people of Papua New Guinea and the Solomons. As one observer put it, they seem to be about one hundred years behind the native people in this part of the South Pacific.[41]

Robert W. Robson wrote:

> Most of the Polynesians are big men; all are sophisticated, dignified, carrying themselves with the easy assurance that comes with pride of race. In this respect, the Fijians, although formally classified as Melanesians, must go in with the Polynesian–Micronesian group.
>
> The Melanesians, on the other hand, are all small men, and even those who are well-educated and accustomed to European contacts, seem shy and bashful.[42]

But these differences did not produce the predicted failure in creating a sense of region among islanders. The conference was in fact viewed as having unforeseen benefits. Nancy Robson concluded that the 'revelation of the east to the west'—in the sense of the 'awakening realisation' among the Melanesians 'of possibilities within themselves'—was 'perhaps the most significant achievement of the Conference'.[43] For Dr John Gunther, Australian adviser to the Papua and New Guinea delegations, the Nasinu

---

40   Robson, 'The Suva Conference of South Pacific Peoples', p. 181.
41   Editorial, *Fiji Times and Herald*, 5 May 1950.
42   Robert W. Robson, 'Sidelights on the South Pacific Conference', *Pacific Islands Monthly*, May 1950: 11.
43   Robson, 'The Suva Conference of South Pacific Peoples', p. 181.

conference demonstrated that the disparities between Melanesians and Polynesians could be useful in showing to white people in Papua and New Guinea what the indigenous inhabitants might achieve if appropriate development were instituted. For him, this was a compelling reason for Australia to hold the next conference in 'Papua and New Guinea'.[44] In terms of overcoming the perceived cultural differences, the experiment was seen as successful. For Colonel F.W. Voelcker, the New Zealand observer, 'the barriers of prejudice, isolation, and language among the Island native peoples were cracking'.[45] The Governor of Fiji concluded that 'the conference had produced overwhelming evidence of the fraternal regard among the Pacific peoples, in spite of obvious but often superficial differences'.[46]

An experiment in manners

The other experiment, which dominated day-to-day reporting, was whether Pacific islanders were sufficiently Westernised to engage in regional discussions of this kind. Public commentary focused almost obsessively on the minutiae of how the delegates behaved, dressed and walked. They reflected on the manners, the confidence, originality, style, bearing, ability to discuss and even length of speeches.[47] While the media commentary focused on dress and manner, the officials were focusing on the capacities exhibited within the meeting. Their concerns—indeed 'fears'—were whether the islanders would be capable of meaningful discussion on the native welfare agenda. Would they speak at all? Would they have sufficient command of English? Would they be able to contribute away from the script provided by their advisers? Would they have the concentration and mental staying power, the diplomatic skills and the sophistication to carry on international discussions of this kind? These were seen as practical

---

44   J.T. Gunther, 'South Pacific Conference: Preliminary Report by Dr J.T. Gunther, Advisor to Papua-New Guinea Delegation and Acting Chairman for Australia', Department of External Affairs, Series A1838/1, item 347/2/6, folio 68, undated (attached to memo to Secretary, Department of External Affairs, dated 17 July 1950, from Secretary, Department of External Territories), National Archives of Australia, Canberra.

45   'NZ Observer Reviews Aims and Results of Conference', *Fiji Times and Herald*.

46   'South Pacific Peoples' Conference', *The Times*.

47   See, for example, 'Curious Mixture of Dressing at South Pacific Conference', *Sydney Morning Herald*, 26 April 1950; 'Sombre Fashion at Talks', *Daily Telegraph*, [Sydney], 26 April 1950; Colin Simpson, 'Native Conference in Fiji Opens Colourfully', *The Argus*, [Melbourne], 26 April 1950; 'Pacific Queen in Limelight', *Melbourne Herald*, 29 April 1950; 'Black-eyed Beauty Bosses Pacific Talks', *Sydney Telegraph*, 30 April 1950.

problems in achieving a sense of region. Judged by the detailed reports on the capacities of delegates, this was regarded as an experiment whose outcome was unknown.[48]

In the officials' minds it was on such an experiment, together with the cultural experiment, that the possibility of an effective regional identity depended. These concerns were particularly focused on the Melanesian representatives, and especially on those from Papua and New Guinea. For Robert W. Robson, the level of education and language difficulties of the Melanesians suggested that an all–South Pacific gathering was premature: '[C]an the natives of Melanesia contribute anything of practical value while these enormous problems … remain unsolved?'[49] There was a perception on the part of observers that what was expected in this forum was a level of diplomatic behaviour not experienced within the Melanesian territories, where political development and indigenous participation in decision-making had been minimal (a view that completely overlooked the schooling in diplomatic, negotiation and speaking skills common in Pacific cultures).

Implicit throughout the commentary is not just how the island delegates performed, but also what this suggested for the possibility of development towards a Western political and social style among Pacific islanders. Behind the experiment in manners was an experiment in the possibility of progress in Westernisation and civilisation. Underlying this, for some observers, was a belief in potential equality between Europeans and those they had colonised. The Nasinu conference was, then, an experiment in putting these beliefs into action. The normal colonial and racial hierarchy between the races was suspended for 10 days. The living arrangement was itself an experiment in tentative equality. Arrangements were made for all delegates, advisers and observers to sleep in the dormitories of the teachers' training college in adjoining cubicles. As it happened, while some Europeans slept at Nasinu, the Samoan delegates set up at the Grand Pacific Hotel, and the Tongan and Cook Islands representatives stayed privately. For those Europeans who stayed at Nasinu, it was remarked on that 'the unthinkable' was being experimented with in Suva against the colonial context of Australia's Papuan and New Guinea territories: white men and islanders sleeping in adjoining cubicles and sharing the same

48   See Burton, 'The South Pacific Conference'; and Gunther, 'South Pacific Conference'.
49   Robson, 'Sidelights on the South Pacific Conference', p. 11.

dining table.[50] The governor even suspended the drinking regulations (making it an offence to serve natives alcohol) for the duration of the conference, following an incident at the Grand Pacific Hotel in which islander delegates were refused wine at dinner.[51]

This experiment in potential equality was generally seen as a surprising success. After the conference, Freeston concluded that 'no longer can it be said that the natives of the Pacific sit in shade and idleness waiting for bananas to ripen and coconuts to drop'.[52] The *Sydney Morning Herald* editorialised that 'native delegates greatly surprised observers by their grasp of the problems with which they were called upon to deal'.[53] Forsyth was reported as saying that he was impressed with 'the fluency, clear thinking and poise of the native delegates'.[54] For the Australian observer, Dr Burton, 'there is only one conclusion: the Conference was an outstandingly successful experiment'. He reported:

> [O]ur fears proved to be dupes. We had thought that the native delegates would have been hesitant to express freely their views in the presence of Europeans ... for our experience of Pacific races had led us to think that it would take them long 'to clear their throats' and to orient their minds to deal with any important subject, especially in unfamiliar surroundings.[55]

McNicoll, reporting his answer to the question 'how were they?', reported:

> [P]eople are obviously disappointed to hear that the native delegates sat around like any white men at a Rotary convention, discussing things quietly in excellent English and displaying perfect knowledge of rules of procedure.
>
> My questioners are even more disappointed to hear that these natives, sitting at a conference which helped prepare a blue-print for their personal civilisation, were dressed—above the waist at least—in a completely Western collar-and-tie fashion.[56]

---

50 'Delegates Gather in Fiji for South Pacific Talks', *Daily Mirror*.

51 See 'Storm in a Glass at Suva: Native Delegates are Refused Drinks', *Melbourne Herald*, 1 May 1950; 'Here's to the Governor', *The Argus*, [Melbourne], 2 May 1950; and 'Temporary Issue of Liquor Permits at Suva', *Fiji Times and Herald*, 11 May 1950.

52 'New Era for South Seas', *Sydney Morning Herald*.

53 'Our Opportunity in South Pacific', *Sydney Morning Herald*.

54 'Praise of Natives: Pacific Talk', *Sydney Morning Herald*, 29 April 1950.

55 Burton, 'The South Pacific Conference'.

56 McNicoll, 'Better Days Ahead for the Natives of South Pacific'.

But for the Australian adviser to the Papua and New Guinea delegations, Dr Gunther, most Melanesians (he particularly excluded the Dutch New Guinea delegates) 'did not contribute, per se, originality being most guided by observers' and 'failed to sustain their initial concentration'. Nevertheless, 'some Papua and New Guinea delegates showed they were able to prepare prescribed subject matter and deliver it without nervousness by reading'.[57]

The widely expressed surprise that the islander representatives had generally proven to be competent in terms of the criteria set by the observers seems to have reflected a turning point in European, and particularly Australian, thinking about Pacific islanders. The commentary seems to suggest a changing view of non-European peoples as potentially equal once development processes had their effect. This is captured in McNicoll's comments:

> The days are almost gone when we can think of the Pacific natives as 'fuzzy wuzzies', as simple, ignorant people too lazy to make anything but indifferent laborers and slipshod servants ... True, the bulk of the Pacific natives are still in the 'fuzzy wuzzy' stage; an enormous preponderance are illiterate; the work of raising their standards is prodigious.

> But the South Pacific Conference was the writing on the wall, the start of better days for these natives whom we would do well to cultivate as our friends as well as our neighbours ... What once was a pipe dream—westernised natives in the Pacific—mightn't be far from a reality.[58]

An experiment in 'regional trusteeship' versus self-determination

There were more fundamental agendas underlying the attempt to forge a regional identity. The Nasinu conference could be seen as the playing out of the politics of the Canberra conference of three years earlier around the question of whether the Pacific island conference would serve as a vehicle

---

57   Gunther, 'South Pacific Conference'.
58   McNicoll, 'Better Days Ahead for the Natives of South Pacific'.

for encouraging political self-determination or as a model of trusteeship. For those supporting self-determination, the Nasinu conference was seen as part of an attempt to deliver a 'new deal' to Pacific peoples.[59]

Here, then, were two countervailing experiments invested in the creation of regional identity among islanders: an experiment in maintaining empire against moves in world opinion, on the one hand, and a possible way of setting in motion ideas that would help to bring empire to an end, on the other. By the time of the Nasinu conference, it was clear that the balance had moved dramatically in favour of an experiment in maintaining empire or at least slowing the divestment of colonial power. In 1949, Labour/ Labor governments in Wellington and Canberra had been replaced with conservative governments less sympathetic to a liberal interpretation of trusteeship principles. Thus, for all government observers, except possibly the United States, the first Pacific island conference represented a showcase for regional trusteeship rather than a move towards self-determination. In pursuit of this objective, Australia and the United Kingdom made an effort to keep a UN observer away from the conference and an Australian official briefing talked of the advantages of the occasion in terms of establishing anticolonial credentials.[60] The leader of Australia's delegation, Dr Burton, indicated that there were fears 'lest the Conference … be used as a sounding board for political dissatisfaction, especially on the part of the restless Samoans and of the Indians in Fiji'.[61]

Although governments had changed in Wellington and Canberra, the experiment of the social democratic governments remained in the air. The very existence of a conference of representatives of island peoples was enough for their experiment to proceed. There are indications that some officials also represented this view. The Secretary-General of the newly formed SPC, Forsyth, had been Evatt's righthand man on Pacific island and trusteeship issues and was the author of the original study advocating a more progressive regional institution. Maude, the member for social development on the commission's Research Council, had been promoting ideas of localisation in his time in the British Colonial Service in the

---

59   See, for example, 'New Deal Talks in Pacific', *The Argus*, [Melbourne], 21 April 1950.
60   Australian Department of External Affairs, 'South Pacific Conference, Brief to the Minister for External Affairs from South West Pacific Section, 27 January 1950', Department of External Affairs, Series A1838/1, item 347/2/1, folio 89, National Archives of Australia, Canberra.
61   Burton, 'The South Pacific Conference'.

Pacific and, as we have seen, the adviser to the Papua and New Guinea delegations saw the conference as a way of moving white opinion in Port Moresby on the possibilities of political development.

For those seeing this as a politically risky event in which self-determination sentiment might be aired, the experiment may have seemed successful. The Samoan and Indo-Fijian representatives, each of whom had been actively anticolonial at home, had not used the occasion to promote their cause or to foster nationalism among others. Burton reported 'only slight evidence of this'.[62] No-one had sought to move away from an agenda focused on health and social development or to interpret these issues liberally to include political points in the way so common at later conferences. Meanwhile, the conference suggested a powerful image of serious 'native welfare' programs involving participation by people of the territories that could help to assuage the critics of colonial rule (and especially the new Government of India) at the United Nations.

Nevertheless, the conference also looked successful for those who aimed to foster political development. Political development did not need to be on the agenda for this to be the case. For those interested in promoting processes of self-determination, the key was that Pacific islanders would find a basis for valuing the creation of links among themselves, that the less developed would gain inspiration from the more developed and that, through out-of-conference meetings, an exchange of experiences would encourage islander agency in the processes of change. We have already seen that the conference brought together a number of people who were already involved in self-determination processes in their own countries and that, for those who had not yet experienced this, it was judged to be a revelation. The very symbolism of a conference in which only Pacific islanders were speaking was not lost on participants—or journalists:

> From the native point of view the main significance of the conference lay in the fact that Europeans for the first time, were officially recognising that the Pacific races would ultimately be able to look after themselves, economically, socially and in future politically.[63]

---

62   ibid.
63   'S. Pacific Natives Find New Outlook', *Melbourne Sun*, 4 May 1950. See also 'Fires of National Ambition Burn in South Pacific', *Sydney Morning Herald*, 6 May 1950.

The commentary in New Zealand's *Daily News* suggested that the impact of the meeting had been in line with New Zealand's views on moving these territories to self-reliance and self-government—'the ultimate transfer of government to the pacific races'.[64] For the New Zealand observer, Voelcker, a 'new era is dawning':

> Seated at the conference table one saw the thoughtful faces of vastly differing races studying earnestly and intelligently the administrative, educational, health, and economic and social problems which have been the concern in the past of administrators, scientists and missionaries.[65]

An experiment in anticommunism

Finally, the Nasinu conference represented an experiment in anticommunism. This was not made explicit by those who devised the idea of creating a Pacific island region in 1947, but the idea of a link between regional security, more generally conceived, and regional trusteeship was there from the beginning.[66] This was clear in the Anzac Pact of 1944, in which the Australian and New Zealand governments set out their proposal for a South Seas commission, as discussed in Chapter 4. It was also evident in Evatt's official statements between 1944 and 1945. The promotion of regional trusteeship was seen as developing the area for defence and meeting the needs of Pacific islanders that might otherwise lead to security problems in the form of an unsympathetic local population in time of war.[67]

Between the South Seas Conference of 1947 and the Nasinu meeting in 1950, the idea of promoting a region among indigenous inhabitants began to reflect the shift from the wartime conceptualisation of global and regional security to one governed by a concern about communism and its possible links to 'Asian nationalism'. Concerns about the spread of communist ideas to the island territories via anticolonial movements meant that regional trusteeship was invested with a new meaning—that

---

64 'The Suva Conference', *The Daily News*, [New Zealand], 6 May 1950.
65 'NZ Observer Reviews Aims and Results of Conference', *Fiji Times and Herald*.
66 The link between 'native welfare' and security in the formation of the SPC is well covered in Herr, 'Regionalism in the South Seas'; and Smith, *South Pacific Commission*.
67 See Australian Department of External Affairs, 'Australian–New Zealand Agreement', clauses 28–31; and Evatt, *Foreign Policy of Australia*, pp. 116, 132, 142.

of keeping 'the natives' satisfied and looking to each other, and to the West. This was seen as applicable to the native welfare programs of the SPC whether or not they involved Pacific island participation. A *New Zealand Herald* editorial, for example, in commending the work of the new commission 'in trying to improve the lot of native communities from Dutch New Guinea to Tahiti', argued:

> In 1947 Asiatic communism was not the danger it has since become. The situation today has changed so much for the worse that the Pacific Powers can neglect no measure that will serve toward checking the red tide that may yet be found flowing south and east from the continental mainland.[68]

Also, for Maude, interviewed in the month after the conference:

> [T]he trend of world events made it all too probable that the Pacific islands peoples would in the not too distant future, be the recipients of skilled and specious propaganda from their near neighbours to the north and west … The best method of meeting this threat was … for the colonial Powers to make immediate and concerted efforts to raise the islanders' social and economic standard of living.[69]

For those with a more conservative view of trusteeship, and who wanted to hold on to empire, the new concern with anticommunism contained a possible challenge to their position. Did the recent Asian experience of nationalism and communism suggest that to resist political development was to play into the hands of the communists or could their commitment to slowing the divestment of colonial territories also be seen as serving their desire to oppose communist influence? A slightly different ambivalence is captured in the *Pacific Islands Monthly*'s coverage of the conference. The editorial, presumably written by Robert W. Robson, argued that in the face of 'communism sweeping across overcrowded Asia, approaching our northwest frontiers', meetings such as the South Pacific Conference diverted energy from the real task of integrating Western forces to contain communism. 'How', the writer asked, 'can we achieve such a combination when so many of our leaders devote so much of their time to the uplift of down-trodden races?'[70] This preoccupation with 'sociological planning' while communism was spreading was so 'much fiddling while Rome

---

68 'The South Pacific Commission', *New Zealand Herald*, [Auckland], 20 February 1950.
69 'Propaganda: South Pacific May Be Deluged by North-West', *Fiji Times and Herald*, 22 June 1950.
70 Editorial, *Pacific Islands Monthly*, May 1950: 1, 6.

burns'.[71] Although Robson's signed article in the same issue indicates the same preoccupation, it argued that 'in the circumstances, it is just as well that per medium of the SP Conference ... the Western nations should guide and direct the Pacific Islanders'. He concluded that 'perhaps in view of events in Asia and Indonesia, we may regard the SP Conference as an insurance'.[72]

A *Daily Mirror* 'special correspondent' pursued a similar theme:

> The conference is being held in an area where there is plenty of potential tinder for the spark of Asiatic communism. For that reason, whatever the conference finally achieves, the gathering of races and colours here at Nasinu must in itself be socially valuable.[73]

And the *Auckland Star* developed a rationale for the connection between regional identity and anticommunism:

> The conference should serve as tangible proof that Western democracy has something worthwhile to offer to the native peoples. It should prove a valuable antidote to the insidious propaganda of the Communist agents who are known to be at work in the Pacific ... In South-east Asia, where there was no such organisation as the South Pacific Conference, the Communist agitators have been able to use the upsurge of nationalism for their own purposes. Only by offering a future that is bright with promise can the various Governments hope to prevent the nationalistic aspirations of the native peoples of the Pacific from being misused in the same way. The South Pacific Conference is a positive move in the right direction. Admittedly, it is an experiment.[74]

Ultimately, however, this seems to have been a rather low-priority experiment for the Australian Government at this time, although regional identity and anticommunism were to be strongly linked in Australia's South Pacific policy later in the Cold War. While the South Pacific figured significantly in Canberra's interests in 1947, by 1950, attention was centrally focused on Asia, largely because of the Chinese revolution and developments in Korea.[75]

---

71   ibid.
72   Robson, 'Sidelights on the South Pacific Conference', p. 11.
73   'Delegates Gather in Fiji for South Pacific Talks', *Daily Mirror*, 24 April 1950.
74   Editorial, *Auckland Star*, 26 April 1950.
75   'Leadership in South Seas', *Sydney Morning Herald*, 8 May 1950; and 'Our Opportunity in South Pacific', *Sydney Morning Herald*, 13 May 1950.

Conclusion

The meanings invested in the European experiment of creating a sense of regional identity among Pacific islanders were many. But they were all related in some way or other to the experience of the recent world war and to the hopes and interests involved in constructing a postwar order. The world war represented a turning point in fundamental ideas: from a wartime conceptualisation of security to the Cold War thinking that was to dominate the next 40 years; from notions of the natural inequality of races to principles of equality and 'civilisability'; from a commitment to perpetual colonialism to the promotion of self-determination; and from diversity and partition within the Pacific to unity and common will. World War II also prompted a shift in the self-image of Australia and New Zealand, from dependency to independent leadership aspirations in the Pacific. While the newly created Pacific island region, like Spate's broader Pacific region, was a 'European artefact', there was no general agreement among European observers about the meaning of the experiment. In particular, the modern South Pacific was born of a tension in the European, and particularly the Australian, mindset between ideas of indigenous self-determination and ideas of hegemonic control—a tension that has continued to underlie attitudes towards South Pacific regional governance ever since.

Pacific island representatives at Nasinu welcomed the experiment, with their enthusiasm couched in terms of a shared need to deal with the rapid changes occurring in their societies. The novelty of Nasinu, as the first regionwide meeting of Pacific island leaders, was reinforced by the lack of opportunities for Pacific islanders to meet each other across colonial boundaries over the previous 50 years. During the first half of the twentieth century, changing European economic practices and colonial control of movement and travel confined Pacific islanders to their territories. With colonialism came internal labour trades, whereby the colonial administrations restricted or banned foreign recruiters. This contrasted with the previous situation, where labourers were typically taken, or opted, to work beyond the confines of their own island group. Colonial restrictions on their mobility were reinforced by the more limited opportunities to join trading vessels. No longer were there the opportunities for long-range travel provided by the whaling vessels or by the large canoes still available in the nineteenth century. Opportunities to come in contact with more distant island groups were, from the 1930s, limited to attendance at the Central Medical School in Suva or, for some Polynesians, mission activity in Melanesia.[76] Prior to the decolonisation period of the 1960s, regional networks were confined to colonial officials and even here were mainly *within* colonial empires rather than *between* them. So, it is not surprising that contemporary opinion viewed Nasinu as a watershed in Pacific history and, for nervous administrators as well as leading Pacific islanders, a social and political experiment of momentous significance.

---

76   I am indebted to Doug Munro for his insights on these points.

6

The decolonisation of regional governance

The key tension inherent in the 'South Pacific experiment' of 1950, and in the establishment of the SPC three years earlier, was between two competing imperial framings of the Pacific—one motivated by the principle of self-determination and the other by continued imperial control but with a commitment to 'native development' and 'native welfare'. The loss of government in 1949 by the main champions of political self-determination for Pacific peoples—the Labor/Labour parties of Australia and New Zealand—meant that self-determination was off the agenda in the 1950s. All colonial governments in the Pacific—the United States, France, the United Kingdom, the Netherlands, Australia and New Zealand—now shared a commitment to continued colonial control within their territories and made only minimal attempts to honour the spirit of the trusteeship arrangements they had entered into or to meet new global norms of self-determination. The strategic imperatives of the Cold War and economic interests took precedence. Britain and the United States were using their Pacific territories as nuclear testing sites; Australia and New Zealand were feeding a postwar agricultural boom with phosphate from their trust territory, Nauru.

This mindset was reflected in the form of regional governance promoted under the auspices of the SPC. Decision-making within the SPC remained dominated by colonial powers and the development agenda promoted by the organisation reflected these interests. Reflecting on the SPC's first decade (the 1950s), Fiji's prime minister Ratu Sir Kamisese Mara (1971–87), the leading player in regional politics from the 1960s to the 1980s, observes that it 'went on benignly and benevolently but unimaginatively treating the South Pacific people as though they were children who were not capable of handling their own affairs'.[1]

From the early 1960s, the contest between imperial control and self-determination resurfaced. This time it was not a contest between progressive and conservative colonial powers but rather a struggle between all of the colonial powers, on the one hand, and the emerging island leaders of Pacific territories undergoing political change, on the other. The new leaders of Fiji, Tonga, Samoa, Niue, Cook Islands and Nauru, in particular, demanded change to the power structure within the SPC. They also moved to establish their own indigenous regional organisations—most importantly, the South Pacific Forum (SPF). Their aim was to establish indigenous control of regional decision-making consistent with the self-determination principle that was being promoted by the United Nations as a global discourse and was starting to impact on Pacific territories. They wanted regional norms to reflect these changing global ideas.

This contest over political agency in regional decision-making from 1962 to 1974 culminated in a new agreement to govern the SPC, guaranteeing formal control by the Pacific island representatives, as well as in the establishment of a new major regional institution controlled by Pacific islanders, the SPF. It was primarily a contest over political agency, but this would, in turn, determine the outcomes of subsequent decisions about the political purpose of the regional community—most notably, about how these emerging Pacific countries would control global economic and political forces and react to continuing colonialism and nuclear testing in the region.

Although the new Pacific island leaders challenged the dominant principles on which regional governance had been based, it is notable that the colonially imposed boundaries of the region were by and large accepted but with important exceptions. The boundaries of the SPC became the outer boundaries of regional consciousness and identity, and the outer limits on action on such issues as nuclear involvement and continued colonial intrusion. However, participation at the regional table required self-determination as the foundation credential. This created a tension between those accepted as belonging to a Pacific regional identity and those

---

1   Mara, 'Regional Co-operation in the South Pacific', p. 2.

accepted as having the right to participate in regional diplomacy. This, in turn, laid the basis for a subsequent contest about self-determination and political agency, which will be examined in Chapter 7.

Decolonisation and regional self-determination

The backdrop to the emergence of a commitment to regional self-determination among key Pacific leaders in the 1960s was the movement in global discourses and commitments concerning decolonisation, and their expression in the gathering pace of decolonisation in Africa and South-East Asia, following the earlier movement in South Asia. The change in British policy towards decolonisation after prime minister Harold Macmillan's 'wind of change' speech to the South African Parliament in Cape Town in February 1960 was a key turning point in this discourse, as was the signing of the UN Declaration on the Granting of Independence to Colonial Countries and Peoples in December of the same year. In this context, it was hard for colonial powers not to make some gesture towards political development within their Pacific territories. New Zealand moved early to change its approach in response to pressure from the United Nations and from the Samoans, who had never accepted colonial rule. The early decolonisation in Samoa (then known as Western Samoa) in 1962 was followed by self-government in Cook Islands in 1965 and Niue in 1968. A very determined campaign by Nauruans for justice after severe exploitation by Australia, New Zealand and Britain, supported by UN pressure, led a reluctant Australia and New Zealand to move Nauru towards independence in 1968.

Britain began to move Fiji to independence from 1965, despite the reluctance of indigenous Fijians; it also moved slowly to create political development in its other smaller Pacific territories (although at this stage full independence was not contemplated). Similarly, in Micronesia, the United States created forms of representation and limited self-government as part of obligations in administering a UN trusteeship. Even in the French territories where there was no recognition of a right or need for self-determination, there was a move to create advisory assemblies and forms of indigenous representation.

The upshot of this activity was a change in the consciousness of key indigenous leaders across the region. Its most dramatic expression was the emergence of four fully independent states (Western Samoa in 1962, Nauru in 1968 and Tonga and Fiji in 1970) and two associated states (Cook Islands in 1965 and Niue in 1968). This change in consciousness was also being experienced by some key figures in territories experiencing some early stages of decolonisation, such as Papua New Guinea.[2]

The particularly important development, for the purposes of this study, was how this idea of self-determination became a regional principle. It became a shared norm promoted by Pacific indigenous leaders as the basis of legitimate *regional* governance, as well as legitimate *national* statehood. The big regional story of the 1960s and early 1970s is how the indigenous regional movement championed self-determination as a legitimating principle in the face of continuing colonial reluctance to change the regional power structures. New Zealand was an early exception because of the change in its own policy. By decade's end, it was joined by Australia, after a change of government in 1972. France and the United States, on the other hand, remained staunch defenders of the colonial regional order throughout the 1960s.

The Pacific leaders' embrace of the regional legitimating principle of self-determination was expressed not just in the effort to gain control of decision-making structures in the regional forums and in establishing indigenous political agency. It was also focused on anticolonialism everywhere within the boundaries of the region, including opposition to nuclear testing at Moruroa and Fangataufa atolls in French Polynesia. There was a developing shared belief in *regional* self-determination as a principle underpinning legitimate regional governance of the regional political community.

This concern with political agency was also about establishing the means to deal with how Pacific islanders were forced to live their lives anywhere in the region. Nuclear testing, for example, was a prime concern from the mid 1960s. Frustration with having discussion of this banned in regional forums was a major part of the story of why island leaders wanted

---

2   The decolonisation of the Pacific is examined comprehensively in the first section of Howe et al., *Tides of History.*

regional structures that could give voice to their concerns. Thus, regional self-determination was seen as vitally related to the moral and political purposes of both regional governance and local societies.

The 'Lae rebellion'

Although there had been earlier isolated instances of islanders' dissatisfaction with their role within the SPC, it was not until the 1962 conference, held at Pago Pago, in American Samoa, that such feelings were widely shared and articulated.[3] The mood influenced the representatives of the colonial powers meeting at the 1964 session of the SPC, which decided that the conference would henceforth be able to make recommendations concerning the work program. Delegates at the sixth conference (in 1965), held in Lae, in Papua New Guinea, were disappointed, however, in how their newly won power worked in practice. This disillusionment was the immediate cause of an outspoken attack on the SPC, expressed in both formal resolutions and supporting speeches.[4]

Islanders thought the resolution proposed by Ratu Mara, the Fijian representative, was an important prerequisite to gaining some control over SPC activities. It was felt that if the territories were able to contribute to SPC funds then they, as representatives of those territories, would have the right to control the commission's activities. These sentiments were reflected in the words of Mariano Kelesi, the British Solomon Islands delegate:

> If we agree to contributions to the Commission's funds we will have more say in this Conference; if we refuse to contribute, we will not have the right to say anything.

Buren Ratieta of the Gilbert and Ellice Islands said: 'I think the feeling we should have about this Commission is that it is ours. We should therefore contribute to the Commission because it is ours.' Thomas Remengesau of the Trust Territory of the Pacific Islands commented that 'this resolution will be regarded as a second step towards the Islanders acquiring more

---

3   For an account of the mood at the Pago Pago conference and of earlier instances of dissatisfaction, see Herr, 'Regionalism in the South Seas', pp. 179–86.
4   Robert Langdon, 'South Seas Regional Council May Grow Out of Lae Talks', *Pacific Islands Monthly*, August 1965: 21; and SPC, *Pacific Forum (Sixth South Pacific Conference, 1965)*, Nouméa: SPC, 1966, p. 36, Resolutions 75(e) and 75(f).

responsibility within the framework of the SPC' (the first step being the acquisition of the right to discuss draft work programs). And Ratu Mara argued that

> to deny them [the territories] this responsibility is not in keeping with the trend that has been taking place in the territories. We are being trained to take more responsibility in our own countries, so why should we be denied responsibility here?[5]

Ratu Mara was the principal protagonist, but nearly all islander delegates supported him. He was later to describe their joint action as a 'rebellion'. He argued that the 'confrontation' with the colonial powers—although 'not an easy thing to do because Fiji was still under colonial rule'—was necessary because

> the powers seemed incapable of realising that the winds of change had at last reached the South Pacific and that we peoples of the territories were no longer going to tolerate the domination of the Commission by the Metropolitan powers. We were sick of having little to say and no authority. Regardless of what we said or did the final decision was always in the hands of the Metropolitan powers.[6]

For both indigenous participants and European observers, the Lae conference represented a watershed in regional affairs. William Forsyth, who was Secretary-General of the SPC at this time, said:

> [T]he year 1964–65 may come to be recognised historically as the point at which in the South Pacific, emphasis moved over from the relationship of dependency to that of local inter-change.[7]

He cites the Lae conference as one of the prime indicators of this development. Robert Langdon, who was the *Pacific Islands Monthly*'s correspondent at the conference, commented at the time that 'the Lae Conference may well prove to be a milestone in Pacific history'.[8]

---

5   SPC, *Pacific Forum (Sixth South Pacific Conference, 1965)*, pp. 7, 23, 27.
6   Mara, 'Regional Co-operation in the South Pacific', p. 7.
7   Forsyth, 'South Pacific', p. 15.
8   Langdon, 'South Seas Regional Council May Grow Out of Lae Talks'. See also R.Q. Quentin-Baxter, 'A New Zealand View', in Mary Boyd, ed., *Pacific Horizons: A Regional Role for New Zealand*, Wellington: Price Milburn for the New Zealand Institute of International Affairs, 1972, pp. 21–31, at p. 22.

These observations have proved correct. Prominent islanders later recognised the Lae conference as the beginning of indigenous political assertion within the SPC. Ratu Mara, in particular, has emphasised the significance of the actions taken in 1965:

> I had solid backing from the representatives of all the territories in that revolt and though what I said then might not have been welcomed by the Colonial leaders of that time, our combined attack on the old system had the effect of bringing democracy into the Commission. The happenings of 1965 eventually led to a reversal of the earlier positions.[9]

Dr Macu Salato, when secretary-general of the SPC, took a similar view. He regards the Lae conference as being the occasion on which 'the voice of Pacific regionalism first began to make itself heard in the Commission'.[10]

The 'rebels' had to wait until 1969 for an answer to their request regarding territorial contributions. The underlying demand of the sixth conference—that islanders should have a more significant role within the SPC—received a prompter response. This demand had been reiterated at the 1966 meeting of the SPC. Ratu Mara, attending as one of the United Kingdom's commissioners, told the meeting that Fiji would have little use for the SPC in the future if it did not regard the territories as equal partners.[11] In response to these demands, at the next conference (in Nouméa in 1967), A.J. Fairclough, the senior commissioner for the United Kingdom, announced, on behalf of the participating governments, a series of arrangements aimed at giving the conference 'a greater role in determining the work of the Commission than it has at present'.[12] Fairclough attributed these changes to Ratu Mara, 'who had pressed hard for the territories to exert influence on the Commission'.[13]

The new arrangements provided for the draft annual budget of the SPC to be submitted to territorial administrations and participating governments prior to the meeting of the conference. The conference was to examine the draft work program and its budgetary implications and recommend

---

9   Mara, 'Regional Co-operation in the South Pacific', p. 8.
10   Salato, 'South Pacific Regionalism', p. 32.
11   Smith, *South Pacific Commission*, p. 203.
12   SPC, *Report of the Seventh South Pacific Conference and Proceedings of the Thirtieth Session of the South Pacific Commission*, Nouméa: SPC, 1967, Annex 1, p. 20.
13   'It's Not an Exclusive Club Now—And the Islanders Like It', *Pacific Islands Monthly*, November 1967: 25.

to the SPC, for its final decision, the particular items to be included.[14] The conference was henceforth to be held annually (it was previously triennial) to enable delegates to carry out these new functions, and the conference was to be followed immediately by an SPC session. But the participating governments took care to emphasise that 'the ultimate authority over the work of the Commission will remain as now with the Participating Governments in the Session'.[15] Another innovation introduced at the seventh conference (in 1967) was that the chairman of the conference was henceforth to be a representative of the territories instead of a commissioner of one of the metropolitan governments, as provided for in the Canberra Agreement.

At the eighth conference (in 1968), the delegates repeated their request for territorial contributions to SPC funds. This was done by way of a resolution. Although there were no other relevant resolutions, there were strong and outspoken attacks made during speeches on the powers of the SPC. Ratu Mara, who was chairing the conference, suggested delegates should have a more direct say in the projects proposed for their benefit. Faletau of Tonga asked: 'Why do the decisions of the Conference end as recommendations to the Commissioners? What right has the session to debate what the Conference puts forward?'[16]

Although the conference recommendations on the work program, the budget and other matters required the approval of the SPC, the eighth conference noted that 'with regard to its recommendations on the Budget and Work Programme, the representatives of the participating Governments have expressed an undertaking to accept these recommendations as put forward'.[17] This certainly was the case in 1968 when the thirty-first session of the SPC, meeting immediately after the eighth conference, approved all the recommendations of the conference. Thus, by 1968, the conference had assumed the SPC's former major annual task: the determination of the budget and work program. Stuart Inder reported that the 1968 conference 'spelled the end of the "exclusive club" charge that was first levelled at the Commissioners by Ratu Mara of Fiji in 1965'.[18]

---

14   SPC, *Report of the Seventh South Pacific Conference*, p. 20.
15   ibid., p. 20.
16   Kathleen Hancock, 'There was Blood and Thunder about More Power for the Islanders', *Pacific Islands Monthly*, November 1968: 30.
17   SPC, *Report of the Eighth South Pacific Conference and Proceedings of the Thirty-First Session of the South Pacific Commission*, Nouméa: SPC, 1968, p. 20, s. 9.
18   Stuart Inder, 'And Now the SPC's Crisis is Over', *Pacific Islands Monthly*, November 1968: 31.

At the 1969 conference, Ratu Mara put forward a proposal to establish a committee to review the activities of the SPC and the South Pacific Conference to see whether further change was desirable. His proposal was supported by the meeting and placed before the SPC, which also approved it.[19] The committee met during 1970 under the chairmanship of Laufo Meti of Western Samoa. The 1969 session of the SPC, meeting shortly after the ninth conference, decided to appoint an islander, Afioga Misimosa, as the next secretary-general.[20] Prior to 1970 only Europeans selected from the metropolitan countries had filled this post. Now, for the first time, an islander was at the head of the Secretariat of the Pacific Community, the body which had significant influence on the content of the draft work program and which was responsible for carrying out the final program as approved by the SPC. It was in 1969, too, that Ratu Mara finally received a response to his demand for territorial contributions. Henceforth, all territorial administrations, except those under French control, were to make financial contributions to the general SPC budget.[21]

The review committee set up by the ninth conference reported to the next annual conference, held in Suva. Two of its recommendations were concerned with increasing the powers of the South Pacific Conference: the conference should elect its own chairman and deputy chairman, who may or may not be a commissioner, and should determine its own rules of procedure and agenda.[22] The first recommendation was put into operation at the end of the conference when the delegates elected the chairman and deputy chairman for the next meeting.[23] The request for control over the agenda and rules of procedure was granted at the thirty-fourth session of the SPC in 1971.[24] At the 1970 conference, the delegates also made a bid for a voice in selection of the principal officers of the Secretariat of the Pacific Community, suggesting appointment by a committee comprising representatives of the territories and of the participating governments.[25] But by this time, the Pacific leaders were also determined to go outside the SPC framework and establish their own form of regional governance.

---

19   Stuart Inder, 'Togetherness Comes to the SPC', *Pacific Islands Monthly*, November 1969: 26.

20   ibid., p. 27.

21   SPC, *South Pacific Report 1969–70*, Nouméa: SPC, 1970, p. l.

22   SPC, *Report of the Tenth South Pacific Conference and Proceedings of the Thirty-Third Session of the South Pacific Commission*, Nouméa: SPC, 1970, p. 32, Resolution 19.

23   ibid., p. 24, s. 33.

24   SPC, *Report of the Eleventh South Pacific Conference and Proceedings of the Thirty-Fourth Session of the SPC*, Nouméa: SPC, 1971, p. 58, Resolution 30.

25   SPC, *Report of the Tenth South Pacific Conference*, pp. 14–16.

Speaking with 'a true island accent'

In the same year as the Lae rebellion (1965), which marked the start of the move by islander leaders to decolonise the SPC, the same island leaders initiated their own modest regional consortium, the Pacific Islands Producers' Association (PIPA).[26] Ratu Mara, then member for natural resources in the Fiji Government, was again the primary force. He saw the need for closer cooperation among island territories supplying bananas to the New Zealand market. Fiji was joined by Western Samoa, Cook Islands, Niue, Tonga and the Gilbert and Ellice Islands.[27] Thus, PIPA really amounted to a Polynesian venture, reflecting the more advanced stage of decolonisation of the eastern part of the Pacific and the fact that the main banana exporters also happened to be Polynesian territories. Although initially formed with the practical objective of improving access and the terms of trade for island bananas into the New Zealand market, it gradually expanded its scope to cover other agricultural products and all steps in the production, transport and marketing cycle.

PIPA was created not merely to work on practical problems of development and trade, although this was the stated objective. Most of the activities undertaken by PIPA could have been approached through the SPC, yet a decision was taken to establish a new organisation. Although PIPA achieved very little in terms of its development brief, it was celebrated in terms of its political symbolism. For example, in his closing speech to the 1971 PIPA conference, Tupua Tamasese said: '[T]his is the strength of our small body ... this is an association of islanders, created by islanders and successful only from the efforts of such.'[28] And Prince Tu`ipelehake, then prime minister of Tonga, later referred to PIPA as being, in its day, the only organisation 'of its kind which spoke with a true island accent'.[29] For Albert Henry, then premier of Cook Islands, PIPA was important as

---

26 Between 1965 and 1968, this organisation was called the Pacific Islands Producers' Secretariat. PIPA's constitution did not become operative until 1971. See Pacific Islands Producers' Association [hereinafter PIPA], *Constitution Establishing the Pacific Islands Producers' Association*, Suva: PIPA, 1971.

27 The details of PIPA's origins and early history are described by H.P. Elder, the executive secretary of the organisation, in PIPA, *Pacific Islands Producers' Association*, Suva: PIPA, March 1971.

28 PIPA, *Sixth Session: Record of Proceedings*, Nuku`alofa: PIPA, April 1971, p. 24.

29 South Pacific Forum Secretariat [hereinafter SPF Secretariat], 'Summary Record and Final Press Communiqué', in SPF Secretariat, *Leaders' Communiqué: Fifth South Pacific Forum, Rarotonga, Cook Islands, 20–22 March 1974*, Suva: SPF Secretariat, 1974, p. 10.

a symbol of Polynesian assertion in particular: '[F]or 200 years, the white man has been exploiting the resources of the Pacific, but now Polynesians are working together for Polynesians.'[30]

PIPA was terminated in 1973 but only because there was by then a more ambitious and wideranging indigenous organisation that could take over its activities. Prince Tu`ipelehake stated that he did not object to PIPA being subsumed by the South Pacific Bureau for Economic Co-operation (SPEC: the research arm and secretariat of the new South Pacific Forum) because he regarded them both as 'speaking the same language'.[31]

Indigenous regional governance

The South Pacific Forum (SPF) was set up in August 1971 to provide the heads of the newly independent Pacific states with a forum to discuss 'matters of general interest'.[32] Its creation was spurred by the frustrations felt with the limits placed on the scope of discussion in the SPC. As we saw in Chapter 4, the Canberra Agreement limited the SPC's scope to economic and social development; political matters had been purposely excluded. This began to annoy islander delegates to South Pacific conferences during the 1960s. Several attempts were made to introduce political issues. At the 1962 conference, for example, Netherlands New Guinea delegates attempted to raise the subject of the Indonesian 'invasion' of their country. The chairman ruled against hearing the issue in view of its political nature. It was reported that this ruling 'caused mutterings of dissent'.[33] The attempt to introduce the subject of the French nuclear tests at the 1970 conference resulted in island delegates repeatedly raising the issue until the French commissioner, M. Nettre, walked out of the conference.[34]

---

30   'Pacific Leaders Make Nuku`alofa a Get-Together to Remember', *Pacific Islands Monthly*, May 1971: 22.
31   SPF Secretariat, 'Summary Record and Final Press Communiqué', p. 7.
32   Ratu Sir Kamisese Mara, 'The South Pacific Forum', Address at the University of the South Pacific, Suva, 25 August 1972, p. 5.
33   'Lae Meeting May Bring Some Get-Up-And-Go to the SPC', *Pacific Islands Monthly*, June 1965: 49.
34   J. Eccles, 'Not So Much Togetherness Now', *Pacific Islands Monthly*, October 1970: 18.

Ratu Mara has emphasised the link between the creation of the SPF and the frustration that island leaders felt about the 'no politics' rule. He said the fact that political matters could not be discussed 'irked the representatives of the territories, especially those which had attained independence or were taking steps towards independence'. As a result of such frustration, he said, 'conviction grew that there must be another organisation to fill the gaps left in the Commission's framework'.[35] Tupua Tamasese Lealofi IV, then prime minister of Western Samoa, made a similar observation. Speaking to the twelfth South Pacific Conference (in Apia in 1972), he commented:

> I believe that no organisation can emerge to flourish without there being a legitimate need for it. Recent developments (the establishment of the Forum) might therefore be pointed to as fair criticism of this organisation of ours [the SPC], because these other bodies could only have grown up to meet needs in the region that were not being catered for, thus inferring a chronic inability on the part of the South Pacific Commission to grow with the times.[36]

The idea of establishing a new regional organisation was first discussed by the leaders of the independent island states, and of those approaching independence, in 'out of conference meetings during the South Pacific Conferences of 1967, 1968 and 1969'. Ratu Mara claims that following these conferences he put out 'feelers' to the New Zealand prime minister to see how he would react to the idea of hosting a meeting of Pacific island leaders. Ratu Mara does not indicate what sort of reception he received. According to Mara, it was at a private meeting of island leaders, held during Fiji's independence celebrations in October 1970, that the SPF was actually 'born'.[37] At this stage, it was evident that the islanders were considering the inclusion of Australia and New Zealand in their proposed meeting. Stuart Inder commented that they 'considered it a good idea that the leaders meet regularly with Australia and NZ and discuss common problems and wants'.[38]

---

35 Mara, 'The South Pacific Forum', p. 5.
36 Tupua Tamasese Lealofi IV, 'Opening Address by the Chairman: Twelfth South Pacific Conference and Thirty-Fifth Session of the South Pacific Commission', Unpublished conference paper, 1972.
37 Mara, 'The South Pacific Forum', p. 5.
38 Stuart Inder, 'Leading from the Rear is Still Leadership', *Pacific Islands Monthly*, September 1971: 27.

At the Commonwealth Prime Ministers' Conference held in Singapore in January 1971, Western Samoa, Fiji and Tonga sought support for their protest against the French nuclear tests. Forsyth argues that

> the slightly dusty answer they got almost certainly strengthened their feeling that it might be time to think about some platform of their own, additional to the Commonwealth and SPC.[39]

Forsyth's argument was supported by the fact that immediately after his return from the Prime Ministers' Conference, Tamasese Lealofi IV called publicly for a meeting of island leaders to discuss matters of interest to them.[40] The *Fiji Times* reported that his statement had the support of Ratu Mara of Fiji and Hammer DeRoburt of Nauru.[41]

The leaders of the independent states took their shared idea of establishing their own organisation a stage further in off-the-record discussions at the sixth PIPA meeting held in Nuku`alofa, Tonga, in April 1971. All the independent island states, except Nauru, which was not a member of PIPA, were present. They decided that Ratu Mara should approach the New Zealand prime minister to see whether he would host a meeting[42] at which island leaders could discuss 'matters of interest to them within the region and in their involvement with Australia and New Zealand'.[43] They intended such a meeting to be an annual event. The New Zealand prime minister, Sir Keith Holyoake, announced in May 1971 that New Zealand would cooperate willingly with the islanders' plan.[44] New Zealand leaders had been advocating that the island leaders form their own organisation since late 1970. This was evident, for example, in a statement made by the Minister for Māori and Island Affairs, Duncan MacIntyre, in December 1970: '[W]hat many Islanders want, and what we should encourage, is a political forum where island countries can meet on equal terms with Australia and New Zealand.'[45]

---

39   W.D. Forsyth, 'Wellington Conference Means New Era of Pacific Alliances', *Pacific Islands Monthly*, August 1971: 12.

40   Robert Keith-Reid, 'Getting Tough in Tonga', *The Bulletin*, [Australia], 24 April 1971: 37.

41   Forsyth, 'Wellington Conference Means New Era of Pacific Alliances'.

42   Ratu Mara later said the reason for choosing Wellington for the first meeting was to avoid accusations that Fiji was 'trying to usurp the leadership of the island region'. See Mara, 'The South Pacific Forum', p. 11.

43   Ratu Mara, quoted in 'Pacific Leaders Make Nukualofa a Get-together to Remember', *Pacific Islands Monthly*, May 1971: 23.

44   Forsyth, 'South Pacific', p. 18.

45   W.D. MacIntyre, cited in M. Margaret Ball, 'Regionalism and the Pacific Commonwealth', *Pacific Affairs*, 46(2), 1973: 232–53, at p. 243.

M. Margaret Ball argues that 'New Zealand was obviously anxious to promote the Forum idea, but the formal initiative came from the Islanders'.[46] The use of the word 'formal' here is misleading as it implies that it was not in fact an islander initiative. The facts point to the SPF idea being not only formally, but also actually, an islander initiative. Islanders' discussions of the idea had already begun when the New Zealand leaders' statements began to appear. Australia also welcomed the islander initiative, and Australia's foreign minister Leslie Bury said Australia would make facilities available for a future meeting. Although the leaders of all five independent Pacific countries were involved with the establishment of the SPF, some played a more significant role than others. Albert Henry of the Cook Islands, Ratu Mara of Fiji and Tamasese of Western Samoa were particularly active. Forsyth describes Henry as 'the Islands leader probably most entitled to the credit of initiating publicly the idea of an Islands political forum'. Henry's views were made known to other island leaders during 1969 and 1970. Forsyth claims:

> [I]t has been easier … for Mr. Henry to take the lead as the Cook Islands have not been involved in the past history of rivalry and reservations which has affected relations between Tonga, Samoa and Fiji.

He also draws attention to the fact that Henry was the president of PIPA when it met in Nuku`alofa in April 1971. This, he argues, 'doubtless … helped to bring about the agreement … to go ahead with the project for a forum'.[47] Tamasese's main contribution was to make a public statement calling for a meeting of island leaders on his return from the Commonwealth Prime Ministers' Conference in January 1971. Ratu Mara's role was to approach the New Zealand prime minister about hosting the first forum meeting. The other two 'founding' leaders did not play active parts. Inder described DeRoburt of Nauru as 'not nearly so interested in the intricacies of political affiliations and inter-government relationships as, say, Ratu Mara and Mr Albert Henry'. Further, he argues:

> Nauru turned up to the Forum with probably even less of an inkling of its possible direction than anyone. Nauru has been a loner, with little time available for, or understanding of the need to mend fences in her own region.[48]

---

46 ibid., p. 243.
47 Forsyth, 'South Pacific', p. 19.
48 Inder, 'Leading from the Rear is Still Leadership'.

Foundation principles

When the heads of government of the five independent Pacific island states assembled for the first South Pacific Forum in the parliament buildings in Wellington in August 1971, it was already clear, in general terms, what ideas they were seeking to promote. As we have seen, these were the same people who for some years had been involved in the annual conferences of the SPC and who had established PIPA, in which they had met since 1965. They had also recently been together at Fiji's independence celebrations in October 1970 and at the Commonwealth Prime Ministers' Conference in Singapore in January 1971. In each of these forums, they had made it known to each other, and to a wider audience, that it was time for a fundamental departure in the principles and practice of regional cooperation.[49]

The individuals concerned were exceptional leaders in national and regional politics. Ratu Mara was an impressive paramount chief who had already established his regional leadership credentials in the campaign to decolonise the structures of the SPC and in his initiative in establishing PIPA. Tamasese held one of the four high chiefly titles of Western Samoa. Henry did not have the high chiefly status of the others but made up for it with his noted oratorical and political skills, honed in trade union politics in New Zealand and on the political hustings in Cook Islands. The two other founding leaders were less prominent in the development and promotion of the new regionalist principles but were nevertheless important players. Tonga's Prince Tuʻipelehake, the brother of the King, had been prime minister since 1965, and DeRoburt, president of Nauru since 1968, had been head chief of his people since 1956 and tenaciously led the successful campaign for independence against a reluctant Australian Government during the 1960s.

The main principle underlying the forum initiative was that of self-determination in regional affairs. In this regard, the establishment of the SPF represented the culmination of a political process rather than a beginning. As we have seen, the representatives of Pacific island territories had been involved, since the early 1960s, in a campaign to decolonise the power structure in the colonial regional organisation, the SPC. The principle of self-determination was seen, then, as a prior concern of

---

49   The standard works on the formation and subsequent activities of the SPC are Smith, *South Pacific Commission*; Herr, 'Regionalism in the South Seas'; and Forsyth, 'South Pacific'.

regional cooperation and the SPF was the most sophisticated institutional expression of it. To underscore this principle, it was not enough that the proposed organisation overcome the constraints on political discussions in the SPC or be structured in such a way that there was equality among members. It was also regarded as essential that only sovereign island states, and Australia and New Zealand, be allowed to participate, thus excluding the dependent territories and the other metropolitan powers, France, the United Kingdom and the United States.

The idea of including Australia and New Zealand in the cooperative process seemed to some observers to abrogate the self-determination principle. If this was to be a move away from colonial governance, why include two countries that were still colonial powers and the main economic forces in the island region? Should not the postcolonial states form their own collective to determine their position in relation to these regional powers, as had occurred in South-East Asia, the Caribbean and Africa? The island leaders recognised that it might appear an unusual step but saw it as a necessary one if they were to maximise their influence over the terms of engagement with these countries. Ratu Mara, for example, later asserted:

> We were happy to be joined by Australia and New Zealand in the Forum ... Indeed, we wanted them for a special reason. For part of the ambitious plan of the Forum ... was no less than to alter the whole balance of the terms of trade.[50]

While the invitation to Australia can be thought of mainly in pragmatic terms, the inclusion of New Zealand was also based on some feelings of close affinity. New Zealand was perceived as having more empathy with the island region. It had a significant Polynesian population, it had been supportive of islander initiatives to reform the SPC and some of the island leaders had close personal and educational links with New Zealand. It was also known that New Zealand's leaders were interested in exploring new multilateral arrangements for dealing with what was fast becoming a postcolonial South Pacific.[51] Significantly, it was New Zealand prime minister Holyoake whom Ratu Mara approached on behalf of the other island leaders about hosting the first SPF.

---

50   Ratu Sir Kamisese Mara, 'Grail Address', Corpus Christi College, Suva, January 1973, as cited in Sandra Tarte, 'Fiji's Role in the South Pacific Forum, 1971–1984', BA(Hons) thesis, Department of Political Science, University of Melbourne, Melbourne, October 1985.
51   Mary Boyd, 'Introduction', in Mary Boyd, ed., *Pacific Horizons: A Regional Role for New Zealand*, Wellington: Price Milburn for the New Zealand Institute of International Affairs, 1972, pp. 7–17, at pp. 9–10; and Ken Piddington, *South Pacific Forum: The First 15 Years*, Suva: South Pacific Bureau for Economic Co-operation, 1986, p. 6.

Further decolonisation of the SPC, 1972–78

The successful creation of their own regional organisation encouraged, rather than deterred, the efforts of Pacific island leaders to decolonise what they saw as the 'exclusive club' of the SPC. Ratu Mara renewed his attack at the 1972 South Pacific Conference when he asked: 'Why should the gentlemen who sit in Paris and in Washington be deciding the pace and extent of the development of the people in this region?'[52] R.G. Ward, an observer at the conference, reported:

> It was clear at the 12th Conference that virtually all the island territories and most of the metropolitan 'Participating Governments' were anxious to see changes in the organisation of the SPC so that the Islanders could have more direct control over the work of the Commission.[53]

The Australian delegation placed a proposal aimed at quelling this anxiety before the 1973 conference. The proposal suggested a '*de facto* merger of the Commission and Conference', which, inter alia, 'should reduce any resentments of Conference members at having their recommendations subject to the approval of a body largely comprised of "metropolitan powers"'.[54] It was proposed that territories and participating governments should each have one vote. The Australian delegation suggested that the change be effected by convention rather than going through the difficult process of getting all participating governments to agree to alter the Canberra Agreement. The Australian proposal, however, still included a provision that maintained the ultimate authority of the participating governments. A participating government could demand in relation to any particular issue that only participating government votes be counted. In the words of the Australian paper to the conference, 'this, hopefully, would be an extreme step that would rarely, if ever, be taken'.[55]

---

52   R.G. Ward, 'Report on South Pacific Commission Conference', Unpublished report, Canberra, 1972, p. 1.
53   R.G. Ward, 'Report on the Thirteenth South Pacific Conference, Guam and a Visit to Manila, September 1973', Unpublished report, Canberra, 1973.
54   Australian Government, *Possible Changes in the Functioning of the South Pacific Commission*, Working Paper No. 4, Presented to Thirteenth South Pacific Conference, Guam, 1–20 September 1973, p. 3.
55   ibid., s. 13.

In the discussion of the proposal by the South Pacific Conference, island delegates made it clear that they would not tolerate anything short of full acceptance of the Australian proposal. France's reluctance to accept change sparked bitter comments from some island delegates. Albert Maori Kiki of Papua New Guinea told the conference that 'it was time for the delegates from colonial governments to "shut up" and let the Pacific Islanders get on with their job'. Bikenibeu Paeniu of the Gilbert and Ellice Islands said the SPC must come under the control of the island governments, and Joe Williams of the Cook Islands commented:

> [I]f France continued to object to the reforms then the Cook Islands would propose that the Commission session be abolished altogether and the Conference put officially in full charge of the SPC.[56]

The conference set up the Future Status Committee to examine ways of implementing the principles espoused in the Australian proposal. The committee accepted the proposal and tabled a resolution that was accepted by the conference, calling on Australia to

> initiate discussion immediately with all participating governments at the highest appropriate level to revise the Canberra Agreement in such a way that it will reflect the needs and aspirations of the Pacific people.[57]

The committee retained the safeguard clause for the participating governments, pending alteration of the Canberra Agreement, and expressed the hope that it would not be invoked. In response to the conference's request, Australia arranged a joint review meeting of participating governments of the SPC in Wellington in March 1974. The meeting approved a memorandum of understanding that was signed by participating governments during the subsequent South Pacific Conference in October.[58]

The memorandum instituted important structural change without formal amendment of the Canberra Agreement. Under the new arrangements, the SPC and the South Pacific Conference were to meet in joint session at

---

56 'All—Except France—Agog for Change—In South Pacific Commission', *Pacific Islands Monthly*, October 1973: 7.

57 SPC, *Report of the 'Future Status' Committee, Thirteenth South Pacific Conference*, Nouméa: SPC Secretariat, September 1973.

58 The text of the memorandum is contained in SPC, *Report of the Fourteenth South Pacific Conference*, Nouméa: SPC, 1974, Annex C, pp. 42–4.

which each country (whether a participating government or a dependent territory) would have one vote. The new joint session, the conference, assumed most of the functions of the SPC—the executive body under the old arrangements. The SPC was reconstituted as a committee of the conference (the Committee of Representatives of Participating Governments, CRPG). The CRPG retained the power to approve the administrative budget and to nominate the principal officers of the SPC. Thus, it did not operate strictly as a committee of the conference. The other major change was the establishment of the Planning and Evaluation Committee, whose function it was to examine the draft work program prior to South Pacific Conference meetings. Significantly, all members of the conference were entitled to representation on this committee.

The arrangements under the memorandum represented the culmination of a decade of demands by island leaders for a more significant role for the South Pacific Conference within the SPC's structure. Although certain powers were retained by the reconstituted SPC (the CRPG), the conference had now become the governing body in the organisation. In view of the fact that, under the pre-memorandum rules, the SPC was the executive body and the conference had only an advisory function, the new arrangements constituted a reversal of roles.

The fifteenth South Pacific Conference (in Nauru in 1975) was the first to operate under the new rules. Ratu Mara dispelled any thought that the memorandum should be construed as having satisfied all islander complaints concerning metropolitan influence within the SPC. He attacked the control that donor countries might exercise over SPC programs through their voluntary contributions to special projects. The metropolitan participating governments, in particular, had been giving voluntary contributions outside their normal budgetary contribution. These voluntary contributions were tagged for particular projects. Ratu Mara argued that the people in the region, not SPC staff and donor countries, should decide where funds should be spent. Ratu Mara also criticised the SPC's work program, claiming it was irrelevant to the needs of the people. His criticisms became a rallying point for other speakers. The object of their attacks was the work program and, by implication, and at times by specific reference, the metropolitan countries and the Secretariat of the Pacific Community, which they held responsible.[59]

---

59   This section is based on personal observations made at the fifteenth conference. They are developed in Gregory E. Fry, 'Report on the Fifteenth South Pacific Conference held in Nauru, 29 September to 10 October 1975', Unpublished report, Canberra, February 1976.

The mood of dissatisfaction culminated in the decision to hold a review conference in May 1976 to 'conduct an exhaustive re-evaluation of the total functions and organisation of the South Pacific Commission'.[60] The review committee's recommendations did not, however, substantially affect the structure of the SPC.[61] They emphasised certain functional areas on which the SPC should concentrate but these did not mark an important departure from past practice. The most important recommendation concerned the structure of the secretariat. It was suggested that the division of the work program into the separate categories of health, social development and economic development be discontinued. It was further suggested that the divisions within the secretariat corresponding to these functional areas be integrated into one unit. The committee also proposed that special projects be incorporated into the general work program—a suggestion that answered Ratu Mara's demands at the fifteenth conference. The review committee's recommendations were all agreed to by the sixteenth conference (in Nouméa in 1976).

A remaining anomaly in post-memorandum arrangements was the plural voting system in use in the CRPG. This system had been in use in the SPC since 1964 and was carried over into the CRPG. The introduction of plural voting had been a condition of France's support for Western Samoa's admission to SPC membership. Under this arrangement, a participating government's number of votes depended on the number of Pacific territories it represented. Thus, France and the United Kingdom were entitled to more votes than, say, Fiji, which was entitled to only one. This created the possibility of metropolitan dominance of the CRPG. Before any significant public expression of islander dissatisfaction could be voiced, the metropolitan powers announced an end to this system, at the 1976 South Pacific Conference.[62]

The attack on what were seen as residual elements of metropolitan dominance did not rest there. At the seventeenth conference (in Pago Pago in 1977), Papua New Guinea's foreign minister, Ebia Olewale, led a critical discussion on the restrictive qualifications for membership of the inner group of the SPC (those who had acceded to the Canberra Agreement and had thereby qualified for membership of the CRPG).

---

60 SPC, *Report of the Fifteenth South Pacific Conference*, Nouméa: SPC, 1975, Resolution 23.
61 See SPC, *Report of the SPC Review Committee, Nauru, 3–7 May 1976*, Nouméa: SPC, 1976.
62 'South Pacific Commission: Sixteenth South Pacific Conference', *Australian Foreign Affairs Record*, November 1976, p. 612.

It was proposed that the agreement be amended to allow all non-self-governing territories to become participating governments. Olewale commented:

> [W]e are no longer in the 40s and 50s when the SPC was regarded as a rich man's club, in which important decisions are made by a small group of people. We can't afford to let this go on.[63]

Even though the SPC had been terminated by the memorandum of understanding, the islanders' statements indicated that they viewed the new CRPG as retaining important functions in which dependent Pacific territories could not participate. The CRPG indicated a willingness to go part of the way in satisfying this demand. At the eighteenth South Pacific Conference (in Nouméa in 1978), they notified their intention to amend the Canberra Agreement to allow the accession of countries which had attained a constitutional status in which they were in 'free association with a fully independent Government'.[64]

At the 1978 conference, there was evidence of continuing opposition to what was perceived as undue metropolitan influence on SPC affairs. Australia provoked the anger of island delegates by referring matters to Canberra for decision and keeping the rest of the conference waiting in so doing.[65] The first occasion was on the question of Tuvalu's accession to the Canberra Agreement. Tuvalu, as a newly independent Pacific country, had qualified to become a participating government in the SPC. The motion inviting Tuvalu to accede to the Canberra Agreement was approved by all member countries except Australia, whose representative said he would have to refer the matter to Canberra for approval. This meant that the decision on Tuvalu's accession had to be delayed for three days. The second occasion concerned a motion on civil aviation. Australia was once again the only country not in a position to give its immediate concurrence. Referring to the Australian actions, the Fijian delegate, Livai Nasilivata, asked:

---

63   J. Carter, 'Horrid Niggling, or Happy Nuptials, for Commission and Forum?', *Pacific Islands Monthly*, November 1977: 10.

64   SPC, *Report of the Eighteenth South Pacific Conference*, Nouméa: SPC, 1978, Item 17, p. 26.

65   These views on the 1978 conference are based on personal observation. They are developed in Gregory E. Fry, 'Report on the Eighteenth South Pacific Conference', Unpublished report, Canberra, 1978. The events described are also reported in C. Ashton, 'Australia Takes a Beating', *The Bulletin*, [Australia], 24 October 1978: 21–2; and in R. Hawkins, 'The Hot Politics of a "Routine" Conference', *Pacific Islands Monthly*, December 1978: 26–9.

> [H]ow much longer are we, the island countries and, in fact, ministers representing island peoples at this conference, to allow ourselves to be treated in this insulting and paternalistic way by some of our partners?[66]

Fiji's attack on Australia was supported by other island delegates. It was not merely the fact that the conference had been kept waiting that angered islander delegates, nor that a delegation had to cable home for instructions. It is evident that at the core of the Fijian objection was the fact that it was a metropolitan country that was doing these things. The appearance was of a conference waiting for a decision to be taken in a metropolitan capital. This was too much of a reminder of a past when metropolitan powers had much more influence.

The events at the 1978 conference indicated that islander leaders were still very sensitive to any metropolitan actions that might be construed as trying to unduly influence the operation of this organisation. This sensitivity remained despite the structural changes, and the changes in work programs and procedures, which gave islanders effective control of the SPC. For many islanders, the SPC would always be seen as an organisation created by the colonial powers and therefore not to be regarded in the same way as 'homegrown' institutions. The presence of metropolitan countries in the South Pacific Conference and the CRPG, and the fact that these countries provided nearly all of the SPC's budget, contributed to a feeling among islanders that whatever changes were made to the SPC, it was still not really theirs. Indeed, in the following decade, some Pacific leaders saw the only solution as being to terminate the SPC and to support instead the institutions they had created themselves.

Sovereignty and regional self-determination

The development of formal regional governance structures based on self-determination principles resulted from the political change within Pacific territories. For those approaching state sovereignty, it also reinforced that national sovereignty. In making statehood the criterion for a seat at the regional table of decision-making, self-determination was equated with sovereign statehood. If colonial regionalism had been dominated by colonial powers, the new regionalism would be determined by postcolonial

---

66   Ashton, 'Australia Takes a Beating', p. 22.

states. The new legitimating principles for regional governance were particularly important in entrenching the sovereignty of associated states. The Cook Islands and Niue had chosen associated statehood rather than independence to continue the advantages of access to New Zealand. This legal status was new in world politics and it became a work in progress for these territories to establish their actual international status. Regional membership established their credentials as international players. Thus, rather than regional governance competing with national sovereignty, the two were mutually constitutive.

But there was a tension inherent in this regional self-determination principle. In setting up political independence as the criterion for full political agency in the new regional society of states, access was denied to those who were content with limited self-government as the end point of decolonisation. As we will see in Chapter 7, this created a tension and contest between independent countries and dependent territories—for example, with Guam and French Polynesia—in the regional arena. While independent countries saw them as belonging to one regional family, they had to be seen to earn their place at the regional decision-making table by first gaining independence. Under the new principles, regional self-determination was extended to all Pacific island peoples, while political agency rested only with those who had an independent state. We return to this tension between identity and agency in Chapter 7.

This also affected sovereignty and anticolonial movements, which wanted to go as far as they could with decolonisation but were limited by being a minority in a larger state. This was the case in West Papua, New Caledonia and Hawai`i. In such cases, recognition by the regional forum of having a right to speak was enormously important in terms of international support for domestic struggles. But while the regional identity embraced by the independent states included the dependent territories, it did not generally extend beyond the SPC's territorial area into the metropolitan countries. Regional support for such sovereignty movements would be supported, rather, by regional NGOs.

The equation of political agency within the new regional governance with state sovereignty also left out NGOs and, over time, was seen as reflecting an elitist top-down regionalism. It is to the broadening out of the postcolonial regional polity, and to the contradictions between agency and identity in 'the new South Pacific' of the 1970s and 1980s, that we now turn.

7

The postcolonial regional polity

Regional governance took a dramatic turn in the early 1970s. The contest over regional self-determination continued but it took place in a very different context, that of a *postcolonial* regional polity. Although the independence of Fiji and Tonga in 1970 brought the number of new Pacific island states to only five, there was already a shared sense among the Pacific leaders that a new political era had begun for the region as a whole. The independent Pacific countries committed themselves to the newly established SPF as a diplomatic focal point for promoting the practical purposes of postcolonial national development and negotiating global relationships, as well as promoting regional self-determination beyond their own territorial borders.

From 1971, the new leaders began meeting in the annual summit of the SPF, together with Australia and New Zealand, and by 1972, they had set up the economic research arm, the SPEC, which soon became the de facto secretariat of the SPF. They assumed, correctly, that it was only a matter of time before they were joined in their regional association by the other dependent territories that fell under the jurisdiction of the SPC. This was encouraged by the certainty that, with a change of government in Canberra, Papua New Guinea would move to independence by 1975, and by Britain's indication that it would soon be leaving its remaining colonies, Solomon Islands, Kiribati and Tuvalu. By the end of the decade, there were 11 independent Pacific countries and they were to be joined by three more in the 1980s.

The sense that this was the beginning of a 'new South Pacific'[1] was also encouraged by the impact of the new regional university established in Suva in 1968. The University of the South Pacific (USP) generated a regional awareness among its students and in parts of the broader community. The sense of a new postcolonial age was further fostered by the emergence of a number of important regional civil society organisations and institutions around churches, women's groups and antinuclear and anticolonial movements. They expressed a shared commitment to regional self-determination and a desire to participate actively in influencing the ideas that underpinned the practices of regional governance.

The emergence of new sovereign states with independent foreign policies and a commitment to joint diplomacy attracted the interest of larger powers that had not previously been active in the area in the colonial era. It also demanded a recalibration of involvement from the former and continuing colonial powers. From 1976, Australia, New Zealand and the United States began to see the region through Cold War lenses. They regarded it as essential that regional governance in the security realm accord with Western interests. They promoted the idea of 'regional security' for the first time in the South Pacific context and linked this to national development and regionalism. France also had to adjust its approach to the region as its nuclear testing at Moruroa and Fangataufa atolls—and its failure to decolonise its Pacific territories—became a key target of the new Pacific collective diplomacy through the SPF. The rapid political change in the South Pacific, together with the prospect of a new law of the sea regime from the mid 1970s, also spurred strong interest and involvement from China, Taiwan, Japan and the European Economic Community (EEC).

The postcolonial regional polity that developed from the early 1970s can be usefully seen as comprising three major groups of actors. At the centre of this new regional polity was what we might term a developing regional 'society of states' with shared purposes around practical concerns of nation-building and negotiating global engagement, together with shared values, particularly around the principles of regional self-determination, sovereign equality and Christianity within a broader 'Pacific way' ideology.[2] A second group, comprising new NGOs with aspirations to

---

1   R.G. Crocombe, *The New South Pacific*, Wellington: Reed Education, 1973.
2   Following Mohammed Ayoob's adaptation of Hedley Bull's international society concept. See Ayoob, 'From Regional System to Regional Society'.

counter deleterious global influences on Pacific societies, constituted an embryonic regional civil society. They were also vitally concerned with regional self-determination. The third group comprised international actors—states and international agencies—seeking to influence the way in which regional security and regional development would be defined in the postcolonial Pacific.

Underpinning some significant aspects of this international influence was the policy-related knowledge created by academics and international agencies around the notion of 'smallness' as a special category in international relations and development, requiring regionalism as a key policy solution. From 1976, a Cold War security framework in which the economic realm was in service of security objectives joined this global framing of the Pacific island region in economic terms.

Changing global context

The context in which regional governance developed in the 1970s and 1980s was influenced very significantly by the decolonisation policies of the United Kingdom, New Zealand and Australia. The changed attitudes underpinning these policies made the 'new South Pacific' possible. In nearly all cases, the pace of decolonisation was faster than that desired by the people of the territory concerned. In only three cases—Nauru, Western Samoa and Vanuatu—was there a concerted demand for independence. For Britain, the pressure to move Fiji to independence by 1970, despite the reluctance of the Fijian population (concerned about Indian dominance in a new state), was driven by its general policy determination to withdraw from all its colonies that were big enough to stand on their own feet. It was only with a changing international attitude to the possibility of decolonising very small territories that Britain then moved in the 1970s to decolonise Gilbert and Ellice Islands into two states, Tuvalu and Kiribati, and Solomon Islands and Vanuatu (which it ruled, with France, as a condominium). The new Australian Labor Government promoted the decolonisation of Papua New Guinea at a similar pace between 1972 and 1975, and New Zealand moved Niue to associated statehood in 1974. Tonga was a special case. As a British protectorate, it chose to reenter 'the comity of nations' in 1970.[3]

---

3   Campbell, *Worlds Apart*, Ch. 17; Howe et al., *Tides of History*, Part 2.

The decolonisation of the British, Australian and New Zealand territories, leaving only the American and French Pacific territories as colonial dependencies, impacted significantly on the nature of the postcolonial regional governance that emerged in the 1970s. It was Suva-centred and English-speaking. Its participating states were members of the Commonwealth. They adopted variations of the Westminster model (except Kiribati) and six of them recognised the Queen of England as head of state.

While the international influences on the emergence of the new regionalism were thus profound, the resulting indigenous regional developments in turn invited new international interest and involvement. The emergence of a significant number of independent Pacific states scattered over a large area of ocean inevitably stimulated interest from outside powers with no former colonial links to the area. New overtures—first evident in the mid 1970s—came mainly from the Soviet Union, China and Japan, and were expressed in the establishment of diplomatic ties, trade links, visits and offers of economic assistance. The Soviet Union and Japan appeared to be motivated primarily by the desire to facilitate the operation of their large fishing fleets in the area. This has to be considered in the context of the move by the newly independent Pacific states to declare 200-mile economic zones under the new Law of the Sea promulgated in 1976. Under such arrangements, most of the independent island states, being archipelagic countries, have sovereignty over a very large area of ocean— so large, in fact, that, taken collectively, they claim control of most of the South Pacific Ocean. The declaration of these zones, the political change within these states and the increasing attractiveness of the South Pacific as a fishing ground compelled distant water fishing nations (DWFNs), such as Japan and the Soviet Union, to develop closer relations with the new island states.

The Soviet Union was particularly concerned to establish a base for its fishing fleet in the region, and in this regard approached Tonga in 1976 with an offer of aid to assist with airport extensions in exchange for port facilities.[4] In the same year, the Soviet Union established diplomatic links with Fiji and Western Samoa. Japan became involved in joint fishing

---

4   Australian Department of Foreign Affairs, 'The South Pacific', Submission to the Senate Standing Committee on Foreign Affairs and Defence Inquiry into the Need for an Increased Australian Commitment to the South Pacific', Canberra: AGPS, March 1977, p. 21. For a Soviet perspective, see Alexander Malyashkin (a journalist of the Novosti Press Agency), 'USSR, the Pacific', *Pacific Islands Monthly*, January 1978: 15–16.

ventures with some Pacific states and gave assistance to their fishing industries through the provision of ships and training.[5] The factors underlying Chinese involvement in Oceania from the mid 1970s are less clear, although the decision to establish diplomatic missions in Fiji and Western Samoa in 1976—the same year as the Soviet initiatives—lends support to the view that China was motivated primarily by the desire to compete ideologically with the Soviet Union. This is also indicated by the public warnings that the Chinese Government made concerning Russian activities in the area.[6] There was also the equally compelling motive of countering Taiwan's growing influence in the region. Three of the Pacific island states—Nauru, Tonga and Tuvalu—recognised Taiwan in the 1970s and Taiwanese trawlers were already active in South Pacific waters.

The metropolitan powers with established or former colonial interests in the area had to readjust their relations with this 'new' Pacific. For all except the United Kingdom (which retained only a token interest after withdrawing from its last major Pacific colony in 1980), strategic interest heightened as the region became more involved in Cold War competition. For the United States and France, their continued involvement in the region was more direct as they had no intention of withdrawing from their Pacific territories. The wide, isolated expanse of French Polynesia provided an ideal setting for nuclear testing at Fangataufa and Moruroa atolls after France was excluded from its Algerian testing site in 1962.[7] Moreover, the Rothschild mining operation in New Caledonia was at this time the world's second largest producer of nickel. For the Americans, the strategically placed Micronesian territories and Guam continued to provide sites for key military, nuclear and communications bases that were seen as crucial for prosecution of the Cold War.

Although they had withdrawn from their own colonies, Australia and New Zealand increased their involvement in the region dramatically as a response to the new, more fluid situation in the decolonised context of the mid 1970s. They were particularly motivated by the Soviet offers of aid to some Pacific countries in 1976. They returned to the longstanding Australasian assertion of a natural right to lead this region. Australia, in

---

5   Japan's economic involvement at this time is explored in a series of articles: 'Japan: Her Role in the South Seas', *Pacific Islands Monthly*, June 1976: 33–47, and 'Japan and the Pacific', *Pacific Islands Monthly*, September 1978: 37–68. See also Yoshio Okawara, 'Japan's Plea: Give Us Access to Your Waters', *Pacific Islands Monthly*, April 1978: 10–11.

6   'Russian Threat in Pacific Claimed', *Sydney Morning Herald*, 1 March 1977.

7   Denoon et al., *The Cambridge History of the Pacific Islanders*, Ch. 10.

particular, saw the Pacific island area as constituting a regional strategic entity with itself as the manager on behalf of the West. There were ongoing attempts by Australia, New Zealand and the United States—as an explicit Australia New Zealand United States (ANZUS) Treaty strategy—to keep the newly independent states under Western influence in the Cold War struggle and to see regional governance as central to this enterprise. These developments are explored in detail in Chapter 9.

In the 1980s, the political stakes became much higher, at least as seen from the position of the metropolitan countries. Regional politics began to attract, for the first time since World War II, the serious attention of the world's largest powers.[8] They began to view the outcomes of SPF deliberations as having significant implications for their grand strategies—France on nuclear testing and its continuing colonial presence in the region, the United States on security issues and Law of the Sea questions and Japan on nuclear waste dumping and driftnet fishing. For such international players, the SPF came to be seen increasingly as the political site where the governing norms and principles of a regional order, as a prevailing pattern of state practice, were being determined. It became the focus of efforts to influence the content to be given to such concepts as regional security and regional development. In 1989, Canada, France, Japan, the United Kingdom and the United States accepted an invitation to participate in a regular post-SPF dialogue. China and Taiwan jealously eyed the one position at the table available to China, seeing it as an important symbol of regional acceptance. In the event, a formula was found where both could be involved in dialogue with SPF members. International agencies also played a much greater role in the regional polity in the 1980s. The World Bank, the International Monetary Fund (IMF), the Asian Development Bank (ADB), the UNDP and the UN Environment Programme all became major influences on regional politics, as we will see in Chapters 10 and 11. Cold War thinking, decolonisation and self-determination ideas, and developmental ideas around the special needs of the small state, provided the large global policy frameworks influencing international involvement in the Pacific in these opening decades of the postcolonial era. Each emphasised regional governance as the focus of their Pacific strategy.

---

8   Fry, 'Regionalism and International Politics of the South Pacific'.

The development of a regional 'society of states'

Against this global backdrop, the leaders of the independent Pacific countries developed what I referred to, in Chapter 2, as a regional 'society of states'. Beginning in 1971, with seven members, it grew to 13 member states by 1980 and to 16 by the mid 1980s. Although there were other important participants in the contest over regional governance, their joint efforts to set up and develop regional organisations and to promote joint diplomacy were the 'main game' of regional politics. I argue that the Pacific regional system that developed in the 1970s and 1980s meets the criteria put forward by Hedley Bull (and adapted to the regional level by Mohammed Ayoob) for the existence of a society of states. Furthermore, I argue that this demonstrates the political significance of this form of regional governance without a high degree of regional integration. These criteria include common interests and practical association, institutional expressions and common values.

Common interests and practical association

The five Pacific island countries which, along with Australia and New Zealand, constituted the membership of the SPF at the time of its first meeting in 1971, were all committed to regional cooperation as a principal, if not *the* principal, avenue for their postcolonial diplomacy. The leaders of these states had worked closely together in establishing indigenous-controlled forms of regional governance in the 1960s. In the post-independence context of the 1970s, and with a new regional forum in existence, this commitment to regional affairs took a more practical turn. Tonga, Samoa and Nauru decided not to join the United Nations and other international agencies but to instead focus their limited diplomatic resources on participation in regional forums. The Cook Islands, as an associated state (with New Zealand), had even more limited diplomatic possibilities. Under the terms of its association status, it could not become a member of the United Nations. Membership of regional organisations was by necessity the only avenue available; it was also one that granted Cook Islands a limited international legal personality. In the regional context, Cook Islands (and later, Niue and the Micronesian associated states) was recognised as equal to the fully independent countries.

Fiji's case was very different. It had the resources to look further afield and participate in international organisations. Fiji joined the United Nations but emphasised that it saw its role as a representative of the Pacific island region. In 1970, in his first statement to the UN General Assembly after Fiji's entry to that organisation, prime minister Ratu Mara, in speaking of the need for a 'Pacific voice' in the General Assembly, said:

> [A]s far as we are authorised by our friends and neighbours, and we do not arrogate to ourselves any role of leadership, we would hope to act as representative and interpreter of that voice.[9]

The Fijian Government claimed that it regarded involvement in world forums as of secondary importance to participation in regional affairs. In his address to the twenty-sixth session of the UN General Assembly in 1971, Fiji's permanent representative S.K. Sikivou said:

> [As] important as our membership of some of these [international] organisations may be, our sense of geographical identity has us [sic] to place greater emphasis on the development of our relations with our immediate island neighbours.[10]

In a similar vein, in his report to parliament on the first three years of foreign affairs as an independent Fiji, prime minister Ratu Mara made it clear that

> in its foreign policy, Government has accorded the highest priority to the development of the closest possible relationships with its South Pacific neighbours and to the extension of practical co-operation to all matters of common interest.[11]

Beyond their general ambition of creating a form of regional governance in which they could speak about any matter of concern to them, the Pacific leaders clearly had two specific interests in promoting cooperation through the SPF. One was to jointly approach the economic development of their newly independent states; the other was to maximise the diplomatic influence of their small countries on political issues such

---

9   Ratu Sir Kamisese Mara, 'Statement to the Twenty-Fifth Regular Session of the UN General Assembly: 1970', in Ratu Sir Kamisese Mara, *Report on Foreign Affairs for the Period 10th October 1970 – 31st December 1973*, Parliamentary Paper No. 19, Suva: Parliament of Fiji, 1974, Appendix iii(a), p. 22.
10   S.K. Sikivou, 'Statement to the Twenty-Sixth Session of the UN General Assembly: 1971', in Mara, *Report on Foreign Affairs for the Period 10th October 1970–31st December 1973*, Appendix 3, p. 26.
11   Mara, 'Statement to the Twenty-Fifth Regular Session', p. 1.

as nuclear testing. It was less clear what notions were held about the form cooperation should take and how far state sovereignty should be subsumed in supranationalist arrangements. Would a customs union, free-trade area or other form of economic community be attempted? Would political union be held out as an ultimate objective, as in the African and European cases?

The Wellington SPF meeting went some way in clarifying these questions. There was no talk of moving towards political unification in the longer term. Collective diplomacy, however, was clearly considered a useful strategy. As part of their first communiqué, the leaders issued an urgent appeal to France to make the current nuclear test series at Moruroa Atoll its last—something they had long wished to do in the SPC, where such a political move was banned. Further, the leaders indicated that they were open to exploring various forms of regional economic integration, including economic union, a regional bulk-purchasing scheme, joint tourism promotion, a regional disaster fund and a regional shipping line.[12]

The SPF gradually expanded its membership as other island states became eligible through the second and third waves of decolonisation in the 1970s and 1980s. By 1980, the founding members had been joined by Niue, Papua New Guinea, Solomon Islands, Tuvalu, Kiribati and Vanuatu; and by the end of the 1980s, with the addition of the Federated States of Micronesia and Marshall Islands from the north Pacific, there were 13 island members (Palau was still to join in the 1990s). As well as introducing additional Polynesian countries (Niue and Tuvalu), the decolonisation of the 1970s and 1980s also introduced Melanesian participants (Papua New Guinea, Solomon Islands and Vanuatu) from the Western Pacific and three more Micronesian countries (Kiribati, Federated States of Micronesia and Marshall Islands) to join Nauru. Although some of these new states were geographically and historically removed from the old Commonwealth club of the central Pacific, their commitment to regionalism was as strong as that of the founding member states. Papua New Guinea, for example, which had other interests to pursue in South-East Asia and could afford other diplomatic channels, opted to make participation in South Pacific cooperation a priority concern. In his 1974 report on foreign affairs to the Papua New Guinea House of Assembly, the Minister for Defence, Foreign Affairs and Trade, Albert Maori Kiki, said:

---

12 SPF Secretariat, *Final Communiqué: South Pacific Forum, Wellington, 5–7 August 1971*, Suva: SPF Secretariat, 1971.

> [W]e feel ... that Papua New Guinea's interests are best served in international affairs by being clearly a member of the community of the South Pacific Island Nations loyal to this community's causes and common initiatives.[13]

Despite the differences in the size and structure of their economies, the island state members all emphasised the importance of shared economic and developmental needs as a primary motivation for working together in these areas. At their regional gatherings in the 1970s, the leaders of the new Pacific states often drew attention to their similar situations with regard to economic development. For example, Tamarii Pierre, a Cook Islands delegate to the fourteenth South Pacific Conference in 1974, said:

> As stated by other speakers before me, whether it be in economic, political, social or educational fields, our developmental problems and aspirations are identical to many, if not all of the islands states within the Pacific.[14]

At the same meeting, Iulai Toma from Western Samoa commented that 'the problems of Western Samoa are very, very similar to those faced by all of us here'.[15] Even Papua New Guinea—a country with a markedly different economic structure and potential to its Pacific neighbours—recognised a shared situation. The new prime minister of Papua New Guinea, Michael Somare, when speaking of his country's relations with the South Pacific, said: '[W]e share the same development problems and aspirations for the future.'[16] For Western Samoa's prime minister, Tupuola Efi, speaking in 1978, the 'attractions for regional action are inviting if not irresistible' given the fact 'the human, natural and economic resources are just not present to enable many small island states to go it alone'.[17]

---

13   Albert Maori Kiki, *Papua New Guinea: An Assessment Report on Foreign Policy by the Minister for Defence, Foreign Relations, and Trade to the House of Assembly, 6 December 1974* [Reprinted as 'Papua New Guinea: An Assessment Report on Foreign Policy', *Australian Foreign Affairs Record*, June 1975: 320–5].

14   Tamarii Pierre, *Address on Special Needs and Problems*, Fourteenth South Pacific Conference Working Papers, Rarotonga: SPC Secretariat, 27 September 1974.

15   Iulai Toma, *Address on Special Needs and Problems*, Fourteenth South Pacific Conference Working Papers, Rarotonga: SPC Secretariat, 27 September 1974.

16   PNG National Broadcasting Commission [hereinafter NBC], 'Papua New Guinea and the Pacific', *Politics in Paradise Radio Series*, Port Moresby: NBC, February 1975, p. 3.

17   Tupuola Efi, 'Statement at the Commonwealth Heads of Government Regional Meeting in Sydney, 14 February 1978', Press release, 16 February 1978, Sydney, p. 2.

The Pacific states' practical commitment to regionalism as a preferred way of approaching their developmental needs should also be seen in the context of the international environment in which the Pacific countries sought development assistance. That environment was one in which donor countries and international agencies regarded a regional approach to the development of the Pacific countries as desirable. In such circumstances, it was in the interests of the Pacific leaders to emphasise their commitment to regional approaches to attract financial support that would otherwise be lost to the region.

Institutional expressions

The focal point of this regional commitment by Pacific leaders was the SPF, later renamed the Pacific Islands Forum (PIF) to reflect the fact that its membership included the island countries of the North Pacific. The SPC—in which these states could now operate as full members alongside France, the United States, the United Kingdom, Australia and New Zealand—continued to operate alongside the SPF network. In addition, a number of other intergovernmental agencies were created: the Honiara-based South Pacific Forum Fisheries Agency (FFA) in 1979, the Honolulu-based Pacific Islands Development Program in 1980, the Suva-based South Pacific Applied Geoscience Commission in 1984, the Apia-based South Pacific Regional Environment Program in 1990 and, in 1988, a coordinating body, the South Pacific Organisations Coordinating Committee, which sought to rationalise the activities of all these institutions. Most of the Pacific island countries were also members of the governing boards of other significant regional institutions and corporations including the USP, Air Pacific and the Pacific Forum Line. The forum network of institutions nevertheless became the main focus for the 'society of states'. It was through this network that the principal integrative schemes were attempted, joint political stances were worked out and a number of regional legal regimes were negotiated on arms control, environmental protection, resource management and international trade. With its entry qualifications of full political sovereignty and regional residence, the SPF was the only regional organisation representing the collective opinion of the independent states of the region.

In 1972, the SPF established the SPEC as its research arm.[18] Australia and New Zealand each contributed one-third of the budget, with the remainder contributed jointly by the island country members. As a subject became of interest to the SPF and required further investigation, it was referred to the SPEC. In its first years of operation, the SPEC's most important tasks were coordinating the negotiation of the terms of association of Western Samoa, Fiji and Tonga with the EEC, promoting regional trade and examining the feasibility of a regional shipping line. It subsequently began to oversee research and programs concerned with such matters as telecommunications and fisheries development.[19]

The region therefore had two organisational networks—one centred on the SPC and the other on the SPF. As will have become evident, there are important distinctions to be made between them. The SPC covered a wider region through its inclusion of dependent territories; it also had greater metropolitan involvement through the participation of France, the United States and the United Kingdom, in addition to Australia and New Zealand. The SPF, on the other hand, restricted its membership to the independent Pacific countries, plus Australia and New Zealand. Another important distinction was that the SPC retained its 'no politics' rule, whereas any subject could be raised in the SPF. Thus, it was only in the SPF that joint positions could be adopted regarding important political issues affecting the region, such as decolonisation and nuclear testing, and that joint approaches could be made to countries and organisations outside the region.

By the end of the 1980s, there were more than 300 full-time staff in the principal regional organisations. The commitment of bureaucratic resources required of each island state was also substantial. Key officials in economic and foreign policy areas were spending a great deal of time on regional governance—in meetings for the FFA, the Pacific Islands Development Program, the Secretariat of the South Pacific Regional

---

18   *Agreement Establishing the South Pacific Bureau for Economic Cooperation*, Suva, 1973.
19   Author's interviews with SPEC staff, Suva, October–November 1975; South Pacific Bureau for Economic Co-operation [hereinafter SPEC], *Director's Annual Report 1973/74*, (74)17, Suva: SPEC, 1974; SPEC, *Director's Annual Report 1974/75*, Suva: SPEC, 1975; SPEC, *Director's Annual Report 1975/76*, Suva: SPEC, 1976; SPEC, *Director's Annual Report 1976/77*, (77)18, Suva: SPEC, 1977; SPEC, *Director's Annual Report 1977/78*, (78)17, Suva: SPEC, 1978; SPEC, *Director's Annual Report, 1979/80*, (80)8, Suva: SPEC, 1980.

Environment Program, the USP, the Pacific Forum Line, the South Pacific Applied Geoscience Commission, the Regional Security Committee, the Regional Trade Committee and the Committee on Small Island States.

The growing complexity and significance of regional governance, by the late 1980s, was also reflected in the establishment of an array of regional legal regimes, including the South Pacific Nuclear-Free Zone Treaty (Rarotonga, 1985), the Convention for the Protection of the Natural Resources and Environment of the South Pacific Region (Nouméa, 1986) and the Convention for the Prohibition of Fishing with Long Driftnets in the South Pacific (Wellington, 1989).

Political differences were moderated by a shared experience of British political and social institutions—whether under Australian, New Zealand or British colonial rule—to the point where the SPF in its first decade was dubbed the 'Commonwealth club'. There were no participants from the French or American Pacific at this stage because of the lack of decolonisation by those powers. These new states also embraced similar developmental models despite some rhetorical differences. And there was none of the border or irredentist disputes common to new states in Africa and Asia. The early participants were therefore able to conduct their negotiations without the complications of serious conflict between countries in the region or spillover tensions from internal instability, at least until the Fiji coup of 1987 and the outbreak of the Bougainville war of 1989.

The diplomatic rituals of the SPF and of the SPC (and South Pacific Conference) in the 1970s supported the principle of respect for the equality of national sovereignties in participation in regional meetings. Much of the ritual was about establishing equality of countries as diverse in size and power as Australia and Niue. This meant that challenges or perceived challenges to this principle by attempts to establish hierarchy as had existed in the old colonial structures were resisted. Fiji's attempt, as seen by some other Pacific states, to put itself at the centre of regionalism was one such provocation; the other was Australia and New Zealand attempting, from 1976, to create a two-tier hierarchical society of states around regional security, with different rights and responsibilities for the leadership tier. We return to each of these tensions in later chapters.

Regional self-determination and regional identity

This commitment to regionalism on the part of all island states was based not only on shared practical purposes of small new countries entering development, nation-building and global relationships. There were also shared values and, in at least certain political contexts, a regional identity. This places the Pacific closer to Ayoob's concept of a regional *community* of states. This may seem counterintuitive in a region that is so culturally and linguistically diverse, with an overlay of different colonial cultural influences. The shared values arose out of the context of colonialism and decolonisation and the shared commitment to regional self-determination. In the postcolonial era of the 1970s and 1980s, Pacific leaders saw legitimate regional governance as resting on the principle of regional self-determination. There was a strong commitment to the idea that regional decision-making should be in the hands of Pacific islanders and that the right of self-determination should extend to all 'Pacific peoples'. They opposed colonialism and wished to control the 'neocolonial' economic engagements, and to reclaim Pacific values and practices.

In the 1970s, in particular, this was captured in the promotion of the phrase the 'Pacific way', which came to encompass a set of ideas about Pacific regional identity based on shared notions of regional self-determination. Ratu Mara was the first to use the phrase, at the UN General Assembly in 1970, and he was also the main person to give content to the ideology associated with it.[20] It gained widespread currency among Pacific leaders in the 1970s. The ideology embraced several key propositions: that regional decision-making structures should be controlled by Pacific states representing Pacific peoples and societies; that remaining colonial intrusion in the region should be opposed; that neocolonial exploitation should be controlled; that Pacific cultural values should be asserted or at least defended in the face of Western cultural values; and that a Pacific cultural affinity had always existed and had been 'interrupted by colonial expansion and rivalry'. In his message to the SPC on its twenty-fifth anniversary in 1972, Ratu Mara asserted:

> [T]he Commission also formed a focus to bring together again what might be called 'long-lost brothers' and to remind us of ancient historical links which had become weakened by incursions in to the region.[21]

---

20   Crocombe, *The Pacific Way*.
21   Mara, 'Twenty-Fifth Anniversary Messages', p. 15.

In the following year, Fiji's representative to the United Nations, S.K. Sikivou, reiterated the theme, saying the growth of a Pacific consciousness 'is not so much a birth as a rebirth or rediscovery of old links and ties temporarily broken by the division of the area into metropolitan spheres of influence'.[22]

Initially, the 'Pacific way' ideology was associated with the small group of leaders who had worked together in the 1960s and early 1970s in pressing for self-determination in regional governance structures. Although it had grown out of the experience of a Fiji-led group of central Pacific territories, which could largely be categorised as Polynesian, Mara was speaking on behalf of all Pacific societies when he promoted the concept. The leaders of new members of the SPF readily adopted the sentiments of the 'Pacific way' concept. Papua New Guinea's endorsement, given its position on the western periphery of the region and as the leading Melanesian state, was particularly telling. At the completion of Ratu Mara's visit to Papua New Guinea in May 1974, Somare and Mara issued a joint communiqué, which among other things, said:

> [B]oth leaders are aware of the destructive effects on traditions, customs and culture caused by rapid economic exploration [sic] of the Pacific peoples' human and natural resources. The leaders saw the solution as one of complete control over one's human and natural resources.[23]

Somare took up this theme in his own right. He asserted that 'the Pacific will be exposed to outside influence. The Forum and its Bureau of Economic Co-operation hold the hopes of the Pacific people to control these influences'.[24] In 1976, at Papua New Guinea's independence celebrations, Somare again voiced this concern. He claimed:

> Unless the countries now set out to foster a Pacific consciousness, one of the consequences would be the intrusion of other countries who would be prepared to get what they could from the Pacific, but without having the interests of the Pacific at heart.[25]

---

22 Sikivou, 'Statement to the Twenty-Eighth Regular Session', p. 32.
23 Mara and Somare, 'Joint Communiqué', p. 2.
24 Michael Somare, 'The Emerging Role of Papua New Guinea in World Affairs', Twenty-Fifth Milne Lecture, Melbourne, 14 June 1974, p. 13.
25 "'Let's get together' says Somare", *Pacific Islands Monthly*, November 1976: 25.

Alongside this 'Pacific way' theme of asserting Pacific control on behalf of Pacific peoples against global economic and political forces seeking to exploit the region, Somare also embraced the theme of cultural brotherhood and ancient links interrupted by colonial partition of the Pacific. Speaking just before independence in 1975, he said:

> Our principal contacts with the outside world have always been with our brothers in the South Pacific region. Culturally, Papua New Guinea and the other South Pacific islands have always been linked … Our basis for building this relationship will be our similar background historically, and our similarities in culture and custom.[26]

Significantly, all leaders of the independent Pacific states openly endorsed a notion of the Pacific region that equated not just to the territory of SPF member states. Rather, the leaders recognised that the territories of the SPF island states formed only part of the region of their imagination. The region they acknowledged was actually the SPC area, with its much wider boundaries. They agreed to make SPF membership open to any Pacific island country in the broader region once it had 'attained nationhood'. In the meantime, they arrogated to themselves the right to speak on behalf of these colonised territories.

This was particularly evident in relation to the two great causes of joint diplomacy of the Pacific states in the 1970s and 1980s examined in Chapter 8: environmental protection (nuclear testing, dumping of radioactive waste and incineration of chemical weapons) and anticolonialism. Although the proposed site for the dumping of Japanese nuclear waste was technically outside even the broader SPC region (in the Marianas Trench), it was still seen as part of the region for the purposes of this regional campaign. Thus, the Pacific states imagined a region that was beyond their legal jurisdiction. They put a very significant diplomatic effort into pursuing objectives that could not be explained by traditional realpolitik or national interest promotion, but rather had everything to do with shared values around *regional* self-determination.

The 'Pacific way' ideology also included notions about the diplomatic culture that should prevail in regional decision-making. These can be distilled to three maxims: decisions should be arrived at through 'consensus' rather than voting, the process should be conducted among those heads

---

26   Michael Somare, interviewed in NBC, 'Papua New Guinea and the Pacific'.

of government who can make decisions for their countries and they should be conducted in an ambience of informality and with a minimum of background bureaucracy and organisation. Significantly, the SPF's establishment was not formalised by international agreement.

The shared values of regional self-determination associated with the experience of colonisation and decolonisation were interwoven with shared Christian values. Although there were large Hindu and Muslim communities in Fiji, all Pacific countries identified as Christian countries. An indigenised Christianity had permeated all traditional societies of the region to the point where Christianity was regarded as part of indigenous culture. While the contest between Christian sects had often been hard-fought and even violent, particularly between Catholicism and Protestantism, Christianity nevertheless provided an important basis for shared values that marked off the Pacific from East Asia.

The perception on the part of the leaders of the postcolonial Pacific states that they shared practical interests and common values was sufficient to invigorate a very active diplomatic effort to establish, develop and support an increasingly complex set of regional institutions, procedural norms and regional law. The acknowledgement that this constituted a regional society of states with real political significance that went well beyond the sum of its parts was demonstrated by the efforts of others to become members of the society and by the recognition accorded to it by the world's largest powers, which, by the end of the 1980s, were queuing up to engage with the regional agenda pursued through the SPF, as well as seeking to influence individual forum members on regional policy.

The emergence of regional civil society

The regional self-determination principle was also at the centre of the attitudes and activities of the various groups and movements that made up what we might term 'regional civil society'. Emerging in the mid 1970s alongside the new regional society of states, they became active participants in regional debates over security, development and anticolonialism. These included the Protestant and Catholic churches, women's groups, anticolonial and antinuclear groups, writers and scholars. Although excluded from formal decision-making within the main interstate regional organisations, they nevertheless became important players in the postcolonial regional polity. They directly influenced the deliberations of these state-based organisations on key regional issues. Just as importantly, they influenced regional governance through their assertion of alternative conceptions of what the regional community should stand for as a set of ideas, who should belong to it and who should have the right to speak. They also influenced the way key ideas about Pacific security and Pacific development should be conceptualised. It was also the case that many of the key regional civil society thinkers of the early 1970s became key players in state-level politics by the end of the decade, including in a prime ministerial role, and thus had a more direct influence on policy.

In each of these new movements, an emergent regional identity was tied to the idea of regional self-determination. Implicit in their concerns for the self-determination of all 'Pacific peoples' was a notion of regional community that was deeper than that embraced in the regional 'society of states'. This accorded with important aspects of an 'imagined community' in the Andersonian sense because it involved deep commitments to peoples and places that individual members had not met or seen.[27] The commitment was to a regional sovereignty rather than state sovereignty per se. The use of such terms as 'Pacific peoples' and 'we Pacific islanders' reflected the new solidarist positions in this concept of regionalism. It also tended to invoke a slightly broader region geographically and politically than that of the society of states, to include indigenous Pacific peoples in New Zealand, Hawai`i and West Papua. The concerns of regional civil society groups nevertheless overlapped with the commitments and underlying principles of state-led regionalism, and in some cases, there was no distinction between state leaders' and civil society's positions on these issues, particularly in the 1970s.

The first most important institutional development providing a base for the emergence of regional civil society was the creation of the regional university with its main campus in Suva. The idea of setting up a university to serve the needs of the English-speaking countries of the South Pacific had its origins in the recommendations of the Higher Education Mission to the South Pacific appointed in 1965 by the British and New Zealand governments.[28] Although the USP was officially established in 1967 under a Fiji Government Ordinance while Fiji was still a British colony,

---

27   Anderson, *Imagined Communities*.
28   Colin M. Aikman, 'Establishment: 1968–74', in Ron Crocombe and Malama Meleisea, eds, *Pacific Universities: Achievements, Problems, Prospects*, Suva: Institute of Pacific Studies, University of the South Pacific, 1988, pp. 35–52.

it was formally inaugurated under royal charter after Fiji's independence in 1970 to recognise the USP's regional, and Commonwealth, character. Under the royal charter, the Governing Council of the USP comprised representatives of 11 Pacific states and territories. As decolonisation proceeded, the Governing Council came to mirror the SPF in its island country membership, except for Papua New Guinea. From the start, this was seen as a regional enterprise. The university's students were drawn from all 11 countries, and they were catered for at the Laucala Bay campus in Suva, as well as at a growing number of USP centres in the member countries, serviced, from the mid 1970s, by a sophisticated distance learning capacity through the Pan Pacific Education and Communication Experiments by Satellite.[29] Its regional nature was emphasised symbolically by the appointment of the King of Tonga as the first chancellor, and of Fiame Mata'afa Faumuina Mulinu'u II, the prime minister of Western Samoa, as pro-chancellor. In 1973, Nauruan president DeRoburt followed the King as chancellor.

The USP's second vice-chancellor, James Maraj, came to the position in 1975 with a very clear regionalist vision:

> The University has a right and duty to cause regionalism to be seen as a way of life and for these islands—an inescapable way—for those who seek a dignified existence as a people.[30]

He proposed that in planning for the future, the university should emphasise the projection of its regional nature and the 'promotion of a distinctive Pacific flavour'.[31] This emphasis was reflected in such developments as the instituting of Pacific Week, the organising of regional conferences, the provision of extension services throughout the region, the establishment of more university centres in member countries, the creation of the Institute of Pacific Studies with an active publishing program by indigenous scholars, the foundation of USP-based Pacific journals and the teaching of compulsory undergraduate courses on Pacific studies.[32]

29   See Pan Pacific Education and Communication Experiments by Satellite, *Peacesat Project: Early Experience—The Design and Early Years of the First Educational Communication Satellite Experiment*, Honolulu: University of Hawai'i, October 1975.
30   James A. Maraj, 'Statement to the University of the South Pacific', Suva, 23 September 1975, p. 3.
31   ibid., p. 7.
32   Author's interview with Dr James Maraj, Suva, 28 November 1975; also see Frank Brosnahan, 'Outreach: 1975–83', in Crocombe and Meleisea, *Pacific Universities*, pp. 55–6.

While the USP is to be seen, therefore, as part of the emerging regional society of states and as an expression of the commitment of its member states to regional cooperation, it was also a very important stimulus to the establishment of regional civil society. From the early 1970s, the USP became the key site for the coming together of intellectuals from all of the English-speaking Pacific, outside Papua New Guinea.[33] In a time of rapid political change in the early to mid 1970s, it was natural that students and staff at the regional university would be vitally involved in intellectual and social movements concerned with countering exploitation of Pacific societies, the questioning of imposed knowledge systems and concepts and the assertion and reclaiming of Pacific ideas about education, development and social organisation. At this time, the 'Pacific way' ideology was one that also appealed to intellectuals working within the USP, in regional civil society groups and even to creative writers. For Epeli Hau`ofa—later a critic of some aspects of the 'Pacific way' ideology—it held substantial attractions at this time:

> When I first came [to the USP] in 1975 the campus was abuzz with creativity and wide-ranging discussions generated by the emergence of the Pacific Way. Whatever one may say about it the Pacific Way was a large and an encompassing idea that became the ideology of its time, perfectly suited to the immediate postcolonial euphoria and expectations of the 1970s.[34]

The Pacific Way conference organised under the auspices of the newly formed South Pacific Social Sciences Association at the USP in 1973, bringing together intellectuals from across the region, was a major expression of this new commitment. The conference brought together leading intellectuals from the church, journalism, academe, the civil service and NGOs from across the Pacific. Illustrating the blurring between civil society and the state that is a feature of Pacific regionalism, six of the participants were later to become prime minister or president of their country, and two were later to become secretaries-general of the SPC. In his summing up, Ron Crocombe asserted that the conference 'did identify considerable areas of consensus among leading Pacific thinkers

---

33   Aikman, 'Establishment'.
34   Epeli Hau`ofa, 'A Beginning', in Eric Waddell, Vijay Naidu, and Epeli Hau`ofa, eds, *A New Oceania: Rediscovering Our Sea of Islands*, Suva: University of the South Pacific, 1993, pp. 126–39, at p. 126.

and a widespread desire to evolve a "Pacific Way".[35] In sentiments similar to those held by leaders of the independent states at this time, one of the organisers, Sione Tupouniua, a USP academic, concluded the conference with this observation:

> Pacific Islanders are searching for a new way of life in which we fully accept the responsibility for creating the social, political, economic and cultural institutions to suit our own particular needs. Such responsibility involves the acceptance of ourselves for what we are, and not imitating others, whether colonial rulers or neo-colonial masters.[36]

A second major development in the institutionalisation of regional civil society was the establishment of the Pacific Conference of Churches in 1961, and its important offshoot, the Suva-based Pacific Theological College, in 1965. The Catholic Church created a parallel regional forum, the Episcopal Conference of the Pacific, in 1968, and a regional training college, the Suva-based Pacific Regional Seminary, in 1972.[37] Although an important part of the development of regional civil society, the Catholic Church–created institutions did not have the same political involvement in the key regional political issues of the day—nuclear issues, decolonisation and development. The Pacific Conference of Churches came to matter more in the context of influencing regional politics.

The Pacific Conference of Churches had its origins in a regional conference of Pacific Protestant churches held at Malua, Samoa, in 1961. Although organised by the London Missionary Society, it was a response to a need for regional organisation identified over the previous decade by island ministers—notably, Sione Havea of Tonga and Setareki Tuilovoni of Fiji.[38] The conference recommended the establishment of a regional interchurch organisation and the establishment of regional theological training. The Pacific Theological College was a direct result of this recommendation.

---

35   Ron Crocombe, 'Seeking a Pacific Way', in Sione Tupouniua, Ron Crocombe, and Claire Slatter, eds, *The Pacific Way: Social Issues in National Development*, Suva: South Pacific Social Sciences Association, 1975, pp. 1–6, at p. 6.

36   Sione Tupouniua, 'Political Independence: An Opportunity to Create', in Tupouniua et al., *The Pacific Way*, pp. 239–47, at p. 239.

37   Pacific Regional Seminary, *Pacific Regional Seminary 2002 Handbook*, Suva: Pacific Regional Seminary, 2002; and John Foliaki, 'Pacific Regional Seminary', in Emiliana Afeaki, Ron Crocombe, and John McClaren, eds, *Religious Cooperation in the Pacific Islands*, Suva: Institute of Pacific Studies, University of the South Pacific, 1983, pp. 84–8.

38   Lorini Tevi, 'The Pacific Conference of Churches', in Afeaki et al., *Religious Cooperation in the Pacific Islands*, pp. 148–56.

It went on to become another major influence on regional consciousness through the training of young ministers from the Anglican, Methodist, Congregational, Lutheran, Presbyterian and Reformed Evangelical churches, from across the region.[39] The other outcome of the Malua conference was the formation of the Pacific Conference of Churches. It held its first assembly in Lifou, New Caledonia, in 1966 and its second in Davuilevu in Fiji in 1971. It established a number of key regional offshoots: a regional publishing arm, Lotu Pasifika, in Suva, and the Pacific Churches Research Centre, in Port Vila, 'to encourage Pacific people to study our own religion, history, culture and social organisation'.[40]

The Pacific Conference of Churches saw its remit as going well beyond the indigenisation and regionalisation of the Christian churches within a spirit of ecumenicalism. It also engaged in a publishing and diplomatic campaign in relation to key regional political issues: development, decolonisation and nuclear questions. It campaigned for integrated human development against other top-down economic planning models. It pressed for the decolonisation of remaining Pacific dependencies, particularly where the local society had made it clear they desired independence. It was also a very active champion of a nuclear-free Pacific—seen most prominently in its support for the establishment of the Nuclear-Free Pacific Conference and subsequent social movement, its declarations against the nuclear activities of France, the United States and Japan, and its influential publication *A Call to a New Exodus: An Anti-Nuclear Primer for Pacific People*.[41] The Pacific Conference of Churches' position on nuclear issues was unequivocal:

> As Christian people committed to stewardship, justice and peace-making, we oppose and condemn the use of the Pacific for the testing, storage, and transportation of nuclear weapons and weapons delivery systems; the disposal of radioactive wastes; and the passage of nuclear-powered submarines and ships.[42]

---

39 Sione `A. Havea and Bruce J. Deverell, 'The Pacific Theological College', in Afeaki et al., *Religious Cooperation in the Pacific Islands*, pp. 75–83.
40 ibid., p. 150.
41 Suliana Siwatibau and B. David Williams, *A Call to a New Exodus: An Anti-Nuclear Primer for Pacific People*, Suva: Lotu Pasfika, 1982. Also see the Pacific Conference of Churches Secretariat, 'The Pacific as an Arena of Increasing Competition, Conflict, and Struggle', in William Coop, comp. and ed., *Pacific People Sing Out Strong*, New York: Friendship Press, 1982, pp. 12–16.
42 As cited in Siwatibau and Williams, *A Call to a New Exodus*, inside cover.

A third major institutional development creating the basis for the emergence of regional civil society began with the Nuclear-Free Pacific Conference, held in April 1975 in Suva. The conference was sponsored most prominently by Fijian-based ATOM (Against Testing on Moruroa), in conjunction with the Christian student movements in Australia, New Zealand and Fiji, the Campaign for Nuclear Disarmament New Zealand, the Campaign against Foreign Military Activities in New Zealand and the Congress for International Cooperation and Disarmament of Australia. Vijay Naidu, a conference participant and later academic commentator, argues that, from 1970 to 1976, ATOM 'provided the vanguard of the protests against nuclear activities'. He points out that ATOM was

> formed by concerned individuals from the Pacific Theological College (PTC), the University of the South Pacific (USP), the Student Christian Movement (SCM), and the YWCA [Young Women's Christian Association], and was, from its inception, backed by the Fiji Council of Churches (and later the Pacific Council of Churches) and the University of the South Pacific Students Association (USPASA).[43]

The conference brought together the representatives of 86 organisations from 22 Pacific countries. Naidu contends that during the conference a large number of participants shifted their thinking about nuclear involvement in the Pacific, from seeing this as an environmental issue to seeing it as one that was first and foremost a political issue linked to colonialism and racism. This was reflected in the 'Fiji Declaration' that summed up the conclusions of the conference:

> The Conference agreed that racism, colonialism and imperialism lie at the core of the issue of the activities of the nuclear powers in the Pacific. The Pacific peoples and their environment continue to be exploited because Pacific islanders are considered insignificant in numbers and inferior as peoples, the delegates stated.[44]

The conference set up the Suva-based Continuation Committee to draft a Pacific nuclear-free zone treaty and to organise the bringing together of the regionwide movement in its next conference, at which the issue would be further advanced. Reflecting the position of the

---

43 Vijay Naidu, 'The Fiji Anti-Nuclear Movement: Problems and Prospects', in Ranginui Walker and William Sutherland, eds, *The Pacific: Peace, Security and the Nuclear Issue*, Tokyo: United Nations University and Zed Books, 1988, pp. 185–95, at p. 185.
44 'Fiji Declaration', cited in ibid., p. 188.

majority of the conference participants in seeing the nuclear issue as primarily one of imperialism and colonialism, some ATOM members of this persuasion established, in 1976, the Suva-based Pacific Peoples' Action Front, which began to produce a newsletter, *Povai*, supporting independence and autonomist movements throughout the region. There was a close correspondence between the membership of the Continuation Committee, which was drafting the treaty, and the Pacific Peoples' Action Front.

The continuing division between those who saw the issue primarily as an antinuclear issue and those who saw it as an independence issue was reflected in the organisation of the second Nuclear-Free Pacific Conference, in Ponape (Pohnpei), in the Federated States of Micronesia, in 1978. The organisers—the Pacific Peoples' Action Front and the Pacific Conference of Churches—set up two conference streams: an antinuclear stream and an 'independence' stream. The organisers intended, however, that both streams would ultimately be grappling with the question: 'What kind of societies do we want for ourselves?'[45] The deliberations of both streams were concerned with developing strategies for influencing national and regional policy. At the 1980 Nuclear-Free Pacific Conference, the two streams were brought back together—in recognition that all participants were accepting that, in the Pacific context, the issue of nuclear involvement was entwined with the independence issue, and therefore gaining any traction on the nuclear issue would require prior action on decolonisation. In the words of the conference report, 'self-determination for Pacific peoples was the key to creating a demilitarized and nuclear-free Pacific'.[46] The 1980 conference also produced the People's Charter for a Nuclear-Free Pacific and established the Pacific Concerns Resources Center in Honolulu. From the time of the 1983 conference, the movement became known as the Nuclear-Free and Independent Pacific movement.

The last major piece in the jigsaw of the emerging regional civil society of the 1970s was the development of women's organising at the regional level. Although there had been earlier ad hoc connections between Pacific women, the Pacific Women's Conference, held in Suva in October 1975, was a key point of departure. Like the Nuclear-Free Pacific Conference, it drew its participants from a broader region including indigenous

---

45   Ronni Alexander, *Putting the Earth First: Alternatives to Nuclear Security in Pacific Island States*, Honolulu: Matsunaga Institute for Peace, University of Hawai`i, 1994, p. 144.
46   As cited in ibid., p. 151.

participants from Hawai`i, New Zealand and Australia. While the conference resolutions included issues that focused on women's roles, they also notably expressed concerns about broader issues of regional self-determination. The conference called on the independent Pacific governments to 'support territories under colonialism wanting to achieve self-government status, namely the independence movements of New Caledonia, New Hebrides, Micronesia and the autonomist parties of French Polynesia'.[47] It also resolved

> that the Conference support a denuclearised Pacific and in particular the proposals of the People's Treaty for a Nuclear Free Pacific formulated by the Conference for a Nuclear Free Pacific, April 1–6, 1975.[48]

The Pacific Women's Association, which was established as a result of the 1975 conference, set up a regional resource centre at the YWCA in Suva. Although the association did not have strong support among women's national organisations at the end of the 1970s, women's organising at the regional level strengthened in the 1980s. With changing support from international agencies, women and development became a prominent topic of regional governance and women began to have more political agency within regional organisations.

Despite their Fiji-centrism, these emerging regional civil society organisations were genuinely regional in membership, leadership, staffing and geographical interests. Importantly, they included other countries' nationals in the key positions in Suva. They were also genuinely concerned with regional issues and their identity included all those islanders within the SPC region and beyond—for example, in New Zealand, Hawai`i and West Papua. Over the next several decades, they engaged with all of the key areas of regional debate: development, security, ecology, globalisation, decolonisation and nuclear issues.

---

47   'Resolutions of the Pacific Women's Conference, Oct. 27 – Nov. 2, 1975', in Vanessa Griffen, ed., *Women Speak Out! A Report on the Pacific Women's Conference*, Suva: Pacific Women's Conference, 2005, p. 140, Resolution 6.

48   ibid., p. 140, Resolution 5.

Conclusion

This chapter has provided a broad description of the nature of regional governance that emerged and developed during the first two decades of the post-independence era. It made the argument that the emergent regional system could be seen as a regional 'society of states' and that this implies considerably more political significance for Pacific regional governance than is often acknowledged. I also outlined the broader emergence and development of a regional civil society. The commitment to regional community evidenced by this development could even support the view that the Pacific regional political community system is more solidarist, and therefore more politically significant, than the 'society of states' descriptor implies.

In Chapters 8, 9 and 10, we examine three important political contests that took place within this regional polity in the first two decades of the postcolonial era. The first concerns regional self-determination—a normative frame promoted by Pacific island leaders and regional civil society. The second is regional security—a contest prompted by the efforts of Western powers to impose a Cold War frame on the region. The third concerns what form development should take in the postcolonial societies of the Pacific—a contest stimulated by the power of global discourses on development to frame Pacific 'development'. As we shall see, the outcomes in the substantive contests over development and security explored in Chapters 9 and 10 are directly related to the contest over the questions of self-determination, political agency and identity explored in Chapter 8.

8

Regional self-determination[1]

While regional self-determination had been recognised as a key legitimating principle for regional governance in the postcolonial era—by the regional 'society of states', regional civil society groups and most of the international actors—it also became a focus of significant political contestation during the 1970s and 1980s. This chapter focuses on the region as a site of political contest over self-determination in relation to three issue areas of regional politics: environmental protection, anticolonialism and political agency within regional decision-making.

Environmental protection

One of the key expressions of the commitment of Pacific states and NGOs to regional self-determination in the 1970s and 1980s was in relation to the issue of environmental protection. The environmental issues that captured the imagination of the Pacific leaders were those to do with the activities of large powers, wherever they took place in the region, rather than those associated with their own national development. State leaders and civil society groups focused on three specific environmental protection issues

---

1   Parts of this chapter incorporates material from Greg Fry, 'International Co-operation in the South Pacific: From regional integration to collective diplomacy', in W. Andrew Axline, *The Political Economy of Regional Cooperation* (London: Pinter, 1994), pp. 136–77.

in the first two decades of the postcolonial period: French nuclear testing, Japan's proposal to dump radioactive wastes in the Marianas Trench and the US proposal to incinerate chemical weapons on Johnston Atoll.

It was in their attempts to influence these activities and proposals that the island states came closest to having a joint foreign policy and closest to the positions of the regional civil society groups. Significantly, these states and civil society groups invested a great deal of diplomatic resources in challenging the most powerful global states on these issues, and they did so in relation to geographical locations within the Pacific that they would not have visited. These sites of nuclear testing, dumping and incineration were isolated locations on the edge of the region—well to the north in the Marianas Trench and on Johnston Atoll, and well to the east in the Tuamotu Archipelago. These regional campaigns illustrated a doggedness, passion and unity not found in relation to other issues, and they were conducted in relation to an imagined region rather than a known space or national interest. They also referred to spaces that were legally outside the jurisdiction of Pacific island states and under the legal jurisdiction of powerful states. They therefore illustrate most effectively the commitment to *regional* self-determination as a fundamental principle of regional governance.

The collective opposition of Pacific island leaders to French nuclear testing in the Tuamotu Archipelago in French Polynesia predated the establishment of the SPF. As we have seen, the inability to raise such concerns during the late 1960s under the 'no politics' constitution of the SPC had in fact strongly influenced the decision to create the SPF.[2] It was therefore not surprising that the communiqué issued after the first SPF in 1971 included an appeal to the French Government to make the current test series its last. The SPF continued to issue this appeal at each of its meetings until 1975. Australia and New Zealand, under Labor/Labour governments from 1972 to 1975, joined the island states in stronger protests outside the formal SPF context. In 1973, the New Zealand Government sent the warship HMNZS *Otago* into the French Government–declared 'danger zone' around Moruroa Atoll; Australian and New Zealand unions established a boycott against French goods and services; the Fiji Trades Union Congress placed a boycott on French-owned UTA Airlines; and Australia, New Zealand and Fiji took France

---

2   Ratu Sir Kamisese Mara, 'Statement to the Thirty-First South Pacific Conference', Nuku`alofa, Tonga, 18 October 1991, p. 1.

to the International Court of Justice. In 1975, partly in response to these actions, France ceased atmospheric testing and moved the program underground at Moruroa Atoll.

In a move aimed at putting further international pressure on the French Government, but also with broader antinuclear objectives in mind, the 1975 SPF meeting 'commended' a New Zealand Government idea of establishing a nuclear-free zone in the South Pacific and agreed that UN backing should be sought for this. Later in the year, New Zealand, Papua New Guinea and Fiji cosponsored a resolution at the UN General Assembly proposing the establishment of such a zone. Although the resolution was passed, the SPF took the initiative no further because of the influence of the more conservative opinions of the new governments in Canberra and Wellington from early 1976.[3]

The anti–nuclear-testing regional campaign gained new energy when Labor/Labour governments returned to power in Canberra, in 1983, and in Wellington, in 1984. The Australian foreign minister's anger at continued French testing was a major stimulus to his government's decision to launch a proposal for a nuclear-free zone in the South Pacific at the Canberra SPF summit in 1983.[4] The zone came into being in 1985 but left the French program unaffected. The French Government did, however, become concerned about the level of regional opposition to its nuclear presence in French Polynesia, particularly following the outrage expressed by South Pacific states at the bombing by French agents of the Greenpeace protest ship *Rainbow Warrior* in Auckland Harbour in July 1985. French president François Mitterrand consequently instituted an active lobbying program to attempt to influence islander opinion.[5] Although the French campaign had some success in parts of Polynesia, the SPF remained firm in its opposition throughout the 1980s. When president Mitterrand suspended the program in 1992, however, he was responding more to political developments within France and Eastern Europe than to protests in the South Pacific region.

---

3   See Greg Fry, 'Australia, New Zealand and Arms Control in the Pacific Region', in Desmond Ball, ed., *The ANZAC Connection*, Sydney: George Allen & Unwin, 1985, pp. 91–118, at pp. 101–3.
4   P. Beard, 'Paris Snub Prompts Hayden to Seek Pacific Nuclear-Free Zone', *The Australian*, 13 May 1983: 4; 'French Nuclear Test at Mururoa Atoll', *Australian Foreign Affairs Record*, May 1983: 186–7, at p. 187.
5   Stephen Henningham, *France and the South Pacific: A Contemporary History*, Sydney: Allen & Unwin, 1992, pp. 299–316.

The Japanese Government's proposal to dump cement-solidified drums of low-level radioactive waste in the high seas north-east of the Ogasawara Islands in the early 1980s aroused as much emotion as the nuclear testing issue.[6] It was also an issue that united all dependent territory administrations and all independent countries, as well as regional civil society organisations such as the Nuclear-Free and Independent Pacific movement and the Pacific Conference of Churches. As with the testing issue, the Australian and New Zealand governments were very supportive of Pacific island concerns, while the United Kingdom, France and the United States—as fellow dumping nations—lined up with Japan. An experimental dumping program was to begin in 1981 but was delayed because of regional opposition. In an effort to placate islander leaders, the Japanese Government sent several missions through the region in the early 1980s.[7] These were not successful in changing the united position of Pacific states and societies. Rather, they simply served to galvanise the opposition of South Pacific states to the proposal.

The campaign against dumping radioactive waste was conducted on several fronts. Kiribati and Nauru represented the region's interests at the London Dumping Convention meetings. In 1983, they put forward a proposal for a global ban on the dumping of low-level radioactive waste. Although the proposal was defeated, it led to a compromise motion, which was passed, calling for a moratorium on dumping until the Nauru/Kiribati proposal could be assessed. The island states also worked to establish a regional antidumping regime.[8] A prohibition on dumping was incorporated in two regional legal regimes: the South Pacific Nuclear Free Zone Treaty and the Convention for the Protection of the Natural Resources and Environment of the South Pacific Region (1986). Although the dumping proposed by Japan fell outside the legal jurisdiction of these regimes, these provisions were seen to be pointing at Japan. In early 1985, on the eve of an official visit to Fiji, the Japanese prime minister, Yasuhiro Nakasone, announced his intention to shelve the dumping proposal in deference to islander sensitivities on this matter.[9]

6 The Japanese Government's intentions are set out in detail in Nuclear Safety Bureau, *Low-Level Radioactive Wastes: Dumping at the Pacific*, Tokyo: Science and Technology Agency, Government of Japan, 1980.
7 Ogashiwa, *Microstates and Nuclear Issues*, pp. 18–19.
8 Pacific Islands Forum Secretariat [hereinafter PIFS], *Leaders' Communiqués: Twelfth Pacific Islands Forum, Port Vila, Vanuatu, 10–11 August 1981, Thirteenth Pacific Islands Forum, Rotorua, New Zealand, 9–10 August 1982* and *Sixteenth Pacific Islands Forum, Rarotonga, Cook Islands, 5–6 August 1985* (Suva: PIFS).
9 Bronwen Jones, 'Japan Seeks Understanding on N-Waste Dumping Plans', *The Canberra Times*, 12 January 1985: 1.

This degree of cohesiveness among South Pacific countries was aroused again at Port Vila, Vanuatu, in 1990 in relation to a proposal by the US Government to use Johnston Atoll as a site for the incineration of chemical weapons. Island leaders were angered by the lack of consultation and very concerned about the possible environmental effects of the proposed program. The 'consultation' mission toured the island states only after their concerns were publicised and when a point of no return had been reached regarding the destruction of chemical weapons already en route from Germany. This islander opposition needs also to be seen against a long history of Pacific islanders being deceived by the United States, the United Kingdom and France about the long-term effects of their nuclear testing programs since 1945 at Bikini, Enewetak, Johnston Atoll, Christmas Island, Moruroa and Fangataufa.

In this case, the South Pacific position was not supported by Australia. At the 1990 SPF meeting in Port Vila, where this issue dominated the agenda, Australia attempted to garner support for the incineration facility on the grounds that it was an important contribution to global disarmament and that it was safe. The island states regarded the Australian efforts, and particularly the way in which prime minister Bob Hawke sought to have his minority view dominate, as unacceptable behaviour.[10]

The island states' strong opposition to the US proposal, voiced by all island leaders at the Port Vila forum, and subsequently by the Secretary-General of the SPF Secretariat—who reportedly accused the United States of treating the Pacific people as 'breadfruits and coconuts' rather than human beings—caught Washington's attention.[11] In October of the same year, president George H.W. Bush invited the leaders of all Pacific island states to a summit in Honolulu. While the meeting covered several aspects of the United States' relationship with the island states, the incineration issue was of the most immediate concern to the island leaders. The US president 'assured' the Pacific leaders:

> [W]e plan to dispose of only the chemical munitions from the Pacific theater currently stored at Johnston Atoll, any obsolete materials found in the Pacific Islands, and those relatively small

---

10   Mary-Louise O'Callaghan, '"Two-Faced": Forum Attacks Hawke', *Sydney Morning Herald*, 3 August 1990: 3; and Karen Magnall, 'A Tale of Two Hotels', *Pacific Islands Monthly*, September 1990: 10–14.

11   Geoff Spencer, 'Forum to Protest Over US Chemical Weapons Plan', *The Age*, [Melbourne], 8 September 1990: 9.

quantities shipped from Germany ... once the destruction is completed, we have no plans to use Johnston Atoll for any other chemical munitions purpose or as a hazardous waste disposal site.[12]

This was a significant concession to the strong Pacific island opposition. The United States would have preferred to have kept its options open, knowing that there would be more weapons to destroy as part of new disarmament agreements and that there would be considerable opposition to the use of mainland US sites.

Anticolonialism

A second key expression of the commitment to regional self-determination as the defining principle of regional governance in this period was the diplomatic energy Pacific leaders injected into opposing continuing colonialism in the Pacific, particularly in the French Pacific. As seen by Pacific leaders and civil society groups, legitimate regional governance should respect the right of self-determination for Pacific peoples wherever they were in the region. Like the regional diplomacy on the environmental question, the sustained regional actions on anticolonialism did not relate to the promotion or defence of the national interest of the Pacific states involved. They were motivated by a commitment to *regional* self-determination.

Support for decolonisation did not appear on the regional agenda in the early 1970s because decolonisation was proceeding relatively smoothly. Far from there being obstructions in the granting of self-determination, there was, if anything, a desire on the part of Australia, New Zealand and the United Kingdom to move to a faster timetable towards independence than desired by significant sections of the island societies they were administering. The exception was the French–British colony of the New Hebrides, where the independence aspirations of the Vanua`aku Party came up against obstruction by the French half of the joint administration. But even here events moved quickly. The forerunner of the Vanua`aku Party was established in 1975; by 1980, Vanuatu (as the New Hebrides was now known) had gained full independence.

---

12   George H.W. Bush, 'Remarks at the Conclusion of the Pacific Island Nations–United States Summit in Honolulu, Hawaii', 27 October 1990.

When the independence issue did begin to feature on the regional agenda, it did so in a selective way. The focus was on support for self-determination efforts in the French territories and, more particularly, in New Caledonia. This partly reflected the fact that, unlike French Polynesia or the American territories such as Guam, American Samoa or Palau, the majority of indigenous people in New Caledonia desired full independence; that, unlike Tokelau, Wallis and Futuna Islands and Pitcairn Islands, New Caledonia was a significant size and was significantly resourced; and that, unlike West Papua and Hawai`i, New Caledonia was not regarded as an integral part of a large country (Indonesia and the United States, respectively). Furthermore, New Caledonia's indigenous people were Melanesian. It was therefore understandable that neighbouring independence-minded Melanesian states, and especially Vanuatu, which had just been through its own independence struggle, would champion its independence.

The collective Pacific diplomatic campaign to oust France from its colonies began in 1978 when the four South Pacific members of the United Nations—Papua New Guinea, Solomon Islands, Fiji and Western Samoa—made a joint attack on continuing colonialism in the region during the thirty-third session of the UN General Assembly.[13] Vaovasamanaia Filipo, Western Samoa's finance minister, was reported as having

> voiced his country's 'deep concern' that some Pacific countries which want to gain independence have yet to do so. In some cases their wish and their right to aspire to independence have not even been acknowledged by the colonial powers concerned. We would wish to see an end to this situation as soon as possible.[14]

Immediately after the 1978 Nouméa South Pacific Conference, Papua New Guinea initiated a political campaign to pressure France into giving independence to its Pacific territories. Papua New Guinea's foreign minister, Ebia Olewale, raised the issue at the July 1979 SPF meeting and was supported by the other independent Pacific states. Australia and New Zealand insisted, however, that the call for the decolonisation of the Pacific territories appear in a watered-down form in the final

---

13   'Pacific Nations Speak Out with One Voice', *Pacific Islands Monthly*, February 1979: 9–10.
14   ibid., p. 9.

communiqué.[15] Olewale continued his campaign in press interviews and at an independence day rally in Tahiti while attending the October 1979 South Pacific Conference in Papeete. He called for decolonisation of the French territories and attacked Australia and New Zealand for not supporting the issue.[16] Even Father Gerard Leymang, the francophone chief minister representing the New Hebrides at the 1979 South Pacific Conference, was supportive of Olewale's sentiments and was openly critical of French attitudes in the Pacific.

At the 1979 SPF meeting, Pacific leaders made the following recommendation:

> Noting the desire of Pacific Island peoples, including those in French Territories, to determine their own future, the Forum reaffirmed its belief in the principle of self-determination and independence applying to all Pacific Island peoples in accordance with their freely expressed wishes. Accordingly, the Forum called on the metropolitan powers concerned to work with the peoples of their Pacific Territories to this end.[17]

In the following year, in his first speech to the UN General Assembly, Vanuatu's prime minister, Father Walter Lini, stated:

> Our difficult colonial past has also prompted in our national experience many concerns, and, with all humility, there may be occasions where a mutual benefit may be derived if those concerns are voiced here. It is the fact that some of our concerns are regional, based on support for what we in Vanuatu regard as a natural expectation held by those Pacific peoples still subject to colonial rule. Their right to be granted a free and unfettered political determination is a principle we shall not abdicate. We shall not forget that this principle is supported by this Assembly on every available opportunity, just as we shall advocate and strive with equal conviction to ensure that our Pacific Ocean be free from nuclear contamination through the practice of the dumping of nuclear waste or the testing of nuclear devices.[18]

---

15   PIFS, *Press Communiqué: Tenth South Pacific Forum, Honiara, Solomon Islands, 9–10 July 1979,* Suva: PIFS.

16   Author's observations at the nineteenth South Pacific Conference, Papeete, French Polynesia, October 1979.

17   SPF Secretariat, *Leaders' Communiqué: Tenth South Pacific Forum.*

18   Walter Hadye Lini, 'Vanuatu Enters the United Nations', in William L. Coop, ed., *Pacific People Sing Out Strong,* New York: Friendship Press, 1982, p. 52.

The New Caledonia question became a major item on the SPF agenda for the next decade. There was general sympathy among forum members for supporting political change, with nearly all members supporting full independence as the ultimate goal. The annual discussions centred on the form that support should take and how hard and fast the issue should be pushed. In the period 1980–86, there was a fundamental division on this question. On the one side, the Melanesian states fully supported the position of the Kanak independence movement, the Front de Libération Nationale Kanak et Socialiste (FLNKS: Kanak and Socialist National Liberation Front). They proposed that FLNKS be given observer status at the SPF and that the forum support the reinscription of New Caledonia on the UN decolonisation committee's list of non-self-governing territories. On the other side were the Australian and New Zealand governments, Fiji and the Polynesian states, who opposed the reinscription strategy on the grounds that it would be counterproductive and that France should be given more time to demonstrate that it was instituting the political change it had promised. They went as far as agreeing to discussions with the French Government and the setting up of a fact-finding mission; however, they did not wish to embarrass the French Government in wider international forums.[19]

The politics changed dramatically following a change of government in Paris in 1986. The determination of Jacques Chirac's centre-right coalition government to reverse the socialists' political reform process in New Caledonia ended this division among the Pacific states. The SPF island states united behind the Melanesian 'reinscription' strategy. At the 1986 SPF meeting, the leaders decided to pursue this strategy vigorously, and in this they were even supported by Australia and New Zealand. On Vanuatu's request, the Non-Aligned Movement (of which it was a member) subsequently agreed to support the reinscription issue at the United Nations, and in December of the same year, the General Assembly passed the SPF states' reinscription resolution by 89 votes to 24.[20]

The turning point in France's New Caledonia policy in 1988, was not, however, provoked by the SPF's efforts to increase international pressure on France but rather by the departure of the Chirac Government and the appointment of Michel Rocard. This once again caused a more progressive

---

19   Stephen Bates, *The South Pacific Island Countries and France: A Study in Inter-State Relations*, Canberra: Department of International Relations, The Australian National University, 1990, Ch. 5.
20   ibid., pp. 86–8.

approach to New Caledonia. In August 1988, the French Government and the FLNKS leadership signed the Matignon Accords, which promised assistance with economic development and political change leading to a referendum on political status in 1998. With the FLNKS willing to give the accords a chance, the SPF took the issue off its agenda until 1990 when, on the request of the FLNKS and the Melanesian Spearhead Group (MSG), it reactivated its interest in overseeing progress made on decolonisation under the Matignon Accords.

Regional decision-making

A third important expression of the commitment to regional self-determination was evident in the various positions taken on the question of political agency in regional decision-making. The postcolonial states built their regional efforts on the regional self-determination principle they had earlier established in their bid to take over the regional organisations. They accepted the regional boundaries of the SPC as the extent of their commitment to regional self-determination but, consistent with this principle, they acknowledged as having a right to speak or decide on regional politics only those Pacific peoples who had gained independence or associated statehood. This interpretation of regional self-determination, which privileged a particular view of who should have a right to political agency in regional governance, was built implicitly on the idea that states are the appropriate bearers of rights and duties in international relations—a fundamental proposition in the 'society of states' conception explained in Chapter 7.

The regional self-determination principle—a foundation principle of the SPF—therefore involved a commitment to political agency in the regional structures being in the hands of Pacific states, and not metropolitan states or former colonial powers. Consistent with this principle, Australia and New Zealand were invited into the SPF on terms set by the Pacific island states; and other non-regional metropolitan powers were excluded.

This view of political agency in regional decision-making became a source of tension both within the 'society of states' and between the 'society of states' and civil society organisations, metropolitan countries and territorial administrations. Territorial governments of the dependent territories of France and the United States demanded equal rights to participate in regional decision-making even though they did not have, nor did they necessarily intend to achieve, full political sovereignty. France and the United States, which wished to retain their influence on regional governance, supported their territories in this struggle, as did some states within the SPF. Civil society groups asserted a right to a political voice in relation to the same set of issues confronting the Pacific governments meeting in the SPF. They asserted a right to participate in the debate over how postcolonial Pacific societies should engage with powerful global structures around issues of development, security and sovereignty.

The tensions over admission criteria in relation to SPF membership first arose when, in 1972, a newly self-governing PNG administration was denied membership. Some observers believed Fiji was behind this decision and surmised that it was trying to block a potential rival for leadership in South Pacific affairs. During a seminar in the same year, Reuben Taureka, Papua New Guinea's Minister for Health, commented:

> We were refused admission by Fiji and its small neighbours to the South Pacific Commission. We have been excluded from the South Pacific Forum. Fiji is afraid for us to enter the South Pacific Forum because she thinks we may dominate her.[21]

Ratu Mara worked extremely hard to overcome these concerns. He visited Papua New Guinea in 1974 to hold talks with Somare, the new chief minister. Having assured his host that Fiji's objection to Papua New Guinea's membership was solely to do with the fact that it was not yet fully independent, he moved to scotch the idea that there was not room for both Papua New Guinea and Fiji in leading roles in regionalism. Papua New Guinea accepted this position and joined the SPF on gaining full independence in 1975.

The issue of the admission criteria arose again in 1978, this time as a conflict within the SPF membership. The occasion was the ninth SPF meeting, held at Niue in September 1978. A Polynesian group, led by Western Samoa's Tupuola Efi, proposed that American Samoa, a dependent territory, be admitted to SPF membership. This proposal was strongly opposed by the Papua New Guinea/Fiji bloc, which, it appears, saw it as threatening indigenous control of the SPF. American Samoa,

---

21 Commentary following U. Sundhaussen, 'Discussion Topic: That PNG Should Try to Play a Significant Role in Both the South-East Asian and South-West Pacific Regions', in James Griffin, ed., *A Foreign Policy for an Independent Papua New Guinea*, Sydney: Angus & Robertson, 1974, pp. 107–17, at p. 110.

as a dependent territory, could not make its own final decisions; it would have to consult Washington. For Papua New Guinea and Fiji, this went against the founding principle of the SPF. They argued that if island countries wanted to enjoy full political agency within the forum, they should first work for independence from their administering power.[22]

The principle of regional self-determination also created a tension between the Pacific states and metropolitan countries when it came to the participation of metropolitan countries in regional decision-making. It also created a division between SPF states over how far to press on this principle. In the postcolonial context of the 1970s, it arose first in relation to a Samoan proposal backed by the Pacific states to admit the United States to the proposed FFA. A Fiji/Papua New Guinea–led Melanesian group objected to US membership partly because the United States did not recognise coastal state sovereignty over migratory species, which was the main resource such an agency would control. Fiji's position was made clear in the month following the 1978 SPF meeting when, in an address to the UN General Assembly, its ambassador, Berenado Vunibobo, stated:

> We have now reached a situation where the formation of such an agency is threatened … The main reason for this sorry state of affairs has been due to the wishes of a dominant power foreign to the region, to join the Agency on its own terms. We view this … as yet another attempt to dominate our region and to dictate to us the terms and conditions in which we should run our affairs.[23]

They particularly objected to the idea that a distant water fishing nation should be a member of an agency controlling the activities of such nations on behalf of the Pacific states. In what turned out to be a victory for the Melanesian bloc in relation to the control of this richest shared resource, the SPF decided to proceed with the establishment of an agency restricted in the first instance to SPF member countries and leaving the question of metropolitan country membership open to further discussion. By the end of the SPF meeting, it was clear that the participants were very aware of the new west/east, Melanesian/Polynesian split that had occurred around the issue of regional self-determination. As a result of these tensions,

22   The SPF proceedings were closed to the public; however, journalists covering the Niue forum reported the rift. See, for example, Bruce Jones, 'US Tuna Fishing a Divisive Issue for Forum Members', *The Canberra Times*, 11 October 1978; and 'Islanders Wary of US Bait', *Sydney Morning Herald*, 24 October 1978.
23   As reported in '"New Colonialism" Over Fishing: Fiji Accuses the US', *The Canberra Times*, 11 October 1978.

the Melanesian states threatened to set up their own fisheries agency and Tom Davis, the Cook Islands premier, was talking of the need for a Polynesian alliance.[24]

The rift between these two groups carried over into the SPC meeting in Nouméa in the following month. Here it was clear that Papua New Guinea and Fiji were determined to weaken the SPC, which they viewed as being tainted with undue metropolitan influence. At the same time, it was evident that they wanted to strengthen the SPF as the regional organisation of choice. The PNG delegate, Father John Momis, used jurisdiction over the proposed South Pacific regional environment program as a test case. His success in having the conference agree to this becoming a joint SPF–SPC venture was regarded as an SPF incursion into traditional SPC territory.[25] Papua New Guinea and Fiji also froze their contributions to the SPC for the next three years. The campaign to strengthen the SPF continued in the 1980s with a proposal to establish a single regional organisation. Dependent territorial administrations, and France and the United States, saw this move as threatening the continuation of the SPC and their political agency within regional politics. They were afraid that any move to a single regional organisation would accord them second-class citizenship. They therefore stymied any such move. By the end of the 1980s, the compromise outcome was the establishment of the South Pacific Organisations Coordinating Committee, to increase cooperation among regional agencies, but stopping short of a single regional organisation.

In the 1970s, civil society groups did not see political agency within the official regional organisations as an issue. State and civil society positions were generally in agreement on a 'Pacific way' ideology that asserted anticolonial and antinuclear positions, and which asserted the right of Pacific peoples to control developments in their region. Moreover, many prominent civil society actors in the 1970s became political leaders by the end of the decade. In such a context, it was hard to draw a firm line between the state and civil society. This accord between civil society and

---

24 Based on discussions with journalists and delegates attending the eighteenth South Pacific Conference, Nouméa, October 1978, and who had attended the SPF meeting earlier in the month.
25 Based on author's observations at the eighteenth South Pacific Conference, Nouméa, October 1978.

official regionalism was also aided by the progressive policies of the Labor/ Labour governments in power between 1972 and 1975 in Australia and New Zealand.

In the 1980s, this civil society perception of official regionalism changed. Alarmed by the more hegemonic positions of Australia and New Zealand after 1976, but particularly in the second Cold War context from 1984, and concerned that some Pacific governments, and particularly Fiji and the Polynesian states, had compromised their position on regional self-determination, civil society groups started to critique the 'Pacific way' as an ideology masking state power, and particularly chiefly power. State representatives meeting regionally were now seen as denying political agency to the 'Pacific people'. This was nowhere clearer than in the development of the People's Charter by the Nuclear-Free and Independent Pacific movement.[26]

By 1980, Pacific women were also demanding political agency within what they saw as a men's club involved in regional decision-making in the SPC and the SPF. At the 1980 South Pacific Conference in Port Moresby, PNG women protested on the other side of a glass wall at the conference venue, with placards asking in effect: 'Where are the women in regional decision-making?'[27] As a result, the SPC instituted a triennial women's conference and established a women's bureau within the secretariat in Nouméa.[28] Other civil society groups did not seek at this stage to become part of the official regional processes of the main institutions, preferring to remain as social movements outside the formal state-centric arenas.

Self-determination and legitimate regional governance

Whether concerned with practical issues and outcomes, and whether promoted by states or civil society organisations, regional governance in the first two decades of the postcolonial era gained its legitimacy from the shared principle of regional self-determination. The question 'what kind of societies do we want for ourselves', which was the focus of the

---

26 *The Peoples' Charter for a Nuclear Free and Independent Pacific*, 1983, available from: www.apc. org.nz/pma/pacchar.htm.

27 Author's observations at the twentieth South Pacific Conference, Port Moresby, Papua New Guinea, 1980.

28 George, 'Pacific Women Building Peace', p. 41.

second Nuclear-Free Pacific Conference in Pohnpei in October 1978, was one that was also being asked by the leaders of the new Pacific states.[29] For both states and civil society groups, the 'ourselves' not only included the citizens of independent states; it also included 'Pacific peoples' in the dependent territories of France and the United States. For some key regional civil society groups, 'Pacific peoples' extended further to include West Papua and the indigenous people of New Zealand, Australia and Hawai`i.

For both Pacific states and civil society groups, this commitment to regional self-determination motivated active and heartfelt political campaigns opposing nuclear testing and proposals to dump radioactive waste and incinerate chemical weapons in the Pacific, as well as opposing continuing colonialism. The strength of this commitment, and the diplomatic resources and time engaged in these campaigns, demonstrated the central importance of regional self-determination as a legitimating principle. This was not explained by national interest or development needs but was rather about promotion of a shared principle. It was focused on territories that were not part of the legal jurisdiction of the SPF members and usually on areas that most would not have had an opportunity to visit. There were, as we have seen, divisions within the society of states and within the Nuclear-Free and Independent Pacific movement over how hard to press, and in relation to which territories, on the question of anticolonialism. But this did not get in the way of united support for decolonisation where the indigenous people desired it.

There were serious divisions within the Pacific society of states, and between the society of states and civil society groups, over the interpretation of political agency in regional decision-making. As we have seen, the experience of the 1960s, with Pacific leaders pitted against colonial powers on this question, had led to a particular interpretation of how this principle should be expressed in postcolonial regional organisations. For Fiji and other founding members of the regional society of states, this meant that only independent states should be involved in regional decision-making, with the proviso that observer status could be arranged for those approaching independence. They invited Australia and New Zealand to participate in the SPF but only on terms of sovereign equality set by the founding members. They did not want a return to the SPC

---

29 Alexander, *Putting the Earth First*, p. 145.

experience of the 1950s and 1960s, when outsiders dominated regional decision-making (or when territorial administrations acted as proxies for those interests). This created tensions with those in the dependent territories of Guam, American Samoa and French Polynesia in particular who wanted to go no further than having 'autonomy' within a continuing colonial context, but who at the same time wanted to participate fully in regional deliberations and be regarded as sovereign entities for this purpose. As we have seen, tensions over political agency within the regional organisations also extended to the contest between supporters of the SPC, on one hand, and supporters of a single regional organisation, centred on the SPF, on the other. The 'society of states' interpretation of who should have political agency to promote regional self-determination was also challenged by civil society groups, particularly women's groups and the nuclear-free Pacific movement.

Contending interpretations of the regional self-determination principle also became a source of tension *within* the regional 'society of states'. By the beginning of the 1980s, it became clear that an emerging Melanesian identity within regional politics was rallying around a commitment to press harder than their Polynesian and Micronesian neighbours on the regional self-determination principle when confronting colonialism, nuclear issues, fisheries exploitation or diplomatic dominance by former colonial powers within the regional organisations.

Australia and New Zealand supported the position of the Pacific island states on the various regional self-determination issues examined in this chapter. They were strong supporters of the establishment and development of the Pacific-controlled SPF. They joined Pacific island states in opposition to nuclear testing and nuclear dumping proposals. They were also very active participants in the regional move to assist in the decolonisation of Vanuatu and New Caledonia. However, along with the Pacific states, they did not go as far as endorsing civil society demands for decolonisation of the American territories. In these areas at least, then, Australia and New Zealand did not challenge the political agency of Pacific states. As we shall see in Chapter 9, the story in relation to the question of regional security was very different in the period from the mid 1970s until the end of the Cold War. Here, Australia, and to a lesser extent New Zealand, attempted to create a two-tiered hierarchical regional governance structure that fundamentally challenged the legitimating principle of regional self-determination and attempted to deny political agency to Pacific island states.

9

Negotiating regional security in the Cold War[1]

In the first two decades of postcolonial regional politics, the normative contest over 'regional self-determination' was joined by an equally significant, and intersecting, contest over 'regional security'. The idea of regional security, as applied to the South Pacific, emerged in 1976 when Australia and New Zealand began to interpret regional events through a Cold War lens and to see the promotion of regionalism, and a particular notion of regional security, as vital to their own security interests, and to those of the West more broadly. After the Grenada crisis in 1983 and the ANZUS crisis of 1984–85 (as discussed later), and in the context of heightened Cold War rivalry in the broader Pacific in the 1980s, Australia and New Zealand were joined by the United States, the United Kingdom and France in attempting to influence how Pacific states should behave in their foreign policies and within their states, if political instability was not to affect Western interests, as they saw them.

This attempt to impose a Cold War regional security order on the Pacific island region or, more accurately, to impose several competing notions of a Cold War order, was a highly significant move at several levels. First, it introduced the idea of regional security as an explicit notion, and one that reinforced the idea that the region was indeed a political community or entity that sat alongside the state in determining outcomes in these

---

1 Parts of this chapter were first published in 'At the Margin: The South Pacific and changing world order', in R. Leaver and J.L. Richardson (eds), *Charting the Post–Cold War Order*, Boulder, CO: Westview Press, 1993, pp. 224–42.

societies. Second, it introduced 'regional security' as a site of political contest over questions such as security for whom? Security from what? How should the region be secured? Third, it placed regionalism at the centre of its proposed solutions to the regional security 'problem'. Fourth, because of the way this approach envisaged the regional governance of security—as a hierarchical and hegemonic structure—it challenged the basic legitimating principle of indigenous regionalism. It attacked the principle of regional self-determination and the principle of sovereign equality that was wrapped up in it. It proposed instead that some states should have more rights and responsibilities than others in the regional society of states. Fifth, it raised the stakes involved in regional governance. And finally, it impacted on regional development because of the assumption that there was a strong connection between regional security and regional development. Economists in aid agencies and international organisations still pursued a separate developmental logic; for security analysts and politicians, however, regional development was to be seen as in service of regional security.

The attempt by the ANZUS members, and the United Kingdom and France, to promote various forms of a Cold War regional order in the Pacific, involving hierarchical and hegemonic forms of regional governance, provoked a strong response from Pacific island state leadership and regional civil society organisations. It is important to note, however, that like the Western countries, the Pacific island states were divided among themselves on their preferred conception of regional security and how it should be promoted. This challenges the idea of there being a simple global/local contestation over impositions by global actors. It was also a policy contest in which the participants had not just different notions of regional security; they actually saw the other party's nominated security *solution* as a security *threat*, antithetical to their own security interests. The stakes could therefore not have been higher in this contest over regional security governance.

At the centre of this political contest over the regional governance of security from the mid 1970s was the nuclear question. The region had been significantly involved in the nuclear aspects of the Cold War since the 1940s, providing nuclear testing sites for the United States, the United Kingdom and France. This nuclear involvement became a *regional* issue for Pacific island leaders in the 1960s when it became their unifying 'regional self-determination' issue. In the 1970s, Australia and New Zealand joined the postcolonial states and the emerging regional civil society groups in opposing French testing in the Pacific. In the 1980s, the nuclear question became tied to the question of regional security in a dramatic way. From 1984, the contest over regional security began to focus on the issue of a nuclear weapons–free zone. The Western positions were complicated by New Zealand's antinuclear policy and the ensuing ANZUS crisis, as well as by the differing conceptualisations and interests of Australia, on the one hand, and France, the United Kingdom and the United States, on the other. The Pacific camp was also divided once the issues moved beyond French nuclear testing. A split developed between Polynesian states and Fiji, on the one hand, and Melanesian states and regional civil society, on the other.

'Nuclear playground'

From the early years of the Cold War, parts of the South Pacific were linked directly to the grand strategies of Western powers in very significant ways. The remoteness of some atolls and the strategic location of others made them attractive sites for nuclear weapons testing and deployment, and imperial control made this easy to achieve. The United States began testing atomic bombs over Bikini Atoll in the Marshall Islands—part of the American-administered Trust Territory of the Pacific Islands—in 1946. Two years later, it began testing at Enewetak Atoll, where the first hydrogen bomb was exploded in 1952. Atmospheric testing continued at these sites until 1958, when the United States moved its testing site to Johnston Atoll, an American island south of Hawai`i. In 1957, Britain moved its nuclear testing program from Australia to Christmas Island (Kiritimati) in its Gilbert and Ellice Islands colony. The United States joined the United Kingdom in testing at Christmas Island five years later. Both the British and American programs moved to the Nevada desert after the 1963 Partial Test Ban Treaty. In the same year, France established its Centre d'expérimentation du Pacifique and conducted 41 atmospheric tests at Moruroa Atoll in French Polynesia before 1974. Meanwhile, the American territory of Guam provided a base for nuclear-armed B52s until 1990, while Kwajalein Atoll in the Marshall Islands became the main testing site for American antiballistic missiles from 1964.[2]

---

2   I examine this nuclear involvement in greater detail in Greg Fry, *A Nuclear-Free Zone for the Southwest Pacific: Prospects and Significance*, Working Paper No. 75, Canberra: Strategic and Defence Studies Centre, The Australian National University, 1983, pp. 11–20.

For particular individuals and societies in the French and American territories, this involvement was disastrous. Chamoro people in Guam and Tinian, and Marshall Islanders in Kwajalein, Bikini and Enewetak, were forced off their land. Bikini and Enewetak people, as well as Christmas Islanders and French Polynesians, suffered the effects of radioactivity associated with the American, British and French tests. All people in the Pacific region potentially suffer from the fallout of the 163 atmospheric tests conducted in the region before 1975. Moreover, the strategic interests of the United States and France severely constrained the self-determination efforts of islanders in these territories.[3]

Aptly dubbed 'the nuclear playground' by prominent Pacific historian Stewart Firth, this nuclear involvement in the Pacific was part of a continuing imperial order.[4] While the Cold War may have influenced the intensity of testing, it is likely the United Kingdom, France and the United States would have been involved in this way in their Pacific territories whether or not there was an ideological competition between East and West and whether the world was 'bipolar' or 'multipolar'. World War II had done little to alter the fact that Pacific island societies remained appendages of large powers. For Pacific island societies not directly affected by nuclear involvement, there was little to suggest any influence of the Cold War. In fact, developments within these British, Australian and New Zealand territories reflected a quite different theme in Western 'world order' thinking: the principle of self-determination. The decision to slowly move these territories towards self-government demonstrates that Cold War thinking could be overridden by other normative principles. A policy dictated solely by Cold War considerations would have left the Pacific islands under direct political control rather than opening them to the possibility of Soviet influence.

For the first 30 years or so of the Cold War, then, the regional order was the legacy of an imperial order established in the late nineteenth century. With colonial sovereignty fixed, South Pacific societies were a strategic backwater, out of bounds to great power rivalry. The gradual emergence of independent island states after 1962 did little to change this imperial

---

3   The impact of this nuclear involvement on Pacific islanders and their societies is documented in Robert C. Kiste, *The Bikinians: A Study in Forced Migration*, Menlo Park, CA: Cummings Publishing Co., 1974; Stewart Firth, *Nuclear Playground*, Sydney: Allen & Unwin, 1987; and Bengt Danielsson and Marie-Thérèse Danielsson, *Poisoned Reign: French Nuclear Colonialism in the Pacific*, 2nd edn, Melbourne: Penguin, 1986.

4   Firth, *Nuclear Playground*.

order. Economic patterns followed previous colonial ties and foreign policy initiatives were few. It was only when a significant portion of the region had been decolonised and more independent foreign policies had begun to be asserted that a post-imperial order could be said to have taken shape. This is the point at which the nuclear issue became 'regionalised'; it is also the point at which it became part of a new notion of 'regional security' built on Cold War assumptions.

The creation of the idea of 'regional security'

The idea of 'regional security', as applied to the Pacific island region, emerged with a change to conservative governments in both Canberra and Wellington in late 1975. The new governments began to view the region through a Cold War lens. Although the Cold War had been under way for three decades, and had dramatically impacted on parts of the region, this was the first time since World War II that the area as a whole was seen as a security region. The conservative Australian and New Zealand governments worked together to develop a new regional security framework. This affected the significance they attached to regional cooperation, the objectives they pursued through their involvement in regional cooperation and the positions they took on regional issues. Conceptually, they began to link regional organisation, regional security and regional development. They began to see regional organisation and regional development as serving regional security—defined in Cold War terms as the exclusion of Soviet influence from the Pacific island region. They also began to see themselves as the leaders of the 'new South Pacific', as the United Kingdom withdrew from its territories, and as representing Western interests in this part of the world.

In promoting this new policy framework aimed at securing the region as a whole, Australia and New Zealand were driven by their concern about the possibility of Soviet influence on the new Pacific states following a reported offer in July 1976 of economic assistance to Tonga in exchange for access for the Soviet fishing fleet. They viewed this report against the backdrop of newly established diplomatic relations between the Soviet Union and Fiji, Tonga and Western Samoa, and more generally against the unsettling new involvement of other powerful international actors in what they had begun to see as an 'ANZUS lake' in the quiet postcolonial years of the early 1970s.[5] They viewed with some concern—although not with the alarm reserved for the Soviet Union—the new economic and diplomatic involvement of China, Taiwan and Japan in the island states south of the equator. In his speech to the SPF immediately after Soviet ambassador Oleg Selyaninov's visit to the Kingdom of Tonga, Australia's representative, Senator Robert Cotton, gave a clear indication of the Australian Government's prime concern:

> Australia was … concerned about the increasing Soviet involvement in the South Pacific and where it might lead. The Soviet Union was bound to seek to exploit any features of the situation to its own advantage … it was important to study Soviet activities with great seriousness, and to be on guard against any developments which might not be in the interests of individual countries or of the region as a whole. The development of large on-shore facilities by the USSR to serve its fishing fleets could open the way for unwelcome longer-term developments.[6]

The Australian Government viewed regionalism not only as the key to establishing a shared notion of regional security that accorded with its own security interests. It also clarified the central role that it accorded to regional cooperation as a way of promoting this concept and the crucial connection it saw between regional security and development. Again, in Senator Cotton's words:

> This [the new external awareness of the region] we feel enhances the need for more intensive cooperation on a regional basis in the South Pacific and emphasises the importance of the existing regional organisations such as the South Pacific Forum, SPEC and the SPC. Australia will continue its efforts to support and strengthen these organisations and to make them as responsive as possible to the needs of the countries of the region.[7]

---

5   Australian Department of Foreign Affairs, 'The South Pacific', p. 21; 'Roubles for Tonga from Russia with Love', *Pacific Islands Monthly*, August 1976: 14–15; and Russell Skelton, 'Soviet Turns Eyes to South Pacific Areas', *The Age*, [Melbourne], 14 July 1976.
6   'A Thundercloud but No Storm over the Forum', *Pacific Islands Monthly*, September 1976: 13.
7   ibid.

A few months after the Soviet offer to Tonga, Australia quadrupled its aid to the South Pacific countries.[8] In 1977, it also increased its diplomatic network and began negotiations for a nonreciprocal, oneway regional free-trade agreement.

At the August 1976 ANZUS Council meeting, New Zealand joined Australia in an attempt to persuade the United States to take a more active role in the Pacific island region south of the equator to counter Soviet influence.[9] This subject reportedly dominated council discussions. The US Deputy Secretary of State, Charles Robinson, later admitted that, as a result of the meeting, he was 'more sensitive' to the need for increased economic assistance to the South Pacific states. In reference to the Soviet moves in the region, he is reported as having said that 'the seriousness of the threat is one of potential, and hopefully it can be contained in a co-operative way'.[10] Illustrating the importance the ANZUS partners attached to the relationship between regional security, regional economic development and regional cooperation, the official communiqué from the meeting 'reaffirmed'

> the importance which it attached to the security of the region and in this connection emphasised the contribution to be made by steady and sustained economic progress. The Council noted the intention of Australia and New Zealand to give greater priority to the South Pacific in their development assistance programs. It also welcomed the growing sense of regionalism among the countries of the South Pacific, as exemplified by the South Pacific Forum and the South Pacific Commission.[11]

The 1977 ANZUS Council meeting echoed these sentiments. It welcomed the 'continuing growth of regional institutions in the South Pacific, and their contribution to the welfare of countries in the region' and promised that these countries 'could expect continued support from the ANZUS

---

8   'Speech by the Australian Minister for Foreign Affairs on the Australian South Pacific Aid Program to the Meeting of the South Pacific Forum in Suva on 12 October, 1976', *Australian Foreign Affairs Record*, October 1976: 556–7.

9   'US Urged to "Watch Pacific"', *The Canberra Times*, 4 August 1976: 9; and 'Red Sails in the South Seas?', *Sydney Morning Herald*, 7 August 1976: 10.

10   Brian Toohey, 'What Russians? Its Economics that Matter', *Australian Financial Review*, 5 August 1976; and Russell Skelton, 'ANZUS to Step Up Aid: Council Acts on Soviet Pacific Move', *The Age*, [Melbourne], 5 August 1976: 3.

11   Australian Department of Foreign Affairs, *Twenty-Fifth ANZUS Council Meeting Communiqué*, News Release No. D16, 4 August 1976, Canberra: Australian Government, p. 12.

partners on a bilateral and regional basis'.[12] Australia's policy approach, in particular, continued along these lines into the early 1980s, further encouraged by global developments in the Cold War. At the beginning of 1980, prime minister Malcolm Fraser made a direct connection between the Soviet invasion of Afghanistan and his government's further doubling of economic assistance to the South Pacific, saying that Australia's duty on behalf of the West was to ensure that the South Pacific was free of Soviet influence.[13]

The central premise of this new security framing of the region was that a desirable regional order would ensure no Soviet involvement of any kind and no developments that could be interpreted as inviting such involvement—an approach later known as 'strategic denial'.[14] This approach drew a conceptual link between 'stability' within a state and *regional* security. It also posited a link between security and development; since economically fragile societies were assumed to be more susceptible to Soviet entanglements. Economic assistance, and even trade and investment, came to be seen as instruments serving regional security. The conceptual link between regional identity and regional security presumed that the identity encouraged through regional organisation would help exclude 'illegitimate' players from decision-making and that regional organisations would be a vehicle for a regional consensus around the desired objective of security.

Canberra and Wellington promoted two organising principles of state behaviour as part of this preferred regional security order. The first was that these smaller states should not exercise their full sovereign rights. They should deny themselves forms of relationship with the Soviet Union common in the West, including embassies, trade links, visits to Moscow and forms of association common elsewhere among postcolonial states, such as membership of the Non-Aligned Movement. Furthermore, they should curb domestic developments that could be seen as providing openings to the Soviet Union. The second organising principle was that Australia and New Zealand should act as 'gatekeepers' on behalf of the

---

12   'ANZUS Council Communiqué', *Australian Foreign Affairs Record*, August 1977: 412.
13   Malcolm Fraser, 'Afghanistan: Australia's Assessment and Response', Department of the Prime Minister and Cabinet News Release, Canberra, 19 February 1980, p. 18.
14   R.A. Herr, 'Regionalism, Strategic Denial and South Pacific Security', *Journal of Pacific History*, 21(4), 1986: 170–82.

West. There was, then, an attempt to establish a pecking order of states within the regional society of states: Australia and New Zealand would act as middlemen between the United States and the island states.

Until 1982, this preferred regional order of Australia and New Zealand largely became *the* regional order accepted and acted on by other Pacific island states. The operating principles appeared to be supported: Australian and New Zealand leadership was encouraged by Washington, and Pacific island states seemed to accept limitations on their sovereignty over dealings with the Soviet Union. Furthermore, the SPF seemed to accept the policy of strategic denial.

There were, however, two prominent issues that provoked concern in Australian policy circles because of their perceived potential to breach this pro-Western regional security community. One was Vanuatu's nonaligned posture, its government's talk of promoting Melanesian socialism and its establishment of diplomatic relations with Cuba and Vietnam. Seen from Canberra, Vanuatu looked to be the weak link in the strategic denial policy it was attempting to build with New Zealand. The Australian Government's other concern was the Soviet offer to undertake hydrographic research in Vanuatu and Solomon Islands waters in 1980. This prompted Australia, at the 1981 SPF meeting, to strongly support a move by Solomon Islands' prime minister, Peter Kenilorea, to forge a regional consensus around the desirability of rejecting all Soviet offers of assistance and to organise a counteroffer by the United States, Australia and New Zealand.[15]

It is difficult to prove whether the strategic denial policy was successful in its own terms and to what extent it denied political agency on the part of the island states. Certainly, no Pacific island government accepted Soviet offers of assistance. Nor did they permit a Soviet embassy on their soil (by contrast, they allowed the establishment of Chinese embassies). But whether this was a result of the strategic denial policy is arguable. By the early 1980s, Pacific island leaders had considerable experience in gaining the attention of Western nations by letting it be known that Soviet offers of assistance were on the table. Further, it is evident that they had their own reservations about Soviet involvement, whether on ideological or religious grounds or on the practical grounds that their own sovereignty could be

15   Russell Skelton, 'Thirteen Pacific Nations Agree to Reject Soviet Aid Offers', *Sydney Morning Herald*, 12 August 1981.

threatened by the possible superpower rivalry that might follow a decision to allow a Soviet presence. While Australian influence may have made a difference on the question of Vanuatu and Solomon Islands accepting the Soviet Union's hydrographic research offer, there is no evidence in the public domain to support prime minister Fraser's claim that during his administration he was able to persuade three Pacific island countries 'to stick with us and New Zealand rather than with the Soviets'.[16]

Cold War thinking and regional strategic denial in the 1980s

The new Labor/Labour governments in Canberra, in 1983, and Wellington, in 1984, promoted the regional strategic denial policy with even greater vigour than their conservative predecessors. The Australian Labor Government's commitment to the strategic denial policy framework was soon evident in its response to supposed Soviet and Libyan involvement in the region. Canberra greeted with dismay the negotiation, and signing, of the Kiribati–Soviet fisheries access agreement in 1985. It saw it as the first breach of the Pacific consensus around strategic denial. The dangers thought to flow from this commercial agreement—despite Australia and New Zealand themselves having such an agreement with the Soviet Union—were those dictated by the logic of strategic denial: it had to be assumed that the Soviets had motives other than fisheries access and this would be the 'thin edge of the wedge', perhaps ultimately leading to widespread economic involvement, the according of legitimacy to a Soviet regional economic presence, a shift to Soviet political influence and perhaps a military base. The Soviet Union's subsequent negotiation, in 1987, of a fisheries access agreement with Vanuatu, with provision for future negotiations concerning landing rights for Aeroflot, was seen as vindicating the correctness of this logic.[17]

---

16   Warren Mirrill and Peter Samuel, 'Soviets May Soon Have Pacific Base, Says Fraser', *The Australian*, 24 April 1985: 3.
17   See, for example, Ean Higgins, 'Pacific Islands Warned About Soviet Threat', *Australian Financial Review*, 4 April 1985: 14; Peter Hastings, 'Aust. Concern as Soviets Offer Vanuatu $2m Deal', *Sydney Morning Herald*, 15 December 1986: 1; 'Hayden Warns of Soviet Infiltration through Fishing Deals', *The Canberra Times*, 14 December 1986: 1.

The strategic denial framework also guided Australia's interpretation of the link between Libya and some key political figures in Vanuatu and New Caledonia in late 1986 and early 1987. Australian policy circles were concerned that such links would expand and, in particular, that a Libyan Peoples' Bureau would be established in Port Vila. They interpreted any involvement by Libya as illegitimate and destabilising. While Canberra's policymakers did not necessarily embrace the thesis that Libya was a surrogate for the Soviet Union, the Australian response nevertheless had a Cold War feel to it.[18] The Australian foreign minister Bill Hayden took the issue very seriously, to the point where he thought it necessary to take a special trip to New Zealand to persuade prime minister David Lange of the need to take some regional action on the matter. An Australian envoy put the case for regional strategic denial of Libyan involvement to the other South Pacific leaders. This Australian diplomacy had a mixed reception. Australia's case was strengthened once it had closed its own Libyan Peoples' Bureau, thus stemming the charge of applying double standards. Papua New Guinea and New Zealand were reportedly sceptical about Australia's concerns.[19] Others were concerned about the precedent of trying to use the SPF as a watchdog over matters that should be the preserve of sovereign states.

While prime minister Walter Lini's subsequent decision not to allow a Libyan Peoples' Bureau to be established in Port Vila seemed to indicate a successful outcome for Australian diplomacy, it is more likely that his decision related to power struggles within his government and within the ruling Vanua`aku Pati. The expulsion of the Libyan-linked Front Uni de Libération Kanak from the FLNKS in New Caledonia can, on the other hand, be seen as a move influenced by Australia's regional diplomacy because the FLNKS leadership saw the Libyan link as a disadvantage in their dealings with the SPF region, and particularly with Australia.

The intensity of the Australian response to Soviet and Libyan involvement can be explained in part by the fact that these developments were viewed against the backdrop of the ANZUS crisis.[20] This created the perception in Canberra of a region signalling vulnerability to the Soviet Union.

---

18   The Libyan involvement in the South Pacific, and the Australian Government's response to it, is examined in David Hegarty, *Libya and the South Pacific*, Working Paper No. 127, Canberra: Strategic and Defence Studies Centre, The Australian National University, 1987.

19   ibid., p. 13.

20   See John Ravenhill, 'Political Turbulence in the South Pacific', in John Ravenhill, ed., *No Longer an American Lake?*, Sydney: Allen & Unwin, 1989: 1–40.

Just as importantly, the ANZUS crisis attracted serious global attention to the region for the first time since World War II. The United States was now looking over Australia's shoulder, no longer confident that it could 'subcontract' its interests in this area to Canberra. As seen from Washington, the combination of a Soviet link with Kiribati, the breakup of the ANZUS Treaty and an antinuclear New Zealand suggested regional vulnerability with implications for its global alliance system.[21] The rising direct interest of larger powers, and particularly the United States and Japan, but also France, the United Kingdom and China, put pressure on the Australian Government to increase its efforts to give leadership to the regional strategic denial policy. Larger countries were losing faith in Australia's ability to lead the region and Australian policymakers were sensing this. They were intent on proving their continuing credentials as the reliable agent of Western interests in the Pacific island region.

From 1983, the question of South Pacific regional security moved significantly up the agenda of the world's most important powers. The issues of how Pacific regional security was defined, how Pacific island states oriented their foreign policies and how internal political developments in these countries might impact on international relations came to be seen as vital questions in metropolitan capitals. There were a number of related developments contributing to this heightened interest and the new era in regional security governance to which it led. As we have seen, a crucial element was the change in government in Canberra in 1983, followed by Wellington in 1984, and the uncertainty this created about whether these new governments were adequately representing vital Western interests as interpreted in Paris, Washington and London. These metropolitan countries now saw it as imperative to attempt to directly influence the way regional security was governed in the Pacific island region if the West's global nuclear posture within the Cold War was not to be weakened. For France, the problem was the growing regional opposition to its continued nuclear testing, which it regarded as the top priority for its national security. For the United States and the United Kingdom, the concern was not only that a proposed nuclear weapons–free zone would possibly affect the movement of their navies, but also that the symbolism of this move would further encourage the antinuclear movement in Europe at a crucial time.

---

21   Henry S. Albinski, 'American Perspectives and Policy Options on ANZUS', in Ravenhill, *No Longer an American Lake?*, pp. 200–2.

This heightened interest on the part of the world's largest powers also has to be viewed against broader global developments in the Cold War: the emergence of an assertive Reagan doctrine, concerns about Soviet naval activity in the Pacific following the opening of Cam Ranh Bay naval base in Vietnam and the rising influence of antinuclear movements in Europe and Japan. It also needs to be seen in the context of the new security thinking in Western capitals following the Grenada security crisis of 1983, which suggested that small state instability could have significant repercussions for Western interests.

'Small is dangerous'

The Grenada crisis of September 1983 sparked a new awareness in Western circles of the vulnerability of very small states to political instability, the potential of such national instability to impact on regional and even global security and the importance of promoting appropriate security governance arrangements at the regional level. It prompted new thinking about microstates as a special category in international relations with a particular security 'personality'.[22] This new thinking built on the assumptions already established in the development literature that such states were particularly vulnerable, dependent and without resources.[23] These economic characteristics were linked to an assumed security characteristic: a lack of resources to deal with even minor security threats. Consequently, instability flowing from this situation could significantly affect regional security as defined in Cold War terms. This 'small is dangerous' diagnosis not only heightened Western interest in South Pacific security; it also reinforced the importance accorded to regional organisation and economic development and encouraged the tendency to link *national* security with *regional* security.

The promotion of a strategic denial strategy was reflected in the rise of an academic industry concerned with analysing regional security, including 'domestic instability', in the South Pacific. It began in 1985 as an offshoot of the studies of the rift in ANZUS caused by New Zealand's antinuclear

---

22   See, for example, George H. Quester, 'Trouble in the Islands: Defending the Micro-States', *International Security*, 8(2), 1983: 160–75; Sheila Harden, ed., *Small is Dangerous: Micro States in a Macro World*, Report from the David Davies Memorial Institute of International Studies, London: Frances Pinter, 1985.
23   See, for example, Commonwealth Consultative Group on the Special Needs of Small States, *Vulnerability: Small States in the Global Society*, Report of a Commonwealth Consultative Group, London: Commonwealth Secretariat, 1985.

decision. Attracting mainly Australian, New Zealand and US defence community scholars, the studies revolved around a series of conferences financed by governments and think tanks.[24] They evinced a common preoccupation with the 'Soviet threat', 'instability' and ways of limiting damage caused to Western regional interests by the ANZUS crisis and Soviet fishing deals. While some contributions to this literature were reflective and cautious, most were alarmist and partial. Most were *not* concerned with South Pacific security for itself, but only as it might threaten Western interests. If there was a fine line between government and academic agendas, it was difficult to discern. Rather than being disinterested studies of contending visions of regional order, they became part of the effort to promote particular Western conceptions of Pacific regional order.

New directions in Australian–New Zealand regional security thinking

While they held to strategic denial and its organising principles, the new Australian and New Zealand governments also introduced antinuclear and self-determination objectives into their framing of a desirable regional order—objectives they saw as consistent with regional security defined in Cold War terms. For example, Australia justified its opposition to France's nuclear testing and its opposition to French colonial policy in New Caledonia in terms of its potential damage to Western interests by their encouragement of the radicalisation of Pacific social movements. New Zealand argued that its new national antinuclear policy was consistent with the aims of the ANZUS alliance and that it did not affect New Zealand's efforts to counter Soviet influence in the region. France, the United Kingdom and the United States did not share these perspectives on a preferred regional Cold War order. They saw the Australian–New

---

24   See, for example, Dennis L. Bark and Owen Harries, eds, *The Red Orchestra: Instruments of Soviet Policy in the Southwest Pacific*, Stanford, CA: Hoover Institution Press, 1989, based on a conference organised by the Hoover Institution in Washington, DC, in March 1987; Leon M. Slawecki, *The United States and the South Pacific: A Conference Report—Apia, Western Samoa, November, 1988*, San Francisco: Asia Foundation Center for Asian Pacific Affairs, 1989; Henry S. Albinski, Robert C. Kiste, Richard Herr, Ross Babbage, and Ian McLean, *The South Pacific: Political, Economic and Military Trends*, Washington, DC: Brassey's, 1990; and the Pacific Forum (Honolulu) Seminar on Strategic Imperatives and Western Responses in the South and Southwest Pacific, Sydney, February 1986.

Zealand conception as not only wrongheaded, but also dangerous and threatening to Western interests. This was particularly the case in relation to Australia's promotion of a regional nuclear-free zone.

The South Pacific nuclear-free zone initiative

The Australian Labor Government was elected to office in 1983 with a commitment to continue with the ANZUS security treaty with the United States as the cornerstone of its security *and* to establish a nuclear-free zone in the South Pacific. It sought to balance these two seemingly contradictory commitments by proposing a partial nuclear weapons–free zone. To reflect the majority view in the Labor Party and the electorate, the Australian proposal had to leave out of the regional initiative any prohibition on US nuclear activity that would have been seen by Washington or the Australian electorate as constituting the dismantling of the security pact with the United States.

The Australian proposal, which was put before the 1983 SPF meeting, therefore added up to a prohibition on the presence of nuclear weapons and on their manufacture or testing anywhere within the territories of South Pacific states up to the 12-mile sea limit. However, there was one very significant qualification to this general prohibition. The treaty specifically allowed each state to make an exception for nuclear weapons that may be aboard ships that were visiting its ports or navigating its territorial sea or archipelagic waters and for weapons that may be aboard aircraft that were visiting its airfields or transiting its airspace.[25]

The debate on this vision for a regional nuclear weapons–free zone developed in a highly charged context. From mid 1984, the New Zealand Government announced a ban on visits to its ports by nuclear-armed or nuclear-powered ships. The New Zealand Government's subsequent enforcement of the ban against US naval ships that would not confirm or deny whether they were carrying nuclear weapons provoked a strong response from Washington. The United States cut defence ties with New Zealand and ANZUS was effectively put in abeyance. For the United States, then, any talk of a regional nuclear-free zone was viewed with

---

25 *South Pacific Nuclear Free Zone Treaty*, 1985, available from: fas.org/nuke/control/spnfz/text/spnfz.htm, art. 5(2).

concern and US Secretary of State, George Shultz, cautioned against it.[26] It was viewed as not only encouraging antinuclear feeling in the Pacific, but also as feeding into the global antinuclear movement. There was concern about its symbolic power.

On the other side, as we have seen, various Pacific governments and the Nuclear-Free and Independent Pacific movement had a long history of promoting a more ambitious regional nuclear-free zone. The most prominent of these earlier proposals was that of the New Zealand Government in 1974, and on that occasion the Australian Government had worked against the proposal because of concerns that it would affect the United States' ability to fulfil its security obligations under the ANZUS Treaty. As we have seen, opposition to French nuclear testing had provided a unified Pacific position on regional self-determination since the late 1960s. There had also been a history of some individual governments adopting more ambitious antinuclear positions such as banning visits by nuclear ships.

By 1984, there was agreement in principle by most Pacific island states to proceed with the Hawke Government's compromise proposal. In 1985, eight SPF members signed the South Pacific Nuclear Free Zone Treaty (known as the Treaty of Rarotonga). The change of government in New Zealand in 1984 assisted with the rapid move from proposal to treaty. The Lange Government wanted a quick and substantial result, whereas there were indications that Australia was more interested in having a negotiation process in place than achieving an end result. France, the United States, the United Kingdom and the Australian opposition parties thought the Treaty of Rarotonga threatened the West's global interests as well as their own individual strategic interests. Some Pacific island governments, and particularly Vanuatu, together with the Australian peace movement and the Nuclear-Free and Independent Pacific movement, thought it represented a sellout of the nuclear-free policy to Australia's commitment to the US global alliance. With Vanuatu wanting a comprehensive zone and Tonga wanting no zone at all for fear of offending France and the United States, the Treaty of Rarotonga represented a compromise position for Pacific island states as well.[27]

26   Milton Cockburn and Amanda Buckley, 'Pacific Treaty Has US Worried', *Sydney Morning Herald*, 3 August 1985: 9; and Michelle Grattan, 'Hawke Courts Kudos for N-Free Treaty', *The Age*, [Melbourne], 7 August 1985: 1.
27   See Paul Malone, 'Reservations on N-Free Zone', *The Canberra Times*, 3 August 1985: 9; Milton Cockburn, 'Nearly Ready for a Nuclear-Free Pacific', *Sydney Morning Herald*, 7 August 1985: l; and 'Nuclear Ships Row on Boil at ASEAN', *Sydney Morning Herald*, 11 July 1985: l.

The reinscription campaign

The other controversial commitment in the Australian–New Zealand vision of regional security was that of promoting self-determination for New Caledonia. Australia's policy was cautious between the 1984 election boycott by the Independence Front and the election of French prime minister Chirac in 1986. It used its influence to moderate the more radical position of the Melanesian countries at the SPF, arguing that the French Government should be given time to implement reform. At the same time, the Australian Government indicated its support for decolonisation of the territory. In taking this position, it pleased neither Paris, which thought it was intervening in its affairs, nor Port Moresby, Port Vila or Honiara, which thought Australia was protecting France. After 1986, feeling that the more progressive policies of the French socialists had been reversed by the Chirac Government, Australia strongly supported the MSG's push for reinscription of New Caledonia on the list of territories overseen by the UN Special Committee on Decolonization (the Committee of 24). Australia played an important role in lobbying at the United Nations, which led to a vote in favour of the SPF's position and against that of France.[28]

Contending Western conceptions of regional order

Washington, London and Paris strongly opposed the promotion of this new view of regional order by Canberra and Wellington, with its emphasis on anticolonial and antinuclear principles. The United States and the United Kingdom shared a view that the Australian Labor Government's approach affected their global strategic interests. They saw a contradiction between Australia's anti-Soviet position, on the one hand, and its promotion of a nuclear-free zone and its attack on French nuclear testing and the French colonial presence, on the other. As seen by these governments, such policies created opportunities for the Soviet Union in the South Pacific. They signalled a further breakdown of Western solidarity following closely from the ANZUS crisis. French control of French Polynesia and New Caledonia, in particular, and the consequent

---

28   Helen Fraser, *New Caledonia: Anti-Colonialism in a Pacific Territory*, Canberra: Peace Research Centre, The Australian National University, 1988, pp. 37–9.

French naval presence in the South Pacific were seen as advantageous for Western interests. It was thought that France's departure would create a vacuum into which leftist regimes (with links to socialist states) could step. The United States and the United Kingdom also saw Australia's continued attack on French nuclear testing as an attack on the Western nuclear deterrent within the global Cold War. As fellow Western nuclear powers, they quietly supported France's testing program at Mururoa.[29] One of Washington's operating principles of a desired regional order—the idea of Australia and New Zealand as 'managers'—now seemed in tatters. Canberra's concept of a desirable regional security order also brought it in direct conflict with the French Government. This culminated in a verbal slinging match between the prime ministers of each country and a banning, by France, of ministerial exchanges with Australia.[30]

This disagreement with Australian policy led to the United States and France developing, for the first time, a policy towards the region outside their Pacific island territories.[31] They used this to promote a different view of what constituted a desirable pro-West regional order.[32] The United States also asked Japan to undertake some burden sharing in this new direct involvement. This resulted in the Kuranari Doctrine of 1987 and the establishment of a substantial Japanese economic assistance program to the Pacific island states.[33]

29 For a different American perspective, downplaying the Soviet threat and emphasising the damage to Western interests caused by French nuclear and colonial involvement, see Robert C. Kiste and R.A. Herr, *The Potential for Soviet Penetration of the South Pacific Islands: An Assessment*, Consultants' Report to the United States State Department, December 1984.

30 Henningham, *France and the South Pacific*, pp. 226–7.

31 For details of the new French policy towards the region, see Bates, *The South Pacific Island Countries and France*, Ch. 6; and Stephen Henningham, 'Keeping the Tricolor Flying: The French Pacific into the 1990s', *The Contemporary Pacific*, 1(1–2), 1989: 97–132, at pp. 113–22.

32 This dominant American perspective was at variance with advice put to the US State Department in a 1984 consultants' report prepared by two prominent Pacific island specialists, who downplayed the Soviet threat and emphasised French nuclear and colonial involvement as damaging to Western interests. For an abridged version of that report, see Kiste and Herr, *The Potential for Soviet Penetration of the South Pacific Islands*; for details of the new French policy, see Bates, *The South Pacific Island Countries and France*, Ch. 6; and Henningham, 'Keeping the Tricolor Flying'.

33 See Isami Takeda, 'New Factors in Japan's ODA Policy: Implications for Australia–Japan Relations', Mimeo, Canberra: Australia–Japan Research Centre, The Australia National University, August 1986; and Tadashi Kuranari, 'Working Towards the Pacific Future Community', Address, Suva, 14 January 1987.

Pacific challenges to Cold War conceptions of regional security

These various Western versions of Cold War regional order did not go unchallenged by the Pacific island states. First, they contested the concept of regional security promoted as the objective of such an order. The Pacific voice was strong and assertive at the Commonwealth-organised South Pacific Colloquium on the Special Needs of Small States held in Wellington in August 1984.[34] The colloquium was specifically designed to elicit Pacific island state opinion on regional security as part of a broader Commonwealth study of the special security needs of small states following the Grenada crisis. The Wellington colloquium became the arena for the first explicit debate about the definition of regional security in the Pacific context and, more specifically, a consideration of such questions as: What is regional security? What are the key security threats to the region? What are the appropriate strategies for dealing with them? What should be the role of regional organisations in responding to them?

The deliberations revealed some surprising conclusions. The Pacific leaders generally held a very different view of regional security than that assumed and promoted by Australia, New Zealand and the wider Western international community. They saw security in economic rather than strategic terms. They did not share the preoccupation with superpower rivalry uppermost in such conceptions: 'they do not perceive any imminent threat or military intervention or interference by a power from either within or outside the region.' Most surprising of all, they concluded that the activities that threatened or potentially threatened their security came from 'countries which already have a presence within the region and with which relations are, or should be, friendly'. They gave examples of the testing of nuclear weapons, the threat of pollution from dumping of nuclear waste, 'relative economic deprivation', 'incursions into EEZs [exclusive economic zones] by foreign fishing vessels' and restraints imposed on the foreign policies of associated states. They emphasised

---

34 'Concluding Statement', Unpublished summary of the South Pacific Colloquium on the Special Needs of Small States, Victoria University of Wellington, 13–14 August 1984; and personal observations of the author, who was a participant in the colloquium.

the importance of continued regional cooperation through the SPF to deal with these issues and downplayed the need for military security arrangements for intervention in Pacific island states.[35]

The Pacific island leaders made it clear that, if pressed, they would define regional security quite differently, with East–West concerns well down the list and economic security and protection of sovereignty near the top. So defined, the United States was seen as the 'enemy' because of the poaching of the islands' main shared resource, the skipjack tuna, by American vessels. The continued assertion by Pacific island leaders through the mid 1980s that economic security was the name of the game, and that the Soviet Union was playing by the rules while the United States was not, resulted in a significant concession from the United States: an agreement to pay for access to tuna fishing grounds, which went against the general principles the United States had been pressing on the jurisdictional rights over highly migratory species of fish.[36]

In a second challenge, in the years following the Wellington colloquium, the Pacific leaders confronted the relatively longstanding operating principles of the Australian and New Zealand approach to regional order, particularly their self-appointed role as regional managers. More conservative Pacific island states criticised Australia and New Zealand for moving outside the anti-Soviet regional order they had themselves constructed, while more radical states condemned Australia in particular for not going far enough on the antinuclear and anticolonial questions, and for being too tied into an order dictated solely by East–West rivalry. The Australian Government was also criticised for its paternalistic diplomatic style, particularly over the issue of Libyan involvement. This resistance grew strongly after the Fiji coups in 1987 because, whether or not they agreed with the military takeover, Pacific island leaders rallied around the right of Fiji to put its own house in order; they therefore opposed moves by Australia and New Zealand to exert pressure through the SPF.[37]

---

35   ibid.
36   ibid.; and personal observations of the author, who was a participant in the colloquium.
37   Roderic Alley, 'The 1987 Military Coups in Fiji: The Regional Implications', *The Contemporary Pacific*, 2(1), 1990: 37–58, at pp. 41–2; Eric Shibuya, 'The Problems and Potential of the Pacific Islands Forum', in Jim Rolfe, ed., *The Asia-Pacific: A Region in Transition*, Honolulu: Asia-Pacific Center for Security Studies, 2004, pp. 102–15.

The Pacific island states also began to question the second-class citizenship assigned to them in the regional security order. Against strong opposition from Canberra and Wellington, first Kiribati, in 1985, and then Vanuatu, in 1987, asserted the right to have a fisheries access agreement with the Soviet Union. Since both Australia and New Zealand had extensive commercial dealings with the Soviet Union, there was general resentment in the region of the denial of that same right to Pacific island states.

NGOs throughout the Pacific—churchpeople, trade unionists, students, women's groups, independence movements and antinuclear groups— also resisted the various brands of Cold War regional order promoted by Australia and New Zealand, and by France, the United Kingdom and the United States. They were organised transnationally across the region in various alliances: the Pacific Trade Union Forum, the Pacific Women's Association, the Pacific Conference of Churches and the Nuclear-Free and Independent Pacific movement. Their vision of an appropriate regional order was one that was nonnuclear, nonaligned, self-determining, nonmilitarist and participatory. At the state level, their positions were variously represented by many of the policies of the Lini Government in Vanuatu until 1987, the Fiji Labour Government of 1987 and the New Zealand Labour Government. Significant social movements within Australia and New Zealand, including a large section of the governing Labor/Labour parties, also supported these positions.

Conclusion

In the mid 1980s, there were, then, at least four contending normative visions of regional security. One was defined in terms of the global concerns of powerful Western countries—the United States, France, the United Kingdom and Japan—and shared by the conservative parties in Australia and New Zealand. It emphasised strategic denial of the Soviet Union and its allies, a continued French presence in the Pacific and opposition to nuclear-free policies. A second vision, promoted by the Labor/ Labour governments in Australia and New Zealand (but with important differences between them on nuclear issues), embraced strategic denial alongside a commitment to countering French nuclear testing and the French colonial presence. A third position represented the shared concerns of Pacific island governments with a more self-determined regional order that might limit infringements of their sovereignty and allow 'legitimate'

Soviet involvement in the region. A fourth vision, emphasising a nuclear-free and economically independent region, was promoted by various NGOs. As we have seen, much of the contest between these contending visions was conducted in the regional organisations and was reflected in decisions about institutional structure, finance, membership, policy outcomes and competition over key regional positions.

The outcome demonstrated that the Pacific island states did have significant sources of power. The Australian and New Zealand governments felt compelled to make important shifts to accommodate the challenge from the region. For example, to gain credibility for its 1987 expectation that Vanuatu should not allow the establishment of a Libyan Peoples' Bureau, the Australian Government bowed to Pacific island state opinion that Australia should close the Libyan bureau on its own soil. In 1988, Australian foreign minister Gareth Evans frankly acknowledged that Australia would have to depart from its established policy approach; he regarded a role of 'agent' for Western interests as no longer workable and advocated 'partnership' instead.[38] Australia and New Zealand also shifted their view of regional security to accord with broader notions emanating from the region. While still holding Cold War concerns uppermost, they had to acknowledge the Pacific island states' concerns with economic security if the damage caused by the breaching of strategic denial were to be contained. The United States also adopted this view after being persuaded that failure to concede might cause Pacific island states to 'go to the Soviets'. Australia also diluted its notion of strategic denial when foreign minister Hayden announced in 1987 that Australia would now welcome 'constructive engagement' in the South Pacific by the Soviet Union.[39]

At the same time, important elements of the Canberra/Wellington vision of regional security prevailed over that propounded by Washington, Paris and London. The establishment of the nuclear-free zone graphically illustrated this, as did the successful campaign to have New Caledonia returned to the purview of the UN Special Committee on Decolonization.

---

38   Gareth Evans, 'Australia in the South Pacific', Address to the Foreign Correspondents' Association, Sydney, 23 September 1988, pp. 9–10. For further elaboration on these points, see Greg Fry, '"Constructive Commitment" with the South Pacific: Monroe Doctrine or New "Partnership"?', in Greg Fry, ed., *Australia's Regional Security*, Sydney: Allen & Unwin, 1991, pp. 120–37.

39   David Hegarty, *South Pacific Security Issues: An Australian Perspective*, Working Paper No. 147, Canberra: Strategic and Defence Studies Centre, The Australian National University, December 1987, p. 1.

The pull, then, was towards conceptions of regional security promoted by the seemingly less powerful states, but not reaching as far as the vision promoted by NGOs. An internal rift within the Vanua`aku Pati in 1987, and the forced removal by the military of Timoci Bavadra's Coalition Government in Fiji in the same year, removed the two Pacific island governments that most shared the regional security vision of the civil society groups.

The Cold War regional security lens was so dominant in Western framings of the Pacific island region from the mid 1970s to the late 1980s that, with its ending, it was difficult for outside powers to continue to imagine the existence of a Pacific island region at all. The idea of region-building had become so attached to the securing of Oceania for Western interests in a global struggle that the end of the Cold War made Western interests question their motives for being involved in region-building. It was as if the idea of region and the imperative to build a stronger regional political community only made sense in the context of existential threat. This was particularly the case in Australia and New Zealand, where there had been a big investment in academic and policy circles in securing the island region according to their own strategic denial vision with its implications for the structure of regional governance.

In Canberra and Wellington, a sense of purpose in Pacific region-building was restored only with the rise of a commitment to establishing a regional economic order based on neoliberal principles from 1994. An economic framing of the islands was now to take over from a security framing for the next two decades. Before we examine this attempt to build a regional economic order on neoliberal principles, we first need to explore the last key strand of the contest over region-building in the 1970s and 1980s— that of the attempt to impose a framing of the regional governance of development on 'modernisation' principles.

10

Negotiating Pacific island development in the post-independence era[1]

In the 'new South Pacific' of the 1970s and 1980s, 'development' sat alongside 'security' and 'self-determination' as one of the key global discourses impacting on the way Pacific island societies were organised. As elsewhere in the postcolonial world, development was the main preoccupation of the new national governments. Much of the debate about what form development should take, what ideas it should contain and how Pacific societies should engage with the global economic order was conducted at the regional level. This debate was explicit in relation to the establishment of development-oriented regional organisations such as the SPEC and regional enterprises such as Air Pacific, and in relation to joint approaches to negotiating Pacific interests in trade and resource protection. It was also implicit in the contending views on Pacific island development contained in regional reports and assessments by international agencies and donor countries, and in the dissenting views and regional assessments of Pacific NGOs. Policy-related academic studies also emphasised a regional discourse on development in their characterisations of, and recommendations for, an idealised Pacific island state economy.

1   Parts of this chapter were first published in 'International Co-operation in the South Pacific: From regional integration to collective diplomacy', in W. Andrew Axline, *The Political Economy of Regional Cooperation* (London: Pinter, 1994). I am grateful to the publishers for permission to reproduce this work.

The leaders of postcolonial states in the 1970s were confronted with inherited colonial economies with a narrow base of primary industries, foreign ownership and a large, vibrant village-based subsistence economy. With low tax revenue, the new states were immediately dependent on the export-oriented industries and markets established in the colonial period, as well as on economic assistance from their departing colonial power. As well as the economic imperative of finding funds to financially support the operations of the new state, the populace had expectations that there would be a focus on development to provide improved education and health services.

The new Pacific states were starting from very different economic bases. There was considerable variation in the size of economies—for example, between the larger and more complex economies of Fiji and Papua New Guinea and the smaller, simpler economies such as those of Tonga and Western Samoa. There was also a significant variation in the main export industry—for example, gold and coffee in Papua New Guinea, sugar and gold in Fiji, copra in Western Samoa, phosphate in Nauru and citrus fruit in Cook Islands. They also had very different land areas and resources. But they held in common the challenges of remoteness from markets and accessibility to appropriate transport. They also had in common a large rural population living in an efficient and self-sustaining subsistence economy. The majority of Pacific islanders produced most of their own food.

The development objective and approach that the Pacific leaders promoted at the regional level in the 1970s reflected a tension between two contending discourses: a global liberal discourse emphasising economic modernisation and growth and the 'Pacific way' discourse with its emphasis on preserving Pacific cultural values and asserting Pacific control of the development agenda.

Liberal 'modernisation' ideas

We saw in Chapter 4 that, in the late colonial era, region-building in the Pacific was associated with particular European ideas of 'native welfare'. The focus was on providing training and education to develop skills in making the transition from a 'traditional' to a 'modern' world. This was particularly reflected in the work program of the SPC in the

1950s and 1960s.[2] At the time of independence, Pacific governments were working in a global context in which particular Western ideas of modernisation as the only path to development for postcolonial states were dominant. A central tenet of this modernisation discourse emphasised *economic* development and self-sustaining economic growth as the ultimate objectives.

However, the economic modernisation discourse of the 1970s was not pure market liberalism of a kind that would be recognised by Adam Smith or later embraced by neoliberals. It departed from pure market liberalism in advocating, or at least allowing for, a significant role for the state sector in the economy and even promoting some aspects of a command economy through the advocacy of development plans. It also encouraged a transfer of economic assistance to kickstart developing economies on the road to self-sustaining economic growth. The agents of this economic modernisation discourse, which dominated all development thinking in newly independent countries, were the departing colonial governments, international agencies, donor countries and development advisers in the national planning offices in Pacific island capitals.

Liberal modernisation theory was also the dominant discourse at the regional level. It was promoted by Western countries, international agencies and the academy as the development norm for region-building. The key liberal idea influencing region-building was the assumption that regional integration was the most effective approach for postcolonial states to achieve economic modernisation.[3] The idea of making one larger economy, following the European experience, was also promoted in Africa, the Caribbean and Latin America. This global discourse was a major influence on the thinking of Pacific leaders as they began to set up their own regional institutions in the early 1970s. This regional integration discourse was based on several seemingly compelling liberal premises: that larger units do better than smaller ones (particularly very small ones); that rationalisation of industry across the region would maximise economies of scale, or at least reduce the diseconomies of scale that would otherwise occur; that small countries could not each afford shipping lines, universities, airlines and development banks; that a free-trade area would be trade-creating for the region; and that cost-cutting

---

2   See Smith, *South Pacific Commission*, Chs 8–10.

3   See, for example, Joseph S. Nye, ed., *International Regionalism: Readings*, Boston: Little, Brown & Co., 1968.

could be achieved through bulk purchasing. These ideas were implicit in the early proposals of the SPF, in the tasks given by the first forum to a committee on trade, which met in 1971, and in the tasks given to the newly created SPEC in its founding agreement.[4]

There were, however, two influential tenets of liberal modernisation theory, applied at the regional level, which departed from classical liberal economic theory. The first was that developing states should be regarded as a special category in the global market, requiring special assistance in regional trade arrangements with the industrialised North. The liberal modernisation paradigm of the 1970s accepted, and indeed promoted, the idea of nonreciprocal preferential regional free-trade schemes—a departure from the assumption of pure liberal free-trade theory. This approach assumed that developing states needed special treatment to enter the market on a fair basis. This was very attractive to Pacific states trying to establish infant industries behind tariff protection. The creation, in the 1970s, of the South Pacific Regional Trade and Economic Co-operation Agreement (SPARTECA) with Australia and New Zealand, and the Lomé Convention with Europe, represented a meeting of minds between Pacific island governments and their Global North partners on this liberal modernisation idea. As we shall see in Chapter 11, this was not the case with subsequent attempts by Northern partners to negotiate replacement free-trade areas based on neoliberal principles.

The second major departure from pure liberal theory was the idea that 'smallness', and especially the small *island* state, should constitute a special category in the global political economy, deserving of special treatment. This was a concession over and above the exceptions granted to developing states in the global market. It involved recognition of the special disadvantages of smallness, island-ness and remoteness, and advocated appropriate additional support in response. This discourse began with a depiction of the small island state 'problem' and ended with region-building as a key solution to the problem.[5] The international community's depiction of an idealised small Pacific island developing state created a highly influential regional preconception for development policy in the Pacific.

---

4 SPF Secretariat, *Final Communiqué: South Pacific Forum, Wellington, 5–7 August 1971*; and *Final Communiqué: South Pacific Forum, Canberra, 23–25 February 1972*.
5 Burton Benedict, 'Introduction', in Burton Benedict, ed., *Problems of Smaller Territories*, London: Athlone Press for the Institute of Commonwealth Studies, 1967, pp. 1–10, at pp. 9–10.

The academic discourse on 'smallness' was primarily initiated and developed by economists and geographers.[6] The policy community in the international agencies such as the United Nations Conference on Trade and Development (UNCTAD) and the Commonwealth Secretariat were also prime agents in developing the 'smallness' concept and category.[7] From the early 1970s, the international community began to recognise that 'developing island states' formed a special category in development terms, sharing problems that were not only quantitatively, but also qualitatively, different from those of larger continental developing countries. This recognition first became evident in the context of UNCTAD III in May 1972. The conference recommended that a panel be set up to examine the special problems faced by developing island countries, giving particular attention to the difficulties associated with isolation.[8] In 1976, UNCTAD IV took the issue further, recommending special assistance for all developing island countries.[9] The following year, the UN General Assembly requested that the relevant UN agencies incorporate UNCTAD IV's recommended actions within their programs.[10]

The United Nations went a step further than merely recognising island states as a special category and implementing special programs for them through its agencies. Particularly important for our present purposes is that the UN agencies came to regard regional cooperation as an effective means of approaching these problems. The panel of experts that emerged as a result of UNCTAD III stated:

---

6   See, for example, Percy Selwyn, *Small, Poor and Remote: Islands at a Geographical Disadvantage*, Discussion Paper 123, Sussex: Institute of Development Studies, 1978; R.T. Shand, ed., *The Island States of the Pacific and Indian Oceans: Anatomy of Development*, Development Studies Centre Monograph No. 23, Canberra: Development Studies Centre, The Australian National University, 1980. For a critical perspective on the usefulness of 'island-ness' as a category/concept in conjunction with 'smallness', see Percy Selwyn, 'Smallness and Islandness', *World Development*, 8(12), 1980: 945–51.

7   See, for example, Edward Dommen, 'Some Distinguishing Characteristics of Island States', *World Development*, 8(12), 1980: 931–43.

8   United Nations Economic and Social Council, *Special Economic Problems and Development Needs of Geographically More Disadvantaged Developing Island Countries*, E/5647, New York: ECOSOC, 27 March 1975, p. 1.

9   United Nations Conference on Trade and Development [hereinafter UNCTAD], *Proceedings of the United Nations Conference on Trade and Development: Fourth Session, Nairobi, 5–31 May 1976. Volume 1: Reports and Annexes*, E.76.II.D.10, New York: United Nations, 1976, available from: unctad.org/en/Docs/td218vol1_en.pdf, Part 1, s. A, Resolution 98 (iv).

10   United Nations General Assembly, *Progress in the Implementation of Specific Action in Favour of Developing Island Countries: Report of the Secretary-General*, A/32/126, New York: United Nations, 28 June 1977, p. 3.

[T]he regional aspect is central to any consideration of developing island problems ... basically regional co-operation between groups of island countries is needed in order to carry out activities which it is difficult or impossible for them to carry out individually.[11]

Significantly, the UN General Assembly, in its thirty-second session (in 1977), urged

the United Nations organisations concerned, in particular the United Nations Development Programme and the regional commissions, to give attention to programmes of regional and sub-regional co-operation in respect of developing island countries.[12]

The Pacific leaders not only embraced this global discourse on 'smallness'; they also took actions to extend its utility in their global economic engagements. In a move obviously aimed at encouraging this developing international recognition of island states as a special category, the eighteenth South Pacific Conference (in 1978) 'called on donor countries and international organisations to accept developing Island countries and territories as a special development group' and 'invited aid donors, both bilateral and multilateral, to initiate and undertake special measures and assistance ... to developing Island countries'.[13]

The singling out of small island states as a special category of development need also took place in the Commonwealth Heads of Government Regional Meeting held in Sydney on 13–16 February 1978. The SPEC Secretariat prepared a paper for the meeting emphasising the shared special needs of Pacific island states. The Pacific was successful in having the meeting recognise the need for special assistance; it requested that the Secretary-General of the Commonwealth examine ways to support such countries.[14]

---

11   UNCTAD, *Developing Island Countries: Report of the Panel of Experts*, New York: United Nations, 1974, p. 20.
12   United Nations General Assembly, Resolution A126, Thirty-Second Session, para. V.
13   SPC, *Report of the Eighteenth South Pacific Conference*, p. 18, Resolution 13.
14   South Pacific Bureau for Economic Co-operation [hereinafter SPEC], *The Special Problems of Small States: The Developing Island Countries of the South Pacific, Commonwealth Regional Meeting, Sydney, 13–16 February 1978*, Suva: SPEC, 30 December 1977; and M.T. Somare, 'Closing Address by the Prime Minister of Papua New Guinea, the Right Honourable M. T. Somare', Press release, Commonwealth Heads of Government Regional Meeting, Sydney, 16 February 1978, pp. 9–10.

In summary, liberal modernisation ideas provided the dominant framing of the objectives and approaches of regional development in the 1970s. However, the 'regional integration', 'smallness' and 'nonreciprocal free trade' discourses heavily influenced the definition of the problem and the desired pathway for moving towards a regional norm of development. While accepting many of the liberal premises of modernisation theory, the Pacific leaders were also influenced by another homegrown discourse in their region-building activities. These ideas moderated the influence of the global discourse of liberal modernisation.

The 'Pacific way' discourse

From the start of the SPF in 1971, and even before, at the creation of PIPA in 1965, Pacific leaders made it clear that their shared goal in regional collaboration was to renegotiate the foundations and terms of the Pacific's engagement with the global economy. This was aimed at getting a better deal within the global liberal capitalist system. As we saw in Chapter 6, the SPF was partly created on the idea of challenging neocolonialism, overcoming dependency and facilitating collective diplomacy to negotiate a better deal within global economic structures.

Allied to this—and forming part of the same 'Pacific way' ideology discussed in Chapter 6—was a commitment on the part of the Pacific leaders to defend Pacific cultural values in any negotiation of the transfer of the economic modernisation model to the Pacific. All Pacific island states protected customary land tenure even as they pursued modernisation. At the regional level, there was also a powerful discourse stressing the importance of not accepting anything in modernisation theory that would unduly damage these cultural traditions. Just after the creation of SPEC in 1973, its Deputy Director-General, Ken Piddington, found it necessary to stress the significance of this commitment to a New Zealand audience:

> The Bureau has been instructed not to transpose 'international' recipes for economic development but rather to work out how these recipes need to be rewritten for the South Pacific … Economic progress is the goal, but it will only be pursued on terms which are acceptable to the Governments and peoples of the Island nations.

> SPEC's message is a simple one; we recognise the need for accelerated economic development in the region; we are convinced that the key to this lies in a collective effort; but it must be pursued in harmony with local values and local attitudes—in brief, economic progress through regional co-operation 'in the Pacific Way'.[15]

For various members of the regional intelligentsia, meeting at the Seminar on Social Issues in National Development conference at the USP in 1973, there was an even stronger expression of these two key aspects of the 'Pacific way' discourse on development. They were concerned both with the need to temper powerful modernisation discourses with social developmental norms drawn from Pacific cultures and with changing the neocolonial economic relations restricting Pacific island states' control of their own economies. Such a stance was indicated in the title, *The Pacific Way*, given to the collection of papers from this important workshop.[16] In his introduction to the collection, Ron Crocombe states that 'the real fear of becoming neo-colonial puppets, subservient and manipulated, concerned many speakers'.[17] More effective regional cooperation was seen as one of the 'essential prerequisites to stem the neo-colonial tide'.[18] A number of speakers—among them John Momis from Bougainville (later its president), Sione Tupouniua from Tonga (an academic) and Francis Bugotu from Solomon Islands (later the Minister for Education)—called for strategies that would lessen neocolonial dependence. As Bugotu put it:

> The challenge for us Pacific Islanders is not to stand wide-eyed at one side of the arena, blankly watching our interests being manipulated and aspirations changed by foreigners … The task is to find a design for a future which serves our interests, and need not necessarily be patterned on western lines, nor serve western strategic, economic or political aims.[19]

At first, in the 1970s, there was a broad meeting of minds between the Pacific island states and regional civil society on the 'Pacific way' discourse on development. The experience of region-building in the 1970s,

---

15   Ken Piddington, *The South Pacific Bureau: A New Venture in Economic Co-operation*, Wellington: New Zealand Institute of International Affairs, 1973, pp. 3, 16.

16   Sione Tupouniua, Ron Crocombe, and Claire Slatter, eds, *The Pacific Way: Social Issues in National Development*, Suva: South Pacific Social Sciences Association, 1975.

17   Crocombe, 'Seeking a Pacific Way', p. 6.

18   ibid., p. 6.

19   Francis Bugotu, 'Decolonising and Recolonising: The Case of the Solomons', in Tupouniua et al., *The Pacific Way*, pp. 77–80, at p. 77.

however, provoked a radical critique of the 'Pacific way' discourse as being complicit with the more exploitative aspects of liberal modernisation. This new gulf between civil society and the government elites on the development question also reflected the growing influence of the global discourse of neo-Marxism as a critique of global capitalism in the 1980s.

Regional integration in practice

In the 1970s, the SPF decided to work actively on regional integration and instructed its research arm, SPEC, to explore and initiate various regional integration projects. In the event, proposals for comprehensive regional economic integration, such as economic union, free trade and industrial rationalisation, did not pass initial inspection by consultants and committees. They failed largely on the basis of the supporting arguments as examined by officials and consultants rather than because of the political positions of member countries in formal negotiations. Industrial rationalisation was thought to be premature when an industrial base simply did not exist in the island countries, except in Fiji. Interisland trade was minimal; their products were either the same (for example, copra, bananas) or, where different, were not the type of product that other island states had the capacity to process (for example, copper, phosphate, gold, nickel). While a regional free-trade area would benefit Fiji's economic development, it would be damaging to the other island economies. Incorporation in a wider free-trade area with Australia and New Zealand had similar implications. The larger countries would simply attract investment and employment, leaving the island economies with little chance for development. Significantly, SPARTECA did not establish a regional free-trade area; instead, it negotiated a Lomé-style agreement, which accorded nonreciprocal access for island products into the Australian and New Zealand markets.[20]

Thus, comprehensive regional economic integration was effectively removed from the regional agenda in the early years of the SPF's activities. Forum states focused instead on sectoral integration, particularly in

---

20 *South Pacific Regional Trade and Economic Co-operation Agreement*, Signed in Tarawa, Kiribati, 14 July 1980, available from: www.forumsec.org/wp-content/uploads/2018/02/South-Pacific-Regional-Trade-and-Economic-Co-operation-Agreement-SPARTECA-1.pdf. For an early critique of SPARTECA, see William Sutherland, 'Australia's Economic Relations with the South Pacific: A Pacific Perspective', in Brendan O'Dwyer, ed., *Australia and the South Pacific*, Canberra: Centre for Continuing Education, The Australian National University, 1982, pp. 63–73.

education and training, and shipping and civil aviation. Some prominent regional institutions, such as the USP and Air Pacific, had already been created in these sectors in the last years of the colonial period. They became controversial in the 1970s as Pacific island leaders outside Fiji began to question whether these Fiji-based institutions were adequately serving their interests.[21] Although conducted by SPF members, the debate over the character of these institutions took place largely outside forum meetings.

It was to be expected that these issues would prove controversial. Decisions about international transport were vital for new island states that were geographically isolated and totally dependent on metropolitan countries for services. Most were on air and sea routes regarded as uneconomic. Furthermore, commitment to a regional arrangement meant that the prestige gained from having a national flag carrier would be forgone. It would also require a substantial commitment of resources.

The idea of a regional airline, based on an expansion of the existing Fiji Airways, was first developed in the late 1960s by the British, Australian, New Zealand and Fiji governments. In 1968, the (British) Western Pacific High Commission on behalf of the British Solomon Islands Protectorate, the Gilbert and Ellice Islands colony and the Kingdom of Tonga, joined the existing shareholders in the consortium—Qantas, Air New Zealand, the British Overseas Airways Corporation (BOAC) and the Fiji Government. In the following year, Western Samoa and Nauru became shareholders and, in 1971, Fiji Airways changed its name to Air Pacific.[22]

By the early 1970s, however, it was evident that, among the island states, only Fiji was keen to develop Air Pacific further as a regional consortium. Despite their shareholdings in Air Pacific, the independent island countries were clearly interested in developing their own national airlines. Nauru had already established Air Nauru in 1969, and Polynesian Airlines, with the Western Samoan Government as majority shareholder, was set up in the same year. In 1972, in a move described as beginning 'the cancer which has eaten away at Air Pacific's strength', Nauru formally withdrew from the board of Air Pacific while retaining its

21   The dissatisfaction with the USP is examined in Ron Crocombe and Uentabo Neemia, 'Options in University Education for the Pacific Islands', *Pacific Perspective*, 12(1), 1983: 5–17.
22   Based on author's interview with Captain P. Howson, former chairman of Air Pacific, Sydney, 19 July 1976.

shareholding.[23] In the following year, the King of Tonga first announced his intention of establishing a national airline and Papua New Guinea established Air Niugini. The other island states demonstrated their lack of commitment to the development of Air Pacific by their reluctance to increase their shareholdings as the metropolitan airlines withdrew and the airline required more capital for expansion. As a result, Fiji became a majority shareholder and the airline became increasingly identified as a national carrier.

After the Rarotonga SPF meeting in March 1974, Ratu Mara had warned that 'the South Pacific Forum will stand or fall on civil aviation … Civil aviation will be the real test of Pacific regional co-operation'.[24] Two months later, he was saying that 'civil aviation is a notable failure'.[25] The idea of a regional carrier was effectively at an end. While various proposals for cooperation among national airlines, such as rationalisation of air routes and cooperation on the purchasing of equipment, would later be countenanced, full sectoral integration in the civil aviation field was effectively off the agenda until proposed again, unsuccessfully, by Australian prime ministers Paul Keating, in 1994, and John Howard, in 2003. The main reason for this failure was the perception held by island states that Air Pacific was dominated by Fiji. They pointed to the fact that it was Suva-based, it had its origins in Fiji, Fiji was the main shareholder and Fijians gained the most from the employment provided by the airline. And, it was claimed, Fiji subsidised internal airfares by setting fares on certain regional routes higher than they should be.[26]

The bitterness this issue engendered was felt not only on one side. It was clear that Fijian leaders took offence at the rising complaints about Fijian dominance. At the 1974 Fiji Tourism Convention, for example, Ratu Sir Penaia Ganilau, the Minister for Communications and Tourism, 'lashed out' at Western Samoa and Tonga. He criticised them for not committing themselves to a 'single regional airline' and complained they both 'benefitted from the Air Pacific consortium and had an influence over Air Pacific's plans, but Fiji received no corresponding benefit from these countries'.[27]

---

23   Stuart Inder, 'Up Front with the Editor', *Pacific Islands Monthly*, June 1974: 3.
24   'Forum Co-op Wanted, Not a Talking Shop', *Pacific Islands Monthly*, May 1974: 105.
25   Mara, 'Regional Co-operation in the South Pacific', p. 13.
26   Inder, 'Up Front with the Editor'.
27   *Pacific Islands Monthly*, June 1974, p. 75.

The failure of the 'one regional airline' concept had important spillover effects on other areas of regional cooperation. The neofunctionalist theory of regional integration underpinning European integration at this time assumed spillover effects in a positive direction as success in one sector influenced success in other sectors. In the Pacific case, however, this was a spillover effect that threatened to take regional integration in the other direction. This was the first major issue causing division among the Pacific island states. Although the negotiations were conducted largely outside SPF meetings, the experience significantly affected the willingness of these states to cooperate on substantive issues within the SPF in its early years. For those Pacific states other than Fiji, their experience of what they saw as Fiji's dominance within Air Pacific affected their perception of Fiji's role within the regional movement more generally.[28]

The experience was also a disillusioning one for Fiji. The lack of support for the consortium and the public criticism of Fiji's role in the venture by its partners caused Fiji to reappraise its attitude to regional integration. By 1975, Ratu Mara had tired of the constant criticism of Fiji's role. In a statement to the press in November of that year, he indicated considerable disillusionment with regionally run organisations such as Air Pacific and the USP. He drew attention to the difficulties associated with joint management of a regional program or institution. In particular, he objected to the fact that under such an arrangement the 'pace of development is determined by the slowest member'. He cited as an example the conflict concerning whether the USP should have chairs in accounting and engineering.[29] Fiji supported this move because of its requirements for such skills while smaller countries opposed it because they did not have economies in which such skills were in demand.

Ratu Mara advocated a move away from joint management of regional institutions to a situation in which the host country was responsible for the running of the regional institution. This, he thought, would ensure that 'development would be determined by the fastest'.[30] When Ratu Mara made this statement, he had in mind the proposed Regional

28 Based on interviews conducted by the author during a fieldtrip through the region, September to December 1975.
29 Fiji Ministry of Information, 'The Prime Minister's Post-Cabinet Press Conference', News Release No. 625, Suva, 13 November 1975.
30 ibid.

Telecommunications Training Project then before the Fiji Cabinet. Significantly, it was subsequently established as a Fiji-run regional organisation with places available for others in the region.

The establishment of a regional shipping line was the only exception to the general trend towards disillusionment and the retreat to nationalistic positions that dominated the early years of the SPF in relation to regional economic governance. Whereas Air Pacific and the USP were part of the colonial inheritance, the shipping line was homegrown. Beginning as a proposal within PIPA in 1971, it was taken over by the newly formed SPEC as a major initiative in 1973. The first proposal considered by SPF countries in the period 1973–74 was for a regional shipping corporation.[31] Some members found it unsuitable because they thought it would require too much capital commitment. In addition, Nauru and Tonga were not keen to sacrifice their national shipping lines for an untried regional line. Consequently, SPEC was sent back to the drawing board to work up a more acceptable proposal.

The proposal that was ultimately accepted was a 'pooling' concept: an operating company that would charter ships from member countries.[32] This overcame most of the obstacles that had confronted the earlier proposal. The capital outlay was not prohibitive, existing national shipping lines were not threatened, shareholdings were equal, profits and losses were to be shared equally and its establishment was based on a detailed market survey showing potential commercial viability. Consequently, the Pacific Forum Line began operations in 1978. Its shareholders—all SPF members except Australia and Niue—contributed only A$12,250 to the share capital of the line. The line initially chartered three vessels from its 'shipping members': Nauru, Tonga, Western Samoa and New Zealand. It was the only significant example of sectoral integration established by the island states, and even here the level of integration was limited to a pooling concept.

Unlike the Air Pacific experience, the significant divisions that occurred among Pacific states in relation to the shipping line concerned its formation and proposed form rather than its operations once established. There were

---

31 Francis Hong Tiy and R.G. Irwin, *A Survey of the Development of Inter-Government Proposals for a Multi-National Regional Shipping Line in the South Pacific*, Discussion Paper for the Papua New Guinea Harbours Board South Pacific Ports Conference, Port Moresby, 17–19 March 1975.
32 SPEC, *Director's Annual Report 1976/77*, pp. 19–20, and *Director's Annual Report 1977/78*, p. 20; "'If We Break Even, We'll Be Laughing': PFL's Modest Aim', *Pacific Islands Monthly*, August 1978: 77–9.

significant variations in the level of enthusiasm for the venture. Western Samoa was the main supporter. Unlike Fiji, it was not well served by shipping and, unlike Tonga and Nauru, it did not have its own national line. Fiji's experience with Air Pacific made it at first reluctant to support the formation of a regional shipping line, but Ratu Mara was reported as having moderated this attitude at the Rarotonga SPF meeting in March 1974:

> [H]e had almost decided not to support a regional shipping line because of Fiji's experience with [the] regional airline, but having heard the afternoon's discussion, he had come around again to supporting it in principle.[33]

From this point it appears that Fiji adopted a position of qualified support—the qualification being that the line should be financially viable. The Air Pacific experience also affected how Solomon Islands initially viewed the proposal. Its perception of a Fiji-dominated Air Pacific made it sceptical about how such a line would operate.[34]

By the end of the 1970s, it was clear that Pacific island states were wary of economic integration schemes requiring high capital outlay, centralisation in one island state or a sacrifice of national autonomy. The USP and the Pacific Forum Line were the only examples of a significant degree of sectoral integration. Under vice-chancellor Maraj's leadership, the USP maintained its regional support during the 1970s by decentralising the campus. New campuses and units—set up in Western Samoa, Kiribati and Tonga and promised at that time for Vanuatu—went some way to placating regional concerns about the uneven distribution of benefits.[35] The Pacific Forum Line succeeded at that time because it did not involve high-level integration. The 'pooling' concept, involving an operating company that would charter ships from member countries, allowed an identifiable national component in this regional scheme and kept capital outlays to a minimum. In most areas of cooperation, the emphasis shifted to the supplementation of national efforts through shared expertise, information and coordination, rather than a more ambitious level of sectoral integration.

---

33   SPF Secretariat, 'Summary Record and Final Press Communiqué'.

34   Based on author's interview with chief minister Solomon Mamaloni, Solomon Islands, September 1975.

35   Ron Crocombe and Malama Meleisea, 'Achievements, Problems and Prospects: The Future of University Education in the South Pacific', in Ron Crocombe and Malama Meleisea, eds, *Pacific Universities: Achievements, Problems, Prospects*, Suva: Institute of Pacific Studies, University of the South Pacific, 1988, pp. 341–87, at p. 359.

The Pacific island states were fortunate they did not venture far down the path of comprehensive or sectoral integration common in other parts of the developing world at this time. Had they done so the experience would have likely poisoned any chance of moving to the more workable forms of cooperation later achieved. Their attempts at significant sectoral integration in tertiary education and civil aviation indicated the kinds of tensions that would have pulled more ambitious schemes apart. Regional management boards are not like corporation boards in the private sector. They are composed of representatives of national governments in a context where the most desirable outcome for 'the region' is not necessarily the most desirable outcome for an individual state or, at least, for the politicians running the state. Moreover, despite the assumption of shared 'smallness', isolation and product range, which has informed the dominant approaches to regional development, there was in fact considerable variation among Pacific island states. These differences quickly revealed a serious rift between the centrally located, relatively large and well-endowed Fiji and the other participating states over the costs and benefits of sectoral integration.[36]

There was not only the issue of equity; there was also the question of whether the individual state could achieve a more cost-effective result outside the regional scheme. There were also the political costs. For politicians, the visible national venture, however irrational in terms of economic theory, was far more likely to earn local support than a regional venture headquartered in some distant island country.

Resetting the terms of global economic engagement

In the 1980s, Pacific cooperation on development found its strength in the shift in emphasis from regional integration to collective diplomacy—joint action aimed at resetting the terms of the Pacific's global economic engagement. Collective diplomacy of this kind was in fact evident right from the start of the SPF; and, by the end of the 1970s, there had already been some significant successes.

---

36   These rifts are examined in Neemia, *Cooperation and Conflict*.

Trade diplomacy

The SPF employed this approach, for example, in relation to negotiations with the EEC over the Lomé Convention. The Pacific Group, coordinated by the SPEC, successfully represented the interests of Pacific island states. Prior to the expiration of the Yaoundé Convention, which governed the economic association between the EEC and the former African colonies of France, Belgium and Italy, the EEC invited these African countries, together with former colonies within the Commonwealth, to negotiate a new association with the community. The Pacific states that qualified for membership were Western Samoa, Fiji and Tonga. Following a SPEC study on 'whether and on what conditions' the three should seek associate status, it was agreed they would 'negotiate with the enlarged Community as a group'.[37] In January 1974, the prime ministers of the Pacific countries 'endorsed the value of the collective approach' to the negotiations that had begun in Brussels in July of the previous year.[38] The SPF leaders gave SPEC the task of coordinating and servicing the group's approach to the negotiations and, in February 1974, SPEC's deputy director established a Pacific Group Secretariat in Brussels.

According to Fiji Government sources, the Pacific Group had a relatively significant impact on the negotiations. They claimed that Ratu Mara, as spokesperson for the group, was influential, particularly in relation to the acceptance of the principle of an export utilisation scheme.[39] Ratu Mara was subsequently appointed chairman of the African, Caribbean and Pacific Group Council of Ministers and, in April 1977, he hosted a meeting of the council in Suva. Significantly, this was the first global grouping hosted in the Pacific. From July 1978, SPEC again became the coordinator of the Pacific Group in negotiations for the successor treaty to the Lomé Convention. This time the Pacific Group included Papua New Guinea, the Gilbert Islands (later called Kiribati), Tuvalu and Solomon Islands.[40]

---

37 'Third South Pacific Forum: Final Communiqué', *New Zealand External Relations Review*, September 1972: 26–30, at p. 28; and Ratu Sir Kamisese Mara, *Report on Foreign Affairs for the Period 10 October 1970 – 31 December 1973*, Parliamentary Paper No. 19, Suva: Parliament of Fiji, 1974, p. 7.
38 SPEC, *Director's Annual Report 1973/74*, p. 6.
39 The Fijian Government, *The Lomé Convention: How It Benefits Fiji*, Suva: Government Printer, 1975.
40 SPEC, *Director's Annual Report 1977/78*, p. 31.

The SPF also facilitated a collective Pacific approach to the Australian and New Zealand markets. As we have seen, the SPF and SPEC, its economic research arm, had been established to, among other things, create a more favourable balance of trade with developing countries. As major trading partners for the island states, Australia and New Zealand were obvious focal points for regional diplomacy. In the early years of the SPF, Ratu Mara led Pacific island state pressure on Australia and New Zealand to consider preferential access into their markets for Pacific island products.[41] Australia and New Zealand resisted this pressure, arguing that any such move would be counter to the most-favoured nation principle under the General Agreement on Tariffs and Trade.[42] Fiji countered with the example of preferential access being negotiated in the proposed Lomé Convention with Europe.

Ultimately, the Pacific island states' argument prevailed. It was significant that the thinking in Canberra had already changed direction in granting the newly independent Papua New Guinea preferential access under the Papua New Guinea–Australia Trade and Commercial Regional Agreement signed in Port Moresby in 1976.[43] Following a study of possible options for industrial development and regional trade, the director of SPEC hinted in his 1977–78 annual report that it was time for SPEC to move on the question of regional trade policy. At the subsequent SPF meeting in September 1978, the Pacific leaders resolved that senior trade officials should meet to consider

> the possibility of a preferential non-reciprocal arrangement between Australia, New Zealand and Pacific island countries as well as other measures aimed at improving trade and industrial development in the region.[44]

With Australia and New Zealand now persuaded, negotiations moved quickly: SPARTECA was signed by most member states in Tarawa, Kiribati, in July 1980. All states had signed by 1982.

---

41 Tarte, 'Fiji's Role in the South Pacific Forum', p. 99.

42 SPF Secretariat, *South Pacific Forum, Suva, Fiji, 12–14 September 1972: Summary Record of Proceedings, (Confidential)*, Suva: SPF Secretariat, 1972, pp. 18–29.

43 *Agreement on Trade and Commercial Relations between the Government of Australia and the Government of Papua New Guinea*, entered into force on 1 February 1977.

44 SPEC, *Director's Annual Report 1977/78*, p. 14; and SPEC, *Press Communiqué: Ninth South Pacific Forum, Alofi, Niue, 29 September 1978*, Suva: SPEC, 1978, p. 2.

SPARTECA was

> a nonreciprocal trade agreement under which the two developed
> nations of the South Pacific Forum, Australia and New Zealand,
> offer duty free and unrestricted or concessional access for virtually
> all products originating from the developing island member
> countries of the Forum.[45]

As such, the agreement was welcomed as a good deal for the Pacific
island states, in that it was seen to have the potential to restructure the
trade relationship and create future opportunities for trade expansion.
The sting, however, was in the detail; the exceptions schedule as well as
country-of-origin provisions meant that the projected change in the trade
balance was not realised. From the mid 1980s, academic critiques joined
the concerns of the Pacific leaders, and of the regional secretariat, on this
question. Writing in 1986, William Sutherland argued that SPARTECA
had not delivered on the key objective of addressing the highly unequal
trade relationship with Australia and New Zealand.[46] On the contrary,
he argued, based on figures prepared for SPEC, New Zealand imports
from SPF island countries decreased in real terms by 4.9 per cent while
Australian imports from SPF island countries decreased by 24.9 per cent.[47]
In the same year, Max Robertson drew attention to three critical points
that were being taken up at the political level by Pacific leaders: that the
liberalisation of access provisions in the initial SPARTECA had not been
very generous; that the value content rules were severe and had been
administered unsympathetically; and that the smaller SPF island countries
considered that SPARTECA had little to offer them.[48]

Law of the Sea and the archipelagic principle

The SPF was also successful in facilitating a collective approach to the Law
of the Sea negotiations during the 1970s. It formed the Oceanic group
that successfully represented the views of the island states, particularly in
relation to the rights of archipelagic countries. From the first SPF meeting

---

45 SPF Secretariat, *SPARTECA: South Pacific Regional Trade and Economic Co-operation
Agreement—A Reference Handbook for Forum Island Country Exporters*, Suva: SPF Secretariat, 1989.
46 William Sutherland, 'Microstates and Unequal Trade in the South Pacific: The SPARTECA
Agreement of 1980', *Journal of World Trade Law*, 20(3), 1986: 313–28.
47 ibid., p. 322.
48 Max Robertson, 'The South Pacific Regional Trade and Economic Cooperation Agreement:
A Critique', in R.V. Cole and T.G. Parry, eds, *Selected Issues in Pacific Island Development*, Canberra:
National Centre for Development Studies, The Australian National University, 1986, pp. 147–75.

in 1971, the Pacific states recognised the advantages to be gained from taking a joint approach to the UN Law of the Sea conferences.[49] A special Law of the Sea Forum was held in May 1974 to develop a common position for the approaching UN conference in Caracas. The special forum meeting decided to promote the setting up of a broader 'island lobby' to support Fiji's 'archipelagic principle'—a key issue for island states. As put to the UN Seabed Committee in New York in March 1973 by the Fiji delegate, S. Nandan, the principle was:

> An archipelagic State, whose component islands and other natural features form an intrinsic geographical, economic and political entity, and historically have or may have been regarded as such, may draw straight baselines connecting the outermost points of the outermost islands and drying reefs of the archipelago from which the extent of the territorial sea of the archipelagic State is or may be determined.[50]

The Oceanic Group, as the SPF grouping came to be known in the context of these negotiations, met prior to UN Law of the Sea meetings in 1975 and 1976. In its joint declaration on the subject in October 1976, the SPF declared the intention of its member countries to establish 200-mile exclusive economic zones and affirmed their interest in a comprehensive Convention on the Law of the Sea, which satisfied 'the special concerns of archipelagic and other island states'.[51] Their successful joint diplomacy on the Law of the Sea set the foundation for later achievements in tuna diplomacy and ocean management.

Resource diplomacy

From the mid 1970s, two major developments drew the attention of the South Pacific states to the possibility of cooperating in the management of their marine resources. One was the large-scale movement into South Pacific waters of the fishing fleets of the United States, South Korea, Japan, Taiwan and the Soviet Union, in search of skipjack tuna. The other

---

49 'South Pacific Forum', *Current Notes on International Affairs*, [Canberra], August 1971: 431; 'South Pacific Forum', *New Zealand External Relations Review*, January 1972: 28; and 'Third South Pacific Forum: Final Communique', *New Zealand External Relations Review*, p. 29.

50 S.N. Nandan, 'Statement to the Meeting of the UN Seabed Committee, New York, 15 March 1973', in Mara, *Report on Foreign Affairs*, Appendix IV, p. 35.

51 SPEC, *Director's Annual Report 1974/75*, p. 19, and *Director's Annual Report 1975/76*, pp. 43–4. The text of the joint declaration was issued with the press communiqué of the October 1976 special SPF meeting. See 'South Pacific Forum', *Australian Foreign Affairs Record*, p. 556.

was the island states' declaration of exclusive economic zones, which, due to the archipelagic nature of the island states, amounted to a joint claim over control of marine resources in nearly the whole of the South Pacific Ocean. Pacific island countries began to recognise that they shared a highly valued marine resource but that if it was to avoid being fished out by the distant water fishing nations (DWFNs), with little return to the island states, it would require joint management.

The negotiations to establish a regional agency to carry out this task were conducted within the SPF between 1976 and 1979. At the 1976 SPF meeting, leaders were stimulated by a paper prepared by the Fiji Government on the implications of developments then taking place in the Law of the Sea negotiations. At the conclusion of the forum, they made a declaration (the Nauru Declaration) in which, among other things, they indicated their intention of exploring the possibility of developing a coordinated approach to negotiations with DWFNs and to maritime surveillance and policing.[52] An SPF officials meeting held later in the year recommended the establishment of a regional fisheries agency and the 1977 SPF meeting endorsed this proposal in the Port Moresby Declaration.[53]

In turning this intention into a convention acceptable to all SPF members, the negotiators ran into two major obstacles over the next two years. One concerned the proposed role of the agency. Was it to be solely a resource management role or was it also to be concerned with maximising the returns on this resource for island states? The other was a related point: should DWFNs be members of the organisation? The draft convention worked up by officials for the 1978 SPF meeting in Niue envisaged a resource management role for the agency. This was unacceptable to most of the leaders at Niue, who asked for a redrafting of the convention to bring it more in line with the sentiments of the Nauru and Port Moresby declarations.[54]

---

52 SPF Secretariat, 'Declaration on Law of the Sea', in *Seventh South Pacific Forum, Nauru, 26–28 July 1976*, Suva: SPF Secretariat, 1976, available from: www.forumsec.org/seventh-south-pacific-forum-nauru-26-28-july-1976-3/.

53 SPF Secretariat, 'Declaration on Law of the Sea and a Regional Fisheries Agency', in *Eighth South Pacific Forum, Port Moresby, Papua New Guinea, 29–31 August 1977*, Suva: SPF Secretariat, 1977, available from: www.forumsec.org/8th-south-pacific-forum-port-moresby-papua-new-guinea-29-31-august-1977/.

54 Florian Gubon, 'History and Role of the Forum Fisheries Agency', in David J. Doulman, ed., *Tuna Issues and Perspectives in the Pacific Islands Region*, Honolulu: East–West Center, 1987.

The question of membership of the proposed agency created a significant rift between Pacific island states at the Niue SPF meeting.[55] US membership was supported by a Western Samoa–led group, while a group led by Papua New Guinea and Fiji—which included Solomon Islands, Kiribati, Nauru and Tonga—took the view that US membership should be opposed on the grounds the United States did not recognise coastal state sovereignty over the highly migratory skipjack tuna, which was the main resource the agency would be controlling. Fiji's position was made clear in the month following the SPF meeting when, in an address to the UN General Assembly, its ambassador, Berenado Vunibobo, stated:

> We have now reached a situation where the formation of such an agency is threatened … The main reason for this sorry state of affairs has been due to the wishes of a dominant power foreign to the region, to join the Agency on its own terms … We view this … as yet another attempt to dominate our region and to dictate to us the terms and conditions in which we should run our affairs.[56]

An additional objection, held particularly by Papua New Guinea, was that the United States, as one of the main DWFNs, should not be a member of an agency controlling the activities of such nations on behalf of the South Pacific states. The issue was not resolved at the SPF. By the end of the meeting, the Papua New Guinea/Fiji group was threatening to set up its own fisheries agency. As a compromise, it was decided to proceed with the establishment of an agency comprising only the SPF countries, leaving the question of DWFN membership for further negotiation. A redrafted convention establishing the new Honiara-based South Pacific Forum Fisheries Agency (FFA) was subsequently signed at the 1979 SPF meeting.[57]

Virtually as the ink was drying on the convention, some of the FFA members were already negotiating the formation of a more exclusive alliance comprising those island states that enjoyed a relatively large share of the region's tuna resources. These discussions culminated in 1981 with the creation of the 'Nauru Group', comprising five Micronesian states (Federated States of Micronesia, Kiribati, Marshall Islands, Nauru and

---

55   Jones, 'US Tuna Fishing a Divisive Issue for Forum Members'; and *Sydney Morning Herald*, 'Islanders Wary of US Bait'.

56   As reported in *The Canberra Times*, '"New Colonialism" Over Fishing'.

57   SPF Secretariat, *Leaders Communiqué: Tenth South Pacific Forum, Honiara, Solomon Islands, 9–10 July 1979*, Suva: SPF Secretariat, 1979, available from: www.forumsec.org/tenth-south-pacific-forum-honiara-solomon-islands-9-10-july-1979/.

Palau) and two Melanesian states (Papua New Guinea and Solomon Islands).[58] Although they made it clear this move was not to be seen as threatening the unity of the FFA, and that the Nauru Group would be working closely with the FFA, it inevitably was seen by some as doing just that. The formation of the Nauru Group reflected a feeling of frustration with the difficulties and time involved in establishing the FFA. These countries particularly wanted to sharpen the resource diplomacy and maritime surveillance aspects of regional fisheries management. The negotiations leading to the creation of the FFA had made them concerned about the commitment of the Polynesian states to move firmly on these issues. They established a regional register of vessels and agreed minimum terms for their bilateral negotiations with DWFNs. They worked closely with the FFA, including FFA representatives in their negotiations and using the FFA as their secretariat. The FFA also took over the Nauru Group's regional register of vessels.[59]

The existence of the Nauru Group pointed to a division in regional politics that was present in the negotiations leading up to the FFA. This was the division between those countries that were resource-rich and those that were resource-poor—geographically, a split between the west and east of the region. It was also present in the attitudes taken to the FFA's most impressive achievement in resource diplomacy, the treaty between the FFA members and the United States. The rift did not, however, appear significant during the 10 rounds of negotiations between 1984 and the treaty's signing in April 1987. The Pacific island states were united in their desire to extract some return for the enormous amount of tuna being taken out of the region by US purse seine vessels. For 10 years, the United States had been seen as the main threat to the resource security of the Pacific island states because of its failure to recognise the jurisdiction of coastal states over highly migratory species. Spurred on by the Soviet fishing deal with Kiribati in August 1985, and urged on by its regional

58   *Nauru Agreement Concerning Co-operation in the Management of Fisheries of Common Interest*, Nauru, 1981.
59   David J. Doulman, 'Fisheries Co-operation: The Case of the Nauru Group', in David J. Doulman, *Tuna Issues and Perspectives in the Pacific Islands Region*, Honolulu: East–West Center, 1987, pp. 257–77; and Roniti Teiwaki, *Management of Marine Resources in Kiribati*, Suva: Institute of Pacific Studies, University of the South Pacific, 1988, pp. 108–12.

allies Australia and New Zealand, the United States ultimately signed a treaty that overrode both its own legislation and its general position on the Law of the Sea.[60]

Although initially heralded as a mighty achievement for the weak against the strong, the terms of the treaty awakened old divisions in the Pacific island community. The seeds of the rising discontent lay in the treaty's provision to distribute a portion of the A$60 million payment equally among the FFA nations, regardless of the location of the resource or size of catch. The resource-rich—particularly those for whom tuna was the primary income earner, such as Kiribati—began to question why those countries which had no tuna should receive the same as those which had a significant resource. There had been some discussion as to whether the resource-rich states would have done better to negotiate bilateral deals with the American Tuna Boat Association.[61]

Such divisions did not plague the other major achievement in resource diplomacy and management, that of gaining the agreement of Japan, South Korea and Taiwan to a prohibition on driftnet fishing in the South Pacific. All SPF members were very concerned about this new fishing practice of the late 1980s, which threatened to seriously deplete the stocks of albacore tuna. The negotiations, held under the auspices of the FFA, began in Suva in November 1988 among island states. At the first meeting of the FFA's members with DWFNs in June 1989, Japan and Taiwan were intransigent, indicating their intention to continue driftnetting. A year later, Japan announced its intention to suspend driftnetting in the region for the 1990–91 season as a response to the 'grave concerns' of the SPF states. Events had moved quickly in the interim. In July 1989, the SPF states signed the Tarawa Declaration, which signalled their intention to develop a convention establishing a regional ban on driftnetting; in

---

60   *Treaty on Fisheries between the Governments of Certain Pacific Island States and the Government of the United States of America*, Port Moresby, 2 April 1987; SPF Secretariat, *Forum Communiqué: Thirteenth South Pacific Forum*; SPF Secretariat, *Forum Communiqué: Fifteenth South Pacific Forum, Funafuti, Tuvalu, 27–28 August 1984*, Suva: SPF Secretariat, 1984, and *Forum Communiqué: Eighteenth South Pacific Forum, Apia, Western Samoa, 29–30 May 1987*, Suva: SPF Secretariat, 1987; Jon Van Dyke and Carolyn Nicol, 'US Tuna Policy: A Reluctant Acceptance of the International Norm', in Doulman, *Tuna Issues and Perspectives*, pp. 105–32; and Teiwaki, *Management of Marine Resources in Kiribati*, pp. 113–15.

61   See, for example, Roniti Teiwaki's comments, as reported in 'Kiribati Gets Too Much Aid; Must Learn to Say "No" Says Opposition Leader', *Pacific Report*, 6(22), 1993: 6.

October, the Guam South Pacific Conference endorsed the Tarawa Declaration and, in an unprecedented move in the 'no-politics' SPC, criticised Japan and Taiwan in a resolution of the conference.[62]

In the same month, the US House of Representatives endorsed the Tarawa Declaration and urged the US Government to support the efforts of the Pacific states. In November 1989, the Convention for the Prohibition of Fishing with Long Driftnets in the South Pacific (known as the Wellington Convention) was signed by seven SPF states following a meeting with DWFNs at which Japan remained intransigent.[63] In December, the United States, together with the SPF states with UN membership and their supporters, placed a resolution for a ban on driftnetting in the South Pacific before the UN General Assembly. Japan responded with its own resolution calling for scientific evidence for the claims concerning the impact of driftnetting. A compromise was found in UN Resolution 44/225 (1989), which called, inter alia, for a cessation of driftnetting in the South Pacific by 1 July 1991, and until such time as there were 'appropriate conservation and management arrangements for South Pacific albacore tuna resources'.[64]

This achievement was viewed as the high-water mark of South Pacific collective diplomacy aimed at resetting global economic engagements and promoting a Pacific regional interest. The gradual forging of coalitions within the region, within the Commonwealth and then at the United Nations, the use of legal conventions and declarations and the embarrassment of Japan and Taiwan at regional conferences—all contributed to the success of this joint policy. Greenpeace, an international NGO, also played a very significant role in educating Pacific island leaders about the impact of driftnetting.[65] Australia and New Zealand also took

---

62   See SPF Secretariat, *Tarawa Declaration*, Suva: SPF Secretariat, 11 July 1989, available from: www.forumsec.org/tarawa-declaration/; Author's observations at the Twenty-Ninth South Pacific Conference, Agana, Guam, 9–11 October 1989.

63   See SPF Secretariat, *Forum Communiqué: Twentieth Pacific Islands Forum, Tarawa, Republic of Kiribati, 10–11 July 1989*, Suva: SPF Secretariat, 1989; *Forum Communiqué: Twenty-First South Pacific Forum, Port Vila, Vanuatu, 31 July – 1 August 1990*; *Forum Communiqué: Twenty-Second South Pacific Forum, Palikir, Pohnpei, Federated States of Micronesia, 29–30 July 1991*; *Pacific Report*, 19 July 1990; and Richard A. Herr, 'The Region in Review: International Issues and Events, 1989', *The Contemporary Pacific*, 2(2), 1990: 350–7, at pp. 353–4.

64   UN General Assembly, *Large-Scale Pelagic Driftnet Fishing and its Impact on the Living Marine Resources of the World's Oceans and Seas*, A/RES/44/225, New York: United Nations, 22 December 1989, available from: digitallibrary.un.org/record/82553?ln=en.

65   See Michael Hagler, 'Driftnet Fishing in the South Pacific', in Ramesh Thakur, ed., *The South Pacific: Problems, Issues and Prospects*, New York: St Martin's Press, 1991, pp. 95–104.

a major part in the coalition-building in wider international forums and in devising an appropriate legal regime. The FFA secretariat, under the leadership of Phillip Muller, played a major part in putting the issue on the regional agenda, in providing information on the driftnetting practice and in organising the negotiations with DWFNs.[66] Furthermore, all Pacific island states were unified in their outspoken opposition to the practice. This was generally a cost-free exercise for SPF members, although Fiji, for one, was concerned that the legalist approach taken to this issue by Australia and New Zealand might needlessly offend Japan, thereby affecting gains in other areas.[67]

Conclusion

In the 1970s and 1980s, Pacific leaders embraced the economic development goal of the liberal modernisation paradigm, but they tempered this acceptance with a commitment to the defence of Pacific cultural values, particularly as seen in the regionwide protection of customary land tenure. There was also a ready adoption of liberal modernisation's depiction of 'smallness' and advocacy of regional integration as the logical remedy. But, with the failure of regional integration schemes in the 1970s, Pacific region-builders began to focus more on the idea of renegotiating the structures of engagement with the global economy. Here, they were more successful in their regional approach to development. As we shall see, both approaches to region-building for development—regional integration and joint diplomacy aimed at renegotiating the terms of engagement with the global economy— revealed tensions between Pacific states, as well as between the outside world and the Pacific island states. In the 1970s, there was broad accord between political leaders and civil society on the promised assertion of a Pacific regional perspective on modernisation. But increasingly, in the 1980s, this consensus broke down as parts of civil society started to question whether the Pacific way and an elite state-driven regionalism was

---

66   David J. Doulman, 'Fisheries Management in the South Pacific: The Role of the Forum Fisheries Agency', in Thakur, *The South Pacific*, pp. 89–92.
67   Jioji Kotobalavu, 'Trends in Perceptions of Security', in David Hegarty and Peter Polomka, eds, *The Security of Oceania in the 1990s. Volume 1: Views from the Region*, Canberra: Strategic and Defence Studies Centre, The Australian National University, 1989, pp. 25–30, at p. 28.

delivering appropriate development for Pacific peoples. We will examine this critique as it becomes more vocal as an alternative framing of Pacific development in Chapter 11, as part of an exploration of the ascendancy of neoliberalism as a development framework.

11

The neoliberal ascendancy and its critics[1]

The normative framing of the Pacific island region changed dramatically after the Cold War. Western states and global institutions began to view Pacific regionalism primarily through an economic development lens rather than the security lens of previous decades. This new lens reflected the rise to global dominance of the neoliberal political economy. Neoliberal ideas had become dominant within Western countries, as seen most prominently in the Thatcherite and Reaganite revolutions in the United Kingdom and the United States in the 1980s. They also became the dominant ideology of the main international agencies forming the basis of the so-called Washington Consensus during the 1990s.

These ideas became powerful in the Pacific because Western countries— and particularly the European Union, Australia and New Zealand— were now committed to imposing these ideas on the region through aid conditionality, trade liberalisation and the promotion of regional economic integration and 'pooled regional governance'. This amounted to a new interventionism in the Pacific economies not evident in the Cold War years, when the main motivation of Western aid donors had been to outbid their Soviet rival rather than attempting to mould how Pacific island states organised their societies and economies.

---

1   Parts of this chapter were first published in 'Climbing Back onto the Map? The South Pacific Forum and the New Development Orthodoxy', in the *Journal of Pacific History* (29[3], 1994: 64–72).

In terms of the region-building theme of this book, the most important expression of this new framing of the Pacific was the attempt by Australia and New Zealand to promote an institutionalised regional economic order based on neoliberal principles. The international agencies played an important part in providing the authoritative *regional* framing that would underpin the promotion of neoliberal policies at the national level. However, it was Australia and New Zealand—recent converts to the neoliberal ideology in their own political economies—that took this forward as a regional project. In 1994, they launched a major initiative to use the SPF as a key vehicle for creating regional norms to govern state behaviour with regard to development and 'good governance'.

While the neoliberal discourse was the dominant normative frame applied to the Pacific island region by powerful outside actors in the period 1990–2018, there were also competing global development discourses, promoting alternative framings of a preferred regional economic order. These included 'human development', 'sustainable development' and 'radical' perspectives. The dominant neoliberal regional normative frame was also contested by Pacific governments and by regional civil society— sometimes deploying one of these alternative global development discourses and, at other times, promoting a local cultural framing of Pacific regional development. It should be noted that although the contest we are examining here is about influencing *regional* norms, these norms were ultimately about how people should live *within* their states and societies.

The rise of neoliberalism

The neoliberal framing of Pacific development promoted by the main global institutions from the early 1990s laid the foundation for ongoing contests over the form and content of regional economic governance over the next three decades. The World Bank and the IMF had promoted such ideas in their 'structural adjustment' programs for individual Pacific island countries in the 1980s, but it was not until the 1990s that these institutions began to promote neoliberal economic governance as a regional project. This approach was first set out in the World Bank's 1992 and 1993 reports on the Pacific island states, in which it provided an authoritative depiction of a Pacific development problem, which, it argued, needed a Pacific-wide solution. It painted the picture of a typical Pacific island economy as one in trouble (as indicated by low growth figures) and therefore in urgent need of neoliberal solutions.[2] As well as providing this authoritative and influential depiction of the Pacific problem as a rationale for neoliberal programs of privatisation, free trade and market deregulation, it also encouraged donor countries to promote this approach in their economic assistance, by toughening the conditions they attached to such assistance.[3] In its 1993 regional report, *Pacific Island Economies: Toward Efficient and Sustainable Growth*, the World Bank introduced the notion of the 'Pacific paradox' to capture the problem:

> Development performance in the PMCs [Pacific Member Countries] during the last decade or so has been marked by a paradox: virtually no growth (0.1% annually) occurred in average real per capita income during this period despite a favourable natural and human resource endowment, high levels of aid, and reasonably prudent economic management.[4]

The bank explained this paradox primarily in terms of the favouring of 'public sector interventions of low effectiveness, rather than more efficient private sector activity'.[5]

As the basis for a regional approach to development, these neoliberal ideas represented a significant departure from the form of economic liberalism that had previously been promoted as part of region-building projects in the 1970s and 1980s. Neoliberal ideas included a dismantling of the state, privatisation and structural adjustment. Ultimately, this perspective promoted market fundamentalism, employing national growth in gross domestic product (GDP) as the key indicator of success. On international trade, its adherents promoted a 'level playing field' in the form of free trade with no special assistance or concession for small island states. By contrast, the modernisation paradigm, which had previously shaped the regional policies of donor states and international agencies, had been tolerant of significant state involvement in development, and indeed advocated development planning. Furthermore—and of particular relevance for the Pacific—proponents of the earlier modernisation ideas were sympathetic to the granting of preferential treatment for small island developing states in global markets, whereas neoliberals were not.

---

2   World Bank, *Pacific Island Economies: Towards Higher Growth in the 1990s*, Washington, DC: The World Bank, 1991; World Bank, *Pacific Island Economies: Toward Efficient and Sustainable Growth. Volume 1: Overview*, Report No. 11351-EAP, Washington, DC: The World Bank, 8 March 1993.
3   World Bank, *Pacific Island Economies: Towards Higher Growth in the 1990s*, p. 85.
4   World Bank, *Pacific Island Economies: Toward Efficient and Sustainable Growth*, pp. ix, 1.
5   ibid., p. 5.

With the failure of the neoliberal structural adjustment programs throughout the Third World from the mid 1990s, the World Bank developed the 'good governance' concept as a key organising idea for its global development programs. The neoliberal economic ideas were retained as part of the new organising concept but there was a new emphasis on seeing their success as dependent on remaking the postcolonial state to ensure an enabling policy environment. The good governance approach 'was articulated in highly managerial and administrative terms, focusing on public sector management, accountability, the legal framework, transparency and information, and civil society'.[6] Citing the *World Bank Development Report 1997: The State in a Changing World*, Anthony Payne and Nicola Phillips argue:

> [T]he World Bank's policy reform prescriptions thus shifted away from an exclusive focus on macroeconomic stabilization and adjustment to the so-called 'second generation' reform agenda, addressing fiscal reform, labor flexibilisation and the 'modernisation of the state'.[7]

The emphasis on 'good governance' in the programs of the global institutions had a major impact on the contests over the normative basis of region-building in the Pacific. As we shall see below, it became a major pillar of the SPF Secretariat's strategic plan, sitting alongside economic growth and sustainable development.

The promotion of the neoliberal framing of the Pacific island region began as an academic endeavour. Its most dramatic expression was contained in the 'Pacific 2010' project at The Australian National University, which became the basis for the Australian Government's promotion of a new regional economic order in the Pacific from 1994.[8] The *Pacific 2010* report emphasised an impending crisis in the Pacific island region. As expressed in the report, the key issue was 'survival' in a completely changed global strategic and economic order. The Pacific island economies, it was asserted, had 'fallen off the map' since the end of the Cold War and were threatened with further marginalisation by rapid changes in the global trading order. Pacific island societies were portrayed as having arrived at a major crossroads: if they continued along their current path, they

---

6   Anthony Payne and Nicola Phillips, *Development*, Cambridge, UK: Polity Press, 2010, p. 97.
7   ibid.
8   Rodney V. Cole (ed.), *Pacific 2010: Challenging the Future*, Canberra: National Centre for Development Studies, The Australian National University, 1993.

would risk ever-decreasing living standards and, ultimately, in the more extreme descriptions, a 'doomsday scenario' or 'Pacific nightmare'. The other path—that of significant structural adjustment and 'sustainable development'—was said to lead not only to an avoidance of crisis, but also to the possibility of a fast-growing, export-based, self-reliant economy linked to the 'new Asia'.[9]

The way to get back on to the map under these new global conditions, it was argued, was by island governments taking hard decisions: to jettison the plea for special treatment based on small size and to implement effective structural adjustment, which would result in a dynamic private sector able to develop niche export markets within the new global trading structure.[10] The Indian Ocean and Caribbean countries were held out as models of what small island states could achieve. This was, at heart, a case for the necessity of adopting the neoclassical economics model. Although the adherents of these ideas measured economic success in terms of the growth in GDP per capita, they did not advocate growth at any cost. From the early 1990s, the proponents of structural adjustment, following World Bank practice, also embraced a particular concept of sustainable development, which in the Pacific context brought together environmental and resource management agendas. The general ideas contained in the resulting model were not entirely new to South Pacific governments. They had been moving along the structural adjustment and sustainable development path at various speeds since the mid 1980s, encouraged by international agencies and their own economic advisers. What was different about the new orthodoxy, then—which in general terms followed evolving World Bank prescriptions—was not the character of the ideas but the level of commitment to serious and urgent implementation of them, and the attachment of stricter conditionality to economic assistance.

---

9   See, for example, Rowan Callick, 'Pacific 2010: A Doomsday Scenario?', in Cole, *Pacific 2010*, pp. 1–11; Rodney Cole and Somsak Tambunlertchai, eds, *The Future of Asia-Pacific Economies: Pacific Islands at the Crossroads?*, Canberra: National Centre for Development Studies, The Australian National University, 1993; Rowan Callick, 'Time to Shift Pacific Goalposts', *Australian Financial Review*, 16 April 1994: 15.
10   See, for example, Andrew Elek, 'The South Pacific Economies in a Changing International Environment', in Cole and Tambunlertchai, *The Future of Asia-Pacific Economies*; and Rodney Cole and Somsak Tambunlertchai, 'Signposts at the Crossroads of Development in the Pacific', in Cole and Tambunlertchai, *The Future of Asia-Pacific Economies*.

Its regional impact was felt largely in policy developments in the SPF, where neoliberal ideas became institutionalised from the mid 1990s. The other major policy expressions of these ideas were Australia's and New Zealand's promotion of a regional free-trade area with the Pacific island states and the European Union's attempts to establish a regional economic partnership agreement with the region. Over time, this mainstream neoliberal discourse expanded and changed to incorporate 'good governance', 'women and development', 'sustainability', 'human development' and cultural tenets, but only in a form consistent with the core beliefs of neoclassical economics.

Competing development discourses

The ascendancy of neoliberal regional norms (with their incorporation of the sustainable development discourse) in the early 1990s prompted several critical responses. In the same year as the establishment of neoliberal ideas as the main framing perspective for Pacific development at the 1994 SPF meeting, the UNDP promoted the 'sustainable human development' perspective as an alternative paradigm for the Pacific region. It was first introduced at a meeting of Pacific island states (with Australia and New Zealand as observers) in Suva in May 1994. Hosted by the UNDP, the meeting's purpose was to consider the *Provisional Pacific Human Development Report*. The meeting endorsed the new concept and 'confirmed that sustainable human development is consistent with the political commitment for people-centred development which already exists in all Pacific island countries'.[11] The meeting adopted the Suva Declaration on Sustainable Human Development in the Pacific, which, among other things, endorsed enhancing the productivity of the rural and subsistence sectors, the promotion of community-based development, improving access to land, addressing inequality and emerging poverty, promoting the advancement of women, ensuring youth involvement, supporting environmental regeneration and establishing effective governance.[12]

---

11   UNDP, 'Foreword', in *Suva Declaration on Sustainable Human Development in the Pacific*, Suva: UNDP, 1994; and UNDP, *Pacific Human Development Report: Putting People First*, Suva: UNDP, 1994.
12   UNDP, *Suva Declaration*.

At the global level, 'human development' had had a major influence on the development debate since the concept was launched in the UNDP's 1990 global *Human Development Report*. As developed in that first report, the concept of 'human development' provided a critique of the World Bank's emphasis on national growth as the indicator of development progress.[13] Beginning in 1990, the UNDP also initiated the Human Development Index as an alternative measurement of development.[14] As explained in the first *Pacific Human Development Report* of 1994, sustainable human development 'seeks to refocus attention on the ultimate objective of development, to increase the opportunities for people to lead productive and satisfying lives'.[15] While the human development paradigm recognises that 'greater economic growth is a prerequisite for a sustained improvement in human development', it posits that 'for a host of reasons there is no guarantee that growth in income alone will be satisfactorily translated into a general improvement in living standards'.[16] It promotes equitable distribution of income, adequate access to health and education services and building on and recognising the strengths of the subsistence sector and cultural identity.

Although the 1994 SPF communiqué endorsed the Suva Declaration, it is clear these ideas did not at this stage challenge the dominance of the neoliberal ideas promoted by Australia and the World Bank.[17] During the 1990s, the human development discourse was expressed mainly through UNDP programs conducted either at the national level or in partnership with regional agencies concerned with technical cooperation. The SPC— with its emphasis on youth, gender, cultural and other human-centred development programs—was a natural partner in this regard. On the other hand, the key ministerial councils set up to take the neoliberal agenda forward within the SPF were not noticeably influenced by these human development ideas in the 1990s. The UNDP nevertheless continued throughout the decade to champion the human development paradigm, most notably in its *Pacific Human Development Report 1999*.[18] The report

---

13   UNDP, *Human Development Report 1990*, New York: Oxford University Press, 1990.

14   UNDP, *Human Development Index*, New York: UNDP, available from: hdr.undp.org/en/content/human-development-index-hdi.

15   UNDP, *Pacific Human Development Report*, p. 1.

16   ibid., p. 5.

17   SPF Secretariat, *Leaders' Communiqué: Twenty-Fifth South Pacific Forum, Brisbane, Australia, 31 July – 2 August 1994*, Suva: SPF Secretariat, 1994, para. 4.

18   UNDP, *Pacific Human Development Report 1999: Creating Opportunities*, Suva: UNDP, June 1999.

emphasises several key themes: the increasing poverty and inequality in the region, the importance of sustainable livelihoods as an objective of development regardless of the level of economic growth and the problems associated with focusing too much on economic growth at the expense of social impacts.[19]

A second, alternative development perspective—which we might dub the 'radical' perspective on development—was associated with civil society groups, churches and the women's movement. It focused on inequality, human development and gender as well as taking a critical view of growth-oriented and deregulation policies focused on national growth at the expense of communities. It was critical of structural adjustment strategies as a way of reorganising Pacific economies and societies. It was most forcefully expressed in *Sustainable Development or Malignant Growth?*, a volume of critical essays written by Pacific women and published in the same year (1994) as the key SPF meeting that launched the neoliberal regional order.[20] These ideas had first entered the regional debate with the Development Alternatives with Women for a New Era (DAWN) conference on women, the environment and development in the Pacific, held in Suva in 1992.[21] In her introductory chapter, Atu Emberson-Bain argues:

> [T]here is little questioning (at the official level at least) of the purpose and ramifications of the free market ideology being peddled by the new-look colonial 'missionaries' of the 1990s—the powerful global financial institutions like the World Bank and the International Monetary Fund (IMF) which are the effective ghost-writers/directors of regional development policy.[22]

Although the critical development perspective presented in the volume appears to share many of the same positions as the 'human development' and 'sustainable development' perspectives, Atu Emberson-Bain is careful to distinguish it from these perspectives. She presents these discourses as having been coopted in the Pacific context by the dominant market (neoliberal) ideology:

---

19   ibid., pp. 4–7.
20   Atu Emberson-Bain, ed., *Sustainable Development or Malignant Growth? Perspectives of Pacific Island Women*, Suva: Marama Publications, 1994.
21   Atu Emberson-Bain, 'Introduction: Sustaining the Unsustainable?', in ibid., p. i.
22   ibid., p. ii.

> The concepts of sustainable and human development take on board the reassuring (politically correct) language of the international community but do not appear to have inspired fundamentally new development approaches. They continue to be guided by the sacrosanct policies of the market and economic growth.[23]

Emberson-Bain argues that the sustainable and human development paradigms, at least as promoted in the Pacific regional institutions, have inherent contradictions because of their stated commitment to free-market and economic growth principles as well as human-centred development. She posits that the economic restructuring associated with free-market policies has disturbing outcomes for human-centred development and for the environment. These include:

> The relinquishment by Pacific island states of their long-held responsibilities for providing basic educational, health and welfare services; the weakening of both modern democratic and traditional cultural institutions by the imposition of market or adjustment policies without community consent, and often in spite of popular resistance; the emergence of a 'new' culture of conflict and violence that embraces state-sponsored militarism, coercive labour practices, and community conflict over resource-revenue benefits; and the openings for greater foreign domination of Pacific Island economies created by privatisation and deregulation policies.[24]

These ideas draw their lineage from the 'Pacific way' critique of development in the 1970s considered in Chapter 10. While they failed to influence the regional policy debate that was taking place in the SPF in the 1990s, their later resurfacing in the context of the Pacific Plan and in relation to free-trade negotiations in the 2000s was more influential. The greater commitment to the inclusion of civil society voices in the region-building project in the second decade of the 2000s created an opportunity not allowed by the state-centric, top-down regionalism of the 1990s.

Taken together, then, these alternative development perspectives did not impact on the ascendancy of the neoliberal paradigm in the 1990s. The human development ideas were treated as an add-on to the main game of promoting neoliberalism through the SPF. Like gender and sustainable development perspectives and (later) 'good governance' commitments,

---

23   ibid., p. iv.
24   ibid., p. vi.

the human development concept was coopted by the neoliberal project and did not challenge the central commitments to economic growth and restructuring and deregulating in line with free-market principles. As we shall see, however, these human-centred perspectives on development reappeared at various points in the regionalism story over the next three decades with ever-increasing influence.

One idea central to both the moderate and the radical critiques of the neoliberal perspective was the need to defend traditional cultural practices and communal land tenure. This was a view also shared by the political leadership of the Pacific island states and it was therefore one that had a major influence on the form of neoliberalism that came to dominate in the Pacific. For example, in October 1994, at the Port Vila South Pacific Conference, Pacific leaders pushed back against the neoliberal policy of moving away from communal land tenure to free up land for investment. At the planned themed discussion on land questions, Melanesian chiefs from several island countries spoke about the cultural significance of communal land tenure. At the end of the meeting, the Australian Minister for Development Cooperation and Pacific Island Affairs, Gordon Bilney, said he had learnt a lot from the discussion. From that point, land reform was dropped from the Australian Government's regional policy on promoting a neoliberal order.[25]

Institutionalising the regional neoliberal economic order

The Australian Labor Government under prime minister Keating was the prime mover in translating neoliberal ideas into a regional policy agenda. From early 1994, Bilney worked towards translating the Pacific 2010 recommendations into a regional strategy. Capitalising on the opportunities offered by Australia's hosting of the Twenty-Fifth South Pacific Forum in Brisbane in July of that year, the minister focused on the meeting as a potential point of departure.

---

25 Based on observations of the author, who attended the South Pacific Conference in Port Vila in 1994.

The tone of the SPF's deliberations had already been set by Bilney's speech to the Foreign Correspondents' Association in Sydney in June 1994.[26] In a declaration that was millenarian in tenor, he said:

> [I]t is our hope that we shall be able to seize the moment [the Brisbane SPF meeting] to launch ourselves with a fresh determination, on the crucial task of preparing our region for the challenges of a new century.[27]

Broadcast by satellite to island capitals, the message was a development of the assumptions contained in the Pacific 2010 project's 'Pacific doomsday scenario' and the 'falling off the map' thesis as well as the World Bank's 'Pacific paradox'. The speech was intended to set a new agenda— to confront directly the failure, as the minister saw it, of Pacific island governments to address seriously sustainable development issues or to adequately prepare their countries for changing global conditions. He saw the solution in public sector reform, private sector development, the possible abandonment or adaptation of 'old social and economic attitudes', making traditional land-use patterns more compatible with the needs of investors and giving consideration to the appropriateness of maintaining costly national airlines. In the post–Uruguay Round international trading environment of diminishing preference margins, Bilney saw 'no realistic alternative to competition and the pursuit of comparative advantage, no matter how daunting these concepts may appear'.[28]

Some prominent islander economists and central bankers reportedly shared the minister's concerns. They had 'recently been urging Australia … to talk frankly and toughly to their own politicians'.[29] In his address at the launch of the National Centre for Development Studies' Pacific 2010 Colloquium at Australia's Parliament House in June, Sir Mekere Morauta, Governor of the Bank of Papua New Guinea, certainly indicated his agreement with the main tenets of Bilney's doomsday scenario. The doomsday scenario, he said, 'is not surrealistic. The seeds of that scenario have been planted in every Melanesian state, and are growing daily.'[30]

---

26   Gordon Bilney, 'Australia's Relations with the South Pacific: Challenge and Change', Address to the Foreign Correspondents' Association, Sydney, 15 June 1994 [published as Briefing Paper No. 34, Canberra: Australian Development Studies Network, The Australian National University, July 1994], available from: openresearch-repository.anu.edu.au/bitstream/1885/9989/1/Bilney_AustraliasRelations 1994.pdf.
27   ibid., p. 6.
28   ibid., p. 5.
29   Rowan Callick, 'Tough Talking in the Pacific', *Australian Financial Review*, 27 June 1994.
30   Sir Mekere Morauta, 'Melanesia in the Twenty-First Century', Address at the Launch of Pacific 2010 Project, Parliament House, Canberra, 30 June 1994, p. 1.

However, some Pacific leaders clearly had reservations about the more extreme claims of a potential 'nightmare' that underlay minister Bilney's position and which were enlarged by the Australian media. In a television interview during a *Lateline* program on 'the Pacific nightmare', the prime ministers of Papua New Guinea, Fiji and the Cook Islands rejected the image of impending crisis and the purely economistic analysis of the 'doomsday' approach.[31] Cook Islands prime minister, Sir Geoffrey Henry, also indicated his concern with the generalised accusations in Bilney's statement:

> There is no question that we must all address the problems facing the region—and each is doing that—but to brush generally over the Pacific and say 'you are all a bunch of failures' … [Bilney] should have named the countries in his speech and not just thrown a net across the Pacific … I know for a fact the speech was not well received in the Pacific.[32]

At the Brisbane SPF meeting in 1994, the Pacific island leaders nevertheless agreed on a series of measures aimed at supporting the implementation of structural adjustment ideas through regional action. The leaders agreed that finance ministers would meet to consider, among other things, 'appropriate policy responses to maximise opportunities and minimise threats resulting from changes to the global economic environment', and directed the SPF Secretariat to take a more active role in advising member governments on private sector development.

A second set of decisions emanating from the twenty-fifth SPF was concerned with promoting regional integration: the consideration of regional free-trade arrangements by trade ministers, exploration of bulk purchasing and the rationalisation of civil aviation. As we have seen, these are very old ideas in the context of South Pacific regional cooperation. Their return after a 20-year absence reflected the new influence of neoliberal ideas within the SPF, particularly as promoted by Canberra and Wellington. The rationale for such an approach was much the same as that which underlay the initial enthusiasm for these ideas—that larger units do

---

31   Kerry O'Brien and Margot O'Neill, 'Pacific Nightmare', *Lateline*, Sydney: Australian Broadcasting Corporation, 1 August 1994, available from: trove.nla.gov.au/work/21232284?q&versionId=25338293.
32   'Cook Islands Prime Minister Applauds Resources Theme of Forum Meeting', *Pacific Report*, 7(15), July 1994: 5.

better than smaller ones; that a free-trade area would be trade-creating for the Pacific area; that small countries cannot each afford a national airline; and that cost-cutting could be achieved through bulk purchasing.

While the neoliberal conception of 'development' was dominant in the decisions of the Brisbane SPF, the leaders departed from a purely neoliberal perspective in supporting a series of environmental measures in line with the sustainable development agenda set at the 1992 UN Conference on Environment and Development in Rio de Janeiro and the 1994 UN Global Conference on Sustainable Development of Small Island States in Barbados. These built on programs and commitments that had been developed under SPF auspices since 1991. Although environmental issues such as nuclear testing and dumping of radioactive waste had featured on SPF agendas for many years, the comprehensive commitment to environmental protection measures under the rubric of sustainable development was a new phenomenon. Spurred by the increased prominence of environmental concerns in mainstream economic thinking, Pacific island states were now supporting, to varying degrees, regional measures aimed at confronting their own environmental problems as well as those caused by larger states. But serious regional input into this effort through the South Pacific Regional Environment Program was still at a very early stage.

Throughout the second half of the 1990s, there was a concerted effort by the Australian and New Zealand governments to institutionalise the new regional development norms established at the 1994 Brisbane SPF meeting. The form of regional governance that began to dominate was the regional harmonisation of national laws, regulations and policies. There was now more emphasis on regional management of the structural reform agenda for Pacific states. Political scientist and former Deputy Secretary-General of the Pacific Islands Forum Secretariat, William Sutherland, argues that 'the increased pace and scope of reforms that occurred in the islands from the mid 1990s onwards cannot be explained outside the context of the donor-driven regional reform agenda'.[33]

To facilitate the new agenda, Australia and New Zealand pushed for the creation of the Forum Finance Ministers Meeting as a new part of the SPF structure. This was agreed at the 1994 SPF meeting and the first Forum Finance Ministers Meeting, financed by Australia, was held in Suva in

---

33   William Sutherland, 'Global Imperatives and Economic Reform in the Pacific Island States', *Development and Change*, 31(2), 2000: 459–80.

February 1995. The Forum Finance Ministers Meeting adopted a procedure of monitoring through reporting on agreed specific objectives—a level of accountability unusual in Pacific regional governance. The reform agenda pursued through the Forum Finance Ministers Meeting focused on the regional harmonisation of national regulations and practices in areas such as privatisation, transparency of investment, lowering of tariffs, accountability and output-based budgeting.[34] The 1996 SPF meeting expanded the scope of the Forum Finance Ministers Meeting deliberations to include all economic issues and changed the name accordingly to the Forum Economic Ministers Meeting (FEMM). The first FEMM was held in Cairns, Queensland, in July 1997. Sutherland argues that

> by the second half of 1998 the regional reform agenda was well and truly in place … the new pattern was clear: for the region as a whole, reforms were now deeper, more extensive and gathering steam.[35]

A key move in setting the reform agenda in place was the Economic Action Plan agreed in 1997 at the Cairns FEMM chaired by the Australian Treasurer. The action plan provided the blueprint for the implementation of neoliberal reforms across the region. Crucially, the action plan encapsulated the finance ministers' agreement to 'encourage the adoption of a set of best practice principles for public accountability' and to 'pursue a common goal of free and open trade and investment'.[36] At the same meeting, the ministers also agreed to the eight principles of accountability, which together became the new regional norm on 'good governance'. SPF secretary-general Noel Levi argued that 'governance and accountability are the core of the Forum Economic Ministers Action Plan'. He went on to argue that 'promoting good governance in all its aspects … is an essential element of the framework within which economies can prosper'. 'Government attitudes and policies towards good governance and accountability', he asserts, 'are also a critical pre-condition to attracting foreign direct investment and to generating sustainable economic growth'.[37] Reviewing the regional impact of these 'good governance' principles in 2001, Levi concludes:

34   ibid., p. 466.
35   ibid., pp. 469–70.
36   FEMM, *Action Plan: Forum Economic Ministers' Meeting, Cairns, 11 July 1997*, Suva: SPF Secretariat, 1997.
37   PIFS, 'The Forum's Eight Principles of Accountability: A Progress to Date', Press statement by Mr W. Noel Levi, Secretary-General of the Pacific Islands Forum, Suva, 27 February 2001, available from: www.pireport.org/archive/2001-07-30.

> Since the adoption of the Eight Principles of Accountability, most
> Pacific Island Countries have undergone substantive public sector
> reform and private sector development strategies and programmes
> designed to generate economic growth and to improve standards
> of living.[38]

The neoliberal framing of Pacific 'development' within the SPF's programs included a core commitment to trade liberalisation. This commitment emerged in the context of the rise of free-trade ideology at the global level from the late 1980s, culminating in the establishment of the World Trade Organization (WTO) in 1995. Australia and New Zealand had also embraced free-trade ideas in their national and Pacific policies, and this was another major contributing factor. The 1997 FEMM proposed that the SPF Secretariat explore free-trade options.[39] Following a consultant's report, the secretariat's advice to member governments was for Pacific island governments to set up a Pacific island country– only free-trade agreement as a stepping stone that would not expose the Pacific to competition from Australia and New Zealand in the first instance. Australia and New Zealand objected strongly to this proposal and fought hard—and some argue overbearingly—to change the terms in which this would occur.[40] This determination on the part of Canberra and Wellington was only partly motivated by economic ideology; it was also about not being left out of any major regional arrangement for strategic reasons. They were also motivated by knowledge of the European Union's intention to negotiate a free-trade agreement with the Pacific.

The outcome was seen as a partial win by both sides. The Pacific island states signed a free-trade arrangement among themselves, the Pacific Island Countries Trade Agreement, and they also signed an agreement with Canberra and Wellington, which would trigger negotiations for a free-trade area with Australia and New Zealand once the Pacific began negotiations on free trade with third parties (the European Union). This was a pyrrhic victory for Australia and New Zealand as it created distrust among the Pacific island leaders concerning their dominance and role in the region—a point we will explore in greater detail in Chapter 13.

---

38   ibid.
39   FEMM, *Action Plan* (1997).
40   Jane Kelsey, *Big Brothers Behaving Badly: The Implications for the Pacific Islands of the Pacific Agreement on Closer Economic Relations (PACER)*, Suva: Pacific Network on Globalisation, 2004.

By the end of the 1990s, then, there was a neoliberal ascendancy in the framing of the regional economic order. The commitments to a neoliberal program of deregulation, accountability ('good governance'), free trade and privatisation had gone beyond agreed declarations and guidelines. It had been institutionalised in the operation of the FEMM and its reporting procedures as well as in the SPF Secretariat's policies. There had been occasional push back from the Pacific leaders against the purely economistic view of development and a concern for a more holistic approach that took in cultural and human values. We saw this in 1994 with the signing of the Suva Declaration and, again, after the Brisbane SPF meeting in 1994, when the leaders made clear their commitment to the defence of communal land tenure in the face of the pressures of neoliberal proposals. Sutherland also notes two occasions in the 1990s when SPF chairs appealed for development with a more human face. The first was in 1997, as SPF host, prime minister Henry of Cook Islands

> suggested that reforms ought to go beyond conventional economic dimensions and urged consideration of the need for Pacific cultural values and norms to be the basic premise and foundation for the whole reform process.[41]

The second occasion was in 1998 when the SPF host, Marshall Islands president Jacob Nena said:

> We as Forum leaders should not reform just for the sake of reform … we must not fall into the trap of encouraging economic growth for growth's sake alone and at the cost of more important aspects of true Pacific prosperity.[42]

The rising challenge from human-centred development

In September 2000, the global community endorsed the UN Millennium Declaration and the human development goals it authorised. This new global consensus signalled the rising influence of the human development paradigm and a serious challenge to the global ascendancy of neoliberalism. This change was reinforced by the failure of neoliberalism

---

41 Sutherland, 'Global Imperatives and Economic Reform in the Pacific Island States', p. 476.
42 ibid., p. 477.

as a development strategy in the 1990s and the growing self-criticism by some key economists who had been part of the promotion of the Washington Consensus in the World Bank and the IMF. In particular, the Asian Financial Crisis had revealed the failures of the neoliberal strategies pursued by these agencies.

This global change in development thinking was reflected in the rising influence of human-centric development ideas in the economic assistance policies of the main development partners of the Pacific states: Australia, New Zealand and the European Union. This, in turn, started to influence the framing of Pacific regional development. As we saw earlier, Pacific island leaders had signed on to human development ideas in their 1994 Suva Declaration, but this commitment had largely been displaced in the 1990s by the efforts of Australia and New Zealand to institutionalise the neoliberal paradigm through the SPF and the FEMM. We saw occasional efforts to assert Pacific cultural positions and to soften the neoliberal reform agenda, but these did not go far. However, with the advent of the Millennium Development Goals (MDGs) at the global level, from 2000, human development ideas began to influence the framing of development in the PIF and the framing of existing human development programs in other regional agencies.

The Pacific leaders signed on to the global millennium declaration in September 2000. In March 2003, a UN and Council of Regional Organisations in the Pacific (CROP) MDG working group was established to provide oversight of the region's response to the global MDG process. It is significant that the PIF Secretariat (PIFS) was one of the organisers, along with the UNDP, the ADB and the SPC, and that, as chair of CROP, PIFS provided the chair of this working group.[43] At the 2003 annual PIF meeting, the leaders:

> Recognised the broad relevance of the Millennium Development Goals to the Pacific … and their usefulness in focusing and improving the integration of planning for sustainable development, and in the monitoring of progress.[44]

---

43 Secretariat of the Pacific Community, 'The Pacific Islands Regional Millennium Development Goals Report', Paper presented to the Thirty-Fourth Meeting of the Committee of Representatives and Administrations, Nouméa, 16–19 November 2004 (SPC/CRGA 34), pp. 1–2.

44 PIFS, *Leaders' Communiqué: Thirty-Fourth Pacific Islands Forum, Auckland, New Zealand, 14–16 August 2003*, Suva: PIFS, 2003, para. 7.

Meanwhile, the SPC, with its longstanding interest in technical cooperation in human development–related issues, became the key regional agency working on the preparation of regional reporting to the global MDG process. The UNDP and SPC jointly prepared the first Pacific regional MDG report in 2004.[45] This was a natural fit. In its 2003–05 corporate plan, the SPC listed 'achieving the international community's development goals in the Pacific' as one of its key objectives.[46] In 2003, the SPC established an MDG taskforce to assist member countries in the development of 'the MDG approach'. The neoliberal frame (including good governance, trade liberalisation and deregulation commitments) was still dominant in the FEMM, but the PIF had begun to take on an oversight role on the MDGs and to give rhetorical commitment to their significance as a new separate framing of Pacific regional development; and the SPC had adopted the MDGs as a new policy frame for its human development programs.

From Pacific Plan to the framework for Pacific regionalism

In 2003, Australia and New Zealand became the principal drivers of a new era of region-building focused on deepening regional integration through a revitalised PIF. Among other things, this was an attempt to take the institutionalisation of the neoliberal economic order to a new level. This amounted to a further ratcheting up of the existing efforts to promote regional economic integration through harmonisation of national laws and target-setting and monitoring through regional ministerial meetings. For Australia, the commitment to a more effective regional effort in promoting a regional neoliberal economic order was explicitly motivated by a security imperative: the 'war against terror'. It was part of the Howard Government's new doctrinal approach to the Pacific, underpinned by its view that Australia had a 'special responsibility' to look after 'our patch'.[47] In the context of developing the rationale for intervention in Solomon

---

45 Secretariat of the Pacific Community, 'Pacific Islands Regional Millennium Development Goals Report', Paper presented to the Thirty-Fourth Meeting of the Committee of Representatives and Administrations, Nouméa, 16–19 November 2004 (SPC/CRGA 34).

46 ibid., p. 1.

47 'Howard: Solomons Could Have Become a Haven for Terrorists', *Sydney Morning Herald*, 23 July 2003; and John Howard, 'Transcript of the Prime Minister the Hon. John Howard MP Interview with Kerry O'Brien, The 7:30 Report, ABC', 25 June 2003.

Islands in mid 2003, Howard promoted the idea of the pooling of regional resources as a means of small nonviable states finding the resources to govern and to avert the longer-term economic problems producing state failure and inviting terrorism.[48]

As the August 2003 PIF meeting approached, Helen Clark, prime minister of New Zealand, also indicated her government's commitment to create a much more effective PIF to confront the issues that her government had been very active in providing assistance with in recent years: development, law and order and conflict situations. While not embracing the 'special responsibility' or 'war on terror' motivations of the Howard Government, the Clark Government, as PIF chair, was very keen to give leadership to the reframing of regionalism as practised by the PIF. Indeed, it was Clark, rather than Howard, who was the main driver of the reform process from the 2003 PIF meeting to the adoption of the Pacific Plan in 2005.[49] Reflecting on this commitment, Clark said it was necessary if the Pacific was not to descend into a 'ghetto of conflict and poverty'.[50]

The other Pacific leaders at the 2003 Auckland PIF meeting agreed to the chair's call for a renewal agenda and agreed to set up the Eminent Persons' Group (EPG) to conduct the first comprehensive review of the PIF.[51] The EPG was chaired by Sir Julius Chan, former prime minister of Papua New Guinea, and comprised several prominent members: Dr Langi Kavaliku of the Kingdom of Tonga; Teburoro Tito, former president of Kiribati; Maiava Iulai Toma, the Samoan ombudsman; and Robert Cotton, a former Australian diplomat and senator. The New Zealand Ministry of Foreign Affairs provided the secretariat.

Reflecting the urgency to act quickly, particularly as seen by the PIF chair (prime minister Clark), the EPG reported to a special PIF meeting in Auckland in April 2004 after consulting widely in the Pacific at both state and civil society levels. At the 2004 PIF meeting, the Pacific leaders had before them an EPG proposal for future directions and an outline of the principles on which a future Pacific 'community of states'

48   'Transcript of the Prime Minister, the Hon. John Howard MP, Press Conference', Canberra, 22 July 2003.
49   Nicola Baker, 'New Zealand and Australia in Pacific Regionalism', in Greg Fry and Sandra Tarte, eds, *The New Pacific Diplomacy*, Canberra: ANU Press, 2015, pp.137–48, at p. 143.
50   Sean Dorney, 'Regional Security and Corruption the Focus of Pacific Forum', *The World Today*, ABC News, 6 April 2004, available from: www.abc.net.au/worldtoday/content/2004/s1082146.htm.
51   PIFS, *Leaders' Communiqué: Thirty-Fourth Pacific Islands Forum*.

should be based.[52] A vision statement outlined the general concept; its implementation awaited the drawing up of the Pacific Plan. The April 2004 special PIF meeting endorsed the EPG report and its vision statement.[53] The EPG envisaged a regional community of states engaged in 'deep integration' and greater cooperation in such areas as transport, information technology, quarantine, customs, security, judicial and public administration and regional law enforcement. It is important to note, however, that the EPG vision also introduced Pacific heritage and cultural identity as guiding principles of a 'refreshed' regionalism alongside the security and development purposes promoted by the Australian and New Zealand governments.[54] It also promoted the participation of dependent territories and civil society groups in regional deliberations and introduced the notion of 'peoples of the region' as key participants if regional community-building was to gain legitimacy.

To develop the Pacific Plan, a taskforce of officials drawn from member countries was appointed with a mandate to consult all key stakeholders and report back to the October 2005 PIF meeting. The resultant Pacific Plan for Strengthening Regional Cooperation and Integration reflected a commitment to a deeper level of regional integration.[55] As presented for endorsement by the October 2005 PIF meeting, the Pacific Plan represented the key aims of those who had driven the process in Canberra and Wellington. Although the earlier Pacific vision of the EPG had introduced cultural heritage and identity as key concerns, it is significant that these did not feature in the final plan. The Pacific Plan looked more like the Australian and New Zealand regional security and economic agenda of the previous decade, but this time to be pursued in an institutional context in which it could be more effectively implemented.[56]

52 The Eminent Persons' Group Review of the Pacific Islands Forum, *The Eminent Persons' Report*, April 2004, available from: www.iri.edu.ar/publicaciones_iri/anuario/CD%20Anuario%202005/Asia/47-pacific%20island%20forum-eminent%20persons%20report%2004.pdf.
53 PIFS, *Leaders' Decisions: Pacific Islands Forum Special Leaders Retreat, Auckland, New Zealand, 6 April 2004*, Suva: PIFS, available from: forumsec.org/pacific-islands-forum-special-leaders-retreat-auckland-6-april-2004-leaders-decisions/.
54 The Eminent Persons' Group Review.
55 PIFS, *Kalibobo Roadmap on the Pacific Plan*, Kalibobo Village, Madang, Papua New Guinea, 26 October 2005, available from: www.forumsec.org/kalibobo-roadmap-on-the-pacific-plan/.
56 ibid.

One significant departure, however, was the introduction of sustainable development as a separate pillar of the work program alongside economic growth, governance and security, rather than incorporating it as part of a neoliberal agenda. The concerns listed under 'sustainable development' were similar to those making up the UNDP's 'human development' paradigm: capacity-building of youth and women, education, health and environmental protection.[57] This reflected the increased influence of the human development agenda on the regional framing of development. However, the plan's designers were not embracing the 1999 *Pacific Human Development Report's* definition of sustainable development objectives such as sustainable livelihoods and individual opportunities;[58] rather, they were seeing sustainable development as capacity-building in service of promoting neoliberal objectives (mirroring the way elements of the human development paradigm had been incorporated in World Bank thinking).

The principal critique from civil society groups was that there had been insufficient consultation. The EPG had talked of the Pacific Plan as a people's document and had talked up inclusivity in the process. This tone was reinforced by the terms of reference for the Pacific Plan and the statements surrounding it, which suggested that this was to be a people's document. Accordingly, there were high expectations that this task would involve a process of deep and inclusive reflection on future approaches to 'development' in the region as it would affect the lives of all Pacific islanders. For NGOs, there was, instead, a sense that this was a consultation on a fait accompli and that there was little movement from the core commitments of the draft.[59]

A second critique was that it was just a repackaging of the long-established PIF agenda and that this in turn reflected the priorities of Australia and New Zealand rather than the Pacific island states and societies. In her cogent critique of the plan, Elise Huffer argues that the objectives were centred uncritically on the pursuit of neoliberal ideas and that the plan 'appears to be mainly a tool for integration by free trade':

---

57   ibid.

58   UNDP, *Pacific Human Development Report 1999*.

59   Claire Slatter, 'The New Framework for Pacific Regionalism: Old Kava in a New Tanoa?', in Fry and Tarte, *The New Pacific Diplomacy*, pp. 49–63, at p. 52; and Elise Huffer, 'The Pacific Plan: A Political and Cultural Critique', in Jenny Bryant-Tokalau and Ian Frazer, eds, *Redefining the Pacific? Regionalism, Past, Present and Future*, London: Routledge, 2006, pp. 172–3.

The July 2005 draft makes this clear when it states that the 'leaders' wish' is to move towards regional integration which is described in purely economic terms as 'the lowering [of] market barriers between countries ... easier access to more consumers by Pacific companies, increasing economies of scale.[60]

Claire Slatter and Yvonne Underhill-Sem take a similar view, describing the plan as 'a framework for deepening neoliberal reform and trade liberalization in the region'.[61]

A third concern was that the cultural identity/heritage pillar of the EPG had been dropped from the Pacific Plan, with significant implications for how development was being defined and approached. Huffer argues:

Integrating culture into the Plan by cutting it up into (non cultural) categories such as good governance and sustainable development rather than making it the foundation of the Plan is a piecemeal and unproductive approach. 'Cultural identity' is an all-encompassing feature of life in the Pacific. What Pacific peoples have in common are the cultural values that they hold, their ways of life and their worldviews.[62]

Huffer goes on to cite the critique of Lopeti Senituli, Director of the Tongan Community Development Trust, that the ethical stance or underpinning of the plan assumes that the problem of the Pacific lies with Pacific cultures' inability to adapt to a liberalised global market and to the values espoused in the good governance agenda. This, he argues,

ignores the fact that there are communities in the region, which live by local and customary values and norms, and which do not espouse the values attached to (neo) liberal politics and economics.[63]

The Pacific Plan became the overarching program for regional governance for the next decade. For the main instigators of the plan, Australia and New Zealand, there was a growing recognition that it was not producing results. It had not captured the imaginations of Pacific island leaders,

---

60   Huffer, 'The Pacific Plan', p. 172.
61   Claire Slatter and Yvonne Underhill-Sem, 'Reclaiming Pacific Island Regionalism: Does Neoliberalism Have to Reign?', in Bina D'Costa and Katrina Lee-Koo, eds, *Gender and Global Politics in the Asia-Pacific*, Basingstoke, UK: Palgrave Macmillan, 2009.
62   Huffer, 'The Pacific Plan', p. 166.
63   ibid.

and it had not been sufficiently inclusive as seen by civil society groups. For Roman Grynberg, senior trade adviser in the PIFS at the time of the Pacific Plan, the legitimacy problem stemmed from the plan's genesis:

> Australian and New Zealand officials basically took the regional aid programs that they were already implementing and renamed them the Pacific Plan. There was also little or no support from islands as it soon became evident that the Plan was merely window dressing, a renaming of whatever Australian and New Zealand bureaucrats were, in any case, planning to do. Thus the Pacific Plan continues to live in name only but failed because it had no obvious island champions nor any real roots in the islands.[64]

This continuation of a commitment to neoliberal objectives is difficult to reconcile with the strong and rising commitment to human development ideas elsewhere in the PIF system. If anything, the influence of the human development paradigm increased over the next few years such that it appeared with equal billing with neoliberal ideas in regional policies without explanation as to the relationship between them. This ambiguity is present, for example, in the Australia-initiated *Cairns Compact on Strengthening Development Co-ordination in the Pacific*, signed by PIF leaders in August 2009. The key objective of the compact is 'to drive more effective co-ordination of available development resources from both Forum Island Countries and all development partners, centred on the aim of achieving real progress against the MDGs'.[65] However, to 'realise this objective', the compact relies on a set of principles that are the familiar neoliberal commitments (including good governance). For example, the first principle is 'a recognition that broad-based, private sector-led growth was essential to achieving faster development progress'.[66]

This seems to suggest an endorsement of human development ends pursued by neoliberal means—an interesting reversal of the PIF's earlier incorporation of human development as a capacity-building means to assist with achieving the neoliberal objective of economic growth. This new regional framing of Pacific development reflected the

---

64   Roman Grynberg, 'The Pacific Plan and Other Failures: What Can Be Learned?', *Pacific Media Centre*, 16 January 2013, available from: pmc.littleisland.co.nz/articles/pacific-plan-and-other-failures-what-can-be-learned.
65   PIFS, 'Annex B: Cairns Compact on Strengthening Development Coordination in the Pacific, August 2009', in *Leaders' Communiqué: Fortieth Pacific Islands Forum, Cairns, Australia, 5–6 August 2009*, Suva: PIFS, 2009.
66   ibid., para. 2.

change in Australian development thinking in particular, where human development goals were now sitting alongside neoliberalism as a powerful second pillar of development thinking. The significance of this shift from the neoliberal ascendancy in Australian policy was most clearly evident in the *Tracking Development and Governance in the Pacific* report of August 2009, which provided the rationale and evidence for the new policy directions in the Cairns Compact.[67] It was also clear in the new Rudd Government's aid policy, as set out in the Port Moresby Declaration of 2008: 'Australia believes that the Millennium Development Goals agreed by the international community … provide an appropriate framework for developing nations world-wide, including in our region'.[68]

The build-up of dissatisfaction with the ineffectiveness of the Pacific Plan led to the commissioning of a review of it in 2013.[69] The Morauta Review recommended a Framework for Pacific Regionalism to replace the Pacific Plan. The main recommendations for change related to the governance of regionalism, and these will be discussed in the next chapter. What is important for the present argument is the way in which the new framework pictured regional development. The framework continues the ambiguities evident in the revised Pacific Plan. On the one hand, human development influences are evident in the vision and values, with their emphasis on social inclusion, equity and the valuing of cultures and traditions. They are also evident in the principal objectives (the four pillars of the old Pacific Plan). Crucially, the 'sustainable development' objective is linked to the ultimate goal of improved livelihoods; the 'economic growth' objective is qualified by the stipulation that it should be inclusive and equitable. However, as Claire Slatter argues, it is clear that elsewhere the framework retains a fundamental commitment to 'deep' economic integration along neoliberal lines.[70] We see this, for example, in the description of the requirements under the forms of regionalism required to achieve economic growth, which is clearly a restatement of the neoliberal agenda.[71] We also see it in the surprising comment in the

---

67 AusAID, *Tracking Development and Governance in the Pacific*, Canberra: AusAID, August 2009.

68 Australian Department of Foreign Affairs and Trade [hereinafter DFAT], *Port Moresby Declaration*, 6 March 2008, available from: dfat.gov.au/geo/pacific/development-assistance/partnerships/Pages/port-moresby-declaration.aspx.

69 PIFS, *Pacific Plan Review 2013: Report to Pacific Leaders. Volume 1*, Suva: PIFS, 2013 [known as the Morauta Review].

70 Slatter, 'The New Framework for Pacific Regionalism', pp. 56–62.

71 PIFS, 'Annex A: The Framework for Pacific Regionalism', in *Leaders' Communiqué: Forty-Fifth Pacific Islands Forum, Koror, Republic of Palau, 29–31 July 2014*, Suva: PIFS, 2014, PIFS (14)10.

Morauta Review report about the lack of basis for alignment between the 'global development agenda' (the MDGs) and the framework. The report concludes that the MDGs 'are not that useful for tracking progress on regional integration and regional cooperation'.[72]

This ambiguity in regional policy framing continued as Sustainable Development Goals (SDGs) replaced MDGs as the main framing process of the global development agenda. The commitment to the SDGs remained central to FEMM economic action plans, alongside neoliberal commitments.[73] Backed by key development partners, the PIF states developed a Pacific region response to the creation and implementation of the SDGs. In a move seemingly at odds with the Morauta Review's earlier position that the MDGs did not easily fit with the framework, in their 2017 PIF communiqué, the leaders stated that

> in endorsing the *Pacific Roadmap for Sustainable Development* (PRSD) [they] reinforced the centrality of the FPR [Framework for Pacific Regionalism] in contextualizing global commitments under the 2030 [SDG] Agenda and the SAMOA [Small Island Developing States Accelerated Modalities of Action] Pathway.[74]

While there remained ambiguity in the overall position on the development approach in the main frameworks of the PIF, it is clear, at the very least, that human development had made major inroads into the neoliberal ascendancy of the previous decades. This result was mainly felt in relation to the regional norms concerning how states should be governed and the balance between economic and social objectives.

Regional trade liberalisation

It was a very different story in relation to the ideas governing trade negotiations between the Pacific states and their primary trading partners in the first two decades of the twenty-first century. In these negotiations, Australia, New Zealand and the European Union were pursuing unadulterated neoliberal positions as they pursued full trade liberalisation

---

72   PIFS, *Pacific Plan Review 2013*, p. 125 ('Alignment with Global Development Agenda').

73   See, for example, FEMM, *2017 Forum Economic Ministers Meeting Action Plan*, Suva: PIFS, 2017, paras 3–6.

74   PIFS, *Leaders' Communiqué: Forty-Eighth Pacific Islands Forum, Apia, Samoa, 5–8 September 2017*, Suva: PIFS, 2017, PIFS 17(10), para. 14.

with the Pacific island states. These free-market positions were not leavened by human development commitments, which is especially surprising after the global discrediting of pure neoliberalism after the 2008 Global Financial Crisis.[75] For the neoliberal proponents from Canberra, Wellington, Washington and Brussels, such trade liberalisation was seen as a major part of the solution to the Pacific development problem, and a necessity if the Pacific was to adapt to an increasingly globalised world.

The Pacific island governments also gave lip-service to a commitment to trade liberalisation. It had appeared as a key goal in the Pacific Plan. However, as the negotiations for comprehensive trade liberalisation proceeded in the 2000s with the European Union, on the one hand, and Australia and New Zealand, on the other, it was clear they did not intend this commitment to be without conditions. The leaders realised that the move to two-way free-trade arrangements brought no obvious trade benefit to their countries and the threats to their economies, and to their sovereignty, were real. This included a possible loss of local industries, as predicted by some Pacific economists, and the introduction of new, unpopular taxes and a decline in government revenue.[76] Thus, any benefits would have to be gained through hard bargaining as additional concessions outside the trade considerations. Their attitude, then, was one of a reluctant adjustment to new global trading realities but with a shared determination to minimise the predicted costs associated with moving from a preferential system to an 'even playing field' and to broaden the negotiations to include new concessions for Pacific island countries in relation to such matters as labour access and trade facilitation.

The regional free-trade agenda was a significant departure from past practices. The opening of island markets through the removal of tariffs clearly had potential implications for small, protected industries such as tobacco, alcohol and biscuit factories. For smaller states, it also meant the removal of a major part of government revenue and, in turn, this meant imposing a politically unpopular new tax on consumer goods to compensate for that loss. This was a major shift from the dominant development thinking in the 1970s and 1980s, when preferential treatment for the island states was written into the regional trading

---

75   Kevin Rudd, 'The Global Financial Crisis', *The Monthly*, February 2009, available from: www.themonthly.com.au/issue/2009/february/1319602475/kevin-rudd/global-financial-crisis.

76   Wesley Morgan, 'Trade Negotiations and Regional Economic Integration in the Pacific Islands Forum', *Asia and the Pacific Policy Studies*, 1(2), 2014: 325–36, at p. 329.

arrangements with Australia and New Zealand under the SPARTECA and with Europe under the Lomé Convention. These were described as one-way free-trade arrangements because they allowed duty-free access for island products to metropolitan markets.

Ironically, in their long resistance to the neoliberal arguments of Canberra, Wellington and Brussels, the Pacific island leaders did not deploy human development arguments or even cultural protection arguments; rather, they opted for an even purer form of the neoliberal argument. They argued for the free movement of labour as a quid pro quo for agreeing to trade liberalisation, which would otherwise hold no benefits for their states.

As we saw above, in the late 1990s, the European Union had signalled its intention to commence negotiations with Africa, the Caribbean and the Pacific countries for a full free-trade replacement for the Lomé Convention, as its preferential provisions had been challenged as falling foul of WTO trade rules. What was proposed was a new arrangement that would grant free access for European products into Pacific markets as well as eliminating any preferential treatment for Pacific products into the European market. The new agreement was to be negotiated on a regional basis. The negotiation of the new economic partnership agreement (EPA), based on the model also being negotiated with the Caribbean and Africa, began in 2004.[77] The Pacific leaders, advised by the PIFS, realised that such an agreement would disadvantage them unless they negotiated special concessions outside the free-trade provisions. In 2006, they submitted a draft agreement to the European Union, which included proposals for

> special temporary access to the EU for a limited number of Pacific Island workers, the establishment of a regional office for the European Investment Bank in a PIC [Pacific island country], sector-specific strategies to encourage European investment in Pacific tourism and agriculture, and a regional fisheries agreement linking fishing rights for European vessels with measures to encourage downstream processing in Island states.[78]

The Pacific also proposed that liberalisation commitments be linked with financing to offset adjustment costs (primarily tariff revenue losses).[79]

---

77   Wesley Morgan, 'Much Lost, Little Gained? Contemporary Trade Agreements in the Pacific Islands', *Journal of Pacific History*, [Online], 4 June 2018: 5–10.
78   ibid., p. 6.
79   ibid., p. 6.

The European Union's response was to reject all of the Pacific's proposals and to propose a counter treaty without any concessions. This was unacceptable to the Pacific. With a stalemate in negotiations of the regional EPA and the expiry date for the WTO waiver covering EU preferences for island exports imminent, Fiji and Papua New Guinea each signed an interim bilateral EPA. Meanwhile, negotiations on the regional EPA between 2007 and 2015 proved acrimonious. The European Union was seen as splitting the Pacific bloc and it was also criticised for not shifting from its position of promoting an orthodox regional free-trade agreement. For its part, the European Union saw the Pacific states' position as untenable and intransigent. Consequently, in May 2015, the European Union proposed a three-year 'pause' in negotiations.[80] Wesley Morgan concludes that 'Pacific governments decided no agreement at all with the EU would be better than a conventional FTA [free-trade agreement]'.[81]

As indicated earlier, Canberra and Wellington had won a concession from the Pacific island states in the form of the Pacific Agreement on Closer Economic Relations (PACER), signed in 2001, which provided for the triggering of negotiations for a new regional free-trade area with Canberra and Wellington if the Pacific started to negotiate free-trade arrangements with the Europeans.[82] In the event, it was not until 2007 that the Australian and New Zealand ministers announced that they intended to negotiate a new regional free-trade arrangement with the Pacific island states now that negotiations were under way with the Europeans. The so-called PACER Plus negotiations took place over the next decade.[83] As with the negotiations with the European Union, the Pacific island states and the regional secretariat approached these negotiations with the knowledge that any gains to be made, or offsets for potential losses, would come from wins on issues outside the free-trade discussions. The Pacific strategy, then, was to broaden discussions beyond a conventional free-trade agenda.

---

80   African, Caribbean, and Pacific Group of States Secretariat, 'Pacific–EU Talks on Hold', Press release, Brussels, 16 May 2015, available from: www.acp.int/content/pacific-eu-trade-talks-hold.

81   Morgan, 'Much Lost, Little Gained?', p. 10.

82   PIFS, *Leaders' Communiqué: Thirty-Second Pacific Islands Forum, Yaren, Republic of Nauru, 16–18 August 2001*, Suva: PIFS, 2001, para. 7; and PIFS, *Pacific Agreement on Closer Economic Relations (PACER)*.

83   For the most authoritative scholarly analysis of the trade negotiations on PACER Plus, see Morgan: 'Trade Negotiations and Regional Economic Integration'; Morgan, 'Much Lost, Little Gained?', pp. 10–19; Wesley Morgan, 'Negotiating Power in Contemporary Pacific Trade Diplomacy', in Fry and Tarte, *The New Pacific Diplomacy*, pp. 251–61.

The Pacific was strongly committed to winning substantive labour access to Australia and New Zealand and this quickly became the main issue for negotiation. Australia and New Zealand argued for dealing with the labour mobility issue outside the free-trade treaty and, accordingly, they each set up new bilateral labour schemes for Pacific islanders: the New Zealand Recognised Seasonal Employer Scheme (from 2007) and the Australian Seasonal Worker Program (from 2009). Wesley cites Curtain et al. as calculating that, by 2015, nearly 12,000 workers from the Pacific were arriving in Australia and New Zealand.[84] With the Pacific negotiators continuing to insist that labour access be included in the agreement itself, and Canberra and Wellington's refusal to move on this issue, this became the sticking point of the negotiations. In the end, compromise was reached by Australia and New Zealand agreeing to more generous labour mobility arrangements outside the trade treaty and the Pacific island leaders agreeing to drop their demand that labour mobility be included in the treaty. In August 2016, Pacific trade ministers endorsed a complete treaty text but, significantly, Fiji and Papua New Guinea did not sign the treaty. The Fiji minister Faiyaz Koya argued that PACER Plus would limit Fiji's ability to support its domestic industry, while PNG prime minister, Peter O'Neill, argued that the treaty would entail a 'net loss' for the PNG economy.[85] The three Micronesian states with compacts of free association with the United States have also not signed the treaty as yet.

While the European Union and Australia and New Zealand had framed these trade negotiations through the neoliberal free-trade prism, the diplomatic outcome could not be clearly delineated as a triumph for neoliberalism. In the case of the negotiations with the Europeans, these ended in stalemate and ultimately rejection by the Pacific. In the case of PACER Plus, the signing of a free-trade agreement in June 2017 was hailed as a successful outcome by Canberra and Wellington.[86] However, the two key economies in the Pacific, Fiji and Papua New Guinea, refused to sign. It is also the case that the Pacific won concessions from Canberra and Wellington on labour access outside the trade treaty. ANU economist

---

84   Richard Curtain, Matthew Dornan, Jesse Doyle, and Stephen Howes, *Labour Mobility the 10 Billion Dollar Prize*, Pacific Possible Series, Washington, DC: The World Bank, 2016, as paraphrased in Morgan, 'Much Lost, Little Gained?', p. 15.

85   Morgan, 'Much Lost, Little Gained?', p. 17.

86   DFAT, *Pacific Agreement on Closer Economic Relations (PACER): About PACER Plus*, Canberra: DFAT, 2017, available from: dfat.gov.au/trade/agreements/not-yet-in-force/pacer/Pages/pacific-agreement-on-closer-economic-relations-pacer-plus.aspx.

Matthew Dornan concludes that, with the signing of the PACER Plus agreement, 'there is not much to celebrate, beyond a deal being struck'.[87] USP political scientist Morgan concludes:

> Ultimately, after decades of discussion, little of substance has been gained from regional trade negotiations. Perhaps, the biggest loss of all was two decades of political and diplomatic energy, spent in acrimonious talks, securing agreements that left much to be desired.[88]

The commitment to trade liberalisation negotiations had been roundly critiqued by civil society since the early 2000s.[89] As the talk about trade liberalisation arrangements with Europe, on the one hand, and Australia and New Zealand, on the other, began to ramp up, several civil society organisations formed the Pacific Network on Globalisation (PANG), in May 2001, to represent their concerns about these developments. While excluded from the formal negotiations, regional civil society nevertheless had an important role in influencing the course of regional trade diplomacy. PANG, in particular, had a major role in raising and publicising the issues at stake in the secret negotiations. It also lobbied Pacific leaders and officials and, in the more inclusive period of the PIF from 2014, attempted to influence PIF deliberations in the last stages of the PACER Plus negotiations.[90]

The key points of this civil society criticism remained constant over the following two decades. First, PANG has criticised the PIF for the secrecy of these negotiations. Second, it criticised the dominance of Australia, New Zealand and the European Union and their alleged manipulation of the process.[91] Third, regional civil society shared the concerns of some Pacific island leaders about the economic impact on local industry and employment. Fourth, there was concern about the impact on the sovereignty of the Pacific island states based on the loss of sovereignty that had occurred in other free-trade agreements. Finally, PANG raised

---

87   Matthew Dornan, 'PACER Plus is Not Much to Celebrate', *East Asia Forum*, 2 June 2017, available from: www.eastasiaforum.org/2017/06/02/pacer-plus-is-not-much-to-celebrate/.

88   Morgan, 'Much Lost, Little Gained?', p. 19.

89   See, for example, Kelsey, *Big Brothers Behaving Badly*; Pacific Network on Globalisation [hereinafter PANG], *A People's Guide to PACER Plus: Understanding What It Is and What It Means for the People of the Pacific Islands*, Suva: PANG, 2017; Waden Narsey, 'PICTA, PACER and EPAs: Where Are We Going?', *Islands Business*, April 2004.

90   See, for example, PANG, *Defending Pacific Ways of Life: A People's Social Impact Assessment of PACER-Plus*, Suva: PANG, June 2016.

91   Kelsey, *Big Brothers Behaving Badly*.

a number of concerns about the social impacts of the proposed agreement. These included the impacts on health and food security, gendered impacts and impacts on indigenous economies and customary landownership.[92]

Conclusion

In the 1990s, Australia and New Zealand strongly promoted a regional economic order based on neoliberal principles. Neoliberalism became the ascendant policy frame in the principal regional institution in that decade. However, from 2000, the PIF appeared to juggle two separate policy frames—one based on neoliberalism and the other on the human development paradigm—on the assumption that they were entirely compatible. However, for the proponents of human-centred development, there had always been the potential for conflict between these two paradigms. The UNDP, for example, argued that economic growth was important for human development but it could also work against it. Economic growth needed to be inclusive and mindful of social goals. As we have seen, radical perspectives go further, saying that these two paradigms are necessarily in conflict. Free-market ideology necessarily contradicts human-centred development. From this perspective, neoliberalism is not just a different approach to development; it also has deleterious impacts on human development objectives. For many neoliberal proponents, the opposite is true. Human development policies are often seen as a problem to be solved if growth is to occur (for example, too much spending on safety nets or education). The PIF has not tried to square this circle to explain how its endorsement of both policy frames overcomes these contradictions or to enter the debate over whether the pursuit of neoliberal goals has influenced the poor regional outcome on the MDGs, as predicted by human-centric development perspectives.

At the very least, it is evident that the early, unchallenged ascendancy of neoliberalism was not sustained in the 2000s. We have seen that, even in their most unadulterated form—in the promotion of trade liberalisation by Australia, New Zealand and Europe—neoliberal ideas have by no means had a clear victory. We now turn to the other major area of regional diplomacy during this period (1990–2018), in which Australia and New Zealand sought to impose a hegemonic form of regional governance that suited their interests: regional security governance.

---

92   PANG, *A People's Guide to PACER Plus*, and *Defending Pacific Ways of Life*.

12

Reframing regional security in the post–Cold War era

Alongside the attempt over the past three decades to create a regional economic order based on neoliberal principles, there has been an equally significant attempt to reframe the regional security order. As with the reframing of economic development, Canberra and Wellington have been the chief promoters of this post–Cold War framing of regional security. The new security framing has involved a reconceptualisation of the regional security 'problem' and a rethinking of regional approaches to its solution.

This rethinking has gone through several phases, responding to global and regional developments, as well as to domestic politics in Canberra. Spurred initially in the early 1990s by global developments in transnational crime, then from 2000 by political crises in some Pacific island states, and then from 2001 by the global war on terror, Australia and New Zealand proposed ever-deepening levels of regional integration to activate regional intervention both preemptively and at times of crisis. They promoted, and gained agreement to, an increasingly institutionalised regional security regime in an attempt to build a regional *cordon sanitaire* against unwelcome transnational influences while building regional mechanisms for intervention in political crises within states. Ultimately, this new security framing was represented in a new regional institutional network coordinated under the Forum Regional Security Committee (FRSC) and in new regional norms agreed to by PIF leaders in a series of regional declarations, agreements and codes of conduct.

This new security framing was also expressed in new regional policies of military and police intervention and in the harmonisation of national laws around regional standards. It culminated in the negotiation of the Biketawa Plus regional security agreement in 2018 and the uneasy contest between two very different security paradigms: Canberra and Wellington's attempt to reestablish the regional strategic denial doctrine of the Cold War era, but this time aimed at China; and the Pacific island country leaders' attempt to promote a human security paradigm with climate change as the priority concern.

Laying the foundations: Honiara to Aitutaki

During the Cold War, Australian and New Zealand policymakers were concerned with countering a perceived Soviet threat and promoting regional strategic denial through the SPF. With the end of the perceived Soviet threat, Canberra began to define regional security in 'small "s" security' terms, with a focus on transnational crime as the principal threat. As put by Douglas Ranmuthugala, a senior intelligence analyst with the Australian Federal Police:

> One reason for this may be that the vast machinery poised to counter threats to security in the conventional sense now found that it was running out of targets. Highly trained and resourced agencies had to face either dramatic cuts or reorient themselves to face newly discovered threats. And suddenly, law enforcement found that it was no longer the Cinderella in the security field, and that it was being wooed by powerful agencies.[1]

This change of 'paradigm', as Ranmuthugala described it, reflected a change in global security thinking following the end of the Cold War. The rich Western countries were indicating their commitment to cracking down on countries that were encouraging the activities of criminal gangs in drug running, money laundering and human trafficking. This was seen, for example, in the recommendations of the Group of Seven (G-7) Financial Action Task Force and new global agreements such as the 1988 UN Convention against Illicit Trafficking in Narcotic Drugs and Psychotropic Substances.[2]

---

1   Douglas Ranmuthugala, 'Security in the South Pacific: The Law Enforcement Dimension', *Revue Juridique Polynesienne*, 1, 2001, p. 172.
2   *United Nations Convention against Illicit Traffic in Narcotic Drugs and Psychotropic Substances*, Vienna, 20 December 1988.

The change of paradigm was also spurred by perceptions of increased transnational crime within the Pacific region. Karl Claxton notes that the Regional Law Enforcement Needs Assessment

> assesses the island states as being attractive as supply routes for drug traffickers dealing in both hard and soft illicit drugs within the Southeast Asia, Australasian, North and Central American regions.

And that:

> Underworld infiltration into island economies as a result of the drug trafficking activities of Australian Mafia, American cartels, Hong Kong triads and Japanese crime gangs is not yet thought to be widespread, although early indications of limited involvement by all those groups has been detected.[3]

If the security threat was now to be seen as transnational crime, the new solution was the creation of a regional *cordon sanitaire* through intelligence sharing, regional harmonisation of laws and practices on law enforcement and institutionalising cooperation through an enhanced FRSC, which would bring existing regional agencies under the PIF's umbrella. It would include appropriate training and capacity-building in law enforcement, customs and intelligence sharing. The new paradigm entered the regional space in 1991 as a review report for the SPF Secretariat undertaken by an Australian consultant.[4] The findings of the Regional Law Enforcement Needs Assessment concluded that

> a broad definition of both 'law enforcement cooperation' and 'security' is necessary; that national resource constraints facing law enforcement agencies mean that regional activities offer tangible benefits; and that in areas where several regional and international initiatives or organisations deal with common issues the Secretariat should seek to provide a coordinating and information analysing facility rather than duplicating the work of existing bodies.[5]

---

3   As reported in Karl Claxton, 'The Nature and Extent of Crime in the South Pacific and the Region's Attempts to Respond to this Challenge', MA (Strategic Studies) Research Essay, The Australian National University, Canberra, 25 February 1994, p. 16.

4   Perry Head, *Regional Law Enforcement Needs Assessment: Prospects for Enhancing Regional Cooperation*, Discussion Paper prepared for the Forum Secretariat, Suva: SPF Secretariat, June 1991.

5   As reported in Claxton, 'The Nature and Extent of Crime', p. 29.

The Forum Island Countries (FICs) indicated their acceptance of these recommendations in signing on to the Honiara Declaration on Law Enforcement Cooperation at the SPF meeting in Honiara in 1992.[6] In the Honiara Declaration, the Pacific leaders recognised that 'the potential impact of transnational crime was a matter for increasing concern to regional states and enforcement agencies' and that 'there was a need for a more comprehensive, integrated and collaborative approach to counter these threats'.[7] They tasked the FRSC with coordinating the work of the specialised regional law enforcement agencies such as the Pacific Islands Law Officers Meeting, the Customs Heads of Administration Regional Meeting and the South Pacific Chiefs of Police Conference.

This Australian project to create a regional transnational security network was joined by another, related, Australian regional security project from 1992. Australia began to promote a broader concept of regional security with greater emphasis on internal political and security crises as the security problem, and preventive diplomacy and other forms of regional intervention as the necessary policy responses. This did not displace the transnational crime agenda; it was seen as complementary. It was another layer in the new regional security thinking in Canberra emphasising internal political stability of the island states as the core concern.

Like the transnational crime agenda, this new agenda was partly inspired by the new global trends in security thinking at the end of the Cold War. In this case, the new global thinking was the discourse on preventive diplomacy, peacekeeping and peacemaking as expressed in the UN Secretary-General's *Agenda for Peace* and its underlying premise 'that the time of absolute and exclusive sovereignty … has passed'.[8] This policy framing was also inspired by developments within the region. Australian policymakers were mindful of the poor governance in some Pacific island states and the breakdown of constitutional government, which occurred with the coup in Fiji in 1987, the 'President's coup' in Vanuatu in 1988 and the Bougainville rebellion in Papua New Guinea, which began in 1989.[9]

---

6   SPF Secretariat, *Declaration by the South Pacific Forum on Law Enforcement Cooperation [Honiara Declaration]*, Suva: SPF Secretariat, 1992.
7   ibid., para. 1.
8   United Nations, *An Agenda for Peace: Preventive Diplomacy, Peacemaking and Peace-Keeping*, Report of the United Nations Secretary-General, A47/277, New York: United Nations, 17 June 1992.
9   Ken Ross, *Prospects for Crisis Prediction: A South Pacific Case Study*, Canberra: Strategic and Defence Studies Centre, The Australian National University, 1990, pp. 91–2.

The translation of this Australian agenda into a regional one, accepted by the Pacific island states, was achieved at the 1997 SPF meeting, where, in the Aitutaki Declaration on Regional Security Cooperation, the SPF leaders 'accepted the need for the region to take on a more comprehensive approach to regional security consistent with the relevant principles of the United Nation's [sic] Agenda for Peace'.[10] As well as placing greater emphasis on internal political crisis as the potential security problem, its principal new commitment was to strengthen regional mechanisms for preventive diplomacy, including the use of the 'good offices of the Forum Secretary-General, eminent persons, fact finding missions and third party mediation'. In another important departure, the SPF leaders also agreed 'that procedures should be developed and put in place which would better facilitate responses by the region's disciplined forces'.[11]

The 'arc of crisis' and the Biketawa Declaration

From 2000, it seemed—at least for Canberra and Wellington—that the concerns of the Aitutaki Declaration with identifying potential internal crises as the key security threat, and with developing regional mechanisms to respond, were not misplaced. The overthrow of democratic and constitutional governments in Fiji and Solomon Islands in 2000 led some commentators to describe the South Pacific island region as an eastern extension of the 'arc of crisis'—identified from the late 1990s as stretching from Aceh, through Timor, Ambon and Irian Jaya (and, in some versions, Papua New Guinea). Other observers found their analogy not in island South-East Asia, but in the Balkans or Africa.[12] Whatever the political analogy, the general message was the same: the South Pacific was now to be seen in Kaplanesque terms—island states at various points on a path to the 'coming anarchy'[13] of ethnic conflict, state breakdown, gun culture, violence, fragmentation and economic collapse. Solomon Islands and Fiji

---

10   SPF Secretariat, *Aitutaki Declaration on Regional Security Cooperation*, Suva: SPF Secretariat, 18 September 1997, available from: www.forumsec.org/aitutaki-declaration-on-regional-security-cooperation/, Clause (3).

11   ibid.

12   Greg Sheridan, 'Breaking Up Brings No Benefit: We Are Witnessing the Balkanisation of the Region', *The Australian*, 9 June 2000, p. 13; and Ben Reilly, 'The Africanisation of the South Pacific', *Australian Journal of International Affairs*, 54(3), 2000: 261–8.

13   Robert Kaplan, 'The Coming Anarchy', *The Atlantic*, February 1994, available from: www.the atlantic.com/magazine/archive/1994/02/the-coming-anarchy/304670/.

were seen as having already arrived at this state, Papua New Guinea as teetering on the edge and the other 11 Pacific island states as developing the symptoms of instability.

The events in Suva in May 2000 were what first prompted commentators to refer to the Pacific as a whole as an extension of the 'arc of crisis' or as a 'region of instability'.[14] The hostage crisis quickly turned into a much deeper political crisis about the future governance of the country. There was a breakdown of shared understandings about the legitimacy of the elected government, of the 1997 constitution, of democratic principles, of Fijian traditional leadership and even of the idea of Fiji as an ongoing unified entity. The rule of law was undermined and the economy seriously affected. The gravity of the situation was accentuated by the fact that this was the second major breakdown in Fijian governance and that there had been enormous effort by all communities to come back from the divisive, unjust and ineffective governance arrangements of 1987–97.

The so-called copycat coup in Honiara two weeks after the hostage-taking in Suva perhaps understandably caused editorialists, commentators and political cartoonists to portray the Pacific as a series of vulnerable island societies ready to follow suit. As in Suva, the hostage crisis in Honiara quickly revealed a wider ethnonationalist claim, this time on behalf of Malaitans. A new government was subsequently formed in dubious circumstances and was seen as backing the militant group behind the hostage-taking, the Malaitan Eagle Force. The conflict between Guadalcanal militants— the Isatabu Freedom Movement—and the Malaita Eagle Force escalated until peacemaking efforts produced a peace agreement in October 2000.[15] As in Fiji, in Solomon Islands, the government of the day was removed, democratic procedure ignored and the very future of a unified state was threatened. Solomon Islands also took a step closer to all-out civil war—a possibility not ruled out in Fiji but fortunately contained.[16]

---

14   Sheridan, 'Breaking Up Brings No Benefit'; and Reilly, 'The Africanisation of the South Pacific'.
15   DFAT, 'Agreement between Solomon Islands, Australia, New Zealand, Fiji, Papua New Guinea, Samoa and Tonga Concerning the Operations and Status of the Police and Armed Forces and Other Personnel Deployed to Solomon Islands to Assist in the Restoration of Law and Order and Security (Townsville, 24 July 2003)', [Townsville Peace Agreement], *Australian Treaty Series*, 17, Canberra: AGPS, 2003.
16   For a more detailed development of this argument, see Greg Fry, 'Political Legitimacy and the Post-colonial State in the Pacific: Reflections on Some Common Threads in the Fiji and Solomon Islands Coups', *Pacifica Review*, 12(3), 2000: 295–304.

Although the concern with how states were governed was part of the neoliberal framing of the Pacific in the 1990s, it was focused not on issues of state failure and defending the constitutional state, but rather on the capacity and efficiency of the state to deliver sound economic management. The concerns were those of the World Bank with efficient and accountable government for neoliberal development rather than that of *democratic* government. The coups in Fiji and Solomon Islands shifted this concern with bolstering a regional norm of good governance to a different level of significance. The focus was now on supporting state stability and the preservation of democracy. As a direct outcome of these crises, and in the spirit of the Aitutaki Declaration, the Forum Foreign Ministers Meeting (FFMM) was held for the first time, in Apia in August 2000, to discuss what role the PIF might take in relation to assisting with a resolution of these crises. Nicola Baker contends that it was the New Zealand Government that dominated the discussions leading to a proposal to develop more effective regional mechanisms for dealing with crises:

> New Zealand's Foreign Minister, Phil Goff, had put forward a proposal that the Forum build on its previous declarations on regional security and develop procedures and processes for dealing with similar situations. The Australian foreign minister did not contribute at all to the ensuing discussion.[17]

At the PIF meeting in October 2000, New Zealand prime minister Clark and Australian prime minister Howard fought hard to gain support from Pacific island leaders for a strongly worded declaration that would capture the recommendations of the Apia meeting. They wanted a declaration that would give the PIF states the facility to impose sanctions, including suspension from the PIF, as a last resort in dealing with a member state which had violated the norms of good governance and democracy. The result was the Biketawa Declaration, which sets out shared regional norms concerning good governance and individual liberty, democracy and the rule of law, and a set of regional mechanisms, which may be activated if these norms are violated.[18] These include a specially convened FFMM to consider possible regional actions, the creation of a ministerial action group, third-party mediation, a fact-finding mission and the convening of a special high-level meeting of the Forum Security Committee.

---

17 Baker, 'New Zealand and Australia in Pacific Regionalism', pp. 142–3.
18 PIFS, *'Biketawa' Declaration*, Suva: PIFS, 28 October 2000, available from: www.forumsec.org/biketawa-declaration/.

The declaration's most potent and controversial clause states that, if, after such actions are taken, the crisis persists: 'convene a special meeting of Forum leaders to consider other options including if necessary targeted measures'.[19] Subsequent interpretations of 'targeted measures' have included intervention by disciplined forces, at the invitation of the member state, in the case of Solomon Islands in 2003, and suspension of a PIF member, in the case of Fiji in 2009.

To gain the agreement of the Pacific island leaders to the proposed declaration, Clark had proposed the substitution of 'targeted measures' for 'sanctions' (in view of Fiji's objection to 'sanctions').[20] She also reluctantly conceded that the Biketawa Declaration would not apply retrospectively to the Fiji and Solomon Islands crises. Australia and New Zealand nevertheless saw this as a great achievement. They saw the declaration as providing, for the first time, a clear set of prescribed measures in the case of a political crisis in a member country. As reported by Stewart Firth:

> [T]he Biketawa Declaration was acclaimed as a breakthrough ...
>
> John Howard thought the Forum had taken 'a quantum leap forward in relevance' and Helen Clark, while disappointed that the Forum took no immediate action against Fiji, claimed the declaration enabled the Forum to become 'a significant regional organisation ... taking a step beyond talk, talk, talk'.[21]

President Tito of Kiribati, PIF chairman and a supporter of the push by New Zealand and Australia for the Biketawa Declaration, made the following assessment of its significance:

> This is the framework to hold our region together. It's like a village where we now agree for the first time in the history of the Pacific that we have some common rules about our village. And these are the rules now; they may not be perfect. We have also agreed on how we should deal with a member of the village who's not complying with the rules of the village. That is the way I see it now.[22]

19   ibid.
20   David Lewis, 'Helen Clark's OE', *Pundit*, 13 February 2009, available from: www.pundit.co.nz/content/helen-clarks-oe.
21   Stewart Firth, 'A Reflection on South Pacific Regional Security, Mid-2000 to Mid-2001', *Journal of Pacific History*, 36(3), 2001: 277–83, at p. 279.
22   'Pacific Islands Forum Takes No Action against Fiji, Sets up Future Crisis', *PINA News*, [Tarawa], 29 October 2000 (as reported in *Pacific Islands Report*, East–West Center, 30 October 2000).

Niue's Premier, Sani Lakatani, was reported to have had a different reaction to the 'consensus' decision, seeing it instead as a decision imposed by Australia and New Zealand. At the leaders' dinner, he reportedly made 'an unprompted, emotional speech about the treatment of small countries by big ones'.[23]

Despite this perceived dominance by the larger metropolitan neighbours in getting their way with the Biketawa Declaration, the new commitments in the declaration made no difference to the way the PIF dealt with the Fiji crisis. As in the case of Fiji's 1987 coup, the Pacific island leaders 'ruled out any action': 'Pacific island members apparently felt Fiji is on the path back to democracy and should be allowed to continue this without outside interference.'[24] The PIF communiqué stated:

> Leaders also welcomed the effort and commitment to date by the Fiji Interim Government to return the country to constitutional democracy and looked forward to further progress in these efforts.[25]

The 'war on terror' and regional intervention[26]

The terrorist attacks of 11 September 2001, and the launching of the global 'war on terror', gave heightened significance to the 'arc of instability' image of the Pacific island region. As seen from Canberra, the potential threats from transnational crime, particularly in relation to money laundering, now took on more urgency. The failure of a number of island governments to act on the commitments entered into under the Honiara Declaration a decade earlier prompted the Australian Government to promote a new regional security declaration focused on the new security environment and calling for action on the Honiara Declaration. In the Nasonini Declaration on Regional Security, signed at the Suva PIF meeting in August 2002, the 'leaders recalled their commitment to good governance practices' and 'their concern about the recent heightened threat to global

23   Audrey Young, 'Clark Leads at Pacific Islands Forum', *New Zealand Herald*, 26 October 2000.
24   'Pacific Islands Forum Takes No Action against Fiji'.
25   PIFS, *Leaders' Communiqué: Thirty-First Pacific Islands Forum, Tarawa, Republic of Kiribati, 27–30 October 2000*, Suva: PIFS, 2000.
26   This section was first published in '"Our Patch": The War on Terror and the New Interventionism', in Greg Fry and Tarcisius Kabutaulaka (eds), *Intervention and State-Building in the Pacific: The Legitimacy of 'Co-operative Intervention'* (Manchester: Manchester University Press, 2008, pp. 72–86).

and regional security following the events of September 11th, 2001, in particular those posed by international terrorism and transnational crime'. They reaffirmed the importance of the Honiara Declaration 'to address these new and heightened threats to security in the region' and

> underlined their commitment to the importance of global efforts to combat terrorism and to implement internationally agreed anti-terrorism measures, such as the United Nations Security Council Resolution 1373 and the Financial Action Task Force Special Recommendations, including associated reporting requirements.

They also noted that,

> while some progress has been made in the implementation of the Honiara Declaration, further urgent action was required of some member states and recommitted to full implementation of relevant legislation under the Honiara Declaration by the end of 2003.[27]

More significantly, the war on terror moved regional intervention from a declaratory possibility under the Biketawa Declaration to an actuality. This was a direct outcome of the impact of the war on terror and related alliance politics on Australia's regional security policy. While the Australian Government did not necessarily fully endorse the more alarmist conclusions of some think tanks about the potential 'terrorist havens' in the 'failed states' of the Pacific, the war on terror undoubtedly led to a dramatic reassessment of Canberra's thinking about the need for more robust intervention in the Pacific island states as part of its regional security approach.[28] In mid 2003, it developed a new doctrine of 'cooperative intervention' and began to plan police-led intervention in Papua New Guinea and Solomon Islands.[29] In sentiments reminiscent of Australian Pacific policy of the 1940s and the 1970s—examined in earlier chapters—prime minister Howard commented:

---

27 PIFS, *Nasonini Declaration on Regional Security*, Suva: PIFS, 2002, available from: www.forum sec.org/nasonini-declaration-on-regional-security/, Clauses 5 and 7.
28 Elsina Wainwright, *Our Failing Neighbour: Australia and the Future of Solomon Islands*, Canberra: Australian Strategic Policy Institute, 10 June 2003.
29 See Greg Fry and Tarcisius Kabutaulaka, 'Political Legitimacy and State-Building Intervention in the Pacific', in Greg Fry and Tarcisius Kabutaulaka, eds, *Intervention and State-Building in the Pacific: The Legitimacy of 'Co-operative Intervention'*, Manchester: Manchester University Press, 2008.

> The rest of the world sees Australia as having a special role in this area and I believe that the Australian Government and the Australian people should assume it … But this is our patch. We have a special responsibility in this part of the world. I believe that very strongly.[30]

However, as Nicola Baker persuasively argues, the Solomon Islands intervention would have remained a unilateral initiative if it were not for Helen Clark's role in persuading Howard to make it a regional intervention under the auspices of the PIF and its Biketawa Declaration.[31] The Howard Government accepted this advice and asked for a regional Forum Foreign Ministers Meeting in Sydney in July 2003 to discuss the Solomon Islands prime minister's request for assistance in the crisis impacting his country. Following the signing of the subsequent Townsville Peace Agreement governing the intervention, the Regional Assistance Mission to Solomon Islands (RAMSI) was established as a regional initiative under the legal jurisdiction of the PIF.[32]

This was a major intervention, which lasted 14 years. It began as a police-led intervention with the support of some Australian and New Zealand military personnel. The police contingent was drawn from all PIF countries. Australia led the mission and Australian personnel dominated the civilian contingent involved in advising the law and order, governance and financial pillars of the intervention, which were aimed at remaking the state. The initial task of reestablishing law and order was very successful, and the mission then settled down to the long haul of rebuilding the state. Given the Australian dominance in materiel, finance and personnel as well as in leadership positions, pressure began to build to review the governance of the mission.[33] A two-person mission recommended a reassertion of PIF jurisdiction.[34] This was done through regular reporting to the FRSC and some readjustments of the nature of the mission to ensure more regional representation at higher levels.

---

30 'Pacific Leaders Back Australian Role', *The Age*, [Melbourne], 9 August 2004.

31 Baker, 'New Zealand and Australia in Pacific Regionalism'.

32 Townsville Peace Agreement.

33 PIFS, *Leaders' Communiqué: Thirty-Seventh Pacific Islands Forum, Nadi, Fiji, 24–25 October 2006*, Suva: PIFS, 2006, available from: www.forumsec.org/wp-content/uploads/2017/11/2006-Forum-Communique%CC%81_-Denarau_-Nadi_-Fiji_-24-25-Oct.pdf, paras 1 and 2.

34 PIFS, *A Review of the Regional Assistance Mission to Solomon Islands: Report of the Pacific Islands Forum Eminent Persons Group*, Suva: PIFS, May 2005.

The RAMSI experience ultimately enhanced the reputation of the Biketawa Declaration. When the Solomon Islands mission ended in 2016, the reviews were generally positive.[35] Even Solomon Islands prime minister Sogavare, who had earlier been very critical of RAMSI, was a strong supporter at the time of RAMSI's departure.[36] He became a champion of the Biketawa Declaration to the point where, in 2017, he called for 'Biketawa-plus'—an enhanced Biketawa—to take account of the new regional security environment.[37] The PIF review, however, raised some issues about the intervention as a regional venture:

> The Office of the Special Coordinator liaised with the Forum and the SIG [Solomon Islands Government], but operations were primarily overseen from Canberra as were controls over key appointments ... Though RAMSI is often seen as a stellar example of regional cooperation, the mission might have been better served by drawing more constructively on that regional element, not simply in terms of personnel, but also as regards command structure.[38]

Australia's new interventionism in the Pacific prompted by the war on terror also had an impact on its commitment to reform Pacific regionalism as practised through the PIF. Apart from supporting an enhanced pooling of regional governance and a further compromise on national sovereignty, Australia was concerned to establish security as one of the pillars of the Pacific Plan, and for the plan to revisit the various regional security objectives it had failed to achieve in the 1990s despite declaratory agreement by Pacific island leaders. This, then, was an effort to give the security agenda new focus and force with new powers for the PIFS. New Zealand shared the commitment to regional reform and a more interventionist regionalism, but from different motives. It is notable that Clark was not embracing Canberra's war on terror motivation, but rather was concerned about internal crises and their impact on poverty.[39]

35   Jon Fraenkel, Joni Madraiwiwi, and Henry Okole, *The RAMSI Decade: A Review of the Regional Assistance Mission to Solomon Islands, 2003–2013*, Honiara: Solomon Islands Government, 14 July 2014.

36   Manasseh Sogavare, 'Message of Appreciation by Prime Minister Hon. Manasseh Sogavare to RAMSI, RAMSI Participating Countries', Prime Minister's Press Secretariat, Honiara, 25 June 2017.

37   Manasseh Damukana Sogavare, 'Solomon Islands Statement by Hon. Manasseh Damukana Sogavare, MP Prime Minister, 72nd Session United Nations General Assembly, General Debate', United Nations, New York, 2017, available from: gadebate.un.org/sites/default/files/gastatements/72/sb_en.pdf; PIFS, *Leaders' Communiqué: Forty-Eighth Pacific Islands Forum*, paras 31–4.

38   Fraenkel et al., *The RAMSI Decade*, p. 79, para. 15.6.

39   'The United States of the Pacific', *Sydney Morning Herald*, 17 March 2004, p. 12.

The war on terror framing of Australia's regional security policy was also expressed in an effort to ramp up regional action on transnational crime. The Australian Federal Police set up a regional network of transnational crime units in Papua New Guinea, Fiji, Tonga and Samoa and, in June 2004, established the Pacific Transnational Crime Coordination Centre (PTCCC) in Suva, which was moved to Apia after the 2006 coup in Fiji. Although the PTCCC was not set up by the PIF leaders or under the auspices of the PIF, Pacific leaders welcomed its establishment at the 2004 PIF meeting.[40]

The suspension of Fiji and the non-intervention principle

In the case of Solomon Islands, the Biketawa Declaration was invoked in a context in which the government had requested regional assistance with a domestic crisis. In 2009, Biketawa was invoked for the first time in applying 'targeted measures' on a member state without the agreement of the affected country. This therefore represented a major departure from the non-intervention principle that had underpinned Pacific regionalism since 1971. The occasion was the decision of the Pacific leaders at a special leaders' retreat in Port Moresby on 27 January 2009.[41] The PIF chair, Toke Talagi, Premier of Niue, announced the decision in a press statement on 2 May 2009. The decision to 'suspend' Fiji 'from full participation in the Pacific Islands Forum' took immediate effect. Premier Talagi added that the 'unanimous' decision of all PIF leaders

> [r]esponds to Commodore Bainimarama's failure to address constructively by 1 May 2009 the expectations of Forum leaders to return Fiji to democratic governance in an acceptable time-frame …

> Respond directly to the confirmation by the military regime in Fiji … that it rejects fundamental Forum obligations and core principles, as outlined in the Biketawa Declaration and other key guiding documents of the Forum. Reflecting on the Leaders Vision Statement of 2004, this involves cooperation through the

40   PIFS, *Leaders' Communiqué: Thirty-Fifth Pacific Islands Forum, Apia, Samoa, 5–7 August 2004*, Suva: PIFS, 2004.
41   PIFS, *Leaders' Decisions: Pacific Islands Forum Special Leaders' Retreat, Port Moresby, Papua New Guinea, 27 January 2009*, Suva: PIFS, 2009.

> Forum to create a Pacific region respected for the quality of its governance, the sustainable management of its resources, the full observance of democratic values and for its defence and promotion of human rights.[42]

Over the previous two years, since the Fiji coup in December 2006, the PIF leaders had been working their way through less intrusive measures under the Biketawa Declaration. They had begun with the establishment of the EPG, which visited Fiji in January 2007. At the October 2007 PIF meeting, Prime Minister of Fiji, Frank Bainimarama, gave an undertaking that an election would be held in the first quarter of 2009. The PIF leaders also called on Fiji to work with the PIF–Fiji Joint Working Group (of officials) to produce a credible roadmap. To this point, the Biketawa measures seemed to be effective. But in June 2008, Commodore Bainimarama announced that he had decided 'that Fiji will no longer participate in the Forum Working Group meetings until such time [as] the positions of Australia and New Zealand are genuine'.[43] Fiji also failed to attend the August 2008 PIF meeting. The communiqué criticised this absence and condemned recent statements from Fiji suggesting that the commitment to hold an election in 2009 would be broken. The PIF also decided to hold a special meeting of leaders to consider special 'targeted measures', including suspension.[44]

It was at this point that the leaders crossed into new territory, in terms of past regional practice and in terms of the non-intervention principle, in particular. When democracy was overthrown in Fiji in 1987, and again in 2000, the Pacific island leaders would not support Australian and New Zealand efforts to have the PIF intervene, not even to discuss diplomatic measures short of intervention. Just as importantly, the Bougainville war raged within a member state for a decade from 1989 to 1999 without being raised at the PIF as a regional security issue with which it should become involved. In this case, Australia and New Zealand joined the island states in their reluctance to discuss this conflict within Papua New Guinea, despite more than 10,000 deaths.

---

42   PIFS, 'Statement by Forum Chair on Suspension of the Fiji Military Regime from the Pacific Islands Forum', Press Statement 21/09, Suva: PIFS, 2 May 2009.

43   'Fiji Drops Out of Forum Working Group', *Fijilive*, 23 June 2008, available from: www.pireport. org/articles/2008/06/23/fiji-drops-out-forum-working-group.

44   PIFS, *Leaders' Communiqué: Thirty-Ninth Pacific Islands Forum, Alofi, Niue, 19–20 August 2008*, Suva: PIFS, 2008.

Nor can we confidently point to the suspension of Fiji as a turning point in practice in upholding regional norms of democracy and the rule of law. First, there is the problem that, although there was apparent unanimity, it is clear that Australia and New Zealand were the main countries pushing for Fiji's suspension. The half-heartedness of the support of many of the island countries was soon revealed when they supported efforts by Fiji to open new forms of dialogue in new regional institutions, including the Engaging with the Pacific, the Pacific Islands Development Forum (PIDF), the reinvigorated MSG and the Pacific Small Island Developing States (PSIDS) grouping at the United Nations.

Second, the failure of the suspension to move Fiji to elections on the timetable set by the PIF, combined with the unsettling impact of Fiji's determination to set up an alternative regionalism, has meant that there is now a question mark over the effectiveness of 'targeted measures' to achieve their objective.

Third, since the suspension of Fiji in 2009, there have been major departures from democracy, the constitution and the rule of law in two other member states, Papua New Guinea[45] and Nauru,[46] and yet Australia and New Zealand did not seek to bring them under the aegis of the Biketawa Declaration, largely because of Australia's interest in keeping on side with the ruling regimes given their importance in hosting Australia's offshore detention centres. Thus, the norm has not been established that antidemocratic moves on the part of PIF members generally prompts regional measures despite the significance of the PIF's intervention in Solomon Islands and Fiji.

---

45 'Papua New Guinea in Crisis as Two Claim to be Prime Minister', *The Guardian*, 14 December 2011; Matt Siegel, 'Papua New Guinea Braces for Unrest with Two Prime Ministers and Cabinets', *The New York Times*, 13 December 2011.

46 Tess Newton Cain, 'Deafening Silence on Rule of Law in Nauru', *The Interpreter*, Sydney: Lowy Institute for International Policy, 21 March 2014, available from: www.lowyinstitute.org/the-interpreter/deafening-silence-rule-law-nauru; Bal Kama, 'Nauru Rule of Law Case and the Implication for the Pacific', *Outrigger: Blog of the Pacific Institute*, Canberra: The Australian National University, 21 March 2014, available from: pacificinstitute.anu.edu.au/outrigger/2014/03/21/australias-blind-eye-while-rule-of-law-under-siege-in-the-pacific/.

Biketawa Plus: Human security versus strategic denial

From 2017, the Pacific island leaders indicated their interest in expanding the concept of regional security to meet new global and regional challenges. This was in the context of having just recognised the importance and success of the existing Biketawa Declaration in providing the conceptual frame and legal basis for RAMSI from 2003 to 2017. At the FFMM in Suva in August 2017, the Solomon Islands Government took the lead in suggesting consideration of a 'RAMSI Plus' to deal with a changing regional and global context. The other foreign ministers were in accord. They agreed to recommend that the leaders consider this proposal at the upcoming PIF meeting in Apia. It was particularly significant that Fiji's Minister for Defence and National Security, Ratu Inoke Kubuabola, publicly endorsed the idea, given Fiji's opposition to the use of the Biketawa Declaration in suspending Fiji from the PIF in 2009. Shortly after the FFMM, minister Kubuabola was reported as saying:

> I wish to lend support to the idea of a Biketawa Plus. I believe that an expansion of the Biketawa Declaration to Biketawa Plus is an acknowledgement of the emergence of new global trends that is posing new and serious threats to peace, security and prosperity of our Pacific peoples and communities.[47]

At the September 2017 PIF meeting in Apia, the leaders agreed with the FFMM's recommendation. They decided to 'build on the Biketawa Declaration and other Forum security related declarations as a foundation for strategic future regional responses'. They agreed that the proposed reframing of regional security should recognise 'the importance of an expanded concept of security inclusive of human security, humanitarian assistance, prioritising environmental security, and regional cooperation in building resilience to disasters and climate change'.[48] The leaders tasked the secretariat with consulting member states and civil society to produce a draft declaration for consideration at the September 2018 PIF meeting.

---

47   Arieta Vakasukawaqa, 'Ratu Inoke Proposes Biketawa Plus After Regional, Global Security Trends', *Fiji Sun Online*, 12 August 2017, available from: fijisun.com.fj/2017/08/12/ratu-inoke-proposes-biketawa-plus-after-regional-global-security-trends/.
48   PIFS, *Leaders' Communiqué: Forty-Eighth Pacific Islands Forum*, Clause 33.

As the PIFS carried out these region-wide consultations, its efforts were complicated by the sudden entry of a new security discourse aimed at taking the reframing of regional security in a very different direction. From early 2018, Canberra and Wellington began to focus on their 'strategic anxieties' about the changing geopolitics of the region. This mainly concerned the assumed implications of dependence on Chinese loans for Pacific state sovereignty. The ultimate concern was that indebtedness to China could lead to a Chinese military base in the region. In the case of Australia, in particular, this very quickly started to look like a return of the 'strategic denial' security paradigm of the Cold War years based on a traditional concept of security emphasising the grand strategy of great powers and countering a perceived military threat.

In early January 2018, the Australian Minister for International Development, Senator Concetta Fierravanti-Wells, told the media that China's influence was 'clearly growing' in the Pacific and Chinese economic assistance was constructing 'useless buildings' and 'roads to nowhere'—intimating that there were other motives behind this assistance.[49] The Samoan Prime Minister, Tuilaepa Sailele, said the Australian minister's comments were 'quite insulting to the leaders of Pacific Island neighbours' and could 'destroy the excellent relationships existing between Australia and the Pacific Island neighbours'.[50] In the face of protests from China and Pacific island leaders, Australian foreign minister Julie Bishop moved to quell the diplomatic upset with an assurance that Australian government policy remained that of working in the Pacific 'with a wide range of development partners, including China, in pursuit of the goal of eliminating poverty in our region and globally'. But she also went some way in supporting her colleague's criticism of Chinese economic assistance by saying that the Australian Government 'welcomes investment in developing nations in the Pacific that supports sustainable economic growth, and *which does not impose onerous debt burdens on regional governments*' (my emphasis).[51]

---

49 Primrose Riordan, 'Coalition Attack on China over Pacific Aid', *The Australian*, 9 January 2018.
50 Bruce Hill, 'Samoan PM Hits Back at Australia's "Insulting" Criticism of China's Aid Program in Pacific', *Pacific Beat*, ABC News, 12 January 2018.
51 Amy Remeikis, 'Julie Bishop in Balancing Act after Colleague Criticises China's Pacific Aid', *The Guardian*, 11 January 2018.

In April 2018, the issue arose again, but this time it was presented not as a development issue around debt burden but rather as a security issue concerning possible Chinese military basing in the Pacific islands on the back of an assumption that indebtedness to China would lead to a 'debt trap' (a debt for equity swap). It began with *Sydney Morning Herald* defence and national security correspondent David Wroe making the dramatic claim that

> China has approached Vanuatu about building a permanent military presence in the South Pacific in a globally significant move that could see the rising superpower sail warships on Australia's doorstep.[52]

The specific claim was that the new Luganville wharf on the northern island of Espiritu Santo, funded by Chinese loans, had the potential to service naval vessels. Wroe argued that 'while no formal proposals have been put to Vanuatu's government, senior [Australian] security officials believe Beijing's plans could culminate in a full military base'. Wroe also introduced the more general claim that

> Australian intelligence and security figures, along with their partners in the United States and New Zealand, have been watching with concern as Beijing deepens its influence with Pacific islands governments through infrastructure building and loans.

While no evidence of actual Chinese plans was adduced to support the conjecture, these claims quickly became the basis of an alarmist response from other commentators in Australian media outlets and think tanks.[53]

Vanuatu's foreign minister Ralph Reganvanu responded that these claims were false: '[N]o-one in the Vanuatu Government has ever talked about a Chinese military base in Vanuatu of any sort'.[54] Pacific commentators also pointed out the fallacies underlying this reported position of Australian senior security officials and the subsequent commentary by security specialists. For example, James Batley, a former senior Australian diplomat to Solomon Islands and Vanuatu and former RAMSI coordinator, called this commentary 'hyperventilation', while ANU economist Matthew

---

52   David Wroe, 'China Eyes Vanuatu Military Base in Plan with Global Ramifications', *Sydney Morning Herald*, 9 April 2018.

53   See Sally Whyte, 'Australia Must Step Up if China Starts Military Build Up in Vanuatu', *Sydney Morning Herald*, 10 April 2018; Tom Steinfort, 'The China Syndrome', *60 Minutes*, Sydney: Nine Entertainment Co., 17 June 2018.

54   ABC News, 'Chinese Military Base in Pacific Would be of "Great Concern", Turnbull tells Vanuatu', *Pacific Beat*, ABC News, 10 April 2018.

Dornan called much of the reporting 'hysterical'.[55] Dornan also questions some of the key assumptions underlying the worst-case analysis of Australia's reporting. For example, the contract between the Chinese Government and the Vanuatu Government did not actually have a debt for equity provision as claimed; nor was Vanuatu's overall indebtedness at risky levels as claimed.[56]

Despite this critique from Pacific specialists, and the denials of the Vanuatu Government, Australia nevertheless moved quickly to promote a new policy approach to regional security based on these premises. In a style reminiscent of the strategic denial paradigm during the Cold War, prime minister Malcolm Turnbull warned Pacific island governments— and presumably China—that Australia 'would view with great concern the establishment of any foreign military bases in those Pacific island countries and neighbours of ours'.[57] Foreign minister Bishop continued the language of strategic denial during her visit to Micronesian island capitals in early June, reportedly asserting that 'we regard the Pacific as our part of the world, this is our region where we can make a difference'.[58]

The new policy approach quickly moved from diplomatic statements to actions. After meeting Vanuatu's Prime Minister, Charlot Salwai, in London, prime minister Turnbull announced that the Australian Government would be funding an undersea fibre-optic cable connecting Solomon Islands and Papua New Guinea to the internet, cutting out the Chinese company Huawei, which was about to fund these projects.[59] Australia extended this offer to support high-speed undersea cable to Vanuatu during Salwai's visit to Australia in late June.[60] At the Commonwealth leaders' meeting in London, Australia was reportedly successful in 'encouraging Britain to extend its aid, trade and diplomatic influence in the south Pacific after it leaves the EU to help counter Chinese influence in the region'.[61] The United Kingdom announced it

---

55   James Batley, *Review: Safeguarding Australia's Security Interests through Closer Pacific Ties*, Sydney: Lowy Institute, 27 April 2018; Matthew Dornan, 'Australia's Pacific Island Myopia', *The Diplomat*, 13 July 2018.

56   Dornan, 'Australia's Pacific Island Myopia'.

57   ABC News, 'Chinese Military Base in Pacific Would be of "Great Concern"'.

58   Primrose Riordan, 'Julie Bishop's Message for China: Pacific is Australia's Patch', *The Australian*, 5 June 2018.

59   Latika Bourke, 'UK to Open Diplomatic Posts in the Pacific, Citing Security Concerns', *Sydney Morning Herald*, 20 April 2018.

60   Catherine Graue, 'Federal Government Flags Willingness to Help Vanuatu with High-Speed Undersea Internet Cable', *Pacific Beat*, ABC News, 27 June 2018.

61   Dennis Shanahan, 'Turnbull Welcomes British Initiatives in South Pacific Region', *The Australian*, 21 April 2018.

would be opening diplomatic posts in Vanuatu, Samoa and Tonga. In the following month, US marines joined Australian warships to visit Pacific island ports as part of military exercises. Later in June, foreign minister Bishop reportedly announced that the Australian Government would 'compete with China's infrastructure development spree in Australia's neighbourhood to help ensure small nations are not saddled with debts that threatens [sic] their sovereignty'.[62]

Although New Zealand commentary did not exhibit the same level of 'hyperventilation', it was evident that, in announcing its 'Pacific reset' foreign policy in March 2018, its foreign minister was influenced by a perception of the security implications of rising Chinese involvement in the region. Foreign minister Winston Peters emphasised the 'strategic anxieties' created by the fact that 'the Pacific has … become an increasingly contested strategic space, no longer neglected by Great Power ambition, and so Pacific Island leaders have more options'. He concluded that 'there has never been a time since 1945 when Australia and New Zealand need to work together more closely in the Pacific'.[63] New Zealand's Prime Minister, Jacinda Ardern, was, however, careful not to jump to conclusions in her response to the *Sydney Morning Herald*'s claim that China had approached Vanuatu about 'establishing a permanent military presence on the island nation'. She replied that she was not aware of this proposal, but 'what I can say is … that New Zealand is opposed to the militarisation of the Pacific generally'.[64]

By June 2018, then, Australia was promoting a framing of regional security that was very different from the human security paradigm being promoted by the Pacific island leaders. Its position had begun to look very much like the Cold War strategic denial doctrine. This is a traditional geopolitical view of security—one of preventing an assumed possibility of a military base that might threaten Australian security interests. It is, then, a regional security concept built on the security interests of Australia and projected on to the regional community rather than one shared by other members of that regional community. This conceptualisation of threat leads to a regional conception of security governance that is necessarily

---

62   David Wroe, 'Australia will Compete with China to Save Pacific Sovereignty, Says Bishop', *Sydney Morning Herald*, 18 June 2018.
63   Winston Peters, '"Shifting the Dial": Eyes Wide Open, Pacific Reset', Speech delivered to the Lowy Institute, Sydney, 2 March 2018.
64   Fergus Hunter and David Wroe, 'New Zealand Opposed to Militarization in the Pacific: Jacinda Ardern', *Sydney Morning Herald*, 10 April 2018.

hegemonic. As operational policy, the attempt to deny Chinese military involvement becomes an attempt to deny the interests of several Pacific island states committing to loans from China. As in the Cold War, when strategic denial of the Soviet Union became an attempt to deny Pacific island states' economic engagement with the Soviets, such a policy of denial is obviously bound to create tension with Pacific island governments.

First, it offends Pacific governments by assuming that they have no discernment or agency in relation to their decisions about Chinese loans. With an obvious reference to recent warnings from Australia and New Zealand, Samoan Prime Minister Sailele said in late August 2018 that

> some might say there is a patronising nuance, believing Pacific nations did not know what they were doing, or were incapable of reaping benefits of close relationships with countries that will be in the region for some time to come.[65]

Second, it asks the Pacific island countries to forgo an opportunity for economic assistance that they greatly value. The leaders of those states recognising China—Papua New Guinea, Vanuatu, Samoa, Tonga, Cook Islands—have all issued statements saying how valuable the Chinese loans are, providing infrastructure development not generally available from other donors. Cook Islands Prime Minister, Henry Puna, argued that 'from a Cook Islands perspective, the Pacific need not be a zero sum game'. He asserted that 'we have partnered with China as their interests into the Pacific have grown and it's been a most mutually beneficial relationship'.[66] In an attempt to reassure Australia, Papua New Guinea's Minister for Foreign Affairs, Rimbink Pato, was reported as saying that

> Papua New Guinea would continue looking for aid and loans from nations like China, particularly to develop infrastructure … the country's long history of receiving Australian aid taught it how to assess and manage foreign funding.[67]

65   Stephen Dziedzic, 'Samoan Prime Minister Tuilaepa Sailele Hits Out at Climate Change Sceptics during Fiery Speech', *ABC News Online*, 31 August 2018, available from: www.abc.net.au/news/2018-08-31/samoan-prime-minister-hits-out-at-climate-change-sceptics/10185142.
66   Henry Puna, 'The Cook Islands, NZ and Free Association: Speech by Hon. Henry Puna, Prime Minister of the Cook Islands', New Zealand Institute for International Affairs, Wellington, 4 April 2018, p. 4, available from: www.nziia.org.nz/Portals/285/documents/lists/259/PM%20Puna%20-%20NZIIA%20speech%20FINAL%20delivered%204%20April%202018.pdf.
67   Eric Tlozek, 'Australia Should Not Fear Chinese Influence in Papua New Guinea, Government Says', *ABC News Online*, 23 January 2018, available from: www.abc.net.au/news/2018-01-23/australia-should-not-fear-chinese-influence-in-png/9349140.

Third, a tension arises because the denial policy expects a level of forbearance on the part of Pacific island states not exercised by Australia and New Zealand. According to a 2018 report, KPMG estimates that 'Australia remains the second largest recipient country of accumulated Chinese investment, after the US, with USD 99 billion since 2008'.[68] *Bloomberg Business* claims that 'Australia is the most China-dependent economy in the developed world', with 35 per cent of its exports going to China.[69]

Fourth, as in the Cold War, this will be seen as an attempt to create a two-tier, hierarchical form of regional security governance in which the Pacific island states are expected to meet regional norms that do not apply to Australia and New Zealand.

What, then, were the implications of this regional strategic denial doctrine for the negotiation of the new regional security arrangements under Biketawa Plus? Some commentators mistakenly saw the Biketawa Plus Declaration negotiations as an Australian initiative to shore up the region and to exclude unwelcome powers—notably, China.[70] This is, however, a misreading of its history. As James Batley points out, the negotiation of a new regional security arrangement, Biketawa Plus, has its origins 'in the minds of thoughtful Pacific islanders following the conclusion of the Regional Assistance Mission to Solomon Islands in mid-2017'.[71] Nevertheless, there was an expectation that the Nauru PIF meeting would be a contest between the China-threat focus of an Australian strategic denial policy approach and the human security orientation of the Pacific island leaders centred on climate change as the priority security concern.[72]

---

68   KPMG, *Demystifying Chinese Investment in Australia: June 2018*, Melbourne: KPMG Australia, available from: home.kpmg.com/au/en/home/insights/2018/06/demystifying-chinese-investment-in-australia-june-2018.html.

69   Michael Heath, 'Australia's Economy Has a Lot to Lose from US–China Trade War', *Bloomberg*, 23 March 2018, available from: www.bloomberg.com/news/articles/2018-03-23/-very-awkward-spot-in-u-s-china-firing-line-for-aussie-economy.

70   See, for example, Primrose Riordan, 'Pacific Pact to Strengthen Regional Security and Counter China Push', *The Australian*, 6 July 2018.

71   Batley, *Review*.

72   See, for example, Jennifer Hayward-Jones, 'Diverging Regional Priorities at the Pacific Islands Forum', *Australian Outlook*, Canberra: Australian Institute of International Affairs, 3 September 2018, available from: www.internationalaffairs.org.au/australianoutlook/diverging-regional-priorities-at-pacific-islands-forum/.

The outcome of this contest of regional diplomacy over the future governance of regional security is the Boe Declaration.[73] The main commitments in this declaration reflect the Pacific island countries' 'human security' position as the conceptual basis for regional security governance. The preamble recognises:

> The importance we placed on an expanded concept of security inclusive of human security, humanitarian assistance, prioritising environmental security, and regional cooperation in building resilience to disasters and climate change.

In paragraph (vii) of the declaration, there is further indication of the list of security issues falling under the expanded concept. It includes human security (including humanitarian assistance), environmental and resource security, transnational crime and cybersecurity.

The most significant expression of the dominance of the Pacific island countries' position is the 'reaffirmation' that

> climate change remains the single greatest threat to the livelihoods, security and wellbeing of the peoples of the Pacific and our commitment to progress the implementation of the Paris Agreement.[74]

This outcome could not be further from Australia's preferred position, which is reflected in the contemporary debate within the governing party about whether to withdraw from the Paris Agreement.

There is no mention of limits on military basing or strategic denial of other powers. The main influence of the Australian position presumably appears in the commitment to reaffirm the 'importance of the rules-based international order' and to strengthen national security strategies through training (paragraph viii). The commitment to 'respect and assert the sovereign right of every Member to conduct its national affairs free of external interference and coercion' (paragraph iv) could apply to interference by Australia and New Zealand as much as to China and thus should not necessarily be seen as evidence of Australian influence on the text in this regard. The tone of the document is suggestive of the

73 PIFS, 'Annex 1: Boe Declaration on Regional Security [Boe Declaration]', in *Leaders' Communiqué: Forty-Ninth Pacific Islands Forum, Yaren, Nauru, 3–6 September 2018*, Suva: PIFS, 2018.
74 'Draft Declaration', reproduced in Fergus Hunter, 'Pacific Nations Push Morrison Government to Pledge Support for Paris Climate Accord', *Sydney Morning Herald*, 29 August 2018, para. (1).

need for Pacific island control of and assertion over regional security governance. Significantly, the preamble recognises 'the need to strengthen regional security cooperation and collective action through the assertion of *Our Will* and the voices of *Our Pacific Peoples*'.[75]

Australia's pursuit of a strategic denial strategy aimed at China has focused instead on creating new regional institutional arrangements outside the Boe Declaration. Before the Nauru PIF meeting, Australia had announced its intention to establish an Australia Pacific Security College with the objective of training a regionwide coterie of like-minded officials in security analysis.[76] The design summary asserts that the Biketawa Plus regional security declaration will be a 'key driver' for the college. The second initiative—'welcomed' by the Pacific leaders at the Nauru meeting—was the creation of a Pacific Fusion Centre. This agency

> will build on current regional frameworks to strengthen information sharing and maritime domain awareness, to better inform security responses to some of the main threats outlined in the Boe Declaration, such as illegal fishing, drugs trafficking and other transnational crimes.[77]

The third proposal is a joint initiative with the Fiji Government and relates to the redevelopment of Fiji's Blackrock Peacekeeping and Humanitarian Assistance and Disaster Relief Camp into 'a regional hub for police and peacekeeping training and pre-deployment preparation'.[78] These regional initiatives complement Canberra's new bilateral diplomatic and economic strategies aimed at moving Pacific island states away from Chinese loans and influence: its counter bid to provide undersea fibre-optic cables for Vanuatu, Papua New Guinea and Solomon Islands; the development of a joint Australia–Papua New Guinea naval base on Manus Island;[79] the increase in military visits; and the encouragement of increased Western diplomatic presence in Pacific island countries.

---

75   ibid., Preamble.

76   DFAT, *Design Summary for the Australia Pacific Security College*, Canberra: DFAT, 1 August 2018, available from: dfat.gov.au/about-us/business-opportunities/Pages/design-summary-for-the-australia-pacific-security-college.aspx.

77   PIFS, *Leaders' Communiqué: Forty-Ninth Pacific Islands Forum, Yaren, Nauru, 3–6 September 2018*, Suva: PIFS, 2018, para. 45.

78   Malcolm Turnbull, 'Regional Training Hub for Fiji', Media release, 22 August 2018, available from: www.malcolmturnbull.com.au/media/regional-training-hub-for-fiji#.

79   Ben Packham, 'Move to Head Off China with Australian Base on PNG', *The Australian*, 20 September 2018; and Greg Sheridan and Cameron Stewart, 'Top Defence Threat Now Lies in the South Pacific from China', *The Australian*, 22 September 2018.

Australia's preferred regional order is one in which it is the leading external security partner to Pacific island states and the undue influence of other metropolitan powers, and particularly China, has been denied. It has also been concerned over many years to ensure that regional commitments on climate change do not go against Australia's interest in doing very little to lower carbon emissions in its own economy. The outcomes of the regional diplomacy at Nauru, and subsequent developments, suggest Australia has failed on both these counts. The development of a joint naval base with Papua New Guinea on Manus Island has taken Australia's strategic denial policy to a much higher level than it promoted during the Cold War in relation to the Soviet Union. Nevertheless, it is clear that it has not had the desired outcome. Key Pacific states such as Papua New Guinea, Fiji and Samoa have increased their engagement with China and have insisted on their right to do so. And, as we have seen, the Pacific has succeeded in making climate change the key priority of the Boe Declaration.

Conclusion

In the first two decades after the Cold War, Australia and New Zealand sought to reframe Pacific regional security to emphasise political stability and good governance inside the state rather than countering external military threats. They saw poor leadership, poor governance, political instability and state failure as making the region vulnerable to nontraditional transnational security threats such as terrorism, drug running, corruption, fraud, money laundering, tax havens and human trafficking. The preferred security solution involved tightening regional security governance and regional borders by establishing regional norms concerning good governance, institutionalising these norms through new regional structures, with the FRSC at the apex, and the promotion of regional harmonisation of laws enforcing border security. As we have seen, these commitments were all expressed in regional treaties and declarations.

This reframing challenged the conception of sovereignty, and the norm of non-intervention, on which the Pacific regional community had been formed in the early 1970s. This new security framing was inspired by a changing global order as well as changing political developments within the region. This was a hegemonic project, led by Australia and New Zealand but with New Zealand taking the lead over the establishment of the Biketawa regime. Taken together with the promotion of the new regional economic order, this effort to build a regional security order inevitably created a hierarchical regional system within the PIF. Despite its presentation as a regional consensus, it was clear who was setting the agenda, who was responsible for the new dominant conceptualisations of security and who took the dominant role in actual interventions.

However, in the decade since 2010, the Pacific states began to collectively assert themselves diplomatically. We examine this 'new Pacific diplomacy' in the next chapter. The key point for our present purposes is that the issues on which the Pacific leaders had shared concerns about promoting included climate change, ocean management, sustainable development and humanitarian assistance. By 2017, the Pacific leaders started to bring these together conceptually as a 'human security' paradigm as the basis for reframing 'regional security' in the Biketawa Plus negotiations.

Meanwhile, as we have seen, from early 2018, Australian and New Zealand concerns about Chinese influence in the Pacific, which had been evident since 2009, began to be the key frame through which Canberra and Wellington viewed Pacific regional security. This was sparked by the supposed revelation by Australian security officials who claimed that China was planning a military base in Vanuatu on the back of growing indebtedness. The reemergence of strategic denial thinking in Canberra, in particular, and its expression in its Pacific policy, involves an attempt to impose hegemonic regional security governance based on two tiers of rights and responsibilities within the Pacific regional community— familiar from the Cold War. However, as we have seen, this intention has come up against a very determined Pacific leadership, focused on regional self-determination and ready to contest hegemonic regionalism and promote an alternative framing of Pacific regional security.

13

The 'new' Pacific diplomacy and the transformation of regionalism

Beginning in 2009, Pacific island leaders embraced two big ideas that have had a transformative effect on contemporary Pacific regionalism. The first is that Pacific islanders should be in control of regional governance and the regional diplomatic agenda. In the words of Kiribati president Anote Tong in 2012:

> I believe the Pacific is entering a new phase—a new paradigm shift where the Pacific needs to chart its own course and lead global thinking in crucial areas such as climate change, ocean governance, and sustainable development.[1]

The idea that the Pacific should 'chart its own course' is not a new one in the long history of indigenous regionalism; it was, as we have seen, the founding principle of the SPF in 1971. The current promotion of this idea can therefore be seen as a reassertion of the key normative underpinning of the regional diplomatic culture of the 1970s, which had been suppressed in the hegemonic regionalism of the 1990s and 2000s. As in its earlier iteration, this principle has found expression in the commitment to reconfigure the regional architecture such that the

---

1   Anote Tong, '"Charting its Own Course": A Paradigm Shift in Pacific Diplomacy', in Greg Fry and Sandra Tarte, eds, *The New Pacific Diplomacy*, Canberra: ANU Press, 2015, pp. 21–4.

key concerns of Pacific island societies can be addressed, and policies determined, without external interference. However, in the contemporary context of a globalised world, the regional self-determination principle has also taken on new expressions. It has also been represented in a shared commitment among Pacific island leaders to developing new ways of projecting a 'Pacific voice' in global diplomacy, and even in exercising global leadership in some diplomatic areas such as ocean management and climate policy.

The second big idea is that Pacific regionalism should be inclusive, by welcoming Pacific civil society and private sector organisations into regional policy deliberations and agenda setting. This has been expressed not only in institutional adjustments to allow such participation, but also in constant rhetorical references to the inclusion of 'the Pacific peoples' more broadly. This has extended to the inclusion of dependent territories in regional deliberations as equal partners. These developments represent a major departure from the founding norm of the SPF—that the Pacific peoples should be represented by sovereign states and therefore representatives of sovereign states are the only legitimate participants at the regional diplomatic table.

As in 1971, this current paradigm shift in relation to how Pacific regionalism should be governed and how regional diplomacy should be conducted has been expressed in a series of attempts to change the regional architecture. Canberra and Wellington have viewed some of these attempts as threatening their place in Pacific regionalism. This was particularly evident in relation to Fiji's attempts, from 2014, to remake the PIF as an island-only organisation by seeking the removal of Australia and New Zealand. Canberra and Wellington saw similar threats in relation to Fiji's attempts to give leadership to the development of new regional organisations that included only Pacific island states (and nonstate actors). This provoked a contest between Australia and New Zealand, on the one hand, and Fiji on the other, about the future of regional governance and the desired shape of the institutional architecture. In the event, Australia and New Zealand prevailed in this contest, in the sense that Fiji did not gain the support of the other Pacific leaders to exclude Australia or New Zealand from the PIF or to support the new Fiji-initiated PIDF to the point of displacing the PIF.

This chapter develops the argument that, despite the failure of these aspects of Fiji's regional project, the 'new' Pacific diplomacy has nevertheless transformed Pacific regionalism in a fundamental way. Furthermore, it argues that the significance of this transformation is of the order of that experienced in the transition from colonial regionalism to postcolonial regionalism. It involves not only a transformed regional architecture, but also, more fundamentally, a transformation of regional diplomatic culture, on which the legitimacy of regionalism depends.

Fiji's suspension from the PIF in 2009 was a key catalyst for these developments. The suspension led Fiji to adopt a very strategic policy to develop an alternative regionalism outside the PIF network. However, to explain why some of these Fijian initiatives have had a transformative impact we need to understand the rising shared discontent with the PIF among most Pacific island leaders in the previous two decades and their predisposition to endorsing moves to create new avenues through which a 'Pacific voice' could be developed and promoted.

Growing frustration with the PIF

At the time of the establishment of the SPF, Australia and New Zealand had a tacit agreement with the Pacific island states on a regional diplomatic culture in which all member states were regarded as equal at the regional diplomatic table, but with an implicit understanding that the Pacific island states had primacy in determining the regional agenda for their region. As Ken Piddington, a New Zealand foreign ministry official and deputy director of the SPEC (the research office of the SPF), stated at the time:

> [The SPF] is an exercise in partnership. Australia and New Zealand sit at the table as equals, and are not dominant partners ... It is tacitly understood that Australia and New Zealand will defer when it comes to deciding the direction which the Forum as a whole should take in asserting its role in the region.[2]

The 1971 political settlement between Australia, New Zealand and the Pacific island states created a form of regional governance that, for the most part, was seen as politically legitimate by most participants for the next two decades. The strength of this legitimacy was reflected in a very active period of joint diplomacy, through the SPF.

---

2   Piddington, *The South Pacific Bureau*, p. 5.

As we saw in previous chapters, Australia, New Zealand and the Pacific island states together took on some of the world's largest powers on key issues of concern to the Pacific island states, and prevailed.

The strength of this legitimacy was also reflected in the fact that there was robust debate among the SPF members on the joint position to be taken on all of these issues. As we have seen, even after the region became more strategically important in the 'second Cold War' of the 1980s, Australia and New Zealand did not dominate the outcomes of the SPF. Although they attempted to assertively promote a particular kind of Cold War order for the region, their views did not always prevail. The outcomes reflected the robust negotiation that occurred within the SPF, and this was testimony to the legitimacy accorded to the understandings reached in 1971 about the foundation principles on which regional governance and diplomacy would be conducted.

However, after the end of the Cold War, there was a gradual unravelling of the understandings about equality and partnership that underlay this legitimacy. Throughout the 1990s and 2000s, Australia and New Zealand increasingly saw the agenda of the SPF (and then the PIF) as an extension of their own foreign policy, and even of their domestic policy, whether it was curbing money laundering, countering radical climate mitigation positions, promoting security harmonisation, constraining the drug trade, countering terrorism, pursuing defence surveillance, countering tax havens or promoting a neoliberal regional economic order.

In his review of the regional architecture for the PIF in 2005, based on regionwide consultation with leaders, Tony Hughes observed:

> Sometimes the confrontational style of political management practised in Canberra and Wellington has intruded on the Forum and grated upon Pacific Island sensibilities. On occasion the strategic priorities of Australia and New Zealand have been too openly assumed by their representatives to be also those of the island states. From time to time such irritations have led to suggestions of a change of membership status for one or both of the two countries. Neither Australia nor New Zealand would welcome such a move … But the idea remains in the PICT [Pacific island countries and territories] subconscious.[3]

---

3   A.V. Hughes, *Strengthening Regional Management: A Review of the Architecture for Regional Co-operation in the Pacific*, Report to the Pacific Islands Forum, Consultative Draft, 2005, available from: gsd.spc.int/sopac/docs/RIF/06_AV%20Hughes%20Report_CONSULTATIVE_DRAFT(1).pdf, p. 10.

For Ratu Mara of Fiji, who made the case in 1971 for the inclusion of Australia and New Zealand in the SPF, the changing role of Australia and New Zealand had become a problem by 2001, on the occasion of the forum's thirtieth anniversary:

> And here I must confess to a certain sense of disappointment with our metropolitan members. They have not always been ready to show understanding of our problems. And they have sought to impose their solutions in an insensitive way, when left to ourselves we could work things out in what we have come to call the Pacific Way.[4]

The hierarchical regional diplomatic culture that developed in the SPF and then the PIF in the 1990s and 2000s made it difficult for Pacific island leaders to assert control over issues that were of great concern to them, such as tuna management, decolonisation, trade and, most of all, climate policy. We have already seen how this played out in relation to Pacific island state concerns over the forum's role in representing the Pacific's interests in trade diplomacy with Australia and New Zealand while these metropolitan countries were, at the same time, members of the forum. This conflict of interest was recognised in the formation of a new regional agency, the Office of the Chief Trade Adviser (OCTA), although its independence was questioned by some commentators who pointed to the attempts by Australia and New Zealand to 'appropriate' the new office for the promotion of their trade agenda.[5] There was some resentment felt towards a more general skewing of the PIFS to the concerns of Australia and New Zealand through their relatively large resources giving them the ability to set agendas and draft communiqués. Roman Grynberg, a former senior trade analyst for the PIF, described the Australian and New Zealand role as tantamount to 'ownership' of the forum.[6]

The rising frustration of the Pacific leaders with the PIF's failure to adequately represent their interests in global forums was also fuelled by the view that the Forum had largely abandoned joint diplomacy in the

---

4   Ratu Sir Kamisese Mara, *Keynote Address by H.E. Rt Hon. Ratu Sir Kamisese Mara, Former Prime Minister and President of Fiji Islands, On the Occasion of the 30th Anniversary of the South Pacific Forum of Leaders, Yaren, Nauru, August 16, 2001*, Press Statement 6301, Suva: PIFS, 2001, available from: www.pireport.org/articles/2001/08/17/keynote-address-he-rt-hon-ratu-sir-kamisese-mara.

5   Wesley Morgan, 'Regional Trade Negotiations and the Construction of Policy Choice in the Pacific Islands Forum (1994–2014)', PhD thesis, School of Political and Social Sciences, University of Melbourne, Melbourne, October 2014, pp. 154–8.

6   Roman Grynberg, 'Who Owns the Forum?', *Fiji Times Online*, 9 March 2009.

1990s and 2000s as a priority of regionalism, preferring a preoccupation with a more inward-looking, regional integration. This emphasis was influenced heavily by Australia and New Zealand and their commitment to promoting 'pooled regional governance' in security and development as key regional projects. This tendency culminated in the Pacific Plan of 2005–13, which focused on regional pooling and integration, omitting collective diplomacy from its definition of regionalism and from the PIF's mandate.

There were also new pressures from global developments in South–South cooperation, which required the Pacific to be organised as a regional Global South grouping to participate. There was a growing realisation among Pacific policymakers that ways had to be found to break out of the constraints of the PIF structure if the Pacific was to work within these Global South coalitions such as the Group of 77 (G-77) and the Alliance of Small Island States (AOSIS) in projecting a 'Pacific voice' in global diplomacy.[7] With Australia and New Zealand as members, the PIF did not qualify to participate in such Global South groupings.

By the end of the first decade of the twenty-first century, there was therefore mounting frustration with the effectiveness of the PIF to meet the diplomatic needs of the island states in negotiating on key global challenges. It is important to note that this frustration did not lead to a commitment to exclude Australia and New Zealand. The comprehensive review of the Pacific Plan in 2012–13, the Morauta Review, reported on the problem of Pacific leaders feeling that they no longer had control of their regional agenda, but it also reported that this problem did not find expression in a view that Australia and New Zealand should not continue to participate as full members of the PIF:

> Most of those interviewed—particularly Leaders—supported their full participation … The consensus among the most sagacious of the Review's interviewees was that the metropolitan countries have a uniquely important role to play in the Forum.[8]

7   Kaliopate Tavola, 'Towards a New Pacific Diplomacy Architecture', in Fry and Tarte, *The New Pacific Diplomacy*, p. 27.
8   PIFS, *Pacific Plan Review 2013: Report to Pacific Leaders. Volume 1*, [known as the Morauta Review], Suva: PIFS, 2013, p. 79.

These frustrations did mean, however, that the Pacific leaders were ready to develop additional regional avenues outside the PIF to create a space for discussion of joint positions and to assist them in promoting a Pacific-determined agenda. They had already shown that they had such a commitment—independent of Fijian leadership—in their joint initiatives in establishing Pacific island–run regional organisations (to be examined below) to pursue shared interests in areas not adequately represented by the PIF. It also meant that they were receptive to new ideas for creating more effective diplomatic pathways to pursue their interests and to complement, but not displace, the work of the PIF.

The climate change issue as a game-changer

The key issue galvanising Pacific leaders to reframe the governance and architecture of regionalism was climate change. For over 25 years, and even before the Kyoto climate conference of 1997, the Pacific island nations have viewed the global climate change problem as a priority issue for their survival. The Pacific leaders have stressed throughout this period that, as they are 'frontline', low-lying ocean states, the issue is ultimately the survival of their countries in the face of rising sea levels and, in the meantime, the defence of their current livelihoods in the face of storm surges, intensified cyclone activity, acidification and seawater inundation of the freshwater table. For the Pacific leaders, the issue is not some future 'maybe' but a current lived reality affecting livelihoods, the survival of particular villages and islands and the forced movement of people.

In many ways, climate change has become the Pacific's nuclear testing issue of the twenty-first century;[9] it has brought an urgency and emotional commitment to regional collaboration. Where the Pacific states might in the past have tolerated some frustration with the domination of the regional agenda by Canberra and Wellington to pursue the war on terror or to promote a regional neoliberal economic order, this tolerance reached its limit in relation to the climate change issue.

From 1997, there was rising concern, particularly among the low-lying atoll states, about the lack of action by the PIF in representing a strong joint position on this question because of the restraining influence of

---

9   I am grateful to Dr Nicole George, School of Political Science and International Studies, University of Queensland, for this insight.

Australia and New Zealand on regional positions on emissions targets. This was particularly evident in relation to the PIF's joint position as key global summits approached within the UN Framework Convention on Climate Change (UNFCCC) process. For example, in relation to the preparation of a Pacific position for the global meeting in Kyoto to discuss binding emissions targets as part of a climate protocol, Eric Shibuya argues that Australian pressure at the Rarotonga SPF meeting in 1997 resulted in a watered down position in the SPF communiqué—an outcome that did not represent the view of the Pacific island leaders:

> Tuvalu's Prime Minister Bikenibeu Paeniu said that after the statement was issued, 'Australia dominates us so much in this region. For once, we would have liked to have got some respect'.[10]

Also speaking of the discussions about the Pacific position on climate change at the Rarotonga SPF meeting, president Kinza Clodumar of Nauru reported:

> The Forum Communique which emerged at the end of the meeting was extremely bland and was painted by Australia ... as something of a victory. I would class it rather as a disaster. It is fair to say that many of the small island states were aghast at the treatment meted out to them. Nauru, however, which has a long history of negotiating with Australia ... was not all that surprised, and certainly would have preferred a different outcome—even a communique which did not include Australia.[11]

The 2009 PIF meeting in Cairns, Queensland, represented another key point in Australian pressure to weaken the Pacific island states' position, this time in the leadup to the Copenhagen global summit on climate change. A number of Pacific leaders wanted a strong commitment to emissions targets in the communiqué but the anodyne final communiqué— following an effective veto under the consensus procedure—instead represented the position held by Australia and New Zealand. Australia and New Zealand refused to sign on to the more radical demand of the

---

10   Bernadette Hussein, 'The Big Retreat', *Pacific Islands Monthly*, November 1997: 11, as cited in Eric Shibuya, 'The Problems and Potential of the Pacific Islands Forum', in Jim Rolfe, ed., *The Asia-Pacific: A Region in Transition*, Honolulu: Asia-Pacific Center for Security Studies, 2004, pp. 102–15, at p. 110.
11   Republic of Nauru, 'Speech by His Excellency, the Hon. Kinza Clodumar, MP, President of the Republic of Nauru, 23 October 1997, National Press Club, Canberra', Media release, 21 October 1997. This is also reported in *Pacific Report*, 10(20): 1.

Pacific island nations to limit global warming to 1.5 degrees Celsius above pre-industrial levels, and this meant the Pacific went to Copenhagen without its premier regional organisation backing their position.[12]

Yasmine Ryan reports that, when a number of Pacific leaders nevertheless promoted the 1.5-degree limit at the Fifteenth Conference of the Parties (COP15) in Copenhagen, Australia pressured them to change their position:

> On the second last day of the conference, Tuvaluan Prime Minister Apisai Ielemia told reporters that the Australian delegation and Prime Minister Kevin Rudd's office had been pressuring small islands to change their position on the temperature limit and on calls for a legally binding agreement. The Tuvaluan delegation had refused to meet with the Australians but other Pacific leaders had been told that 'they agree to the 2 degree limit and (climate change adaptation) funding will be on the table'.[13]

As the 2015 Paris global summit on climate change approached, the new Abbott Government's reactionary climate policy raised Pacific concerns about Australia's position and its potential constraining influence on the Pacific position. In 2015, the Australian Government announced an emissions target of 26–28 per cent below 2005 levels by 2030, which was well below the 40–60 per cent target recommended by the Australian Climate Change Authority as necessary to keep warming below 2°C, and well short of that required to meet the 1.5-degree level supported by island states. For Tony de Brum, then foreign minister of the Marshall Islands, 'Australia's weak target is another serious blow to its international reputation'. He argued: 'If the rest of the world followed Australia's lead, the Great Barrier Reef would disappear. So would my country, and the other vulnerable atoll nations on Australia's doorstep'.[14]

---

12   Nic Maclellan, 'Pacific Leaders Contradict Cairns Climate Deal', *The Interpreter*, Sydney: Lowy Institute for International Policy, 5 October 2018; Shirley Atatagi, 'Forget Watergate, We Now Have Cairns'Gate', Blog, Sydney: Greenpeace, 7 August 2009, available from: www.greenpeace.org.au/blog/forget-watergate-we-now-have-cairnsgate/; Bernard Keane, 'How We Discouraged Pacific Islands from Tough Emissions Stance', *Crikey*, 21 September 2009, available from: www.crikey.com.au/2009/09/21/leaked-document-oz-discouraged-pacific-islands-from-tough-emissions-stance/.
13   Yasmine Ryan, 'COP15 and Pacific Island States: A Collective Voice on Climate Change', *Pacific Journalism Review*, 16(1), 2010: 193–203, at p. 198.
14   Catherine Graue, 'Marshall Islands Foreign Minister Slams Australia's "Weak" Carbon Target', *Pacific Beat*, ABC News, 11 August 2015, available from: www.abc.net.au/news/programs/pacific-beat/2015-08-11/marshall-islands-foreign-minister-slams-australias/6690570.

The Pacific leaders were also angered by the Abbott Government's efforts to actively work against a global effort to curb global warming. Of particular concern to Pacific leaders over the 2013–15 period was Australia's failure to turn up to global climate change summits, the attempt to form a Canadian–Australian global alliance to work against climate action, the cancellation of the Australian carbon emissions trading scheme, the attack on alternative energy schemes within Australia, the attempt to dismantle the Australian Climate Commission and the statement by the Government's chief business adviser that climate change was a UN 'hoax'. The last straw was prime minister Abbott's announcement that coal was 'good for humanity', and his commitment to opening new coalmines just as the Kiribati Government called for a global ban on new coalmines.[15]

On the eve of the 2015 PIF meeting, at which the Pacific position for the Paris conference on climate change was to be discussed, president Tong of Kiribati was reported as issuing an 'ultimatum', declaring that 'we cannot negotiate this, no matter how much aid. We cannot be bought on this one because it's about the future.'

> [He] raised the prospect of either states walking out or Australia being asked to leave the forum if its two more powerful members forced a compromise on the commitment of island states to the goal of limiting global warming to 1.5 degrees Celsius.

He is reported as going on to say that 'we expect them, as big brothers, not bad brothers, to support us on this one because our future depends on it'.[16] Tuvalu's Prime Minister, Enele Sopoaga, asserted that president Tong's sentiments were 'strongly shared by leaders of smaller island states'.[17]

Reflecting on Australia's actions to dilute 'the strength of previous regional declarations on climate change', Palau's national climate change coordinator, Xavier Matsutaro, said Australia's relationship with the Pacific was 'dysfunctional'. He went on to say:

---

15   For the sources for these claims, see Greg Fry, 'Pacific Climate Diplomacy and the Future Relevance of the Pacific Islands Forum', *Devpolicy Blog*, 4 September 2015, available from: devpolicy. org/pacific-climate-diplomacy-and-the-future-relevance-of-the-pacific-islands-forum-20150904/.
16   Michael Gordon, '"We Cannot be Bought on Climate Change": Pacific Island Leader Warns Tony Abbott', *Sydney Morning Herald*, 8 September 2015.
17   ibid.

Australia is a bit of an anomaly, because on the floor [of climate summits] they're basically sometimes as far right as [US President Donald] Trump in some of their views on climate change, at one point they even denied it existed … But then on a regional basis they've actually given a lot of support to our region … it's like you are in a relationship and you get abused by your spouse but at the same time they feed you and clothe you and things like that … You could say it's a bit of a dysfunctional relationship.[18]

Building island-run regional institutions

Into this context of rising frustration among Pacific leaders came a very determined Fiji Government, committed to developing an alternative regional system. From the time of Fiji's suspension from the PIF in 2009, the Bainimarama regime worked assiduously to reframe Pacific regionalism to serve its own national interests. As seen from Suva, Australia and New Zealand were attempting to cut off various avenues for Fiji's global and regional engagement and financial support. What Fiji needed therefore was 'survival diplomacy' to navigate this new isolation and the loss of 'old friends'. It pursued policies explicitly aimed at ensuring that Fiji was seen as the hub of the Pacific and, in global circles, as its chief spokesperson. It committed itself to the development of an effective regional architecture based on the principles of self-determination and inclusion of all Pacific island 'peoples'.[19]

The implementation of this regional strategy began with Fiji's hosting of a meeting open to all Pacific island states with the theme 'Engaging with the Pacific' at Natadola in July 2010. The meeting met Fiji's objectives of demonstrating that the Pacific leaders supported a continued regional dialogue with Fiji despite its suspension from the PIF, and that 'the Leaders agreed that Fiji's Strategic Framework for Change is a credible home-grown process for positioning Fiji as a modern nation and to hold true democratic elections'.[20] The meeting was attended by 10 of the 14

18   Kate Lyons, 'Australia's Relationship with Pacific on Climate Change "Dysfunctional" and "Abusive"', *The Guardian*, 5 September 2018.
19   Sandra Tarte, 'Fiji's Search for New Friends', *East Asia Forum*, 13 January 2011; Makereta Komai, 'Fiji's Foreign Policy and the New Pacific Diplomacy', in Fry and Tarte, *The New Pacific Diplomacy*, pp. 111–21.
20   The Fijian Government, 'The Natadola Communiqué', Press release, 23 July 2010, Suva, available from: www.fiji.gov.fj/Media-Center/Press-Releases/The-Natadola-Communiqu%C3%A9.aspx, paras 1, 15, 18.

Pacific island state members of the PIF (Samoa, Palau, Niue and Cook Islands were absent). The Natadola meeting also provided the opportunity for Fiji to launch an ongoing alternative regional forum based on the 'Pacific way of *talanoa*, or frank discussion and dialogue'—a format that appealed to other leaders. The focus of the dialogue—sustainable development, climate change and the 'green economy'—also struck a chord with other leaders. Engaging With the Pacific Leaders (EWPT) became an annual meeting.

Fiji proposed the theme of 'A United and Distinctive PSIDS Voice' for the third EWTP meeting, in Nadi in 2012. PSIDS referred to Pacific Small Island Developing States, thus excluding Australia and New Zealand. The leaders supported the Fijian initiative and, in an obvious reference to the PIF, 'noted the challenges facing PSIDS in effectively addressing their common interests through existing regional and international groupings due to competing interests and differing levels of developmental needs of the members' and 'recognized the need for PSIDS to take a united position on issues of priority to its members at the United Nations'.[21] They also agreed to a Fijian proposal to launch a new formal regional organisation, the PIDF, to carry forward the ideas developed in the EWTP meetings in a more organised manner.

The PIDF was launched in Nadi in August 2013. In his opening speech to the new forum, Fiji's Interim Prime Minister, Frank Bainimarama, asked:

> Why do we need a new body, a new framework of cooperation? Because the existing regional structure for the past four decades— the Pacific Islands Forum—is for governments only and has also come to be dominated only by a few.[22]

The strong Pacific-wide support for the Fijian initiative was indicated by the attendance of 10 of the 14 PSIDS (of the absentees, only Samoa spoke against the PIDF initiative). Reflecting a significant redrawing of the regional boundaries, Timor-Leste was also included as a participant, and Timorese prime minister Xanana Gusmão was 'Chief Guest'. In another major departure from PIF practice, Fiji included representatives

---

21   The Fijian Government, 'Engaging with the Pacific Leaders Meeting: Nadi Communiqué', Press release, 27 August 2012, Suva, available from: www.fiji.gov.fj/Media-Center/Press-Releases/ENGAGING-WITH-THE-PACIFIC-LEADERS-MEETING—NADI-C.aspx.
22   Samisoni Pareti, 'Fiji Pushes for Alternative to Pacific Islands Forum', *ABC News*, 6 August 2013.

of dependent territories, civil society and the private sector as equals at the diplomatic table. International development partners (including Australia and New Zealand) were also present, but only as observers.

The new organisation was heralded as pathbreaking in Pacific regionalism in its inclusivity. The *Fiji Sun* newspaper reported on its front page 'we are all Equal Now'—a reference to the equality between states and nonstate actors at the PIDF diplomatic table.[23] 'Inclusion' also extended to Pacific island administrations in dependent territories. The PIDF's agenda was a continuation of that of the EWTP meetings: a focus on green growth and sustainable development, climate change and decolonisation.[24] In the next few years, a number of formal steps were taken to build the PIDF as a formal regional institution: the establishment of a secretariat in Suva, a constitution with provisions for a directing council, a founding agreement and gradual recognition by global partners. The costs for the PIDF conferences were largely provided by China, Russia, the United Arab Emirates, Kuwait and Timor-Leste. Fiji provided the headquarters and seconded staff from its foreign ministry. As we shall see, the high point of the PIDF was reached in 2015 when the annual conference played a major part in the Pacific preparation for the Paris climate conference.

A second strand of Fiji's post-suspension regional diplomatic strategy was to give leadership to the way the Pacific organised at the United Nations so that a 'distinctive Pacific voice' could be projected in global forums. In practice, this amounted to energising the already existing PSIDS grouping at the United Nations, which had been formed to 'raise funds for projects around climate change adaptation and mitigation, renewable energy and pollution'.[25] The PSIDS was reenergised and retasked to the point where it displaced the PIF as the preferred regional coalition for the Pacific island states at the United Nations and as the globally recognised voice for the Pacific island region. After its suspension from the PIF in 2009, Fiji had pursued a very successful 'friends to all' global strategy, aimed particularly at China, India and Russia. It joined the Non-Aligned Movement and opened new missions in major countries in each region. This resulted in global recognition for Fiji as the leading voice for the Pacific—expressed most prominently in Fiji's election to chair the G-77

23 Jyoti Pratibha, 'All Equal Now', *Fiji Sun*, 7 August 2013.
24 Sandra Tarte, 'A New Pacific Regional Voice? The Pacific Islands Development Forum', in Fry and Tarte, *The New Pacific Diplomacy*, pp. 79–88.
25 Fulori Manoa, 'The New Pacific Diplomacy at the United Nations: The Rise of the PSIDS', in Fry and Tarte, *The New Pacific Diplomacy*, pp. 89–98, at p. 80.

in 2010. Fiji was able to leverage this new global prominence to give leadership to a campaign to change the name of the Asian group at the United Nations to the Asia-Pacific Small Island Developing States grouping (or Asia-Pacific grouping for short).[26]

This major recognition for the PSIDS in 2012 galvanised the Pacific island states to use the PSIDS grouping as their primary regional caucus at the United Nations rather than the PIF. By pooling their resources and bargaining power, the Pacific island states achieved the equivalent of a medium-sized mission at the United Nations. This dramatically increased the visibility and influence of the Pacific island region, and was demonstrated through significant global recognition for the PSIDS and the effective displacement of the PIF as the key Pacific grouping at the United Nations. Fiji's role as a regional hub rose with the visibility of the PSIDS and vice versa. The world's most powerful leaders—most prominently, President Xi Jinping of China and Prime Minister Narendra Modi of India—began to visit Fiji from 2014.[27]

Fiji's third major regional strategy was to use its chairmanship of the MSG from 2011 to 2013 to give leadership to a revamp of this existing organisation. The resultant expansion in its range of activities and governance councils started to make the MSG look more like the PIF in structure and function. As the MSG includes the region's largest countries in terms of land, population and economies—Fiji and Papua New Guinea—this was seen in some quarters as a major potential challenge to the primacy of the PIF. Significant achievements in regional free trade and free movement of professional workers, spurred by cooperation between Papua New Guinea and Fiji in this period, were supported by the other Melanesian states.[28]

Fiji's leadership was very important, but the role of other Pacific leaders should not be overlooked. In each of these cases, the legitimacy of the new or reframed institutions was dependent on the support of the other Pacific leaders. Other leaders had also initiated island-run regional institutions. In 2009, the Pacific leaders demanded a new island-run

---

26   ibid.
27   'Fiji Prime Minister Frank Bainimarama Looks Forward to Visits from China and India's Leaders', *ABC News Online*, 17 November 2014.
28   Tess Newton Cain, 'The Renaissance of the Melanesian Spearhead Group', pp. 151–60, and Sovaia Marawa, 'Negotiating the Melanesia Free Trade Area', pp. 161–74, both in Fry and Tarte, *The New Pacific Diplomacy*.

trade negotiation body, the OCTA, to serve the FICs in their negotiations with Australia and New Zealand over PACER Plus. Established in Port Vila in 2010, the OCTA was fully owned by the FICS. And in 2012, Papua New Guinea's prime minister O'Neill, with the support of Solomon Islands prime minister Gordon Lilo, led an initiative to create the new Pacific members of the African, Caribbean and Pacific group (PACP) secretariat outside the PIFS so that Fiji could participate in PACP discussions relating to their relations with Europe—focused particularly on negotiation of the regional EPA.[29] Papua New Guinea's *The National* newspaper reported that

> PNG would provide funding for the PACP to be based in Port Moresby and it would operate separately from the Pacific Islands Forum Secretariat … The PACP meeting decided that the group would operate separately from the Pacific Islands Forum to ensure Fiji's inclusion.[30]

The most significant move to create an island-run regional body outside the PIF framework was in relation to tuna fisheries. This was a move by the tuna-rich states to create an international organisation around the existing membership of the Nauru Group. Papua New Guinea led the initiative and provided the initial funds to set up the secretariat. Under the leadership of Dr Transform Aqorau, the Parties to the Nauru Agreement (PNA) quickly became a highly effective organisation, raising incomes for tuna states dramatically. This was achieved through the introduction of a Vessel Day Scheme based on the jurisdictional rights of host states. The PNA introduced a business model that did not require dependence on metropolitan funds. It has become a model of a cost-effective island-run organisation. The PNA developments occurred without Fijian membership, emphasising the fact that the 'new' Pacific diplomacy was not simply a product of Fiji's PIF suspension.[31]

29　'PM Welcomes New PACP Secretariat Formation', *Solomon Star*, 23 November 2012; 'Forum Secretariat Wrong: PM', *Fiji Sun*, 4 December 2012.

30　'PNG Offers to Provide for PACP Secretariat', *The National*, [Port Moresby], 23 November 2012, available from: www.thenational.com.pg/png-offers-to-provide-for-pacp-secretariat/.

31　Transform Aqorau, 'How Tuna is Shaping Regional Diplomacy', in Fry and Tarte, *The New Pacific Diplomacy*, pp. 223–35; Sandra Tarte, 'Regionalism and Changing Regional Order in the Pacific Islands', *Asia and the Pacific Policy Studies*, 1(2), 2014: 315–18.

The contest over regional governance

By 2014—as a result of the Fiji-led institutional developments and the moves by other Pacific island leaders to form the PNA, the OCTA and PACP—there were now two regional systems. One was the established system of organisations, with the PIF at its centre, which had gradually developed over the four decades since 1971. Coordinated by the Council of Regional Organisations of the Pacific (CROP), this system included the PIF, the Pacific Community (formerly the SPC), the FFA, the Secretariat of the Pacific Regional Environment Programme (SPREP) and the USP. This system was largely financed by Australia and New Zealand (for example, they finance 95 per cent of the PIFS' core and regular budget) and each organisation within it includes Australia and New Zealand as member states.

A second grouping of new Pacific-run organisations sits outside the CROP system. It comprises the PSIDS, the PIDF, the MSG, the PNA, the OCTA, the PACP, the Micronesian Chief Executives' Summit, the Micronesian Presidents' Summit and the Polynesian Leaders' Group. Though not formally, or even informally, coordinated, they have in common that they are island-driven and controlled; they do not include Australia and New Zealand as members. With the exception of the PIDF and the OCTA, they also have in common that they are not financially dependent on Australia and New Zealand or indeed any other larger, metropolitan states.

A further key distinction between these two regional 'systems' is that the new institutions are primarily concerned with engaging in global diplomacy and representing a Pacific voice in global arenas. The CROP system, on the other hand, had been focused in the previous two decades on regional economic integration in the security and economic arenas around an Australian–New Zealand agenda. The PIF had moved away from the globally assertive diplomacy of the 1970s and 1980s. The institutions in the new island-run system, on the other hand, were attempting to have diplomatic agency and influence at the global level on issues that mattered to the Pacific. Together, the new agencies covered key global diplomatic issues impacting the Pacific: climate policy, ocean management, trade and decolonisation.

From 2014, the question before Pacific leaders was: How would these two regional systems fit together? Would they be two competitive systems or could they fit together in a new 'patchwork' regional architecture? The view that the two systems were in competition was encouraged by Fiji's challenge, from 2014, that it would not return to the PIF unless Australia and New Zealand withdrew or were expelled. This atmosphere of contest between Fiji, on the one hand, and Australia and New Zealand, on the other, over the control of regional governance was further increased by Fiji's promotion of the PIDF as an all-island alternative to the PIF—at least as seen by Canberra and Wellington.

The most dramatic part of Fiji's regional strategy was its demand that Australia and New Zealand be excluded from the PIF as the condition for Fiji resuming its membership. In September 2013, Prime Minister Bainimarama was reported as saying:

> We are not interested in going back [to the PIF] until it stops being the play thing of the Aussies and Kiwis. When it becomes a genuine expression of the will of the Pacific islanders themselves, then we will go back, then we will think about rejoining the Forum.[32]

Later in 2014, following the Fiji elections in September, and the invitation to resume its membership of the PIF in October, newly reelected Prime Minister Bainimarama made clear that his demand remained: Australia and New Zealand should leave the PIF as the condition for Fiji's return.[33]

For Canberra and Wellington, Fiji's demand created an issue of highest priority for their Pacific policies. Australia and New Zealand see the PIF as the main vehicle for regional management, and their own membership of the PIF as crucial to that management. As foreign minister Bishop warned in a press conference in Suva in November 2014, she was 'not going to take that [the proposed exclusion] lying down'.[34] In the following months, several Pacific leaders came out publicly in support of Australia and New Zealand. In November 2014, Tommy Remengesau, Jr, chair of the PIF and President of Palau, was reported as having 'stressed the continuing

---

32 'Fiji Says It Won't Rejoin Pacific Islands Forum Unless There Are Changes', *Radio New Zealand International News*, 13 September 2013.
33 'Fiji Will Not Return to Forum', *Pacnews*, 26 October 2014, available from: www.pina.com.fj/?p=pacnews&m=read&o=1608789720544d6db65d45a93939d3.
34 'Fijian PM Support Sydney Meet, No Talk on Pacific Islands Forum', *Pacnews*, 2 November 2014, available from: www.pina.com.fj/?p=pacnews&m=read&o=11573914165456a5c206ecc584e739.

importance of New Zealand and Australia at the regional body'.[35] In the same month, Papua New Guinea's Prime Minister also indicated his support for the inclusion of Australia and New Zealand:

> Mr O'Neill told Radio Australia's Pacific Beat program that the structure of the Pacific Islands Forum does not need changing. 'We must make sure that we don't forget that we all live in the same region and Australia and New Zealand are very much part of that region.'[36]

On 3 April 2015, *Radio New Zealand* reported that the 'new government in Tonga says it is opposed to moves initiated by Fiji to push New Zealand and Australia out of the Pacific Islands Forum'. The new Prime Minister of Tonga, 'Akilisi Pōhiva, was reported as saying that 'as many Tongans live in Australia and New Zealand, it would be unwise to turn around and consider Fiji's position to form a new regional organisation'.[37]

After Bainimarama had reiterated his position in April 2015, prime minister John Key of New Zealand rejected Bainimarama's call, 'saying it is a joke' and asking, 'Where would they get the money to do anything, and the answer is nowhere'.[38] Samoan Prime Minister Sailele said that '"John Key is right" … and went on to say that "it's not as if any money comes from Fiji. It's the money we get from New Zealand and Australia we are using for our stuff"'.[39]

By this time, it was very clear that the Fijian campaign to exclude Australia and New Zealand from the PIF had failed. Fiji's subsequent decision to participate in PIF meetings, including trade negotiations for PACER Plus, did not signal, however, that Bainimarama was dropping his ultimate demand. In May 2015, he announced:

> We will continue to participate in all Forum activities at the public service, technical and ministerial levels … As Head of Government, I will not participate in any Forum Leaders' Meeting

---

35 'Remengesau Stresses Pacific Forum Unity', *Radio New Zealand*, 5 November 2014.

36 'Papua New Guinea PM Peter O'Neill Dismisses Fiji's Push to Remove Australia from Pacific Islands Forum', *ABC News*, 28 November 2014, available from: www.abc.net.au/news/2014-11-28/png-pm-wants-australia-to-remain-in-pacific-regional-body/5926014.

37 'Tonga Opposed to Forum Exclusions', *Radio New Zealand*, 3 April 2015, available from: www.pireport.org/articles/2015/04/06/tonga-opposed-forum-exclusions.

38 'I Can't Stand You Bainimarama: PM Tuilaepa', *Samoa Observer/Pacnews*, 19 April 2015, available from: www.pina.com.fj/?p=pacnews&m=read&o=404430711553476ec71af7e07c0b22.

39 ibid.

until the issue of the undue influence of Australia and New Zealand and our divergence of views is addressed … Australia and New Zealand, PIF's major funders, are not island nations but more development partners … This is not some ill-considered position based on resentment against Australia and New Zealand for their punitive attitude towards our reform programme that produced the first genuine democracy in Fijian history … This is not me 'mouthing off', as the New Zealand Prime Minister so condescendingly put it.[40]

The second aspect of Fiji's regional strategy, which was contested by Australia and New Zealand, was the attempt to create an island-controlled regional organisation to compete with, or even displace, the PIF. Canberra saw Fiji's efforts to reenergise the MSG, and to set up a series of meetings and functions emulating the PIF, as potentially threatening to the PIF. But the real game-changer as seen from Canberra and Wellington was when Fiji's annual EWTP meeting morphed into the creation of a new regional organisation, which excluded Australia and New Zealand, and which was seemingly supported by 10 of the 14 Pacific island states. The PIDF appealed to many island leaders who supported it with their presence over the next few years. But although they supported the PIDF for many reasons, these did not include a desire to see the new organisation displace the PIF. As Samoan newspaper editor Kalafi Moala commented:

> The popular sentiment, among Pacific nations however is that PIDF does not need to replace PIF, but can be complimentary [sic] by having a different focus and being inclusive in its membership [of nonstate actors].[41]

Samoan Prime Minister Sailele was reported as saying the PIDF 'will never replace PIF'.[42] The Pacific leaders had just been through a decade-long review process within the PIF and the fruits of that process were now beginning to show. In such circumstances, there was no enthusiasm to abandon the PIF for the PIDF. In an interview in November 2014, PNG prime minister O'Neill captured this widely held sentiment to uphold the PIF as the preeminent regional institution:

---

40   Liam Fox, 'Frank Bainimarama to Shun Pacific Island Forum over "Undue Influence" of Australia, NZ', *ABC News*, 6 May 2015.
41   Kalafi Moala, 'Regionalism Debate Becoming Contentious', Online Forum, 8 April 2015, Port Vila: Pacific Institute of Public Policy.
42   ibid.

We just had a review of the Pacific Plan which was adopted by the leaders in Palau. We need to start implementing some of these strategies that we are putting in place rather than talking about creating a new structure that is going to be costly and [a] duplication.[43]

Transformation of the regional architecture

The failure of these more dramatic expressions of the 'new' Pacific diplomacy, and the strong reendorsement of the PIF as the preeminent regional agency for collective political leadership, should not be interpreted, however, as meaning that there is a return to the status quo ante. The new ideas and institutional developments have had a fundamentally transformative impact on the shape of the regional architecture and on the underlying norms making up the regional diplomatic culture. In relation to the shape of the regional architecture, by 2017, it was clear that a new 'patchwork' regional architecture (to employ Tess Newton Cain and Matthew Dornan's useful descriptor) had emerged—an amalgam of old and new.[44] Several of these institutions were developing new roles and purposes within the overall patchwork structure. Rather than competing, separate systems, on the one hand, or a fully integrated new system, on the other, this was something in between. It is still a work in progress, but the new architecture allows the flexibility required by the Pacific leaders. It keeps Australia and New Zealand at the regional diplomatic table (and providing the bulk of the funds) in the PIF, ensuring the continued preeminence of the PIF as the key site of regional governance by Pacific leaders, while allowing alternative spaces for Pacific island–only deliberation as well as global projection of a more authentic 'Pacific voice'.

This has not eliminated competition between regional agencies, or suspicions and jealousies, but by and large, it has settled into a cooperative system. As the same Pacific island leaders are on the governing boards of all of these organisations, whether new or old, it is not surprising that these alternative systems could merge cooperatively into a patchwork structure. This does not mean that there will not be further institutional changes as the politics of regionalism proceeds. There are, for example, significant strains between Fiji and some other island countries such as

---

43   ABC News, 'Papua New Guinea PM Peter O'Neill Dismisses Fiji's Push to Remove Australia'.
44   Matthew Dornan and Tess Newton Cain, 'Regional Service Delivery among Pacific Island Countries: An Assessment', *Asia and the Pacific Policy Studies*, 1(3), 2014: 541–60, at p. 555.

Papua New Guinea and Vanuatu, which have emerged since 2016 and which are weakening the MSG.[45] We are also yet to see whether the PIDF will be accepted as having a long-term role within this new architecture.

A key aspect of this transformation is the regional and global acceptance of the PSIDS as the global diplomatic voice for the Pacific island states, displacing the PIF as the significant diplomatic actor in UN forums and global summits. The PSIDS has been recognised widely by other states seeking voting support at the United Nations, and as a coalition of Global South states it works effectively within other such coalitions as the G-77, the AOSIS and the Asia-Pacific grouping at the United Nations. The PSIDS can now point to several major diplomatic successes: the change of name of the Asia grouping at the United Nations to the Asia-Pacific grouping; the inclusion of ocean management and climate policy as SDGs and the organisation of Pacific diplomacy at the Paris climate conference. Significantly, there appears to have been acceptance of this new situation by Australia and New Zealand and by the PIFS.

Second, there has been acceptance of subregionalism as a useful alternative venue for pursuing common interests. Such efforts are no longer seen as threatening the wider regional cooperation pursued in the PIF. According to the Morauta Review:

> [T]he recent establishment of new sub-regional groups in Polynesia and Micronesia, along with the success of the Melanesian Spearhead Group (MSG) in making progress on issues where it has eluded the larger Forum grouping, has been construed by some as a threat to the Pacific Plan and the Forum.

Such a conclusion, it goes on to argue, 'is a mistake'. The leaders interviewed by the Morauta Review 'saw these groupings as benefiting the regional project by illuminating both the challenges of regionalism and ways to overcome them successfully'.[46] And from within the MSG, one of its founding fathers, Sir Michael Somare, made it clear in his twenty-fifth anniversary lecture that the MSG and wider regionalism should be seen as 'mutually reinforcing'.[47]

---

45   Gordon Nanau, 'The Melanesian Spearhead Group and Pacific Regional Co-operation', *Pacific Studies*, 39(3), 2016: 290–3, 303; and George Carter and Stewart Firth, 'The Mood in Melanesia after the Regional Assistance Mission to Solomon Islands', *Asia and the Pacific Policy Studies*, 3(1), 2016: 16–25, at p. 21.
46   PIFS, *Pacific Plan Review 2013*, p. 95.
47   Michael Somare, 'Melanesian Spearhead Group: The Last 25 Years', in Fry and Tarte, *The New Pacific Diplomacy*, pp. 291–98.

The key to the acceptance of this transformation of the regional architecture lies in the position of the Pacific leaders other than Fiji's. They have rejected Fiji's position of excluding Australia and New Zealand but they value alternative diplomatic pathways when there is a blockage in pursuing Pacific island interests through the PIF. They all share the core principles of the new Pacific diplomacy for an assertive Pacific voice in global diplomacy. The new patchwork system therefore suits them. It makes sense also in terms of the governance of each of these institutions. They are all mainly run by the same people—the leaders of the Pacific island states. It is therefore very logical and practical for the Pacific leaders to see the PSIDS as the natural global voice and to have the PIF accept this. Australia and New Zealand have had to step back in the face of this transformation, but so has Fiji. The Pacific island leaders have prevailed in creating a more flexible and effective regional architecture, which gives them diplomatic options. They realise that there is also further work to be done in rationalising this complex system, but the transformation has been embraced.

The road to Paris

This transformation of the regional architecture and of diplomatic practice is well illustrated by the way in which the 'Pacific voice' was projected on the diplomatic road to the Paris conference on climate change in December 2015. Various island state–run forums provided an opportunity to agree on a cogent and shared climate policy agenda and strategy. Most prominent was the PIDF meeting in Suva in August of that year, although there were also other important gatherings such as the Polynesian Leaders' Meeting and the Small Islands States Grouping. The Suva meeting of the PIDF allowed two days of deliberations and consultations without the presence of Australia and New Zealand and inclusive of civil society organisations and the private sector. The Suva Declaration became the main statement of Pacific island demands and expectations going into Paris.

On the other hand, the meeting of the PIF in Port Moresby the following month produced the usual stalemate between the Pacific island nations aiming to ensure their survival and Australia and New Zealand seeking to not commit to anything that would affect their economies. What was different from previous PIF meetings, however, was the outcome. Reflecting the different positions of Australia and New Zealand, on the one hand, and the Pacific island states, on the other, the declaration included an acknowledgement of 1.5°C as the target if survival was to be ensured and also endorsed a preferred target of 1.5°C or 2°C. The leaders agreed to disagree in Paris. This was not ideal, but it was at least a departure from the usual watering down of the communiqué to reflect the position of Australia and New Zealand.

What happened in Paris suggested not two competing regionalisms but the coming together of a complex set of institutions under one body. The Pacific found its collective voice for the first time in UNFCCC history at the Paris conference. They had shared objectives, shared strategies and tactics and organisation. They elected a spokesperson, and they generally kept to shared positions. They achieved most of their key goals and were given substantial recognition by key players. This eventuated because the Pacific operated as one patchwork system.

How did this work? The Pacific island nations all supported the PSIDS as the main diplomatic vehicle for working out strategies and tactics as the negotiations progressed day by day. The PSIDS had 'convening power'. Significantly, the PIFS supported this new joint approach even though Australia and New Zealand were not included in the meetings and the central demand of a 1.5-degree warming threshold was not shared by Australia and New Zealand. Sitting around the table were representatives of most of the agencies in the new patchwork system. Also present were NGOs. For the first time, the PIFS was openly supporting the Pacific island nation position at a UNFCCC meeting. It provided secretarial support to the PSIDS meetings. Indeed, the PIF Secretary-General, Dame Meg Taylor, came out publicly in support of the 1.5-degree threshold—an unthinkable move at previous conferences of parties. Overall, the Pacific island nations were clearly in charge of their own climate diplomacy for the first time and there was de facto recognition of this shift in power. Moreover, they had success in achieving most of their major diplomatic objectives.

A reformed PIF

Arguably the most transformative impact of the new Pacific diplomacy principles on the regional architecture has occurred in the PIF itself. It remains at the centre of the new patchwork system as the preeminent policy body for Pacific island leaders, together with Australia and New

Zealand. But it is a transformed PIF, having been influenced by the same big ideas—regional self-determination and inclusion—that have influenced the formation of the island-only institutions.[48] While the PIF is seen as the centre of the old Pacific regionalism, financed by Australia and New Zealand, it was already on its own journey of reform when Fiji initiated the PIDF in 2013. The 2013 Morauta Review was a response to the disenchantment of Pacific island leaders with the Pacific Plan.

Under the new, dynamic leadership of Dame Meg Taylor, reform was implemented on the basis of two key principles: control of the regional agenda by Pacific island leaders and inclusion of broader Pacific society in working for 'Pacific peoples'. This return to the self-determination principle, which had been at the centre of the PIF's origins, and the embrace of the inclusion principle, meant that PIF reform was very much in accord with the principles of the new Pacific diplomacy even while the organisation might have been seen (at least in Canberra) as in contest with the PIDF for the hearts and minds of Pacific leaders.

The 'Blue Pacific' narrative

From the outset of her tenure as PIF Secretary-General, Dame Meg, a former vice-president of the World Bank Group and former PNG ambassador, emphasised that the PIF was being reformed to better serve the Pacific island leaders and also to make a place for hearing the Pacific 'peoples' voice'. She based the new reform program on the findings of the Morauta Review of the Pacific Plan, which reflected a broad consultation with Pacific leaders and civil society:

> One of the key issues that Sir Mekere has reiterated is who makes the decision for what happens in this region and then who takes on the responsibility. And then in his conduct of the review, it was very clear to him that a lot of the decisions that are made in this region are not made by our leaders …

---

48 The case for a fundamental transformation within the PIF is also made by Helen Leslie and Kirsty Wild, 'Post-Hegemonic Regionalism in Oceania: Examining the Development Potential of the New Framework for Pacific Regionalism', *Pacific Review*, 31(1), 2018: 20–37; Tim Bryar and Anna Naupa, 'The Shifting Tides of Pacific Regionalism', *The Round Table*, 106(2), 2017: 155–64; and Meg Taylor, 'The Future of the Pacific Islands Forum and the Framework for Pacific Regionalism', in Fry and Tarte, *The New Pacific Diplomacy*, pp. 39–47.

> ... it's quite revolutionary in the way you do it but other parts of
> the world have taken this on, setting the agenda for themselves
> ... and have really shifted the way developments happen in their
> own region.[49]

Dame Meg has constantly emphasised the theme of Pacific leaders controlling their own agenda as she has promoted the new 'Framework for Pacific Regionalism'—the major recommendation of the Morauta Review:

> It is through the Framework that I believe we are in the early and
> formative stages of what is a new era for Pacific regionalism. One
> that will strengthen our ability to charter our own destiny.[50]

Under Dame Meg's tenure, the PIF also took on 'inclusion' as a major principle underpinning the new regionalism:

> Pacific island leaders have ... recognized the need for a new
> inclusive and game changing approach to Pacific regionalism ...
> At the heart of this new approach is an emphasis on inclusive
> policy development and implementation ...

> The Framework places strong emphasis on the fact that achieving
> impact requires us to work together, not just as states, but in ways
> that include all actors in the region. The new Pacific Regionalism
> has to be inclusive so that we have access to the breadth of
> experience and insight that exists in our people.[51]

There are still limitations on civil society participation and the jury is still out on whether the PIF's efforts on the inclusion agenda will earn legitimacy among the peoples of the Pacific.[52] This nevertheless amounts to an important paradigm shift in the norms underpinning regional governance within the PIF.

---

49   'Donors Influence Development Decisions: Forum SG', *Pacnews*, 16 April 2015, available from: news.pngfacts.com/2015/04/donors-influence-development-decisions.html.
50   Meg Taylor, 'Keynote Address', Australian Council for International Development (ACFID) National Conference, Melbourne, 26 October 2016.
51   ibid.
52   Maureen Penjueli, 'Civil Society and the Political Legitimacy of Regional Institutions: An NGO Perspective', in Fry and Tarte, *The New Pacific Diplomacy*, pp. 65–78; Slatter, 'The New Framework for Pacific Regionalism'.

From 2017, the assertion of the regional self-determination principle within the PIF moved to another level. Pacific leaders embraced the theme of the 'Blue Pacific: Our Sea of Islands' promoted by the Samoan Government at the Apia PIF meeting in September of that year. Prime Minister Sailele welcomed the delegates as 'descendants of the continent moana, our sea of islands joined to the umbilical cord of our cultures, heritage, resources and identification as people of the Ocean'.[53] He went on to develop the value of adopting the 'Blue Pacific' as the all-embracing 'narrative' of Pacific regionalism pursued through the PIF:

> This new narrative calls for inspired leadership by the Forum and a long-term commitment together as one Blue Continent, has the potential to define a Blue Pacific economy, ensures a sustainable, secure, resilient and peaceful Blue Pacific, as well as strengthens Blue Pacific Diplomacy to protect the value of our Ocean and peoples.[54]

In their communiqué, the Pacific leaders supported Prime Minister Sailele's proposal. They endorsed 'the Blue Pacific identity' as 'the core driver of collective action' and they 'recognised The Blue Pacific as a new narrative that calls for … a long-term Forum foreign policy commitment to act as one "Blue Continent"'.[55] Significantly, they 'recognised The Blue Pacific as being about all Pacific peoples comprising our ocean of islands'.[56]

This new narrative was very quickly adopted in PIF policies and communications. The new discourse had several strands. First, it was about promoting Oceanic identity and solidarity around stewardship of the ocean along the lines argued by Epeli Hau`ofa in 1997 in his famous essays 'Our Sea of Islands' and 'The Ocean in Us'.[57] Second, it promoted an image of solidarity and connectedness in the idea of the reclamation of an Oceanic continent, building on the concept promoted by Albert Norman in 1949.[58] Third, it is clearly talking about the assertion of regional self-determination. And finally, it is signalling an identity mainly

---

53   Tuilaepa Dr Sailele Malielegaoi, 'Let Us Recapture the Essence of Our Blue Pacific', *Samoa Observer*, 7 September 2017.

54   ibid.

55   PIFS, *Leaders' Communiqué: Forty-Eighth Pacific Islands Forum*, para. 6.

56   ibid., para. 7.

57   Hau`ofa, 'Our Sea of Islands'; and Epeli Hau`ofa, 'The Ocean in Us', *The Contemporary Pacific*, 10(2), 1998: 392–410.

58   Albert Norman, 'The Reclamation of Oceania', *Christian Science Monitor*, 4 June 1949.

among the island-state membership of the PIF. This is evident not only in the 'sea of islands' reference above, but also in Dame Meg's reference, in an August 2018 address to the USP:

> The Blue Pacific narrative helps us to understand, *in our own terms, based on our unique customary values and principles*, the strategic value of our region. It guides our political conversations towards ensuring we have a strong and collective voice, a regional position and action, on issues vital to our development as a region and as the Blue Pacific continent.[59]

At the forty-ninth PIF meeting in Nauru in September 2018, there were several significant indications that the diplomatic culture of the PIF was undergoing further transformation based on the principle of regional self-determination. This was clearly expressed in the theme of the meeting, which was 'Building a Strong Pacific: Our People, Our Islands, Our Will'.[60] Second, it was evident in the historic decision to change the financing of the core budget to ensure that Pacific island states control over 50 per cent.[61] Third, the Pacific island states prevailed—against Australia's preferred outcome—in achieving a PIF consensus that climate change was the 'single greatest threat to the livelihoods, security and wellbeing of the peoples of the Pacific' and a reaffirmation by leaders of a commitment 'to progress the implementation of the Paris Agreement'.[62] Finally, for the first time in PIF history, the communiqué contained a declaration agreed to by FICs. Faced with Australian opposition to a proposal to have the PIF call on the United States to return to the Paris Agreement, the Pacific island leaders insisted on the inclusion of a FIC-only declaration.[63] Prior to this, if Australia had a contrary position, the FICs' position would have to be altered to meet Canberra's wishes or dropped from the communiqué in the name of consensus.

---

59   Meg Taylor, 'Introductory Remarks by Dame Meg Taylor, Secretary-General', Research Week, USP Laucala Campus, Fiji, 27 August 2018.
60   PIFS, *Leaders' Communiqué: Forty-Ninth Pacific Islands Forum*, para. 4.
61   ibid., Annex 2.
62   ibid., Annex 1, para. (1).
63   ibid., para. 17.

Conclusion

This powerful 'framing of the islands' as the Blue Pacific, and the linking of this promotion of regional solidarity and Oceanic identity to Pacific island ownership of regional governance, is in many ways to be seen as a renaissance of the ideology underpinning the establishment of the SPF network in the early 1970s. This new framing of the region as solidly connected 'large ocean states' with strategic weight and a determination to ensure indigenous control of the regional agenda has been expressed clearly in the fundamental transformation of the regional architecture, in regional diplomacy outcomes such as climate policy, in the new conceptualisation of regional security in the Boe Declaration and in the way in which a 'Pacific voice' has been asserted in global forums since 2012.

The transformation of regionalism has not proceeded on the lines advocated by Fiji. The PIF has not disappeared and Australia and New Zealand are still supported by all island countries as members. But neither has regionalism reverted to the status quo ante. The Pacific island states have made it very clear that regional diplomacy—pursued through a reformed PIF and a very active PSIDS—is very much under Pacific island control on key issues such as climate policy, decolonisation, ocean management and regional security. Dialogue, debate and support from Australia and New Zealand within the PIF are valued but attempts to frustrate the pursuit of fundamental shared objectives of 'the Blue Pacific' are no longer tolerated. As Dame Meg warned in her address to the State of the Pacific conference in September 2018 regarding the Australian position on climate policy:

> The Blue Pacific belongs to all of us and its value can only be effectively realised collectively. We cannot afford to have one or two of us acting in ways that place the wellbeing and potential of the Blue Pacific Continent at risk.[64]

Since 2012, we have also seen a transformation of regionalism in relation to which Pacific islanders are included in regional diplomacy. There is a new norm concerning the interpretation of how the peoples of the Pacific should be represented. There had always been a norm of having regional

---

64   Meg Taylor, 'Keynote Address', 2018 State of the Pacific Conference, The Australian National University, Canberra, 8 September 2018, available from: www.forumsec.org/keynote-address-by-secretary-general-meg-taylor-to-the-2018-state-of-the-pacific-conference/.

diplomacy work for the Pacific peoples, but, as interpreted from 1971 to 2012, PIF members assumed this to be taken care of by the sovereign states speaking on behalf of the people at the regional diplomatic table. What we have seen since 2012 is a transformation of this norm to one of more direct inclusion of the 'Pacific peoples'. We have seen such inclusion as a founding principle of the PIDF and declared as one of the key principles underpinning new approaches in the PIF. Ironically, we have also seen it in the inclusion of Pacific islanders from dependent territories at the top table of regional diplomacy, via membership of the PIF. The admittance of French Polynesia and New Caledonia as full members of the PIF is a dramatic departure from the longstanding principle of sovereignty as a condition of participation in the Pacific leaders' meetings. But it does fit with the new norm of inclusion of all Pacific peoples in the region, demonstrating a tension between the self-determination and inclusion norms associated with the new Pacific diplomacy.

14

Conclusion: Power and diplomatic agency in Pacific regionalism

The previous chapters have traced the politics and diplomacy of Pacific regionalism against the backdrop of changing global influences, and changing local politics, from the colonial period to recent times. In this concluding chapter, I return to the overriding question motivating this study: what is the political meaning of Pacific regionalism? To unpack this question, I propose to focus on the two key puzzles I raised at the outset.

The first puzzle is the key question of how we should understand the political significance of Pacific regionalism in a context in which the region-building project has not moved along the path of European-style regional integration. Can it, for example, still be seen as a form of political community with real and independent political significance? Seemingly without settled governance or coercive capacity, is it more than an arena for diplomatic talk? If it is, what is the nature and the source of this political significance? How should we understand the power of the regional political community in the Pacific context?

The second puzzle follows from the first: If Pacific regionalism does have political significance, whom has it served? Who has diplomatic agency in this regional enterprise? In particular, how much political agency have Pacific states and societies had in shaping the agenda, structures and policy outcomes of the Pacific political regional community? Is it, rather, the case that, in 'framing the islands' in particular ways, external regional players are setting up Pacific islanders for outcomes not of their making? These thoughts arise from the reality that the pattern of power underlying and surrounding Pacific regionalism at least suggests the possibility of either an Australian and New Zealand regional hegemony or, more broadly, the dominance of globalisation over local interests. This expectation is particularly encouraged by the knowledge that this is a region comprising many of the world's smallest states.

Political significance

The road not travelled

Our starting point in this inquiry was that conventional analyses of regionalism miss the significance of Pacific regionalism because they look for a high level of regional integration or evidence that the region-building effort is on a pathway to that goal. The comparative model for such a judgement is usually the European experience and the indicator of political significance is usually the degree of regional integration achieved by the regional project. Seen through such a conceptual lens, regional integration implies the development of a coercive capacity to ensure state compliance with regional regulations. From this perspective, the creation of state-like attributes at the regional level implies the derogation of national sovereignty.

While there has been constant lip-service paid to the integration goal in the pursuit of the Pacific regional project, the idea has failed to have any serious purchase on the practice of Pacific regionalism. Against those who would conclude that there is therefore little of political significance to see in the Pacific regional project, I argue that the *longue durée* of Pacific regionalism in the twentieth and twenty-first centuries has shown that the Pacific regional entity has had real political significance. This can be seen in the various political roles that have been performed by the regional entity: the constitution of a strategic political arena for the negotiation of globalisation, the provision of regional governance, the building of a regional political community and the operation of a regional diplomatic bloc.

Strategic political arena

It is clear that the Pacific regional entity has acted as a key political arena for diplomatic contests over how people should live their lives and how societies should be organised in the Pacific. The regional arena has not displaced the national political arena, but it has become an important site of politics affecting all aspects of Pacific lives, including security, development, resource management, environmental protection, rights, governance, gender equality, youth and health. In particular, the strategic location of the Pacific regional arena between 'the global' and 'the local' has enabled it to become a valued site for the negotiation of global ideas and processes. As we have seen, global actors such as the international agencies and global powers see the regional arena as a strategic location for promoting their preferred policy agenda and policy knowledge across the Pacific island region. They have seen regional diplomacy as a crucial part of their effort to influence policy within individual Pacific countries. Pacific island countries, on the other hand, have regarded the regional arena as a key place to engage global forces and ideas impacting on their societies, with a view to either moderating such pressures or defending themselves against undesired influences. This has, therefore, been an important political arena for regional diplomacy; it has determined key outcomes for small states in a globalised world; it has been a place where they have negotiated globalisation.

As a result of this diplomatic activity over the past 70 years, we have seen the gradual development of a highly complex regional institutional system. As we have seen, colonial regionalism centred on the South Pacific Commission and its advisory offshoot, the South Pacific Conference. Leaders of independent Pacific island states created the South Pacific Forum in 1971, which, over subsequent decades, became the centre of an elaborate system of regional institutions focused on various aspects of regional governance: fisheries, the environment, technical cooperation and research. From 2009, another burst of institution-building occurred as an expression of what we have here described as the 'new Pacific diplomacy'. By 2016, this new array of regional and subregional organisations was largely accepted as part of the patchwork regional governance system described in Chapter 13. These institutions now cover almost every aspect of governance, including economic development, trade promotion, resource protection, the environment, natural disasters, human rights, governance, security, conflict management, cultural heritage, sustainable human development and decolonisation. They jointly employ more than 1,000 regional public servants to carry out their programs. By any measure apart from the European model, this is a significant regional diplomatic and governance system.

Regional governance

For the sceptics, though, the real issue for establishing political significance is whether this regional activity leads to a form of regional governance that influences what happens within Pacific states. If it has not produced European-style integration and the derogation of state sovereignty, can the Pacific regional community be regarded as having an impact on what happens within states? I argue that the diplomatic contest within these organisations has produced significant outcomes that can be seen as a form of regional governance. However, as explained in Chapter 2, the outcome of this diplomatic activity has been a form of governance not easily recognised through the European integration lens. Its significance derives from the authority of the settled regional norms, which are the cumulative outcomes of regional diplomatic contests in a particular era. These carry authority. While they do not require formal surrendering of sovereignty or compliance, they derive their authority from the power of dominant discourses, international agreements and policy knowledge. This study has focused on how this changing regional governance has mattered, in particular, in three key areas: development, security and climate policy. In each case, we saw how the regional regime constrained or influenced state behaviour, as well as how it impacted on the policies pursued by regional institutions.

Regional political community

Yet the political significance of Pacific regionalism goes beyond its role as an arena for and a source of governance. I argue that it also constitutes a regional political community—a term that connotes a deep level of commitment, affiliation and identity beyond the nation-state. The justification for using the term 'political community' to characterise the resultant political entity starts with the case I made in Chapter 7 for seeing the new regional polity of the 1970s and 1980s as a 'regional society of states'. The shared values, institutions and ideology constituting that society of states already suggested a form of regional political community. This was not just an instrumental ad hoc association of states, but rather one with a commitment to shared communal values. The aptness of the notion of 'political community' was further strengthened in the 1970s and 1980s by the addition of an emergent regional civil society as an active participant in the regional polity. Island state leaders and civil society representatives shared the regional identity promoted through the SPF at this time, as represented in the 'Pacific way' ideology and the concern shown for Pacific peoples outside the formal national jurisdiction of the member states.

As seen in Chapters 11–13, the 1990s and 2000s saw the advent of a more technocratic and instrumental regional political system under Australian and New Zealand hegemony. This lacked the sense of regional community among Pacific island states and regional civil society developed over the previous two decades. The perceived lack of political ownership of the regional agenda and regional organisation contributed to this lack of commitment to building a regional community. The departure of the post-independence leaders and their shared authority, commitment and values was another major causal factor. Pacific island leaders came to see Australia and New Zealand less as partners in a regional community with a shared commitment to pursuing island interests in regional self-determination. They were instead increasingly seen as the dominant members of the regional diplomatic system, pursuing their own very different interests and values. Nowhere was this more evident than in relation to climate policy.

However, in the 1990s, there did emerge two important harbingers of the need to return to a thicker idea of community in regional relations. Epeli Hau`ofa, writing in his now famous essays, 'Our Sea of Islands' (1993) and 'The Ocean in Us' (1998), made a plea for a less technocratic regionalism based on a shared Oceanic identity. In a similar spirit, at the fortieth South Pacific Conference in Canberra in 1997, Senator Berenado Vunibobo of Fiji made a plea for renaming the South Pacific Commission 'The Pacific Community' to capture the organic ties and human relations the island leaders wanted to emphasise. Vunibobo argued that the 'commission' label, which was being promoted by the Australian secretary-general, smacked of the imposed colonial regionalism of the past and certainly did not evoke sufficiently the familial ties of 'community'. The other Pacific leaders supported his call. This emerging commitment on the part of Pacific leaders to return the regional project to a broader-based regional community on behalf of Pacific peoples was evident in the Pacific Leaders' Vision of 2004, which I examined in Chapter 11. It was not, however, until the second decade of the twenty-first century that a determination to return to this deeper kind of regional political community came fully to the fore with a display of the strong connection and shared values among Pacific leaders and the evocation of 'one Pacific continent' in the 'Blue Pacific' ideology, described in detail in Chapter 13.

Diplomatic bloc

Perhaps the most unrecognised, significant political role for Pacific regionalism has been demonstrated when the regional community has acted as a diplomatic bloc promoting a Pacific voice in global arenas or negotiating as a group with larger powers in regional arenas. This has long been a major part of the Pacific regionalism story. I surveyed in Chapters 6–9 some of the extraordinary successes of collective diplomacy in the 1970s and 1980s against some of the world's most powerful states. There has been an unfortunate tendency to write this significant role out of analyses of Pacific regionalism because in the 1990s and 2000s regionalism began to be defined more narrowly, even within the region itself, as regional integration. In these decades, the Forum Secretariat dropped the emphasis on the forum as a diplomatic bloc in global arenas. Collective diplomacy thus did not appear as part of the definition of regionalism in the 2005 review of regionalism or in the proposed functions of the PIF set out under the Pacific Plan.

This political role returned in the second decade of the twenty-first century as part of the movement of ideas that Sandra Tarte and I have labelled the 'new Pacific diplomacy'.[1] A major part of that transformation—described in Chapter 13—was the revitalisation of Pacific regionalism as a bloc for diplomatic purposes in global arenas. The key move was the repurposing of the PSIDS at the United Nations. This organisation of Pacific island ambassadors (without Australia and New Zealand) became the globally recognised voice for Pacific diplomacy, displacing the PIF in this role. Whereas the role of diplomatic bloc in the 1970s and 1980s was expressed mainly in negotiations with one great power—for example, the United States on tuna fishing and Japan on driftnet fishing and the dumping of radioactive waste—the new Pacific diplomacy was concerned with projecting a Pacific voice in global multilateral negotiations. This required new skills and techniques, such as building coalitions, cultivating

---

1   Greg Fry and Sandra Tarte, eds, *The New Pacific Diplomacy*, ANU Press, 2015.

Global South alliances, obtaining strategic leadership in UN committees and framing agendas within niche areas such as ocean management and climate change. By 2018, the Pacific leaders had reestablished the regional diplomatic bloc as a major element in the political significance of Pacific regionalism.

Pacific regionalism and state power

As noted, efforts to build regionalism are usually seen as diluting state power and sovereignty. While this is so when and where regionalism takes the form of regional integration, it has not been the case in the forms of regional activity described here. For Pacific regionalism, I argue that regionalism and state power are mutually constitutive. Indeed, I see regional diplomatic contests as being intimately entwined with state-building. This study has shown that the regional governing ideas, and the debates about them, have been as much about how states should be run as they have been about building a regional community. We have also seen how the regional diplomatic bloc can bolster national interests in global negotiations. Finally, we saw how appeals to the authority of the regional political community were frequently used to assert or bolster claims to national sovereignty on the part of associated states, sovereignty movements and dependent territories. Ultimately, then, Pacific regionalism has provided another important layer of politics above the nation-state that has proved politically significant in each of the ways outlined above, and without requiring the surrender of national sovereignty.

Whose Pacific regionalism?

As noted, the second puzzle about the political meaning of Pacific regionalism follows directly from the first. If Pacific regionalism matters, for whom has it mattered? Who has had the power? To what extent can it serve the interests of Pacific islanders in the face of global actors set on influencing regional diplomatic outcomes? In diplomatic contests involving such large players, the expectation would be that small states would be no more than pawns in this regional game, with larger states always dominating if they need to do so. The prospects for a regional level of politics in which Pacific agency features do not, at first glance, look likely. These are, after all, among the world's smallest countries and among the most highly dependent on economic assistance. Australia and New

Zealand have rarely been reluctant to use Pacific regionalism to promote their own interests, while there have long existed larger players who have tried to influence outcomes at particular times, including the European Union, the United States, France, Japan and China.

There are several potential answers to the puzzle of 'whose Pacific regionalism?'. I consider here three possible candidates for apt characterisation of the dominant influence operating within and on Pacific regionalism: that it has been a vehicle for an Australian–New Zealand hegemony; that it has worked as an agent for globalisation at the expense of local interests; and that it has permitted Pacific island agency in regional and global politics. I then propose to make the case for seeing the answer to this puzzle as a fourth characterisation—namely, an entanglement of the other three 'answers' in a more contingent view of power in Pacific regionalism.

Hegemonic power

Any superficial glance at the history and characteristics of Pacific regionalism might suggest that the power relations in this regional community are best described as an Australian and New Zealand hegemony. Australia and New Zealand have had a longstanding desire to manage the Pacific island region. In the late nineteenth century, Otto von Bismarck called this intention the Australasian Monroe doctrine. In 1883, concern about building capacity to flex muscle in managing security in the Pacific island region was the prime motive for organising the intercolonial convention to create the Australian nation. We noted in Chapter 4 Australia and New Zealand's role in the 1940s in initiating the idea of Pacific regionalism and establishing and financing the colonial regional system. In Chapters 6–10, we noted that they continued to have a crucial role in the new regional system created by the Pacific island leaders in 1971. They became the only metropolitan members of the new SPF and supplied most of the financial support for the Forum's budget. They became the main supporters of subsequent expansion of the regional architecture in such organisations as the FFA and SPREP.

From the mid 1970s, Australia and New Zealand made it clear that they saw Pacific regionalism as a key vehicle for pursuing their foreign policies in the region. As we saw in Chapter 9, this was particularly focused on regional security. They viewed the shaping of regional security as their special responsibility on behalf of the Western alliance and particularly the United States. This was certainly how Washington also viewed the relationship: a delegated responsibility for Western leadership of the regional security order.

The influence of Australia and New Zealand was mainly exercised through agenda-setting, the staffing of regional organisations, financial control and the making of regional declarations on security. They also had an effective veto on positions pursued by the Pacific island leaders that they deemed to be hostile to their interests, such as in climate policy. The various moves made by the islands to check their dominance, such as the rise of the new Pacific diplomacy analysed in Chapter 13, also demonstrate that Pacific islanders recognised the impact of this hegemonic power on their interests.

This Australian and New Zealand intention to dominate Pacific regionalism was present throughout the history of Pacific regionalism. It was reinforced by the dependence of Pacific island countries on their bilateral economic assistance from Canberra and Wellington and, in general, the superior resources and capacity of Australia and New Zealand to set the agenda and prepare the outcomes of meetings. Australia and New Zealand were responsible for the creation of many of the new governance mechanisms within the regional architecture, such as the FFMM and the FEMM. They were responsible for nearly all the treaties and declarations, such as the Biketawa Declaration on intervention, PACER Plus on regional free trade, the South Pacific Nuclear Free Zone on nuclear issues and the Aitutaki Declaration on law and order. They also attempted to impose major regional policy frames on the Pacific in relation to development and security. For example, we examined in some detail in Chapter 11 the attempt to create a regional economic order based on neoliberal ideas and policies.

However, these intentions did not always translate into clear hegemonic power. History shows instead a more complex and contingent characterisation. This is most tellingly revealed in the area of highest Australian commitment to a hegemonic system—that of defining regional security and regional security governance. As we saw in Chapter 9, Australia was ultimately unsuccessful in pursuing its preferred Cold War order. The Pacific countries rejected the policy of strategic denial and the two-tier hierarchical regional system promoted as part of the Australian system. By 1989, Australian foreign minister Gareth Evans realised that, although Australia was leading, nobody was following and, accordingly, it was time for a new partnership approach that recognised this fact.

We noted in Chapter 12 that the Australian effort to promote a new strategic denial policy against China in 2018 and a new conceptualisation of regional security was ultimately stymied by a different security narrative promoted by Pacific island states. It was this latter interpretation the PIF leaders enshrined in the Boe regional security declaration in 2018.

On balance, Australia and New Zealand have had enormous influence on Pacific regionalism—on its finances, agenda, policy directions and institutional development. This was most evident in the 1990s and 2000s, which could accurately be labelled an era of hegemonic regionalism. But, even in this post–Cold War period, when Australia and New Zealand seemingly succeeded in creating a regional economic order and a regional security order in accord with their interests, we saw, in Chapters 11 and 12, how they were constantly frustrated in areas where they thought they had agreement from the Pacific island states. With their combined economic and military power—Australia alone is the thirteenth largest economy in the world—compared with the very small economies of the island states, and their longstanding determination to shape the regional agenda and be seen as the natural leaders of the regional community, it might be expected that this would produce over time a more unqualified hegemonic regional system. This study has shown, however, that Pacific regionalism cannot be described as being ultimately determined by hegemonic power. Power as capacity has not easily translated into power as legitimate influence.

The power of globalisation

A second possible answer to the puzzle of 'whose Pacific regionalism?' is to see Pacific regionalism as an agent of globalisation, broadly defined to include all processes and discourses with global reach. In the long history we have just investigated, we have repeatedly noted that large shifts in global epochs, and their defining ideas, create powerful frames that are imposed on Pacific regionalism. Indeed, we saw in Chapter 3 that the idea of the Pacific itself was a global framing of ancient island societies into a new identity and social construction as a result of European exploration, geography and imperial management. We observed that each global epoch seemed to produce a different Pacific regionalism. Global ideas and global power provided the backdrop for the political contests over regional governance, often by generating the big ideological frames within which regional politics was played out. Some of these global influences on the course of regionalism have been geopolitical—for example, colonialism and its ending, World War II, the Cold War, the war on terror and the rise of China. In each era, we also noted powerful global discourses—such as neoliberalism, Darwinism, self-determination, gender equality and human development—which created the parameters of the regional contest of ideas about how Pacific societies should be organised. We also described and analysed the major global processes and activities in the Pacific region that prompted a response from the Pacific political community—for example, nuclear testing, driftnet fishing, the activities of DWFNs, continuing colonialism and climate change.

However, this has never been the case of a unified globalisation process using regionalism to dominate local Pacific societies. The first qualification to enter is that global framing does not represent a homogeneous globalisation process. As we saw in Chapter 3, as early as the nineteenth century, there were contending global discourses about how to characterise Pacific island societies and what policies to pursue on that basis. This extended through to the modern period, where, as we saw in Chapter 9, there was an attempt to impose three different and competing Western conceptions of a Cold War regional order on the Pacific—one supported by France, the United Kingdom and the United States, one by Australia and another by New Zealand. We also discussed, in Chapter 11, this diversity in global framing in the contest between neoliberal and human development discourses on regional development over the past two decades. Another more recent example is provided by the different global views on climate policy, with certain international agencies and parts of global civil society supporting the collective Pacific island state position and other global discourses opposing the Pacific view.

The second qualification is that there is not always one 'local' in this supposed global–local contestation. Some local groups have deployed particular global discourses against other local groups or states—for example, women's groups using global feminist positions against island state positions. And, as we saw in Chapter 9 in relation to Cold War regional security, although the 'local' position prevailed over the most powerful Western countries, the 'local' was also differentiated. Regional civil society allied itself with global civil society actors and some Melanesian states in opposition to Australia, New Zealand and some Polynesian states on the question of the nuclear weapons–free zone for the South Pacific. Meanwhile, Tonga allied itself with the American/British/French position in supporting French nuclear testing in the Pacific.

The third qualification is that these imposed framings are negotiated and mediated, and thereby given Pacific characteristics, behind a seeming acquiescence in the prevailing global discourse. There is a 'messy entanglement' similar to that recognised by Pacific historians and anthropologists in relation to nineteenth-century engagements between colonialists and local societies. For example, behind the seeming acceptance of the neoliberal regional economic order, the Pacific island states made clear they would not accept any change to communal land tenure. This became a 'no-go area' for the subsequent promotion of a regional reform agenda. Overall, then, this study has shown that global ideas and processes may set the agenda and some parameters of action, but they do not necessarily control specific outcomes.

Pacific island diplomatic agency

A third possible answer to the puzzle under discussion is to argue that Pacific islanders—state leaders and civil society representatives—have had the upper hand in the building of regional community. The case for this interpretation is built on the history of the indigenous regional movement, the shared commitment of the region's leaders, the shared regional identity, the negotiation of a regional diplomatic culture that has sometimes enabled Pacific island control of the regional agenda, the successes achieved in promoting a Pacific voice in global and regional diplomatic arenas and the mediation of powerful hegemonic norms in relation to security, development and climate policy.

The regional diplomatic culture is an important determinant of the diplomatic outcomes of the regional political community, and therefore a key site for understanding the deep politics of the regional diplomatic system. Because it deals with the norms about who can speak, how decisions are made and what is regarded as a legitimate procedure, it determines the answers to the fundamental political questions of who controls the regional agenda and the regional diplomatic process. It therefore gets to the heart of the power politics of the regional system.

Drawing from the history of Pacific regionalism set out in the previous chapters, we can trace a long-term trajectory from a hegemonic diplomatic culture under colonialism to a diplomatic culture emphasising regional self-determination, equality and Pacific agency. This achievement was due to the joint efforts of Pacific leaders. As we saw in Chapter 6, from 1965, emerging Pacific island leaders challenged the legitimacy of the colonial diplomatic culture based on racial hierarchy. While this political movement gradually succeeded in bringing about institutional reform that, by the end of the 1960s, allowed greater Pacific agency, the region's leaders remained frustrated that there was no movement on the key principles and practices of a colonial diplomatic culture that excluded the Pacific island peoples, except in an advisory capacity. This led to their diplomatic efforts to create a new forum for regional diplomacy with a very different diplomatic culture, the SPF. Pacific island state leaders, with Australia and New Zealand, agreed on a new set of norms governing diplomacy in the regional arena. There was a strong commitment to self-determination, non-intervention, sovereignty, equality and partnership. This regional diplomatic culture remained in place through the 1970s and 1980s.

In the 1990s and 2000s, Australia and New Zealand imposed a new hegemonic regional diplomatic culture in the PIF that was seemingly accepted by the Pacific island leaders. As we saw in Chapters 11–13, this became possible because Australia and New Zealand started to see regional governance as an extension of their foreign and domestic policies and accordingly raised the stakes by seeking to get their way more often in relation to agendas, financial control and staffing. They also misused consensus procedures, turning them into a veto power for themselves. This hierarchical diplomatic culture affected outcomes on climate policy, the war on terror and trade. The establishment of this hierarchical diplomatic culture was also a product of the loss of the strong, first-generation Pacific island leadership. Yet, behind the scenes, there was mounting evidence that Pacific leaders did not accord this diplomatic culture full legitimacy.

In Chapter 13, I showed how a 'new' Pacific diplomacy challenged and transformed this hegemonic diplomatic culture. I argued that this action in effect created a new regional diplomatic culture embracing the principles of regional self-determination and inclusiveness. It was expressed in the establishment of new institutions and the reform of existing institutions, such that the fundamental norms of how diplomatic dialogue would henceforth be conducted were transformed. The hegemonic regional diplomatic culture of the previous two decades was overthrown, but without excluding Australia and New Zealand from the Pacific regional community. This has been an important win for Pacific island agency within the Pacific regional community.

Another key site for establishing evidence of Pacific island agency within Pacific regionalism is to be found in relation to the Pacific community acting as a diplomatic bloc. Earlier in this chapter, we noted the significance of this role. But what do the diplomatic outcomes say about the success of this regional activity in promoting Pacific island interests against larger powers? This study has traced this successful collective diplomacy throughout the post-independence period since 1971. In Chapter 5, we noted the political success of the Pacific leaders acting in unison in relation to negotiations to establish a Pacific-controlled regionalism in the late 1960s. We then explored, in Chapters 7–10, their successful joint diplomacy, under Forum auspices, in relation to the Law of the Sea, within the UN General Assembly on decolonisation and on trade with the European Union in the Lomé Convention and with Australia in respect of the SPARTECA.

These highly significant outcomes against some of the most powerful states continued throughout the 1980s, with the Pacific achieving a ban on driftnet fishing by large fishing states and a ban on Japanese plans to dump radioactive waste in the Pacific. Most impressive of all was the collective action taken by the Pacific islands against the United States on their right to jurisdiction over their tuna resources. The extraordinarily successful outcome that was eventually achieved involved opposing the US position on the Law of the Sea, its domestic legislation and its powerful fishing industry. Yet the Pacific island states prevailed, and the resulting deal was enshrined in international agreement.

Following the diplomatic doldrums of the 1990s and 2000s, when the Australia/New Zealand–dominated regional diplomatic culture constrained collective diplomacy, and instead emphasised regional integration, the Pacific island states began to use joint diplomacy successfully again. As we saw in Chapter 13, there was a new era of diplomacy. This time it faced an even more difficult test. Whereas the issues of the 1970s and 1980s were usually negotiated in a context in which the Pacific collective faced only one large power, the new agenda—trade, decolonisation, climate policy, sustainable development—tended to be negotiated in large global multilateral settings. Although this created new challenges, the Pacific island states proved adept in deploying new methods to build coalitions and assert a Pacific voice at key global meetings such as Rio-Plus, the UN General Assembly and the UNFCCC. Their achievements since 2012 have included gaining recognition for PSIDS in the creation of the Asia-Pacific grouping as a regional bloc at the

UN General Assembly; the inclusion of ocean management and climate change as SDGs; the inclusion of Pacific priorities in the final outcomes of Rio+20; and the reinscription of French Polynesia on the list of dependent territories under the purview of the UN decolonisation committee. The PSIDS also coordinated a very effective Pacific campaign at the Paris UNFCCC conference, which resulted in achievement of nearly all the diplomatic objectives the Pacific leaders had set themselves in the Suva Declaration. The resultant high standing of the Pacific diplomatic bloc has also been evident in the recognition the PSIDS has been given by global actors and international agencies, particularly in the ocean management and climate change arenas.

A third site in which we can explore the degree of Pacific agency in Pacific regionalism is in relation to regional governance, the governing regional norms and the making of regional policies in areas such as security, development and climate policy. In relation to regional security, we saw in Chapter 12 the way in which Pacific leaders prevailed in the contest with Australia and New Zealand over conceptualising regional security in the Boe Declaration of 2018. The emphasis in the declaration on climate change and human security, rather than on a geopolitical conceptualisation of threat, represented a victory for Pacific island leaders. Australia and New Zealand have also sought to promote a policy of regional strategic denial against China outside the PIF. The Pacific leaders have also asserted themselves against this position, pressing their right to continue their productive relations with China while maintaining their links with Australia and New Zealand.

In relation to economic governance, we saw in Chapter 10 that, during the early decades of the SPF, the Pacific leaders were considerably influenced by a global liberal discourse emphasising economic modernisation and growth, but they qualified and moderated its impact by promoting the 'Pacific way' discourse that emphasised the preservation of Pacific cultural values and the assertion of Pacific control of the development agenda. After 1990, Australia and New Zealand promoted a neoliberal regional economic order, but as we saw in Chapter 11, this was not accepted without mediation and qualification by the Pacific leaders. Again, they promoted a cultural perspective, particularly on the question of land, and in relation to the PACER Plus agreement on regional free trade, the island states with the two biggest economies, Papua New Guinea and Fiji, refused to join. Others joined only as a way of gaining other diplomatic objectives in relation to labour access.

In relation to regional climate policy, the Pacific island leaders have demonstrated their political agency since 2015. For the previous 25 years, the regional climate policy was dominated by Australia and New Zealand. As examined in Chapter 13, the Pacific island states were always hamstrung in producing a PIF climate policy that truly represented what they desperately wanted to promote. This was because the consensus decision-making style of the PIF effectively meant that Australia and New Zealand could veto positions that they saw as working against their interests as big carbon emitters. This in turn meant the Pacific island states were constrained in working collectively through the PIF at UNFCCC meetings. This changed dramatically in 2015. As in earlier PIF meetings, the Port Moresby meeting failed to produce a strong position supporting the Pacific island states' position leading up to the Paris climate conference. This time, however, the Pacific island leaders used their recently repurposed PSIDS (without Australia and New Zealand) to organise and successfully project a Pacific voice in Paris. This gave them a strong collective voice on climate policy on the global stage for the first time.

Contingent and entangled power

I propose therefore to argue that the best answer to the puzzle of where power lies in Pacific regionalism is to be found in a more complex amalgam of the three plausible characterisations surveyed above. In this answer, I move beyond these fixed and static views of power based on assumptions about homogeneous agents—the West, Australian and New Zealand hegemony, globalisation and Pacific islanders. I also move beyond the conventional assumption that larger powers will necessarily prevail over small island states or that powerful global discourses will naturally eclipse local cultural values and interests. What we have seen in this study is a much more complex engagement in which the Pacific island states have sometimes prevailed in shaping Pacific regionalism and at other times managed to mediate global discourses through regional action.

Furthermore, I argue that how these complex power relations are resolved within Pacific regionalism at any given time is highly contingent—that is, they are dependent on a complex set of circumstances. I am using the term 'contingent power' to refer to circumstances that, in certain combinations, can influence outcomes, and I am thus avoiding the conceptual trap of seeing power as a fixed capacity based on material factors or size. This consideration of the long history of Pacific regionalism has allowed us to see what these contingent factors are and how they operate to influence the power politics of Pacific regionalism in different epochs. There are several, but they can easily be identified.

First, there are the changing dominant global discourses, which provide powerful mega framings of how the Pacific (and other regions of the world) should be ordered. As we have seen, it has mattered for Pacific regionalism whether the dominant global discourse is self-determination or Darwinian racial hierarchy, or whether it is neoliberalism or human development. The dominant discourse sets the framing parameters.

A second important contingent factor is changing geopolitics at the global level, which directly impacts on the power politics of regionalism. This includes, for example, the impact of World War II on the decision to establish Pacific regionalism, the Cold War and its impact on the use of the region as a 'nuclear playground' and the challenge to an indigenous regional identity based on antinuclear sentiment. It also includes such developments as the global war on terror and perceptions of China's rise, each of which changed the power relations within Pacific regionalism.

Third, we should note the importance of state sovereignty as a contingent factor. We saw how the Law of the Sea extended sovereign jurisdiction to 200 nautical miles and, collectively for Pacific states, to most of the central and southern Pacific Ocean. This collective sovereignty in turn became the basis for many powerful actions and claims by Pacific states in relation to tuna management. It also became the basis of the contemporary collective identity based on the 'one Pacific continent' narrative and the powerful rebranding of Pacific island states as large ocean states, and to recognition in global arenas of that collective identity as a diplomatic leader in ocean management. Sovereignty also gives small island states the power to say no to signing on to regional programs initiated by larger states, such as PACER Plus and the EPA with the European Union.

Fourth, there is the important element of leadership. We saw that Pacific leadership was smart, strategic, stable and confident in the 1970s and 1980s. This was a major factor affecting its success in overthrowing the colonial regional system. This continued throughout the 1970s and 1980s, when strong Pacific island leadership asserted itself within the SPF against attempts by Australia and New Zealand to assert a two-tier system during the Cold War. It was also seen in relation to Pacific collective diplomatic efforts in relation to the United States, Japan and France. Equally, we saw the importance of the loss of strong island state leadership in the 1990s and 2000s because of political instability within many of the member states and the retirement or defeat of the independence-era leaders.

Fifth, we have seen how the prevailing regional diplomatic culture is an important contingent factor, particularly when it is expressed in the shape of the institutional architecture. We saw the importance of the establishment of the SPF in 1971 in allowing Pacific agency not permitted under the rules of the colonial organisation. We also saw, for example, how the revamping of PSIDS as a global diplomatic voice opened up the possibility of an effective Pacific diplomacy representing Pacific island interests when the PIF avenue was closed off by Australian and New Zealand influence on consensus positions.

Finally, we should note the importance of the political positions coming out of Canberra and Wellington on their relationship to Pacific regionalism. This has always depended on which parties are in government in Canberra and Wellington. For example, the Australian Coalition governments under prime ministers Abbott, Turnbull and Scott Morrison have pursued a climate policy that has been diametrically opposed to the interests of the Pacific island states. This makes it impossible for Canberra to be accepted as a legitimate leader or even a member of the regional community. On the other hand, in the 1970s and 1980s, Canberra and Wellington supported the efforts by Pacific island states to promote their interests through Pacific regionalism in global and regional arenas. This encouraged a degree of regional identity and shared communal values, which made for a very different power relationship than exists under current Australian policies. New Zealand's recent shift on climate policy under the Ardern Government has meant that New Zealand again has a chance of acceptance in the Pacific community.

The future of Pacific regionalism

Although we can expect metropolitan powers, international agencies and economic consultants to continue to call for regional economic integration in the Pacific, past responses suggest that the Pacific island states will not seriously commit to a trajectory towards European-style integration. On the other hand, we can expect that the political roles outlined in this chapter—strategic arena, regional governance, political community and diplomatic bloc—will continue to be politically significant. As shown in Chapter 13, Pacific regionalism is currently on a trajectory towards a deeper regional community among Pacific island peoples, and its role as a diplomatic bloc is on an upward curve of success, recognised by key players in global forums and in key 'wins' in multilateral negotiations. Regional governance of security, development and climate policy will also continue to grow in importance based on current trends outlined in Chapters 11–13. For the reasons developed throughout this study, Pacific regionalism will continue to be a contested political space defining regional norms about how Pacific islanders should live.

The question of the nature of the power relations within this contested regional diplomatic space and, most importantly, whose interests prevail will depend on the contingent factors outlined above. Based on current trends, there are several contingent factors pointing in the direction of deeper regional community among the Pacific island states and peoples for the foreseeable future. These also suggest a continuation of the trend of greater control of Pacific regionalism by Pacific islanders and, conversely, less control by Australia and New Zealand.

The impact of the global context is an important starting point for understanding this trend. The current and prospective impacts of climate change on the low-lying island societies of the Pacific are so profound they will continue to create a rallying cry for the Pacific island regional community and the need for a strong Pacific voice in global affairs. This will also ensure continuing resistance to any attempt by Australia, in particular, to dilute Pacific solidarity on this existential issue. And, importantly, the climate change issue ensures that Pacific solidarity includes regional civil society as well as island state leaders.

The changing geopolitical context will also continue to be an enabler of Pacific island solidarity and successful political agency. As we saw in the Cold War context, when the West sees a threat to its interests in the Pacific at a time of global rivalry, the Pacific island states have greater bargaining power. This was graphically illustrated in the case of the Pacific tuna agreement with the United States. It was also evident in Australia's retreat from promoting a hegemonic regional security order, as examined in Chapter 9. We would therefore expect a continuation of the kind of assertion of Pacific views of security evident in the Boe Declaration of 2018, as examined in Chapter 12, and not just a ready acceptance by Pacific island states of Australia's positions on China's rise in the Pacific.

Another key contingent factor affecting the rise of Pacific islander agency in Pacific regionalism is the reemergence of strong Pacific island leadership. The important role of such leaders as Tuilaepa of Samoa, Bainimarama of Fiji, Sogavare of Solomon Islands, Tong of Kiribati, O'Neill of Papua New Guinea or Sopoaga of Tuvalu has played a part in a more assertive Pacific voice at the global level. But this contingent factor could change. Given the high turnover of leaders, we could see a change to less effective leaders or to ones who are less committed to regional solidarity, or less committed to a regional leadership role for their nation, in the case of Fiji and Papua New Guinea.

The emergence of strong, assertive Pacific leaders can also point in another direction. The tensions between some of these leaders have started to become evident and, although this has not yet led to less solidarity when confronting climate change or Australian hegemony on security, it may do so in the future. This is most likely in relation to Fiji's role. As we saw in the 1970s, the other island states saw Fiji as moving too far out in front as self-appointed regional spokesperson. In the same way, we are seeing a building resentment among other Pacific island states of Fiji's actions as self-appointed regional spokesperson under Bainimarama's leadership. This came to a head at the 2017 climate change talks in Bonn, where Fiji as chair had not adequately consulted other Pacific states and started to represent what were Fijian rather than Pacific positions. We can also see evidence of a souring of relations within the subregional MSG over Fiji's actions, and a cooling of support for the Fiji-created PIDF because of these tensions with Fiji. This tension is the most likely contingent factor that could derail Pacific island solidarity.

On the other hand, the Pacific leaders did not let these tensions derail their solidarity in 2018 in countering Australian efforts to have them curtail their relations with China or promote their own regional security narrative around a solid identity based on a regional 'Pacific continent' in seeking to give leadership to global ocean management. Continued solidarity and assertive agency are also supported by the enabling institutional changes the Pacific leaders achieved in the period 2012–14. These provide alternative Pacific island–controlled regional arenas and diplomatic pathways that have been recognised by global powers. The most important institution in this regard is the PSIDS. As we have seen, this has had extraordinary success in the past five years in projecting a Pacific voice in UN forums, including the UNFCCC, and in obtaining results and recognition by other states as the legitimate voice of the region. Above all, this is an enabling mechanism for continued Pacific island agency vis-a-vis the hegemonic aspirations of Australia and New Zealand going into the future. It would not be easily overturned given its acceptance by other players in global forums and its role in taking Pacific positions into broader Global South coalitions such as the AOSIS and the G-77.

As argued in Chapter 13, the 'new Pacific diplomacy' transformed Pacific regionalism. We are now in a new era of Pacific regionalism, characterised by a new regional diplomatic culture, a transformed institutional architecture and the dominance of the principles of self-determination and inclusion. There is also refreshed commitment to a regional identity around a shared ocean. This new rhetoric of the 'Blue Pacific continent' and the collective of 'large ocean states' has caught the Pacific imagination as a symbol of regional identity. These are also ideas that have purchase in regional civil society.

Australia and New Zealand are not emotionally part of this regional identity, although they claim to be leaders of the regional community. They are not seen as part of this fundamental transformation, partly because of their position on climate change and partly because of their position on China and regional security. But, even more importantly, they are now being judged by the way they seek to promote their regional positions without showing respect to the majority Pacific island state position. In many ways, the Pacific island states retain a surprisingly generous stance towards Canberra and Wellington. They still describe them as 'big brothers' and see them as part of the Pacific 'family', even if they currently feel they are acting as 'bad brothers' and not conducting dialogue within the family in a respectful way. A major contingent factor for the future of Pacific regionalism is therefore the degree to which Australia can overcome the preconceptions that have always flowed from its tendency to see this region as its 'own patch'.

Over the past 100 years, there has been an extraordinary effort on the part of many diverse actors to turn 'the idea of the Pacific' into a regional political community. Powerful global actors have sought to 'frame' the thousands of islands scattered across this vast ocean in at least three senses: first, in the sense of framing a picture, they have drawn geographical boundaries around them for purposes of making generalisations about Pacific island peoples and societies that fall within these boundaries; second, in the sense of framing a house, they have promoted normative policy frames intended to shape the lives of Pacific islanders in particular ways; and finally, in the colloquial sense of 'framing', they have often sought to set up Pacific islanders for outcomes not of their making. This study has shown that Pacific islanders have a long history of successfully entering this contest of ideas in regional diplomacy with their own powerful normative framings of Oceania. We can expect this regional arena to continue to be a key political site, alongside that of the nation-state, for the negotiation of globalisation into the future. This study has shown that we should not discount the political agency of Pacific island state leaders and regional civil society in shaping this diplomatic contest. Regional self-determination will remain a key theme in this indigenous effort to build a legitimate regional political community in the Pacific in the face of global pressures.

Bibliography

ABC News, 'Fiji Prime Minister Frank Bainimarama Looks Forward to Visits from China and India's Leaders', *ABC News Online*, 17 November 2014.

ABC News, 'Papua New Guinea PM Peter O'Neill Dismisses Fiji's Push to Remove Australia from Pacific Islands Forum', *ABC News*, 28 November 2014, available from: www.abc.net.au/news/2014-11-28/png-pm-wants-australia-to-remain-in-pacific-regional-body/5926014.

ABC News, 'Marshall Islands Foreign Minister Slams Australia's "Weak" Carbon Target', *Pacific Beat*, ABC News, 11 August 2015, available from: www.abc.net.au/news/programs/pacific-beat/2015-08-11/marshall-islands-foreign-minister-slams-australias/6690570.

ABC News, 'Chinese Military Base in Pacific Would be of "Great Concern", Turnbull Tells Vanuatu', *Pacific Beat*, ABC News, 10 April 2018.

Acharya, Amitav, *The Quest for Identity: International Relations of Southeast Asia*, Singapore: Oxford University Press, 2000.

Acharya, Amitav, *Whose Ideas Matter? Agency and Power in Asian Regionalism*, Ithaca, NY: Cornell University Press, 2009. doi.org/10.7591/9780801459757.

African, Caribbean, and Pacific Group of States (ACP) Secretariat, 'Pacific–EU Talks on Hold', Press release, Brussels, 16 May 2015, available from: www.acp.int/content/pacific-eu-trade-talks-hold.

The Age, 'Pacific Native Chiefs Gather at Suva', *The Age*, [Melbourne], 24 April 1950.

The Age, 'Historic Gathering: First "Parliament of the South Pacific"', *The Age*, [Melbourne], 26 April 1950.

The Age, 'Indian Problem Worries Fiji's Administrators', *The Age*, [Melbourne], 3 May 1950.

The Age, 'Talks End on S. Pacific: Results Pleasing to Delegates', *The Age*, [Melbourne], 6 May 1950.

The Age, 'Pacific Leaders Back Australian Role', *The Age*, [Melbourne], 9 August 2004.

Agreement Amending the Agreement Establishing the South Pacific Commission of 6 February 1947, London, 6 October 1964.

Agreement Establishing the South Pacific Bureau for Economic Cooperation, Suva, 1973.

Agreement Establishing the South Pacific Commission, Canberra, 6 February 1947.

Agreement Extending the Territorial Scope of the South Pacific Commission, Nouméa, 7 November 1951.

Agreement on Trade and Commercial Relations between the Government of Australia and the Government of Papua New Guinea, entered into force on 1 February 1977.

Aikman, Colin M., 'Establishment: 1968–74', in Ron Crocombe and Malama Meleisea, eds, *Pacific Universities: Achievements, Problems, Prospects*, Suva: Institute of Pacific Studies, University of the South Pacific, 1988, pp. 35–52.

Alagappa, Muthiah, 'Regionalism and Conflict Management: A Framework for Analysis', *Review of International Studies*, 21(4), 1995: 359–87. doi.org/10.1017/S0260210500117966.

Albinski, Henry S., 'American Perspectives and Policy Options on ANZUS', in John Ravenhill, ed., *No Longer an American Lake?*, Sydney: Allen & Unwin, 1989, pp. 187–210.

Albinski, Henry S., Robert C. Kiste, Richard Herr, Ross Babbage, and Denis McLean, *The South Pacific: Political, Economic and Military Trends*, Washington, DC: Brassey's, 1990.

Alexander, Ronni, *Putting the Earth First: Alternatives to Nuclear Security in Pacific Island States*, Honolulu: Matsunaga Institute for Peace, University of Hawai`i, 1994.

Alley, Roderic, 'The 1987 Military Coups in Fiji: The Regional Implications', *The Contemporary Pacific*, 2(1), 1990: 37–58.

Anderson, Benedict, *Imagined Communities: Reflections on the Origin and Spread of Nationalism*, London: Verso, 1983.

Aqorau, Transform, 'How Tuna is Shaping Regional Diplomacy', in Greg Fry and Sandra Tarte, eds, *The New Pacific Diplomacy*, Canberra: ANU Press, 2015, pp. 223–35. doi.org/10.22459/NPD.12.2015.18.

The Argus, 'New Deal Talks in Pacific', *The Argus*, [Melbourne], 21 April 1950.

The Argus, 'Here's to the Governor', *The Argus*, [Melbourne], 2 May 1950.

Ashton, C., 'Australia Takes a Beating', *The Bulletin*, [Australia], 24 October 1978: 21–2.

Atatagi, Shirley, 'Forget Watergate, We Now Have Cairns'gate', Blog, Sydney: Greenpeace, 7 August 2009, available from: www.greenpeace.org.au/blog/forget-watergate-we-now-have-cairnsgate/.

Auckland Star, 'Editorial', *Auckland Star*, 26 April 1950.

AusAID, *Tracking Development and Governance in the Pacific*, Canberra: AusAID, August 2009.

Australia, 'South Pacific Commission', *The Round Table: The Commonwealth Journal of International Affairs*, 48(189), 1957: 87–93. doi.org/10.1080/00358535708452108.

Australian Department of External Affairs, 'Australian–New Zealand Agreement', *Current Notes on International Affairs*, [Canberra], 15(1)(January), 1944: 2–9.

Australian Department of External Affairs, 'South Pacific Conference, Brief to the Minister for External Affairs from South West Pacific Section, 27 January 1950', Department of External Affairs, Series A1838/1, item 347/2/1, folio 89, National Archives of Australia, Canberra.

Australian Department of Foreign Affairs, *Twenty-Fifth ANZUS Council Meeting Communiqué*, News Release No. D16, Canberra: Australian Government, 4 August 1976.

Australian Department of Foreign Affairs, 'The South Pacific', Submission to the Senate Standing Committee on Foreign Affairs and Defence Inquiry into the Need for an Increased Australian Commitment to the South Pacific, Canberra: AGPS, March 1977.

Australian Department of Foreign Affairs and Trade (DFAT), 'Agreement between Solomon Islands, Australia, New Zealand, Fiji, Papua New Guinea, Samoa and Tonga Concerning the Operations and Status of the Police and Armed Forces and Other Personnel Deployed to Solomon Islands to Assist in the Restoration of Law and Order and Security (Townsville, 24 July 2003)', [Townsville Peace Agreement], *Australian Treaty Series*, 17, Canberra: AGPS, 2003.

Australian Department of Foreign Affairs and Trade (DFAT), *Port Moresby Declaration*, 6 March 2008, available from: dfat.gov.au/geo/pacific/development-assistance/partnerships/Pages/port-moresby-declaration.aspx.

Australian Department of Foreign Affairs and Trade (DFAT), *Pacific Agreement on Closer Economic Relations (PACER): About PACER Plus*, Canberra: DFAT, 2017, available from: dfat.gov.au/trade/agreements/not-yet-in-force/pacer/Pages/pacific-agreement-on-closer-economic-relations-pacer-plus.aspx.

Australian Department of Foreign Affairs and Trade (DFAT), *Design Summary for the Australia Pacific Security College*, Canberra: DFAT, 1 August 2018, available from: dfat.gov.au/about-us/business-opportunities/Pages/design-summary-for-the-australia-pacific-security-college.aspx.

Australian Foreign Affairs Record, 'South Pacific Forum', *Australian Foreign Affairs Record*, October 1976: 556.

Australian Foreign Affairs Record, 'Speech by the Australian Minister for Foreign Affairs on the Australian South Pacific Aid Program to the Meeting of the South Pacific Forum in Suva on 12 October, 1976', *Australian Foreign Affairs Record*, October 1976: 556-7.

Australian Foreign Affairs Record, 'South Pacific Commission: Sixteenth South Pacific Conference', *Australian Foreign Affairs Record*, November 1976.

Australian Foreign Affairs Record, 'ANZUS Council Communiqué', *Australian Foreign Affairs Record*, August 1977: 412.

Australian Foreign Affairs Record, 'French Nuclear Test at Mururoa Atoll', *Australian Foreign Affairs Record*, May 1983: 186-7.

Australian Government, *Possible Changes in the Functioning of the South Pacific Commission*, Working Paper No. 4, Presented to Thirteenth South Pacific Conference, Guam, 1–20 September 1973.

Axline, W. Andrew, ed., *The Political Economy of Regional Cooperation: Comparative Case Studies*, London: Pinter Press, 1994.

Ayoob, Mohammed, 'From Regional System to Regional Society: Exploring Key Variables in the Construction of Regional Order', *Australian Journal of International Affairs*, 53(3), 1999: 247-60. doi.org/10.1080/00049919993845.

Baker, Nicola, 'New Zealand and Australia in Pacific Regionalism', in Greg Fry and Sandra Tarte, eds, *The New Pacific Diplomacy*, Canberra: ANU Press, 2015, pp. 137–48. doi.org/10.22459/NPD.12.2015.12.

Ball, M. Margaret, 'Regionalism and the Pacific Commonwealth', *Pacific Affairs*, 46(2), 1973: 232–53. doi.org/10.2307/2756171.

Bark, Dennis L., and Owen Harries, eds, *The Red Orchestra: Instruments of Soviet Policy in the Southwest Pacific*, Stanford, CA: Hoover Institution Press, 1989.

Bates, Stephen, *The South Pacific Island Countries and France: A Study in Inter-State Relations*, Canberra Studies in World Affairs No. 26, Canberra: Department of International Relations, The Australian National University, 1990.

Batley, James, *Review: Safeguarding Australia's Security Interests through Closer Pacific Ties*, Sydney: Lowy Institute, 27 April 2018.

Beard, P., 'Paris Snub Prompts Hayden to Seek Pacific Nuclear-Free Zone', *The Australian*, 13 May 1983: 4.

Benedict, Burton, 'Introduction', in Burton Benedict, ed., *Problems of Smaller Territories*, London: Athlone Press for the Institute of Commonwealth Studies, 1967, pp. 1–10.

Bhagwati, Jagdish, 'Regionalism and Multilateralism: An Overview', in Jaime de Melo and Arvind Panagariya, eds, *New Dimensions in Regional Integration*, Cambridge: Cambridge University Press, 1993, pp. 22–51. doi.org/10.1017/CBO9780511628511.004.

Bilney, Gordon, 'Australia's Relations with the South Pacific: Challenge and Change', Address to the Foreign Correspondents' Association, Sydney, 15 June 1994 [published as Briefing Paper No. 34, Canberra: Australian Development Studies Network, The Australian National University, July 1994], available from: openresearch-repository.anu.edu.au/bitstream/1885/9989/1/Bilney_AustraliasRelations1994.pdf.

Borofsky, Robert, ed., *Remembrance of Pacific Pasts: An Invitation to Remake History*, Honolulu: University of Hawai`i Press, 2000.

Bourke, Latika, 'UK to Open Diplomatic Posts in the Pacific, Citing Security Concerns', *Sydney Morning Herald*, 20 April 2018.

Boyd, Mary, 'Introduction', in Mary Boyd, ed., *Pacific Horizons: A Regional Role for New Zealand*, Wellington: Price Milburn for the New Zealand Institute of International Affairs, 1972, pp. 7–17.

Brosnahan, Frank, 'Outreach: 1975–83', in Ron Crocombe and Malama Meleisea, eds, *Pacific Universities: Achievements, Problems, Prospects*, Suva: Institute of Pacific Studies, University of the South Pacific, 1988, pp. 55–72.

Bryar, Tim, and Anna Naupa, 'The Shifting Tides of Pacific Regionalism', *The Round Table*, 106(2), 2017: 155–64. doi.org/10.1080/00358533.2017.1296712.

Bugotu, Francis, 'Decolonising and Recolonising: The Case of the Solomons', in Sione Tupouniua, Ron Crocombe, and Claire Slatter, eds, *The Pacific Way: Social Issues in National Development*, Suva: South Pacific Social Sciences Association, 1975, pp. 77–80.

Burton, J.W., *The Call of the Pacific*, London: Charles H. Kelly, Every Age Library, 1912.

Burton, J.W., *Brown and White in the South Pacific: A Study in Culture Conflict*, Sydney: Australian Institute of International Affairs, 1944.

Burton, J.W., 'The South Pacific Conference, Held at Nasinu, Fiji, May 1950: Report by the Australian Observer, Rev. J. W. Burton (for the Minister of State for External Affairs and External Territories)', Sydney, June 1950, Department of External Affairs, Series A1838/1, file 347/2/6, 1950, folio 79, National Archives of Australia, Canberra.

Bush, George H.W., 'Remarks at the Conclusion of the Pacific Island Nations–United States Summit in Honolulu, Hawaii', 27 October 1990.

Buzan, Barry, *People, States and Fear: The National Security Problem in International Relations*, Brighton, UK: Wheatsheaf, 1983.

Buzan, Barry, *People, States and Fear: An Agenda for International Security Studies in the Post–Cold War Era*, 2nd edn, London: Harvester Wheatsheaf, 1991.

Callick, Rowan, 'Pacific 2010: A Doomsday Scenario?', in Rodney Cole, ed., *Pacific 2010: Challenging the Future*, Canberra: National Centre for Development Studies, The Australian National University, 1993, pp. 1–11.

Callick, Rowan, 'Time to Shift Pacific Goalposts', *Australian Financial Review*, 16 April 1994: 15.

Callick, Rowan, 'Tough Talking in the Pacific', *Australian Financial Review*, 27 June 1994.

Campbell, Ian C., *Worlds Apart: A History of the Pacific Islands*, Christchurch, NZ: Canterbury University Press, 2003.

The Canberra Times, 'US Urged to "Watch Pacific"', *The Canberra Times*, 4 August 1976: 9.

The Canberra Times, '"New Colonialism" Over Fishing: Fiji Accuses the US', *The Canberra Times*, 11 October 1978.

The Canberra Times, 'Hayden Warns of Soviet Infiltration through Fishing Deals', *The Canberra Times*, 14 December 1986: 1.

Carew-Reid, Jeremy, *Environment, Aid and Regionalism in the South Pacific*, Pacific Research Monograph No. 22, Canberra: National Centre for Development Studies, The Australian National University, 1989.

Carter, George, and Stewart Firth, 'The Mood in Melanesia after the Regional Assistance Mission to Solomon Islands', *Asia and the Pacific Policy Studies*, 3(1), 2016: 16–25. doi.org/10.1002/app5.112.

Carter, J., 'Horrid Niggling, or Happy Nuptials, for Commission and Forum?', *Pacific Islands Monthly*, November 1977: 10.

Chand, Satish, ed., *Pacific Islands Regional Integration and Governance*, Canberra: ANU E Press and Asia Pacific Press, 2005. doi.org/10.26530/OAPEN_459431.

Claxton, Karl, 'The Nature and Extent of Crime in the South Pacific and the Region's Attempts to Respond to this Challenge', MA (Strategic Studies) Research Essay, The Australian National University, Canberra, 25 February 1994.

Cockburn, Milton, 'Nearly Ready for a Nuclear-Free Pacific', *Sydney Morning Herald*, 7 August 1985: 1.

Cockburn, Milton, and Amanda Buckley, 'Pacific Treaty Has US Worried', *Sydney Morning Herald*, 3 August 1985: 9.

Cole, Rodney, and Somsak Tambunlertchai, eds, *The Future of Asia-Pacific Economies: Pacific Islands at the Crossroads?*, Canberra: National Centre for Development Studies, The Australian National University, 1993.

Cole, Rodney, and Somsak Tambunlertchai, 'Signposts at the Crossroads of Development in the Pacific', in Rodney Cole and Somsak Tambunlertchai, eds, *The Future of Asia-Pacific Economies: Pacific Islands at the Crossroads?*, Canberra: National Centre for Development Studies, The Australian National University, 1993.

Cole, Rodney V., ed., *Pacific 2010: Challenging the Future*, Canberra: National Centre for Development Studies, The Australian National University, 1993.

Commonwealth Consultative Group on the Special Needs of Small States, *Vulnerability: Small States in the Global Society*, Report of a Commonwealth Consultative Group, London: Commonwealth Secretariat, 1985.

'Concluding Statement', Unpublished summary of the South Pacific Colloquium on the Special Needs of Small States, Victoria University of Wellington, 13–14 August 1984.

Crocombe, Ron, 'Seeking a Pacific Way', in Sione Tupouniua, Ron Crocombe, and Claire Slatter, eds, *The Pacific Way: Social Issues in National Development*, Suva: South Pacific Social Sciences Association, 1975, pp. 1–6.

Crocombe, Ron, *The Pacific Way: An Emerging Identity*, Suva: Lout Pasifika Productions, 1976.

Crocombe, Ron, and Malama Meleisea, 'Achievements, Problems and Prospects: The Future of University Education in the South Pacific', in Ron Crocombe and Malama Meleisea, eds, *Pacific Universities: Achievements, Problems, Prospects*, Suva: Institute of Pacific Studies, University of the South Pacific, 1988, pp. 341–87.

Crocombe, Ron, and Uentabo Neemia, 'Options in University Education for the Pacific Islands', *Pacific Perspective*, 12(1), 1983: 5–17.

Crocombe, Ron G., *The New South Pacific*, Wellington: Reed Education, 1973.

Current Notes on International Affairs, 'South Pacific Forum', *Current Notes on International Affairs*, [Canberra], August 1971: 431.

Curtain, Richard, Matthew Dornan, Jesse Doyle, and Stephen Howes, *Labour Mobility: The 10 Billion Dollar Prize*, Pacific Possible Series, Washington, DC: The World Bank, 2016.

Daily Mirror, 'Delegates Gather in Fiji for South Pacific Talks', *Daily Mirror*, [Sydney], 24 April 1950.

The Daily News, 'The Suva Conference', *The Daily News*, [New Zealand], 6 May 1950.

Daily Telegraph, 'Pidgin Editors for Suva Talks', *Daily Telegraph*, [Sydney], 21 April 1950.

Daily Telegraph, 'Sombre Fashion at Talks', *Daily Telegraph*, [Sydney], 26 April 1950.

Danielsson, Bengt, and Marie-Thérèse Danielsson, *Poisoned Reign: French Nuclear Colonialism in the Pacific*, 2nd edn, Melbourne: Penguin, 1986.

D'Arcy, Paul, *The People of the Sea: Environment, Identity, and History in Oceania*, Honolulu: University of Hawai`i Press, 2006.

Davidson, J.W., 'Problems of Pacific History', *Journal of Pacific History*, 1(1), 1966: 5–21. doi.org/10.1080/00223346608572076.

Davidson, J.W., *Samoa Mo Samoa: The Emergence of the Independent State of Western Samoa*, Melbourne: Oxford University Press, 1967.

Deakin, Alfred, *The Federal Story: The Inner History of the Federal Cause, 1880–1900*, Melbourne: Robertson & Mullins, 1944.

de Bougainville, Louis Antoine, *A Voyage Round the World*, trans. J. R. Forster, London: Printed for J. Nourse and T. Davies, 1772.

Denoon, Donald, Malama Meleisea, Stewart Firth, Jocelyn Linnekin, and Karen Nero, *The Cambridge History of the Pacific Islanders*, Cambridge: Cambridge University Press, 1997. doi.org/10.1017/CHOL9780521441957.

Deutsch, K.W., *Political Community and the North Atlantic Area: International Organization in the Light of Historical Experience*, Princeton, NJ: Princeton University Press, 1957.

Diderot, Denis, *Supplement au Voyage de Bougainville*, 1796.

Dommen, Edward, 'Some Distinguishing Characteristics of Island States', *World Development*, 8(12), 1980: 931–43. doi.org/10.1016/0305-750X(80)90085-6.

Dornan, Matthew, 'PACER Plus is Not Much to Celebrate', *East Asia Forum*, 2 June 2017, available from: www.eastasiaforum.org/2017/06/02/pacer-plus-is-not-much-to-celebrate/.

Dornan, Matthew, 'Australia's Pacific Island Myopia', *The Diplomat*, 13 July 2018.

Dornan, Matthew, and Tess Newton Cain, 'Regional Service Delivery among Pacific Island Countries: An Assessment', *Asia and the Pacific Policy Studies*, 1(3), 2014: 541–60. doi.org/10.1002/app5.45.

Dorney, Sean, 'Regional Security and Corruption the Focus of Pacific Forum', *The World Today*, ABC News, 6 April 2004, available from: www.abc.net.au/worldtoday/content/2004/s1082146.htm.

Doulman, David J., 'Fisheries Co-operation: The Case of the Nauru Group', in David J. Doulman, *Tuna Issues and Perspectives in the Pacific Islands Region*, Honolulu: East–West Center, 1987, pp. 257–77.

Doulman, David J., 'Fisheries Management in the South Pacific: The Role of the Forum Fisheries Agency', in Ramesh Thakur, ed., *The South Pacific: Problems, Issues and Prospects*, New York: St Martin's Press, 1991, pp. 81–94. doi.org/10.1007/978-1-349-12519-7_5.

Dziedzic, Stephen, 'Samoan Prime Minister Tuilaepa Sailele Hits Out at Climate Change Sceptics During Fiery Speech', *ABC News Online*, 31 August 2018, available from: www.abc.net.au/news/2018-08-31/samoan-prime-minister-hits-out-at-climate-change-sceptics/10185142.

Eccles, J., 'Not So Much Togetherness Now', *Pacific Islands Monthly*, October 1970: 18.

Efi, Tupuola, 'Statement at the Commonwealth Heads of Government Regional Meeting in Sydney, 14 February 1978', Press release, Sydney, 16 February 1978.

Elek, Andrew, 'The South Pacific Economies in a Changing International Environment', in Rodney Cole and Somsak Tambunlertchai, eds, *The Future of Asia-Pacific Economies: Pacific Islands at the Crossroads?*, Canberra: National Centre for Development Studies, The Australian National University, 1993.

Elkin, A.P., *Wanted: A Charter for the Native Peoples of the South-West Pacific*, Sydney: Australasian Publishing Co., 1943.

Emberson-Bain, Atu, 'Introduction: Sustaining the Unsustainable?', in Atu Emberson-Bain, ed., *Sustainable Development or Malignant Growth? Perspectives of Pacific Island Women*, Suva: Marama Publications, 1994.

Emberson-Bain, Atu, ed., *Sustainable Development or Malignant Growth? Perspectives of Pacific Island Women*, Suva: Marama Publications, 1994.

The Eminent Persons' Group Review of the Pacific Islands Forum, *The Eminent Persons' Report*, April 2004, available from: www.iri.edu.ar/publicaciones_iri/anuario/CD%20Anuario%202005/Asia/47-pacific%20island%20forum-eminent%20persons%20report%2004.pdf.

Emmerson, Donald K., '"Southeast Asia": What's in a Name?', *Journal of Southeast Asian Studies*, 5(1), 1984: 1–21. doi.org/10.1017/S0022463400012182.

Ethier, Wilfred J., 'The New Regionalism', *Economic Journal*, 108(449), 1998: 1149–61. doi.org/10.1111/1468-0297.00335.

Evans, Gareth, 'Australia in the South Pacific', Address to the Foreign Correspondents' Association, Sydney, 23 September 1988.

Evatt, H.V., *Foreign Policy of Australia: Speeches by H.V. Evatt*, Sydney: Angus & Robertson, 1945.

The Evening Post, 'Delegates Meet in Suva to Discuss Broad Programmes for Native Welfare', *The Evening Post*, [Wellington], 21 April 1950.

Falk, Richard, 'Regionalism and World Order after the Cold War', *Australian Journal of International Affairs*, 49(1), 1995: 1–15. doi.org/10.1080/103 57719508445142.

Fawcett, Louise, and Andrew Hurrell, 'Introduction', in Louise Fawcett and Andrew Hurrell, eds, *Regionalism in World Politics: Regional Organization and International Order*, Oxford: Oxford University Press, 1995.

Fawcett, Louise, and Andrew Hurrell, eds, *Regionalism in World Politics: Regional Organization and International Order*, Oxford: Oxford University Press, 1995.

The Fijian Government, *The Lomé Convention: How It Benefits Fiji*, Suva: Government Printer, 1975.

The Fijian Government, 'The Natadola Communiqué', Press release, Suva, 23 July 2010, available from: www.fiji.gov.fj/Media-Center/Press-Releases/The-Natadola-Communiqu%C3%A9.aspx.

The Fijian Government, 'Engaging with the Pacific Leaders Meeting: Nadi Communiqué', Press release, Suva, 27 August 2012, available from: www.foreignaffairs.gov.fj/media-publications/media-release/518-engaging-with-the-pacific-leaders-meeting-nadi-communique.

Fijilive, 'Fiji Drops Out of Forum Working Group', *Fijilive*, 23 June 2008, available from: www.pireport.org/articles/2008/06/23/fiji-drops-out-forum-working-group.

Fiji Ministry of Information, *The Prime Minister's Post-Cabinet Press Conference*, News Release No. 625, Suva: Ministry of Information, 13 November 1975.

Fiji Sun, 'Forum Secretariat Wrong: PM', *Fiji Sun*, 4 December 2012.

Fiji Times and Herald, 'More Delegates to Conference at Nasinu', *Fiji Times and Herald*, 22 April 1950.

Fiji Times and Herald, 'Pacific History Made Today', *Fiji Times and Herald*, 25 April 1950.

Fiji Times and Herald, 'Editorial', *Fiji Times and Herald*, 5 May 1950.

Fiji Times and Herald, 'NZ Observer Reviews Aims and Results of Conference', *Fiji Times and Herald*, 9 May 1950.

Fiji Times and Herald, 'Temporary Issue of Liquor Permits at Suva', *Fiji Times and Herald*, 11 May 1950.

Fiji Times and Herald, 'Propaganda: South Pacific May be Deluged by North-West', *Fiji Times and Herald*, 22 June 1950.

Firth, Stewart, *Nuclear Playground*, Sydney: Allen & Unwin, 1987.

Firth, Stewart, 'A Reflection on South Pacific Regional Security, Mid-2000 to Mid-2001', *Journal of Pacific History*, 36(3), 2001: 277–83.

Foliaki, John, 'Pacific Regional Seminary', in Emiliana Afeaki, Ron Crocombe, and John McClaren, eds, *Religious Cooperation in the Pacific Islands*, Suva: Institute of Pacific Studies, University of the South Pacific, 1983, pp. 84–8.

Forsyth, W.D., 'Wellington Conference Means New Era of Pacific Alliances', *Pacific Islands Monthly*, August 1971: 12.

Forsyth, W.D., 'South Pacific: Regional Organisation', *New Guinea and Australia, the Pacific and South-East Asia*, 6(September–October), 1971: 6–23.

Forum Economic Ministers Meeting (FEMM), *1997 Forum Economic Ministers Action Plan*, Suva: South Pacific Forum Secretariat, 1997.

Forum Economic Ministers Meeting (FEMM), *2017 Forum Economic Ministers Action Plan*, Suva: Pacific Islands Forum Secretariat, 2017.

Fox, Liam, 'Frank Bainimarama to Shun Pacific Island Forum over "Undue Influence" of Australia, NZ', *ABC News*, 6 May 2015.

Fraenkel, Jon, Joni Madraiwiwi, and Henry Okole, *The RAMSI Decade: A Review of the Regional Assistance Mission to Solomon Islands, 2003–2013*, Honiara: Solomon Islands Government, 14 July 2014.

Fraser, Helen, *New Caledonia: Anti-Colonialism in a Pacific Territory*, Canberra: Peace Research Centre, The Australian National University, 1988.

Fraser, Malcolm, 'Afghanistan: Australia's Assessment and Response', Department of the Prime Minister and Cabinet news release, Canberra, 19 February 1980.

Frater, M., 'Why Not a South Pacific Confederation?', *Pacific Islands Monthly*, 15 May 1940.

Fry, Greg, *A Nuclear-Free Zone for the Southwest Pacific: Prospects and Significance*, Working Paper No. 75, Canberra: Strategic and Defence Studies Centre, The Australian National University, 1983.

Fry, Greg, 'Australia, New Zealand and Arms Control in the Pacific Region', in Desmond Ball, ed., *The ANZAC Connection*, Sydney: George Allen & Unwin, 1985, pp. 91–118.

Fry, Greg, '"Constructive Commitment" with the South Pacific: Monroe Doctrine or New "Partnership"?', in Greg Fry, ed., *Australia's Regional Security*, Sydney: Allen & Unwin, 1991, pp. 120–37.

Fry, Greg, 'At the Margin: The South Pacific and changing world order', in R. Leaver and J.L. Richardson, eds, *Charting the Post–Cold War Order*, Boulder, CO: Westview Press, 1993, pp. 224–42.

Fry, Greg, 'Climbing Back onto the Map? The South Pacific Forum and the New Development Orthodoxy', in the *Journal of Pacific History*, 29(3), 1994: 64–72.

Fry, Greg, 'International Co-operation in the South Pacific: From regional integration to collective diplomacy', in W. Andrew Axline, *The Political Economy of Regional Cooperation* (London: Pinter, 1994), pp. 136–77.

Fry, Greg, 'The South Pacific Experiment: Reflections on the Origins of Regional Identity', in the *Journal of Pacific History*, 32(2), 1997: 180–202.

Fry, Greg, 'Political Legitimacy and the Post-Colonial State in the Pacific: Reflections on Some Common Threads in the Fiji and Solomon Islands Coups', *Pacifica Review*, 12(3), 2000: 295–304. doi.org/10.1080/713604485.

Fry, Greg, 'Pacific Climate Diplomacy and the Future Relevance of the Pacific Islands Forum', *Devpolicy Blog*, 4 September 2015, available from: devpolicy.org/pacific-climate-diplomacy-and-the-future-relevance-of-the-pacific-islands-forum-20150904/.

Fry, Greg, and Tarcisius Kabutaulaka, 'Political Legitimacy and State-building Intervention in the Pacific', in Greg Fry and Tarcisius Kabutaulaka, eds, *Intervention and State-Building in the Pacific: The Legitimacy of 'Co-operative Intervention'*, Manchester: Manchester University Press, 2008.

Fry, Greg, and Sandra Tarte, eds, *The New Pacific Diplomacy*, Canberra: ANU Press, 2015. doi.org/10.22459/NPD.12.2015.

Fry, Gregory E., 'Report on the Fifteenth South Pacific Conference Held in Nauru, 29 September to 10 October 1975', Unpublished report, Canberra, February 1976.

Fry, Gregory E., 'Report on the Eighteenth South Pacific Conference', Unpublished report, Canberra, 1978.

Fry, Gregory E., 'South Pacific Regionalism: The Development of an Indigenous Commitment', MA thesis, Department of Political Science, The Australian National University, Canberra, 1979.

Fry, Gregory E., 'Regionalism and International Politics of the South Pacific', *Pacific Affairs*, 54(3), 1981: 455–84. doi.org/10.2307/2756789.

Fry, Gregory E., 'Whose Oceania? Contending Visions of Community in Pacific Region-Building', in Michael Powles, ed., *Pacific Futures*, Canberra: Pandanus Books, 2006, pp. 204–15.

Furnas, J.C., *Anatomy of Paradise: Hawaii and the Islands of the South Seas*, London: Victor Gollancz, 1950.

Gamble, Andrew, and Anthony Payne, 'Conclusion: The New Regionalism', in Andrew Gamble and Anthony Payne, eds, *Regionalism and World Order*, Basingstoke, UK: Macmillan, 1996, pp. 247–64.

Gamble, Andrew, and Anthony Payne, eds, *Regionalism and World Order*, Basingstoke, UK: Macmillan, 1996.

Garrett, Jemima, *Island Exiles*, Sydney: Australian Broadcasting Corporation, 1996.

George, Nicole, 'Pacific Women Building Peace: A Regional Perspective', *The Contemporary Pacific*, 23(1), 2011: 37–71. doi.org/10.1353/cp.2011.0001.

Gonschor, Lorenz, *A Power in the World: The Hawaiian Kingdom in Oceania*, Honolulu: University of Hawai'i Press, 2019.

Gordon, Michael, '"We Cannot be Bought on Climate Change": Pacific Island Leader Warns Tony Abbott', *Sydney Morning Herald*, 8 September 2015.

Graham, Kennedy, ed., *Models of Regional Governance for the Pacific: Sovereignty and the Future Architecture of Regionalism*, Christchurch, NZ: Canterbury University Press, 2008.

Grattan, C. Hartley, *The Southwest Pacific to 1900: A Modern History*, Ann Arbor: University of Michigan Press, 1963.

Grattan, C. Hartley, 'Australia and New Zealand and Pacific-Asia', in F.P. King, ed., *Oceania and Beyond: Essays on the Pacific Since 1945*, Westport, CT: Greenwood Press, 1976, pp. 79–116.

Grattan, Michelle, 'Hawke Courts Kudos for N-Free Treaty', *The Age*, [Melbourne], 7 August 1985: 1.

Graue, Catherine, 'Federal Government Flags Willingness to Help Vanuatu with High-Speed Undersea Internet Cable', *Pacific Beat*, ABC News, 27 June 2018.

Grugel, Jean, and Wil Hout, eds, *Regionalism Across the North–South Divide: State Strategies and Globalization*, Abingdon, UK: Routledge, 1999.

Grynberg, Roman, 'Who Owns the Forum?', *Fiji Times Online*, 9 March 2009.

Grynberg, Roman, 'The Pacific Plan and Other Failures: What Can Be Learned?', *Pacific Media Centre*, 16 January 2013, available from: pmc.littleisland.co.nz/articles/pacific-plan-and-other-failures-what-can-be-learned.

The Guardian, 'Papua New Guinea in Crisis as Two Claim to be Prime Minister', *The Guardian*, 14 December 2011.

Gubon, Florian, 'History and Role of the Forum Fisheries Agency', in David J. Doulman, ed., *Tuna Issues and Perspectives in the Pacific Islands Region*, Honolulu: East–West Center, 1987, pp. 245–56.

Gunson, Niel, 'Early Society and Authority Systems', in Brij V. Lal and Kate Fortune, eds, *The Pacific Islands: An Encyclopedia*, Honolulu: University of Hawai`i Press, 2000, pp. 132–9.

Gunther, J.T., 'South Pacific Conference: Preliminary Report by Dr J.T. Gunther, Advisor to Papua-New Guinea Delegation and Acting Chairman for Australia', Department of External Affairs, Series A1838/1, item 347/2/6, folio 68, undated (attached to memo to Secretary, Department of External Affairs, dated 17 July 1950, from Secretary, Department of External Territories), National Archives of Australia, Canberra.

Haas, E.B., *The Uniting of Europe: Political, Social and Economic Forces, 1950–57*, Stanford, CA: Stanford University Press, 1958.

Hagler, Michael, 'Driftnet Fishing in the South Pacific', in Ramesh Thakur, ed., *The South Pacific: Problems, Issues and Prospects*, New York: St Martin's Press, 1991, pp. 95–104. doi.org/10.1007/978-1-349-12519-7_6.

Hancock, Kathleen, 'There was Blood and Thunder about More Power for the Islanders', *Pacific Islands Monthly*, November 1968: 30.

Hanlon, David, 'Patterns of Colonial Rule in Micronesia', in Kerry R. Howe, Robert C. Kiste, and Brij V. Lal, eds, *Tides of History: The Pacific Islands in the Twentieth Century*, Sydney: Allen & Unwin, 1994.

Harden, Sheila, ed., *Small is Dangerous: Micro States in a Macro World*, Report from the David Davies Memorial Institute of International Studies, London: Frances Pinter, 1985.

Hasluck, Paul, *The Government and the People*, Canberra: Australian War Memorial, 1970.

Hastings, Peter, 'Aust. Concern as Soviets Offer Vanuatu $2m Deal', *Sydney Morning Herald*, 15 December 1986: 1.

Hau`ofa, Epeli, 'Our Sea of Islands', in Eric Waddell, Vijay Naidu, and Epeli Hau`ofa, eds, *A New Oceania: Rediscovering Our Sea of Islands*, Suva: University of the South Pacific, 1993, pp. 2–16.

Hau`ofa, Epeli, 'A Beginning', in Eric Waddell, Vijay Naidu, and Epeli Hau`ofa, eds, *A New Oceania: Rediscovering Our Sea of Islands*, Suva: University of the South Pacific, 1993, pp. 126–39.

Hau`ofa, Epeli, 'Our Sea of Islands', *The Contemporary Pacific*, 6(1), 1994: 148–61.

Hau`ofa, Epeli, 'The Ocean in Us', *The Contemporary Pacific*, 10(2), 1998: 392–410.

Hau`ofa, Epeli, 'Epilogue: Pasts to Remember', in Robert Borofsky, ed., *Remembrance of Pacific Pasts: An Invitation to Remake History*, Honolulu: University of Hawai`i Press, 2000, pp. 453–71.

Hau`ofa, Epeli, *We Are the Ocean: Selected Works*, Honolulu: University of Hawai`i Press, 2008.

Havea, Sione `A., and Bruce J. Deverell, 'The Pacific Theological College', in Emiliana Afeaki, Ron G. Crocombe, and John McClaren, eds, *Religious Cooperation in the Pacific Islands*, Suva: Institute of Pacific Studies, University of the South Pacific, 1983, pp. 75–83.

Hawkesworth, John, *An Account of the Voyages Undertaken by the Order of His Present Majesty for Making Discoveries in the Southern Hemisphere*, London, 1773.

Hawkins, R., 'The Hot Politics of a "Routine" Conference', *Pacific Islands Monthly*, December 1978: 26–9.

Hayward-Jones, Jennifer, 'Diverging Regional Priorities at the Pacific Islands Forum', *Australian Outlook*, 3 September, Canberra: Australian Institute of International Affairs, 2018, available from: www.internationalaffairs.org.au/australianoutlook/diverging-regional-priorities-at-pacific-islands-forum/.

Head, Perry, *Regional Law Enforcement Needs Assessment: Prospects for Enhancing Regional Cooperation*, Discussion Paper prepared for the Forum Secretariat, Suva: South Pacific Forum Secretariat, June 1991.

Heath, Michael, 'Australia's Economy Has a Lot to Lose from US–China Trade War', *Bloomberg*, 23 March 2018, available from: www.bloomberg.com/news/articles/2018-03-23/-very-awkward-spot-in-u-s-china-firing-line-for-aussie-economy.

Hegarty, David, *Libya and the South Pacific*, Working Paper No. 127, Canberra: Strategic and Defence Studies Centre, The Australian National University, 1987.

Hegarty, David, *South Pacific Security Issues: An Australian Perspective*, Working Paper No. 147, Canberra: Strategic and Defence Studies Centre, The Australian National University, December 1987.

Henningham, Stephen, 'Keeping the Tricolor Flying: The French Pacific into the 1990s', *The Contemporary Pacific*, 1(1–2), 1989: 97–132.

Henningham, Stephen, *France and the South Pacific: A Contemporary History*, Sydney: Allen & Unwin, 1992.

Henningham, Stephen, 'France in Melanesia and Polynesia', in Kerry R. Howe, Robert C. Kiste, and Brij V. Lal, eds, *Tides of History: The Pacific Islands in the Twentieth Century*, Sydney: Allen & Unwin, 1994, pp. 119–46.

Hereniko, Vilsoni, 'Indigenous Knowledge and Academic Imperialism', in Robert Borofsky, ed., *Remembrance of Pacific Pasts: An Invitation to Remake History*, Honolulu: University of Hawai`i Press, 2000, pp. 78–91.

Herr, Richard A., 'Regionalism in the South Seas: The Impact of the South Pacific Commission 1947–1974', PhD dissertation, Duke University, Durham, NC, 1976.

Herr, Richard A., 'Regionalism, Strategic Denial and South Pacific Security', *Journal of Pacific History*, 21(4), 1986: 170–82. doi.org/10.1080/002233 48608572541.

Herr, Richard A., 'The Region in Review: International Issues and Events, 1989', *The Contemporary Pacific*, 2(2), 1990: 350–7.

Herr, Richard A., 'Regionalism and Nationalism', in Kerry R. Howe, Robert C. Kiste, and Brij V. Lal, eds, *Tides of History: The Pacific Islands in the Twentieth Century*, Sydney: Allen & Unwin, 1994, pp. 283–99.

Hettne, Björn, and András Inotai, *The New Regionalism: Implications for Global Development and International Security*, Helsinki: United Nations University World Institute for Development Economics Research, 1994.

Higgins, Ean, 'Pacific Islands Warned about Soviet Threat', *Australian Financial Review*, 4 April 1985: 14.

Hill, Bruce, 'Samoan PM Hits Back at Australia's "Insulting" Criticism of China's Aid Program in Pacific', *Pacific Beat*, ABC News, 12 January 2018.

Howard, John, 'Transcript of the Prime Minister the Hon. John Howard MP Interview with Kerry O'Brien, The 7:30 Report, ABC', 25 June 2003.

Howard, John, 'Transcript of the Prime Minister, the Hon. John Howard MP, Press Conference', Canberra, 22 July 2003.

Howe, Kerry R., 'The Fate of the "Savage" in Pacific Historiography', *New Zealand Journal of History*, 11(2), 1977: 137–54.

Howe, Kerry R., *Where the Waves Fall: A New South Sea Islands History from First Settlement to Colonial Rule*, Sydney: Allen & Unwin, 1984.

Howe, Kerry R., 'Preface', in Kerry R. Howe, Robert C. Kiste, and Brij V. Lal, eds, *Tides of History: The Pacific Islands in the Twentieth Century*, Sydney: Allen & Unwin, 1994, pp. xi–xiv.

Howe, Kerry R., *Nature, Culture and History: The 'Knowing' of Oceania*, Honolulu: University of Hawai`i Press, 2000.

Howe, Kerry R., Robert C. Kiste, and Brij V. Lal, eds, *Tides of History: The Pacific Islands in the Twentieth Century*, Sydney: Allen & Unwin, 1994.

Huffer, Elise, 'The Pacific Plan: A Political and Cultural Critique', in Jenny Bryant-Tokalau and Ian Frazer, eds, *Redefining the Pacific? Regionalism, Past, Present and Future*, London: Routledge, 2006.

Hughes, A.V., *Strengthening Regional Management: A Review of the Architecture for Regional Co-operation in the Pacific*, Report to the Pacific Islands Forum, Consultative Draft, 2005, available from: gsd.spc.int/sopac/docs/RIF/06_AV%20Hughes%20Report_CONSULTATIVE_DRAFT(1).pdf.

Hunter, Fergus, 'Pacific Nations Push Morrison Government to Pledge Support for Paris Climate Accord', *Sydney Morning Herald*, 29 August 2018.

Hunter, Fergus, and David Wroe, 'New Zealand Opposed to Militarization in the Pacific: Jacinda Ardern', *Sydney Morning Herald*, 10 April 2018.

Hussein, Bernadette, 'The Big Retreat', *Pacific Islands Monthly*, November 1997: 11.

Inder, Stuart, 'And Now the SPC's Crisis is Over', *Pacific Islands Monthly*, November 1968: 31.

Inder, Stuart, 'Togetherness Comes to the SPC', *Pacific Islands Monthly*, November 1969: 26–7.

Inder, Stuart, 'Leading from the Rear is Still Leadership', *Pacific Islands Monthly*, September 1971: 27.

Inder, Stuart, 'Up Front with the Editor', *Pacific Islands Monthly*, June 1974: 3.

Jayasuriya, Kanishka, ed., *Governing the Asia Pacific: Beyond the 'New Regionalism'*, New York: Palgrave Macmillan, 2004.

Jones, Bronwen, 'Japan Seeks Understanding on N-Waste Dumping Plans', *The Canberra Times*, 12 January 1985: 1.

Jones, Bruce, 'US Tuna Fishing a Divisive Issue for Forum Members', *The Canberra Times*, 11 October 1978.

Kama, Bal, 'Nauru Rule of Law Case and the Implication for the Pacific', *Outrigger: Blog of the Pacific Institute*, Canberra: The Australian National University, 21 March 2014, available from: pacificinstitute.anu.edu.au/outrigger/2014/03/21/australias-blind-eye-while-rule-of-law-under-siege-in-the-pacific/.

Kaplan, Robert, 'The Coming Anarchy', *The Atlantic*, February 1994, available from: www.theatlantic.com/magazine/archive/1994/02/the-coming-anarchy/304670/.

Katzenstein, Peter J., *A World of Regions: Asia and Europe in the American Imperium*, Ithaca, NY: Cornell University Press, 2005.

Keane, Bernard, 'How We Discouraged Pacific Islands from Tough Emissions Stance', *Crikey*, 21 September 2009, available from: www.crikey.com.au/2009/09/21/leaked-document-oz-discouraged-pacific-islands-from-tough-emissions-stance/. doi.org/10.1353/cp.0.0029.

Keesing, Felix M., *The South Seas in the Modern World*, New York: John Day Company, 1946.

Keith-Reid, Robert, 'Getting Tough in Tonga', *The Bulletin*, [Australia], 24 April 1971: 37.

Kelsey, Jane, *Big Brothers Behaving Badly: The Implications for the Pacific Islands of the Pacific Agreement on Closer Economic Relations (PACER)*, Suva: Pacific Network on Globalisation, 2004.

Keohane, Robert, and Joe Nye, 'International Interdependence and Integration', in F.I. Greenstein and N.W. Polsby, eds, *International Politics*, Reading, UK: Addison-Wesley Publishing, 1975, pp. 363–414.

Kiki, Albert Maori, *Papua New Guinea: An Assessment Report on Foreign Policy by the Minister for Defence, Foreign Relations, and Trade to the House of Assembly, 6 December 1974*, [Reprinted as 'Papua New Guinea: An Assessment Report on Foreign Policy', *Australian Foreign Affairs Record*, June 1975: 320–5].

Kirch, Patrick, *On the Road of the Winds: An Archaeological History of the Pacific Islands before European Contact*, Berkeley, CA: University of California Press, 2000.

Kiste, Robert C., *The Bikinians: A Study in Forced Migration*, Menlo Park, CA: Cummings Publishing Co., 1974.

Kiste, Robert C., and R.A. Herr, *The Potential for Soviet Penetration of the South Pacific Islands: An Assessment*, Consultants' Report to the United States State Department, December 1984.

Kohli, Atul, Peter Evans, Peter J. Katzenstein, Adam Przeworski, Susanne Hoeber Rudolph, James C. Scott, and Theda Skocpol, 'The Role of Theory in Comparative Politics: A Symposium', *World Politics*, 48(1), 1995: 1–49. doi.org/10.1353/wp.1995.0002.

Komai, Makereta, 'Fiji's Foreign Policy and the New Pacific Diplomacy', in Greg Fry and Sandra Tarte, eds, *The New Pacific Diplomacy*, Canberra: ANU Press, 2015, pp. 111–21. doi.org/10.22459/NPD.12.2015.10.

Kotobalavu, Jioji, 'Trends in Perceptions of Security', in David Hegarty and Peter Polomka, eds, *The Security of Oceania in the 1990s. Volume 1: Views from the Region*, Canberra: Strategic and Defence Studies Centre, The Australian National University, 1989, pp. 25–30.

KPMG, *Demystifying Chinese Investment in Australia: June 2018*, Melbourne: KPMG Australia, 2018, available from: home.kpmg.com/au/en/home/insights/2018/06/demystifying-chinese-investment-in-australia-june-2018.html.

Kuranari, Tadashi, 'Working Towards the Pacific Future Community', Address, Suva, 14 January 1987.

Lake, David A., and Patrick M. Morgan, eds, *Regional Orders: Building Security in a New World*, University Park, PA: Pennsylvania State University Press, 1997.

Lal, Brij V., 'The Passage Out', in Kerry R. Howe, Robert C. Kiste and Brij V. Lal, eds, *Tides of History: The Pacific Islands in the Twentieth Century*, Sydney: Allen & Unwin, 1994, pp. 435–61.

Langdon, Robert, 'South Seas Regional Council May Grow Out of Lae Talks', *Pacific Islands Monthly*, August 1965: 21.

Langdon, Robert, 'Harry Maude: Shy Proconsul, Dedicated Pacific Historian', in Niel Gunson, ed., *The Changing Pacific: Essays in Honour of H.E. Maude*, Melbourne: Oxford University Press, 1978, pp. 1–21.

Legge, J.D., *Australian Colonial Policy: A Survey of Native Administration and European Development in Papua*, Sydney: Angus & Robertson under the auspices of the Australian Institute of International Affairs, 1956.

Leslie, Helen, and Kirsty Wild, 'Post-Hegemonic Regionalism in Oceania: Examining the Development Potential of the New Framework for Pacific Regionalism', *Pacific Review*, 31(1), 2018: 20–37. doi.org/10.1080/095127 48.2017.1305984.

Lewis, David, 'Helen Clark's OE', *Pundit*, 13 February 2009, available from: www.pundit.co.nz/content/helen-clarks-oe.

Lini, Walter Hadye, 'Vanuatu Enters the United Nations', in William L. Coop, ed., *Pacific People Sing Out Strong*, New York: Friendship Press, 1982.

Lyons, Kate, 'Australia's Relationship with Pacific on Climate Change "Dysfunctional" and "Abusive"', *The Guardian*, 5 September 2018.

McDonald, A.H., ed., *Trusteeship in the Pacific*, Sydney: Angus & Robertson, published under the auspices of the Australian Institute of International Affairs and the Institute of Pacific Relations, 1949.

Maclellan, Nic, 'Pacific Leaders Contradict Cairns Climate Deal', *The Interpreter*, Sydney: Lowy Institute for International Policy, 5 October 2018.

McNicoll, David, 'Better Days Ahead for the Natives of South Pacific', *Daily Telegraph*, [Sydney], 12 May 1950: 6.

Magnall, Karen, 'A Tale of Two Hotels', *Pacific Islands Monthly*, September 1990: 10–14.

Malielegaoi, Tuilaepa Dr Sailele, 'Let Us Recapture the Essence of Our Blue Pacific', *Samoa Observer*, 7 September 2017.

Malinowski, Bronislaw, *Argonauts of the Western Pacific*, London: George Routledge & Sons, 1922.

Malone, Paul, 'Reservations on N-Free Zone', *The Canberra Times*, 3 August 1985: 9.

Malyashkin, Alexander, 'USSR, the Pacific', *Pacific Islands Monthly*, January 1978: 15–16.

Mander, Linden A., *Some Dependent Peoples of the South Pacific*, Leiden: E.J. Brill for Institute of Pacific Relations, 1954.

Manoa, Fulori, 'The New Pacific Diplomacy at the United Nations: The Rise of the PSIDS', in Greg Fry and Sandra Tarte, eds, *The New Pacific Diplomacy*, Canberra: ANU Press, 2015, pp. 89–98. doi.org/10.22459/NPD.12.2015.08.

Mara, Ratu Sir Kamisese, 'Twenty-Fifth Anniversary Messages: South Pacific Commission', *South Pacific Bulletin*, 21(Second Quarter), 1972: 15–19.

Mara, Ratu Sir Kamisese, 'The South Pacific Forum', Address at the University of the South Pacific, Suva, 25 August 1972.

Mara, Ratu Sir Kamisese, 'Grail Address', Corpus Christi College, Suva, January 1973.

Mara, Ratu Sir Kamisese, 'Regional Co-operation in the South Pacific', Address at the University of Papua New Guinea, Port Moresby, 27 May 1974.

Mara, Ratu Sir Kamisese, *Report on Foreign Affairs for the Period 10 October 1970 – 31 December 1973*, Parliamentary Paper No. 19, Suva: Parliament of Fiji, 1974.

Mara, Ratu Sir Kamisese, 'Statement to the Twenty-Fifth Regular Session of the UN General Assembly: 1970', in Ratu Sir Kamisese Mara, *Report on Foreign Affairs for the Period 10th October 1970 – 31st December 1973*, Parliamentary Paper No. 19, Suva: Parliament of Fiji, 1974.

Mara, Ratu Sir Kamisese, 'Statement to the Thirty-First South Pacific Conference', Nuku`alofa, Tonga, 18 October 1991.

Mara, Ratu Sir Kamisese, *The Pacific Way: A Memoir*, Honolulu: University of Hawai`i Press, 1997.

Mara, Ratu Sir Kamisese, *Keynote Address by H.E. Rt Hon. Ratu Sir Kamisese Mara, Former Prime Minister and President of Fiji Islands, On the Occasion of the 30th Anniversary of the South Pacific Forum of Leaders, Yaren, Nauru, August 16, 2001*, Press Statement 6301, Suva: PIFS, 2001, available from: www.pireport.org/articles/2001/08/17/keynote-address-he-rt-hon-ratu-sir-kamisese-mara.

Mara, Ratu Sir Kamisese, and Michael Somare, 'Joint Communiqué', Port Moresby, 27 May 1974.

Maraj, James A., 'Statement to the University of the South Pacific', Suva, 23 September 1975.

Marawa, Sovaia, 'Negotiating the Melanesia Free Trade Area', in Greg Fry and Sandra Tarte, eds, *The New Pacific Diplomacy*, Canberra: ANU Press, 2015, pp. 161–74. doi.org/10.22459/NPD.12.2015.14.

Maude, Harry E., 'The South Pacific Commission', *Australia's Neighbours*, Fourth Series, No. 5, Melbourne: Australian Institute of International Affairs, June 1963.

Meaney, Neville, *A History of Australian Defence and Foreign Policy, 1901–23. Volume 1: The Search for Security in the Pacific, 1901–1914*, Sydney: Sydney University Press, 1976.

Melbourne Herald, 'Pacific Queen in Limelight', *Melbourne Herald*, 29 April 1950.

Melbourne Herald, 'Storm in a Glass at Suva: Native Delegates are Refused Drinks', *Melbourne Herald*, 1 May 1950.

Melbourne Sun, 'S. Pacific Natives Find New Outlook', *Melbourne Sun*, 4 May 1950.

Mirrill, Warren, and Peter Samuel, 'Soviets May Soon Have Pacific Base, Says Fraser', *The Australian*, 24 April 1985: 3.

Moala, Kalafi, 'Regionalism Debate Becoming Contentious', Online Forum, Port Vila: Pacific Institute of Public Policy, 8 April 2015.

Moorehead, Alan, *The Fatal Impact: An Account of the Invasion of the South Pacific, 1767–1840*, Harmondsworth, UK: Penguin, 1968.

Morauta, Sir Mekere, 'Melanesia in the Twenty-First Century', Address at the Launch of Pacific 2010 Project, Parliament House, Canberra, 30 June 1994.

Morgan, Wesley, 'Regional Trade Negotiations and the Construction of Policy Choice in the Pacific Islands Forum (1994–2014)', PhD thesis, School of Political and Social Sciences, University of Melbourne, Melbourne, October 2014.

Morgan, Wesley, 'Trade Negotiations and Regional Economic Integration in the Pacific Islands Forum', *Asia and the Pacific Policy Studies*, 1(2), 2014: 325–36. doi.org/10.1002/app5.34.

Morgan, Wesley, 'Negotiating Power in Contemporary Pacific Trade Diplomacy', in Greg Fry and Sandra Tarte, eds, *The New Pacific Diplomacy*, Canberra: ANU Press, 2015, pp. 251–61. doi.org/10.22459/NPD.12.2015.20.

Morgan, Wesley, 'Much Lost, Little Gained? Contemporary Trade Agreements in the Pacific Islands', *Journal of Pacific History*, [Online], 4 June 2018: 5–10.

Morrell, W.P., *Britain in the Pacific Islands*, London: Oxford University Press, 1960.

Munro, Doug, and Richard A. Herr, 'Island Confederation and George Westbrook', *ANU Historical Journal*, 9(December), 1972: 10–18.

Naidu, Vijay, 'The Fiji Anti-Nuclear Movement: Problems and Prospects', in Ranginui Walker and William Sutherland, eds, *The Pacific: Peace, Security and the Nuclear Issue*, Tokyo: United Nations University, 1988, pp. 185–95.

Nanau, Gordon, 'The Melanesian Spearhead Group and Pacific Regional Co-operation', *Pacific Studies*, 39(3), 2016: 290–93, 303.

Nandan, S.N., 'Statement to the Meeting of the UN Seabed Committee, New York, 15 March 1973', in Ratu Sir Kamisese Mara, *Report on Foreign Affairs for the Period 10 October 1970 – 31 December 1973*, Parliamentary Paper No. 19, Suva: Parliament of Fiji, 1974.

Narsey, Waden, 'PICTA, PACER and EPAs: Where Are We Going?', *Islands Business*, April 2004.

The National, 'PNG Offers to Provide for PACP Secretariat', *The National*, [Port Moresby], 23 November 2012, available from: www.thenational.com.pg/png-offers-to-provide-for-pacp-secretariat/.

Nauru Agreement Concerning Cooperation in the Management of Fisheries of Common Interest, Nauru, 1981.

Neemia, Uentabo Fakaofo, *Cooperation and Conflict: Costs, Benefits and National Interests in Pacific Regional Cooperation*, Suva: Institute of Pacific Studies, University of the South Pacific, 1986.

Neumann, Iver, *Uses of the Other: 'The East' in European Identity Formation*, Minneapolis: University of Minnesota Press, 1999.

New Zealand Department of External Affairs, *Report of the New Zealand Delegation on the Conference Held at Canberra, 28 January – 6 February, 1947, for the Purpose of Establishing an Advisory Commission for the South Pacific*, Publication No. 26, Wellington: Government Printer, 1947.

New Zealand External Relations Review, 'South Pacific Forum', *New Zealand External Relations Review*, January 1972: 28.

New Zealand External Relations Review, 'Third South Pacific Forum: Final Communiqué', *New Zealand External Relations Review*, September 1972: 26–30.

New Zealand Herald, 'The South Pacific Commission', *New Zealand Herald*, [Auckland], 20 February 1950.

Newton Cain, Tess, 'Deafening Silence on Rule of Law in Nauru', *The Interpreter*, Sydney: Lowy Institute for International Policy, 21 March 2014, available from: www.lowyinstitute.org/the-interpreter/deafening-silence-rule-law-nauru.

Newton Cain, Tess, 'The Renaissance of the Melanesian Spearhead Group', in Greg Fry and Sandra Tarte, eds, *The New Pacific Diplomacy*, Canberra: ANU Press, 2015, pp. 151–60. doi.org/10.22459/NPD.12.2015.13.

Norman, Albert, 'The Reclamation of Oceania', *Christian Science Monitor*, 4 June 1949.

Nuclear Safety Bureau, *Low-Level Radioactive Wastes: Dumping at the Pacific*, Tokyo: Science and Technology Agency, Government of Japan, 1980.

Nye, Joseph S., ed., *International Regionalism: Readings*, Boston: Little, Brown & Co., 1968.

Nye, Joseph S., 'Patterns and Catalysts in Regional Integration', in Joseph S. Nye, ed., *International Regionalism: Readings*, Boston: Little, Brown & Co., 1968, pp. 333–49.

O'Brien, Kerry, and Margot O'Neill, 'Pacific Nightmare', *Lateline*, Sydney: Australian Broadcasting Corporation, 1 August 1994, available from: trove. nla.gov.au/work/21232284?q&versionId=25338293.

O'Callaghan, Mary-Louise, '"Two-Faced": Forum Attacks Hawke', *Sydney Morning Herald*, 3 August 1990: 3.

Ogashiwa, Yoko S., *Microstates and Nuclear Issues: Regional Cooperation in the Pacific*, Suva: Institute of Pacific Studies, University of the South Pacific, 1991.

Okawara, Yoshio, 'Japan's Plea: Give Us Access to Your Waters', *Pacific Islands Monthly*, April 1978: 10–11.

Oliver, Douglas L., *The Pacific Islands*, Cambridge, MA: Harvard University Press, 1961.

Osborne, Robin, *Indonesia's Secret War: The Guerilla Struggle in Irian Jaya*, Sydney: Allen & Unwin, 1985.

Pacific Conference of Churches Secretariat, 'The Pacific as an Arena of Increasing Competition, Conflict, and Struggle', in William L. Coop, ed., *Pacific People Sing Out Strong*, New York: Friendship Press, 1982, pp. 12–16.

Pacific Islands Forum Secretariat (PIFS), *Press Communiqué: Tenth South Pacific Forum, Honiara, Solomon Islands, 9–10 July 1979*, Suva: PIFS, 1979.

Pacific Islands Forum Secretariat (PIFS), *Leaders' Communiqué: Twelfth Pacific Islands Forum, Port Vila, Vanuatu, 10–11 August 1981*, Suva: PIFS, 1981.

Pacific Islands Forum Secretariat (PIFS), *Leaders' Communiqué: Thirteenth Pacific Islands Forum, Rotorua, New Zealand, 9–10 August 1982*, Suva: PIFS, 1982.

Pacific Islands Forum Secretariat (PIFS), *Leaders' Communiqué: Sixteenth Pacific Islands Forum, Rarotonga, Cook Islands, 5–6 August 1985*, Suva: PIFS, 1985.

Pacific Islands Forum Secretariat (PIFS), *Leaders' Communiqué: Thirty-First Pacific Islands Forum, Tarawa, Republic of Kiribati, 27–30 October 2000*, Suva: PIFS, 2000.

Pacific Islands Forum Secretariat (PIFS), *'Biketawa' Declaration*, Suva: PIFS, 28 October 2000, available from: www.forumsec.org/biketawa-declaration/.

Pacific Islands Forum Secretariat (PIFS), 'The Forum's Eight Principles of Accountability: Progress to Date', Press statement by Mr W. Noel Levi, Secretary-General of the Pacific Islands Forum, Suva, 27 February 2001, available from: www.pireport.org/archive/2001-07-30.

Pacific Islands Forum Secretariat (PIFS), *Leaders' Communiqué: Thirty-Second Pacific Islands Forum, Yaren, Nauru, 16–18 August 2001*, Suva: PIFS, 2001.

Pacific Islands Forum Secretariat (PIFS), *Pacific Agreement on Closer Economic Relations (PACER)*, Suva: PIFS, 2001.

Pacific Islands Forum Secretariat (PIFS), *Nasonini Declaration on Regional Security*, Suva: PIFS, 2002, available from: www.forumsec.org/nasonini-declaration-on-regional-security/.

Pacific Islands Forum Secretariat (PIFS), *Leaders' Communiqué: Thirty-Fourth Pacific Islands Forum, Auckland, New Zealand, 14–16 August 2003*, Suva: PIFS, 2003.

Pacific Islands Forum Secretariat (PIFS), *Leaders' Decisions: Pacific Islands Forum Special Leaders Retreat, Auckland, New Zealand, 6 April 2004*, Suva: PIFS, 2004, available from: forumsec.org/pacific-islands-forum-special-leaders-retreat-auckland-6-april-2004-leaders-decisions/.

Pacific Islands Forum Secretariat (PIFS), *Leaders' Communiqué: Thirty-Fifth Pacific Islands Forum, Apia, Samoa, 5–7 August 2004*, Suva: PIFS, 2004.

Pacific Islands Forum Secretariat (PIFS), *A Review of the Regional Assistance Mission to Solomon Islands: Report of the Pacific Islands Forum Eminent Persons Group*, Suva: PIFS, May 2005.

Pacific Islands Forum Secretariat (PIFS), *Kalibobo Roadmap on the Pacific Plan*, Kalibobo Village, Madang, Papua New Guinea, 26 October 2005, available from: www.forumsec.org/kalibobo-roadmap-on-the-pacific-plan/.

Pacific Islands Forum Secretariat (PIFS), *Leaders' Communiqué: Thirty-Seventh Pacific Islands Forum, Nadi, Fiji, 24–25 October 2006*, Suva: PIFS, 2006, available from: www.forumsec.org/wp-content/uploads/2017/11/2006-Forum-Communique%CC%81_-Denarau_-Nadi_-Fiji_-24-25-Oct.pdf.

Pacific Islands Forum Secretariat (PIFS), *Leaders' Communiqué: Thirty-Ninth Pacific Islands Forum, Alofi, Niue, 19–20 August 2008*, Suva: PIFS, 2008.

Pacific Islands Forum Secretariat (PIFS), *Leaders' Decisions: Pacific Islands Forum Special Leaders' Retreat, Port Moresby, Papua New Guinea, 27 January 2009*, Suva: PIFS, 2009.

Pacific Islands Forum Secretariat (PIFS), *Statement by Forum Chair on Suspension of the Fiji Military Regime from the Pacific Islands Forum*, Press Statement 21/09, Suva: PIFS, 2 May 2009.

Pacific Islands Forum Secretariat (PIFS), 'Annex B: Cairns Compact on Strengthening Development Coordination in the Pacific, August 2009', in *Leaders' Communiqué: Fortieth Pacific Islands Forum, Cairns, Australia, 5–6 August 2009*, Suva: PIFS, 2009.

Pacific Islands Forum Secretariat (PIFS), *Pacific Plan Review 2013: Report to Pacific Leaders. Volume 1*, Suva: PIFS, 2013.

Pacific Islands Forum Secretariat (PIFS), 'Annex A: The Framework for Pacific Regionalism', in *Leaders' Communiqué: Forty-Fifth Pacific Islands Forum, Koror, Republic of Palau, 29–31 July 2014*, Suva: PIFS, 2014.

Pacific Islands Forum Secretariat (PIFS), *Leaders' Communiqué: Forty-Eighth Pacific Islands Forum, Apia, Samoa, 5–8 September 2017*, Suva: PIFS, 2017.

Pacific Islands Forum Secretariat (PIFS), 'Annex 1: Boe Declaration on Regional Security [Boe Declaration]', in *Leaders' Communiqué: Forty-Ninth Pacific Islands Forum, Yaren, Nauru, 3–6 September 2018*, Suva: PIFS, 2018, available from: www.forumsec.org/forty-ninth-pacific-islands-forum-nauru-3rd-6th-september-2018/.

Pacific Islands Forum Secretariat (PIFS), *Leaders' Communiqué: Forty-Ninth Pacific Islands Forum, Yaren, Nauru, 3–6 September 2018*, Suva: PIFS, 2018, available from: www.forumsec.org/forty-ninth-pacific-islands-forum-nauru-3rd-6th-september-2018/.

Pacific Islands Monthly, 'Plea for Co-operation in Pacific Affairs', *Pacific Islands Monthly*, 24 September 1936: 53–4.

Pacific Islands Monthly, 'Fijians and Indians: How Should They Be Represented at South Pacific Conference?', *Pacific Islands Monthly*, January 1950 [from a correspondent in Suva, 19 December 1949].

Pacific Islands Monthly, 'Editorial', *Pacific Islands Monthly*, May 1950: 1, 6.

Pacific Islands Monthly, 'Lae Meeting May Bring Some Get-Up-And-Go to the SPC', *Pacific Islands Monthly*, June 1965: 49.

Pacific Islands Monthly, 'It's Not an Exclusive Club Now—And the Islanders Like It', *Pacific Islands Monthly*, November 1967: 25.

Pacific Islands Monthly, 'Pacific Leaders Make Nuku`alofa a Get-Together to Remember', *Pacific Islands Monthly*, May 1971: 22.

Pacific Islands Monthly, 'All—Except France—Agog for Change in South Pacific Commission', *Pacific Islands Monthly*, October 1973: 7.

Pacific Islands Monthly, 'Forum Co-op Wanted, Not a Talking Shop', *Pacific Islands Monthly*, May 1974: 105.

Pacific Islands Monthly, 'Japan: Her Role in the South Seas', *Pacific Islands Monthly*, June 1976: 33–47.

Pacific Islands Monthly, 'Roubles for Tonga from Russia with Love', *Pacific Islands Monthly*, August 1976: 14–15.

Pacific Islands Monthly, 'A Thundercloud but No Storm over the Forum', *Pacific Islands Monthly*, September 1976: 13.

Pacific Islands Monthly, '"Let's Get Together" Says Somare', *Pacific Islands Monthly*, November 1976: 25.

Pacific Islands Monthly, '"If We Break Even, We'll Be Laughing": PFL's Modest Aim', *Pacific Islands Monthly*, August 1978: 77–9.

Pacific Islands Monthly, 'Japan and the Pacific', *Pacific Islands Monthly*, September 1978: 37–68.

Pacific Islands Monthly, 'Pacific Nations Speak Out with One Voice', *Pacific Islands Monthly*, February 1979: 9–10.

Pacific Islands Producers' Association (PIPA), *Constitution Establishing the Pacific Islands Producers' Association*, Suva: PIPA, 1971.

Pacific Islands Producers' Association (PIPA), *Pacific Islands Producers' Association*, Suva: PIPA, March 1971.

Pacific Islands Producers' Association (PIPA), *Sixth Session: Record of Proceedings*, Nuku`alofa: PIPA, April 1971.

Pacific Network on Globalisation (PANG), *Defending Pacific Ways of Life: A People's Social Impact Assessment of PACER-Plus*, Suva: PANG, June 2016.

Pacific Network on Globalisation (PANG), *A People's Guide to PACER Plus: Understanding What It Is and What It Means for the People of the Pacific Islands*, Suva: PANG, 2017.

Pacific Regional Seminary, *Pacific Regional Seminary 2002 Handbook*, Suva: Pacific Regional Seminary, 2002.

Pacific Report, 'Cook Islands Prime Minister Applauds Resources Theme of Forum Meeting', *Pacific Report*, 7(15)(July), 1994: 5.

Pacific Women's Conference, 'Resolutions of the Pacific Women's Conference, Oct. 27 – Nov. 2, 1975', in Vanessa Griffen, ed., *Women Speak Out! A Report on the Pacific Women's Conference*, Suva: Pacific Women's Conference, 2005, pp. 136–40.

Packham, Ben, 'Move to Head Off China with Australian Base on PNG', *The Australian*, 20 September 2018.

Pacnews, 'Fiji Will Not Return to Forum', *Pacnews*, 26 October 2014, available from: www.pina.com.fj/?p=pacnews&m=read&o=1608789720544d6db65d45a93939d3.

Pacnews, 'Fijian PM Support Sydney Meet, No Talk on Pacific Islands Forum', *Pacnews*, 2 November 2014, available from: www.pina.com.fj/?p=pacnews&m=read&o=11573914165456a5c206ecc584e739.

Pacnews, 'Donors Influence Development Decisions: Forum SG', *Pacnews*, 16 April 2015, available from: news.pngfacts.com/2015/04/donors-influence-development-decisions.html.

Palmer, Norman D., *The New Regionalism in Asia and the Pacific*, Lexington, MA: Lexington Books, 1991.

Pan Pacific Education and Communication Experiments by Satellite, *Peacesat Project: Early Experience—The Design and Early Years of the First Educational Communication Satellite Experiment*, Honolulu: University of Hawai`i, October 1975.

Papua New Guinea National Broadcasting Commission (NBC), 'Papua New Guinea and the Pacific', *Politics in Paradise Radio Series*, Port Moresby: NBC, February 1975.

Pareti, Samisoni, 'Fiji Pushes for Alternative to Pacific Islands Forum', *ABC News*, 6 August 2013.

Payne, Anthony, 'Globalization and Modes of Regionalist Governance', in Jon Pierre, ed., *Debating Governance: Authority, Steering, and Democracy*, Oxford: Oxford University Press, 2000, pp. 201–18.

Payne, Anthony, and Nicola Phillips, *Development*, Cambridge, UK: Polity Press, 2010.

Peebles, Dave, *Pacific Regional Order*, Canberra: ANU E Press and Asia Pacific Press, 2005. doi.org/10.26530/OAPEN_459432.

Penjueli, Maureen, 'Civil Society and the Political Legitimacy of Regional Institutions: An NGO Perspective', in Greg Fry and Sandra Tarte, eds, *The New Pacific Diplomacy*, Canberra: ANU Press, 2015, pp. 65–78. doi.org/10.22459/NPD.12.2015.06.

The Peoples' Charter for a Nuclear Free and Independent Pacific, 1983, available from: www.apc.org.nz/pma/pacchar.htm.

Peters, Winston, '"Shifting the Dial": Eyes Wide Open, Pacific Reset', Speech to Lowy Institute, Sydney, 2 March 2018.

Piddington, Ken, *The South Pacific Bureau: A New Venture in Economic Co-operation*, Wellington: New Zealand Institute of International Affairs, 1973.

Piddington, Ken, *South Pacific Forum: The First 15 Years*, Suva: South Pacific Bureau for Economic Co-operation, 1986.

Pierre, Tamarii, *Address on Special Needs and Problems*, Fourteenth South Pacific Conference Working Papers, Rarotonga: South Pacific Commission Secretariat, 27 September 1974.

PINA News, 'Pacific Islands Forum Takes No Action Against Fiji, Sets up Future Crisis', *PINA News*, [Tarawa], 29 October 2000.

Pratibha, Jyoti, 'All Equal Now', *Fiji Sun*, 7 August 2013.

Puna, Henry, 'The Cook Islands, NZ and Free Association: Speech by Hon. Henry Puna, Prime Minister of the Cook Islands', New Zealand Institute for International Affairs, Wellington, 4 April 2018, available from: www.nziia.org.nz/Portals/285/documents/lists/259/PM%20Puna%20-%20NZIIA%20speech%20FINAL%20delivered%204%20April%202018.pdf.

Quentin-Baxter, R.Q., 'A New Zealand View', in Mary Boyd, ed., *Pacific Horizons: A Regional Role for New Zealand*, Wellington: Price Milburn for the New Zealand Institute of International Affairs, 1971, pp. 21–31.

Quester, George H., 'Trouble in the Islands: Defending the Micro-States', *International Security*, 8(2), 1983: 160–75. doi.org/10.2307/2538600.

Radio New Zealand, 'Fiji Says It Won't Rejoin Pacific Islands Forum Unless There Are Changes', *Radio New Zealand International News*, 13 September 2013.

Radio New Zealand, 'Remengesau Stresses Pacific Forum Unity', *Radio New Zealand*, 5 November 2014.

Radio New Zealand, 'Tonga Opposed to Forum Exclusions', *Radio New Zealand*, 3 April 2015, available from: www.pireport.org/articles/2015/04/06/tonga-opposed-forum-exclusions.

Ramsden, Eric, 'The Pacific is on the Move: Personalities at First Peoples' Conference', *The Auckland Star*, 20 April 1950.

Ramsden, Eric, 'Sons of Stone Age Peoples Delegates to Fiji Conference', *The Auckland Star*, 27 April 1950.

Ranmuthugala, Douglas, 'Security in the South Pacific: The Law Enforcement Dimension', *Revue Juridique Polynesienne*, 1, 2001.

Ravenhill, John, 'Political Turbulence in the South Pacific', in John Ravenhill, ed., *No Longer an American Lake?*, Sydney: Allen & Unwin, 1989, pp. 1–40.

Reilly, Ben, 'The Africanisation of the South Pacific', *Australian Journal of International Affairs*, 54(3), 2000: 261–8. doi.org/10.1080/0004991002001 2552.

Remeikis, Amy, 'Julie Bishop in Balancing Act after Colleague Criticises China's Pacific Aid', *The Guardian*, 11 January 2018.

Republic of Nauru, 'Speech by His Excellency, the Hon. Kinza Clodumar, MP, President of the Republic of Nauru, 23 October 1997, National Press Club, Canberra', Media release, 21 October 1997.

Riordan, Primrose, 'Coalition Attack on China Over Pacific Aid', *The Australian*, 9 January 2018.

Riordan, Primrose, 'Julie Bishop's Message for China: Pacific is Australia's Patch', *The Australian*, 5 June 2018.

Riordan, Primrose, 'Pacific Pact to Strengthen Regional Security and Counter China Push', *The Australian*, 6 July 2018.

Robertson, Max, 'The South Pacific Regional Trade and Economic Cooperation Agreement: A Critique', in R.V. Cole and T.G. Parry, eds, *Selected Issues in Pacific Island Development*, Canberra: National Centre for Development Studies, The Australian National University, 1986, pp. 147–75.

Robson, Nancy, 'The Suva Conference of South Pacific Peoples', *Australian Outlook*, 4(3), 1950: 179–85. doi.org/10.1080/10357715008443743.

Robson, Peter, 'The New Regionalism and the Developing Countries', *Journal of Common Market Studies*, 31(3), 1993: 329–48. doi.org/10.1111/j.1468-5965.1993.tb00467.x.

Robson, Robert W., 'Need for a Closer Relationship between Territories', *Pacific Islands Monthly*, 17 January 1931: 1–2.

Robson, Robert W., 'Plea for Co-operation in Pacific Affairs', *Pacific Islands Monthly*, 24 September 1936: 53–4.

Robson, Robert W., 'Sidelights on the South Pacific Conference', *Pacific Islands Monthly*, May 1950: 11.

Ross, Angus, *New Zealand Aspirations in the Pacific in the Nineteenth Century*, Oxford: Clarendon Press, 1964.

Ross, Ken, *Prospects for Crisis Prediction: A South Pacific Case Study*, Canberra: Strategic and Defence Studies Centre, The Australian National University, 1990.

Rostow, W.W., 'The Coming Age of Regionalism: A "Metaphor" for our Time?', *Encounter*, 74(5), 1990: 3–7.

Rudd, Kevin, 'The Global Financial Crisis', *The Monthly*, February 2009, available from: www.themonthly.com.au/issue/2009/february/1319602475/kevin-rudd/global-financial-crisis.

Ryan, Yasmine, 'COP15 and Pacific Island States: A Collective Voice on Climate Change', *Pacific Journalism Review*, 16(1), 2010: 193–203.

Said, Edward W., *Orientalism*, New York: Vintage Books, 1979.

Salato, E. Macu, 'South Pacific Regionalism: "Unity in Diversity"', *South Pacific Bulletin*, 26(Fourth Quarter), 1976: 30–5.

Samoa Observer and Pacnews, 'I Can't Stand You Bainimarama: PM Tuilaepa', *Samoa Observer/Pacnews*, 19 April 2015, available from: www.pina.com.fj/?p=pacnews&m=read&o=404430711553476ec71af7e07c0b22.

Scarr, Deryck, *Fragments of Empire: A History of the Western Pacific High Commission 1877–1914*, Canberra: Australian National University Press, 1967.

Scarr, Deryck, *The History of the Pacific Islands: Kingdoms of the Reefs*, Melbourne: Macmillan, 1990.

Secretariat of the Pacific Community, *Pacific Islands Regional Millennium Development Goals Report*, Nouméa: Secretariat of the Pacific Community, 2004.

Secretariat of the Pacific Community, 'The Pacific Islands Regional Millennium Development Goals Report', Paper presented to the Thirty-Fourth Meeting of the Committee of Representatives and Administrations, Nouméa, 16–19 November 2004 (SPC/CRGA 34).

Selwyn, Percy, *Small, Poor and Remote: Islands at a Geographical Disadvantage*, Discussion Paper 123, Sussex: Institute of Development Studies, 1978.

Selwyn, Percy, 'Smallness and Islandness', *World Development*, 8(12), 1980: 945–51. doi.org/10.1016/0305-750X(80)90086-8.

Shanahan, Dennis, 'Turnbull Welcomes British Initiatives in South Pacific Region', *The Australian*, 21 April 2018.

Shand, R.T., ed., *The Island States of the Pacific and Indian Oceans: Anatomy of Development*, Development Studies Centre Monograph No. 23, Canberra: Development Studies Centre, The Australian National University, 1980.

Sheridan, Greg, 'Breaking Up Brings No Benefit: We Are Witnessing the Balkanisation of the Region', *The Australian*, 9 June 2000.

Sheridan, Greg, and Cameron Stewart, 'Top Defence Threat Now Lies in the South Pacific from China', *The Australian*, 22 September 2018.

Shibuya, Eric, 'The Problems and Potential of the Pacific Islands Forum', in Jim Rolfe, ed., *The Asia-Pacific: A Region in Transition*, Honolulu: Asia-Pacific Center for Security Studies, 2004, pp. 102–15.

Siegel, Matt, 'Papua New Guinea Braces for Unrest with Two Prime Ministers and Cabinets', *The New York Times*, 13 December 2011.

Sikivou, S.K., 'Statement to the Twenty-Sixth Session of the UN General Assembly–1971', in Ratu Sir Kamisese Mara, *Report on Foreign Affairs for the Period 10th October 1970 – 31st December 1973*, Parliamentary Paper No. 19, Suva: Parliament of Fiji, 1974.

Sikivou, S.K., 'Statement to the Twenty-Eighth Regular Session of the UN General Assembly–1973', in Ratu Sir Kamisese Mara, *Report on Foreign Affairs for the Period 10th October 1970 – 31st December 1973*, Parliamentary Paper No. 19, Suva: Parliament of Fiji, 1974.

Simpson, Colin, 'Native Conference in Fiji Opens Colourfully', *The Argus*, [Melbourne], 26 April 1950.

Siwatibau, Suliana, and B. David Williams, *A Call to a New Exodus: An Anti-Nuclear Primer for Pacific People*, Suva: Lotu Pasfika, 1982.

Skelton, Russell, 'Soviet Turns Eyes to South Pacific Areas', *The Age*, [Melbourne], 14 July 1976.

Skelton, Russell, 'ANZUS to Step Up Aid: Council Acts on Soviet Pacific Move', *The Age*, [Melbourne], 5 August 1976: 3.

Skelton, Russell, 'Thirteen Pacific Nations Agree to Reject Soviet Aid Offers', *Sydney Morning Herald*, 12 August 1981.

Slatter, Claire, 'The New Framework for Pacific Regionalism: Old Kava in a New Tanoa?', in Greg Fry and Sandra Tarte, eds, *The New Pacific Diplomacy*, Canberra: ANU Press, 2015, pp. 49–63. doi.org/10.22459/NPD.12.2015.05.

Slatter, Claire, and Yvonne Underhill-Sem, 'Reclaiming Pacific Island Regionalism: Does Neoliberalism Have to Reign?', in Bina D'Costa and Katrina Lee-Koo, eds, *Gender and Global Politics in the Asia-Pacific*, Basingstoke, UK: Palgrave Macmillan, 2009. doi.org/10.1057/9780230617742_12.

Slawecki, Leon M., *The United States and the South Pacific: A Conference Report—Apia, Western Samoa, November, 1988*, San Francisco: Asia Foundation Center for Asian Pacific Affairs, 1989.

Smith, Bernard, *European Vision and the South Pacific 1768–1850: A Study in the History of Art and Ideas*, Oxford: Clarendon Press, 1960.

Smith, T.R., *South Pacific Commission: An Analysis after Twenty-Five Years*, Wellington: Price Milburn for the New Zealand Institute of International Affairs, 1972.

Söderbaum, Fredrik, 'Modes of Regional Governance in Africa: Neoliberalism, Sovereignty Boosting, and Shadow Networks', *Global Governance*, 10(4), 2004: 419–36. doi.org/10.1163/19426720-01004004.

Söderbaum, Fredrik, and Timothy M. Shaw, 'Conclusion: What Futures for New Regionalism?', in Fredrik Söderbaum and Timothy M. Shaw, eds, *Theories of New Regionalism: A Palgrave Reader*, Basingstoke, UK: Palgrave Macmillan, 2003, pp. 211–25. doi.org/10.1057/9781403938794_12.

Sogavare, Manasseh, 'Message of Appreciation by Prime Minister Hon. Manasseh Sogavare to RAMSI, RAMSI Participating Countries', Prime Minister's Press Secretariat, Honiara, 25 June 2017.

Sogavare, Manasseh Damukana, 'Solomon Islands Statement by Hon. Manasseh Damukana Sogavare, MP Prime Minister, 72nd Session United Nations General Assembly, General Debate', United Nations, New York, 2017, available from: gadebate.un.org/sites/default/files/gastatements/72/sb_en.pdf.

Solomon Star, 'PM Welcomes New PACP Secretariat Formation', *Solomon Star*, 23 November 2012.

Somare, Michael, 'Let's get together', *Pacific Islands Monthly*, November 1976: 25.

Somare, Michael, 'The Emerging Role of Papua New Guinea in World Affairs', Twenty-Fifth Milne Lecture, Melbourne, 14 June 1974.

Somare, Michael, 'Melanesian Spearhead Group: The Last 25 Years', in Greg Fry and Sandra Tarte, eds, *The New Pacific Diplomacy*, Canberra: ANU Press, 2015, pp. 291–98.

Somare, Michael T., 'Closing Address by the Prime Minister of Papua New Guinea, the Right Honourable M.T. Somare', Press release, Commonwealth Heads of Government Regional Meeting, Sydney, 16 February 1978.

South Pacific Bureau for Economic Co-operation (SPEC), *Director's Annual Report 1973/74*, (74)17, Suva: SPEC, 1974.

South Pacific Bureau for Economic Co-operation (SPEC), *Director's Annual Report 1974/75*, Suva: SPEC, 1975.

South Pacific Bureau for Economic Co-operation (SPEC), *Director's Annual Report 1975/76*, Suva: SPEC, 1976.

South Pacific Bureau for Economic Co-operation (SPEC), *Director's Annual Report 1976/77*, (77)18, Suva: SPEC, 1977.

South Pacific Bureau for Economic Co-operation (SPEC), *The Special Problems of Small States: The Developing Island Countries of the South Pacific, Commonwealth Heads of Government Regional Meeting, Sydney, 13–16 February 1978*, Suva: SPEC, 30 December 1977.

South Pacific Bureau for Economic Co-operation (SPEC), *Director's Annual Report 1977/78*, (78)17, Suva: SPEC, 1978.

South Pacific Bureau for Economic Co-operation (SPEC), *Press Communiqué: Ninth South Pacific Forum, Alofi, Niue, 29 September 1978*, Suva: SPEC, 1978.

South Pacific Bureau for Economic Co-operation (SPEC), *Director's Annual Report, 1979/80*, (80)8, Suva: SPEC, 1980.

South Pacific Commission (SPC), *Report of the Secretary-General of the South Pacific Commission on the First South Pacific Conference, 25 April – 5 May 1950, Suva*, Wellington: Government Printer for the SPC, 1950.

South Pacific Commission (SPC), *Round Table*, 48(December), 1957: 87–93. doi.org/10.1080/00358535708452108.

South Pacific Commission (SPC), *Seventh Session: Proceedings*, Nouméa: SPC, 1957.

South Pacific Commission (SPC), *Pacific Forum (Sixth South Pacific Conference, 1965)*, Nouméa: SPC, 1966.

South Pacific Commission (SPC), *Report of the Seventh South Pacific Conference and Proceedings of the Thirtieth Session of the South Pacific Commission*, Nouméa: SPC, 1967.

South Pacific Commission (SPC), *Report of the Eighth South Pacific Conference and Proceedings of the Thirty-First Session of the South Pacific Commission*, Nouméa: SPC, 1968.

South Pacific Commission (SPC), *Report of the Tenth South Pacific Conference and Proceedings of the Thirty-Third Session of the South Pacific Commission*, Nouméa: SPC, 1970.

South Pacific Commission (SPC), *South Pacific Report 1969–70*, Nouméa: SPC, 1970.

South Pacific Commission (SPC), *Report of the Eleventh South Pacific Conference and Proceedings of the Thirty-Fourth Session of the South Pacific Commission*, Nouméa: SPC, 1971.

South Pacific Commission (SPC), *Report of the 'Future Status' Committee, Thirteenth South Pacific Conference*, Nouméa: SPC Secretariat, September 1973.

South Pacific Commission (SPC), *Report of the Fourteenth South Pacific Conference*, Nouméa: SPC, 1974.

South Pacific Commission (SPC), *Report of the Fifteenth South Pacific Conference*, Nouméa: SPC, 1975.

South Pacific Commission (SPC), *Report of the South Pacific Commission Review Committee, Nauru, 3–7 May 1976*, Nouméa: SPC, 1976.

South Pacific Commission (SPC), *Report of the Eighteenth South Pacific Conference*, Nouméa: SPC, 1978.

South Pacific Forum Secretariat, *Final Communiqué: South Pacific Forum, Wellington, 5–7 August 1971*, Suva: South Pacific Forum Secretariat, 1971.

South Pacific Forum Secretariat, *Final Communiqué: South Pacific Forum, Canberra, 23–25 February 1972*, Suva: South Pacific Forum Secretariat, 1972.

South Pacific Forum Secretariat, *South Pacific Forum, Suva, Fiji, 12–14 September 1972: Summary Record of Proceedings, (Confidential)*, Suva: South Pacific Forum Secretariat, 1972.

South Pacific Forum Secretariat, *Fifth South Pacific Forum, Rarotonga, Cook Islands, 20–22 March 1974*, Suva: South Pacific Forum Secretariat, 1974, available from: www.forumsec.org/fifth-south-pacific-forum-rarotonga-cook-islands-20-22-march-1974/.

South Pacific Forum Secretariat, 'Summary Record and Final Press Communiqué', in *Leaders' Communiqué: Fifth South Pacific Forum, Rarotonga, Cook Islands, 20–22 March 1974*, Suva: South Pacific Forum Secretariat, 1974.

South Pacific Forum Secretariat, 'Declaration on Law of the Sea', in *Seventh South Pacific Forum, Nauru, 26–28 July 1976*, Suva: South Pacific Forum Secretariat, 1976, available from: www.forumsec.org/seventh-south-pacific-forum-nauru-26-28-july-1976-3/.

South Pacific Forum Secretariat, 'Declaration on Law of the Sea and a Regional Fisheries Agency', in *Eighth South Pacific Forum, Port Moresby, Papua New Guinea, 29–31 August 1977*, Suva: South Pacific Forum Secretariat, 1977, available from: www.forumsec.org/8th-south-pacific-forum-port-moresby-papua-new-guinea-29-31-august-1977/.

South Pacific Forum Secretariat, *Leaders' Communiqué: Tenth South Pacific Forum, Honiara, Solomon Islands, 9–10 July 1979*, Suva: South Pacific Forum Secretariat, 1979, available from: www.forumsec.org/tenth-south-pacific-forum-honiara-solomon-islands-9-10-july-1979/.

South Pacific Forum Secretariat, *Leaders' Communiqué: Twelfth South Pacific Forum, Port Vila, Vanuatu, 10–11 August 1981*, Suva: South Pacific Forum Secretariat, 1981.

South Pacific Forum Secretariat, *Leaders' Communiqué: Thirteenth South Pacific Forum, Rotorua, New Zealand, 9–10 August 1982*, Suva: South Pacific Forum Secretariat, 1982.

South Pacific Forum Secretariat, *Leaders' Communiqué: Fifteenth South Pacific Forum, Funafuti, Tuvalu, 27–28 August 1984*, Suva: South Pacific Forum Secretariat, 1984.

South Pacific Forum Secretariat, *Leaders' Communiqué: Sixteenth South Pacific Forum, Rarotonga, Cook Islands, 5–6 August 1985*, Suva: South Pacific Forum Secretariat, 1985.

South Pacific Forum Secretariat, *Leaders' Communiqué: Eighteenth South Pacific Forum, Apia, Western Samoa, 29–30 May 1987*, Suva: South Pacific Forum Secretariat, 1987.

South Pacific Forum Secretariat, *Leaders' Communiqué: Twentieth South Pacific Forum, Tarawa, Republic of Kiribati, 10–11 July 1989*, Suva: South Pacific Forum Secretariat, 1989.

South Pacific Forum Secretariat, *SPARTECA: A Reference Handbook for Forum Island Country Exporters*, Suva: South Pacific Forum Secretariat, 1989.

South Pacific Forum Secretariat, *Tarawa Declaration*, Suva: South Pacific Forum Secretariat, 11 July 1989, available from: www.forumsec.org/tarawa-declaration/.

South Pacific Forum Secretariat, *Leaders' Communiqué: Twenty-First South Pacific Forum, Port Vila, Vanuatu, 31 July – 1 August 1990*, Suva: South Pacific Forum Secretariat, 1990.

South Pacific Forum Secretariat, *Leaders' Communiqué: Twenty-Second South Pacific Forum, Palikir, Pohnpei, Federated States of Micronesia, 29–30 July 1991*, Suva: South Pacific Forum Secretariat, 1991.

South Pacific Forum Secretariat, *Declaration by the South Pacific Forum on Law Enforcement Cooperation [Honiara Declaration]*, Suva: South Pacific Forum Secretariat, 1992.

South Pacific Forum Secretariat, *Leaders' Communiqué: Twenty-Fifth South Pacific Forum, Brisbane, Australia, 31 July – 2 August 1994*, Suva: South Pacific Forum Secretariat, 1994.

South Pacific Forum Secretariat, *Aitutaki Declaration on Regional Security Cooperation*, Suva: South Pacific Forum Secretariat, 18 September 1997, available from: www.forumsec.org/aitutaki-declaration-on-regional-security-cooperation/.

South Pacific Nuclear Free Zone Treaty, 1985, available from: fas.org/nuke/control/spnfz/text/spnfz.htm.

South Pacific Regional Trade and Economic Co-operation Agreement, Signed in Tarawa, Kiribati, 14 July 1980, available from: www.forumsec.org/wp-content/uploads/2018/02/South-Pacific-Regional-Trade-and-Economic-Co-operation-Agreement-SPARTECA-1.pdf.

Spate, O.H.K., 'The Pacific as an Artefact', in Niel Gunson, ed., *The Changing Pacific: Essays in Honour of H.E. Maude*, Melbourne: Oxford University Press, 1978, pp. 32–45.

Spate, O.H.K., *The Pacific Since Magellan. Volume 1: The Spanish Lake*, Canberra: Australian National University Press, 1979.

Spate, O.H.K., *The Pacific Since Magellan. Volume 3: Paradise Found and Lost*, Canberra: Australian National University Press, 1988.

Spencer, Geoff, 'Forum to Protest Over US Chemical Weapons Plan', *The Age*, [Melbourne], 8 September 1990: 9.

Stanner, W.E.H., *The South Seas in Transition: A Study of Post-War Rehabilitation and Reconstruction in Three British Pacific Dependencies*, Sydney: Australasian Publishing Company, 1953.

Steinfort, Tom, 'The China Syndrome', *60 Minutes*, Sydney: Nine Entertainment Co., 17 June 2018.

Subramani, 'The Oceanic Imaginary', *The Contemporary Pacific*, 13(1), 2001: 149–62. doi.org/10.1353/cp.2001.0035.

Sunday Telegraph, 'Kokoda Trail Carrier Is Now Leader–Envoy for His People', *Sunday Telegraph*, [Sydney], 23 April 1950.

Sundhaussen, U., 'Discussion Topic: That PNG Should Try to Play a Significant Role in Both the South-East Asian and South-West Pacific Regions', in James Griffin, ed., *A Foreign Policy for an Independent Papua New Guinea*, Sydney: Angus & Robertson, 1974, pp. 107–17.

Sutherland, William, 'Australia's Economic Relations with the South Pacific: A Pacific Perspective', in Brendan O'Dwyer, ed., *Australia and the South Pacific*, Canberra: Centre for Continuing Education, The Australian National University, 1982, pp. 63–73.

Sutherland, William, 'Microstates and Unequal Trade in the South Pacific: The SPARTECA Agreement of 1980', *Journal of World Trade Law*, 20(3), 1986: 313–28.

Sutherland, William, 'Global Imperatives and Economic Reform in the Pacific Island States', *Development and Change*, 31(2), 2000: 459–80. doi.org/10.1111/1467-7660.00162.

Sydney Morning Herald, 'Pacific Talks', *Sydney Morning Herald*, 20 April 1950.

Sydney Morning Herald, 'South Seas Experiment in Co-operation', *Sydney Morning Herald*, 24 April 1950.

Sydney Morning Herald, 'Curious Mixture of Dressing at South Pacific Conference', *Sydney Morning Herald*, 26 April 1950.

Sydney Morning Herald, 'Praise of Natives: Pacific Talk', *Sydney Morning Herald*, 29 April 1950.

Sydney Morning Herald, 'Fires of National Ambition Burn in South Pacific', *Sydney Morning Herald*, 6 May 1950.

Sydney Morning Herald, 'New Era for South Seas: Success at Suva', *Sydney Morning Herald*, 6 May 1950.

Sydney Morning Herald, 'Leadership in South Seas: Australian Failure', *Sydney Morning Herald*, 8 May 1950.

Sydney Morning Herald, 'Our Opportunity in South Pacific', [Editorial], *Sydney Morning Herald*, 13 May 1950.

Sydney Morning Herald, 'Red Sails in the South Seas?', *Sydney Morning Herald*, 7 August 1976: 10.

Sydney Morning Herald, 'Russian Threat in Pacific Claimed', *Sydney Morning Herald*, 1 March 1977.

Sydney Morning Herald, 'Islanders Wary of US Bait', *Sydney Morning Herald*, 24 October 1978.

Sydney Morning Herald, 'Nuclear Ships Row on Boil at ASEAN', *Sydney Morning Herald*, 11 July 1985: 1.

Sydney Morning Herald, 'Howard: Solomons Could Have Become a Haven for Terrorists', *Sydney Morning Herald*, 23 July 2003.

Sydney Morning Herald, 'The United States of the Pacific', *Sydney Morning Herald*, 17 March 2004.

Sydney Telegraph, 'Black-Eyed Beauty Bosses Pacific Talks', *Sydney Telegraph*, 30 April 1950.

Takeda, Isami, 'New Factors in Japan's ODA Policy: Implications for Australia–Japan Relations', Mimeo., Canberra: Australia–Japan Research Centre, The Australia National University, August 1986.

Tarte, Sandra, 'Fiji's Role in the South Pacific Forum, 1971–1984', BA(Hons) thesis, Department of Political Science, University of Melbourne, Melbourne, 1985.

Tarte, Sandra, 'Negotiating a Tuna Management Regime for the Western and Central Pacific: The MHLC Process 1994–1999', *Journal of Pacific History*, 34(3), 1999: 273–80. doi.org/10.1080/00223349908572912.

Tarte, Sandra, 'Fiji's Search for New Friends', *East Asia Forum*, 13 January 2011.

Tarte, Sandra, 'Regionalism and Changing Regional Order in the Pacific Islands', *Asia and the Pacific Policy Studies*, 1(2), 2014: 315–18. doi.org/10.1002/app5.27.

Tarte, Sandra, 'A New Pacific Regional Voice? The Pacific Islands Development Forum', in Greg Fry and Sandra Tarte, eds, *The New Pacific Diplomacy*, Canberra: ANU Press, 2015, pp. 79–88. doi.org/10.22459/NPD.12.2015.07.

Tate, Merze, 'The Australasian Monroe Doctrine', *Political Science Quarterly*, 76(2), 1961: 264–84. doi.org/10.2307/2146220.

Tavita, Tupuola Terry, 'Samoa PM Talks About the Polynesian Leaders Group', *Savali*, 28 November 2011, available from: www.pireport.org/articles/2011/12/01/samoa-pm-talks-about-polynesian-leaders-group.

Tavola, Kaliopate, 'Towards a New Pacific Diplomacy Architecture', in Greg Fry and Sandra Tarte, eds, *The New Pacific Diplomacy*, Canberra: ANU Press, 2015. doi.org/10.22459/NPD.12.2015.03.

Taylor, Meg, 'The Future of the Pacific Islands Forum and the Framework for Pacific Regionalism', in Greg Fry and Sandra Tarte, eds, *The New Pacific Diplomacy*, Canberra: ANU Press, 2015, pp. 39–47. doi.org/10.22459/NPD.12.2015.04.

Taylor, Meg, 'Keynote Address', Australian Council for International Development (ACFID) National Conference, Melbourne, 26 October 2016.

Taylor, Meg, 'Introductory Remarks by Dame Meg Taylor, Secretary-General', Research Week, USP Laucala Campus, Fiji, 27 August 2018.

Taylor, Meg, 'Keynote Address', 2018 State of the Pacific Conference, The Australian National University, Canberra, 8 September 2018, available from: www.forumsec.org/keynote-address-by-secretary-general-meg-taylor-to-the-2018-state-of-the-pacific-conference/.

Teiwaki, Roniti, *Management of Marine Resources in Kiribati*, Suva: Institute of Pacific Studies, University of the South Pacific, 1988.

Teiwaki, Roniti, 'Kiribati Gets Too Much Aid; Must Learn to Say "No" Says Opposition Leader', *Pacific Report*, 6(22), 1993: 6.

Tevi, Lorini, 'The Pacific Conference of Churches', in Emiliana Afeaki, Ron Crocombe, and John McClaren, eds, *Religious Cooperation in the Pacific Islands*, Suva: Institute of Pacific Studies, University of the South Pacific, 1983, pp. 148–56.

Thaman, Konai Helu, 'Decolonizing Pacific Studies: Indigenous Perspectives, Knowledge, and Wisdom in Higher Education', *The Contemporary Pacific*, 15(1), 2003: 1–17. doi.org/10.1353/cp.2003.0032.

Thomas, Nicholas, *Entangled Objects: Exchange, Material Culture, and Colonialism in the Pacific*, Cambridge, MA: Harvard University Press, 1991.

Thomas, Nicholas, *Colonialism's Culture: Anthropology, Travel and Government*, Princeton, NJ: Princeton University Press, 1994.

Thomas, Nicholas, *In Oceania: Visions, Artifacts, Histories*, Durham, NC: Duke University Press, 1997.

The Times, 'South Pacific Peoples' Conference: Successful Experiment', *The Times*, [London], 6 May 1950.

Tiy, Francis Hong, and R.G. Irwin, *A Survey of the Development of Inter-Government Proposals for a Multi-National Regional Shipping Line in the South Pacific*, Discussion Paper, Papua New Guinea Harbours Board South Pacific Ports Conference, Port Moresby, 17–19 March 1975.

Tlozek, Eric, 'Australia Should Not Fear Chinese Influence in Papua New Guinea, Government Says', *ABC News Online*, 23 January 2018, available from: www.abc.net.au/news/2018-01-23/australia-should-not-fear-chinese-influence-in-png/9349140.

Toma, Iulai, *Address on Special Needs and Problems*, Fourteenth South Pacific Conference Working Papers, Rarotonga: South Pacific Commission Secretariat, 27 September 1974.

Tong, Anote, '"Charting its Own Course": A Paradigm Shift in Pacific Diplomacy', in Greg Fry and Sandra Tarte, eds, *The New Pacific Diplomacy*, Canberra: ANU Press, 2015, pp. 21–4. doi.org/10.22459/NPD.12.2015.02.

Toohey, Brian, 'What Russians? It's Economics that Matter', *Australian Financial Review*, 5 August 1976.

Treaty on Fisheries between the Governments of Certain Pacific Island States and the Government of the United States of America, Port Moresby, 2 April 1987.

Tupouniua, Sione, 'Political Independence: An Opportunity to Create', in Sione Tupouniua, Ron Crocombe, and Claire Slatter, eds, *The Pacific Way: Social Issues in National Development*, Suva: South Pacific Social Sciences Association, 1975, pp. 239–47.

Tupouniua, Sione, Ron Crocombe, and Claire Slatter, eds, *The Pacific Way: Social Issues in National Development*, Suva: South Pacific Social Sciences Association, 1975.

Tupua Tamasese Lealofi IV, 'Opening Address by the Chairman: Twelfth South Pacific Conference and Thirty-Fifth Session of the South Pacific Commission', Unpublished conference paper, 1972.

Turnbull, Malcolm, 'Regional Training Hub for Fiji', Media release, 22 August 2018, available from: www.malcolmturnbull.com.au/media/regional-training-hub-for-fiji#.

United Nations, *An Agenda for Peace: Preventive Diplomacy, Peacemaking and Peace-Keeping*, Report of the United Nations Secretary-General, A47/277, New York: United Nations, 17 June 1992.

United Nations Conference on Trade and Development (UNCTAD), *Developing Island Countries: Report of the Panel of Experts*, New York: UNCTAD, 1974.

United Nations Conference on Trade and Development (UNCTAD), *Proceedings of the United Nations Conference on Trade and Development: Fourth Session, Nairobi, May 1976. Volume 1: Reports and Annexes*, E.76.II.D.10, New York: United Nations, 1976, available from: unctad.org/en/Docs/td218vol1_en.pdf.

United Nations Convention against Illicit Traffic in Narcotic Drugs and Psychotropic Substances, Vienna, 20 December 1988.

United Nations Development Programme (UNDP), *Human Development Index*, New York: UNDP, available from: hdr.undp.org/en/content/human-development-index-hdi.

United Nations Development Programme (UNDP), *Human Development Report 1990*, New York: Oxford University Press, 1990.

United Nations Development Programme (UNDP), 'Foreword', in *Suva Declaration on Sustainable Human Development in the Pacific*, Suva: UNDP, 1994.

United Nations Development Programme (UNDP), *Pacific Human Development Report: Putting People First*, Suva: UNDP, 1994.

United Nations Development Programme (UNDP), *Pacific Human Development Report 1999: Creating Opportunities*, Suva: UNDP, June 1999.

United Nations Economic and Social Council (ECOSOC), *Special Economic Problems and Development Needs of Geographically More Disadvantaged Developing Island Countries*, E/5647, New York: ECOSOC, 27 March 1975.

United Nations General Assembly, *Progress in the Implementation of Specific Action in Favour of Developing Island Countries: Report of the Secretary-General*, A/32/126, New York: United Nations, 28 June 1977.

United Nations General Assembly, *Large-Scale Pelagic Driftnet Fishing and its Impact on the Living Marine Resources of the World's Oceans and Seas*, A/RES/44/225, New York: United Nations, 22 December 1989, available from: digitallibrary.un.org/record/82553?ln=en.

Vakasukawaqa, Arieta, 'Ratu Inoke Proposes Biketawa Plus After Regional, Global Security Trends', *Fiji Sun Online*, 12 August 2017, available from: fiji sun.com.fj/2017/08/12/ratu-inoke-proposes-biketawa-plus-after-regional-global-security-trends/.

Van Dyke, Jon, and Carolyn Nicol, 'US Tuna Policy: A Reluctant Acceptance of the International Norm', in David J. Doulman, ed., *Tuna Issues and Perspectives in the Pacific Islands Region*, Honolulu: East–West Center, 1987, pp. 105–32.

Wainwright, Elsina, *Our Failing Neighbour: Australia and the Future of Solomon Islands*, Canberra: Australian Strategic Policy Institute, 10 June 2003.

Ward, John M., *British Policy in the South Pacific*, Sydney: Australasian Publishing Co., 1948.

Ward, R.G., 'Report on South Pacific Commission Conference', Unpublished report, Canberra, 1972.

Ward, R.G., 'Report on the Thirteenth South Pacific Conference, Guam and a Visit to Manila, September 1973', Unpublished report, Canberra, 1973.

Watt, Alan, *The Evolution of Australian Foreign Policy 1938–1965*, Cambridge: Cambridge University Press, 1968.

Whyte, Sally, 'Australia Must Step Up if China Starts Military Build Up in Vanuatu', *Sydney Morning Herald*, 10 April 2018.

World Bank, *Pacific Island Economies: Towards Higher Growth in the 1990s*, Washington, DC: The World Bank, 1991.

World Bank, *Pacific Island Economies: Toward Efficient and Sustainable Growth. Volume 1: Overview*, Report No. 11351-EAP, Washington, DC: The World Bank, 8 March 1993.

Wroe, David, 'China Eyes Vanuatu Military Base in Plan with Global Ramifications', *Sydney Morning Herald*, 9 April 2018.

Wroe, David, 'Australia Will Compete with China to Save Pacific Sovereignty, Says Bishop', *Sydney Morning Herald*, 18 June 2018.

Wyatt-Walter, Andrew, 'Regionalism, Globalization, and World Economic Order', in Louise Fawcett and Andrew Hurrell, eds, *Regionalism in World Politics: Regional Organization and International Order*, Oxford: Oxford University Press, 1995, pp. 74–121.

Young, Audrey, 'Clark Leads at Pacific Islands Forum', *New Zealand Herald*, 26 October 2000.

Young, John M.R., ed., *Australia's Pacific Frontier: Economic and Cultural Expansion into the Pacific, 1795–1885*, Melbourne: Cassell Australia, 1967.

Index

Abbott, Tony 283, 284, 322
Acharya, Amitav 28, 29, 37
Africa 7, 103, 137, 253
    economic association 116, 133,
        193, 206, 243
    regionalism 24, 26, 28
African, Caribbean and Pacific group
    243, 289
    see also Pacific members of the
        African, Caribbean and Pacific
        group
African, Caribbean and Pacific Group
    Council of Ministers 206
Against Testing on Mururoa (ATOM)
    147, 148
Ahnon, Eluida 84
Air Nauru 200
Air New Zealand 200
Air Niugini 201
Air Pacific 135, 191, 200–2, 203, 204
Aisi, Frank 84, 87n.35
Aitutaki Declaration on Regional
    Security Cooperation 253, 255,
    313
Alliance of Small Island States
    (AOSIS) 280, 295, 325
America, *see* Latin America, North
    America, United States
American Samoa 12, 55, 57, 58,
    77n.2, 78, 82, 83, 88n.37, 105,
    157, 161–2, 166
Amnesty International 34, 40, 41

Anapu, Faipule 83
Anderson, Benedict 29, 142
annexation, of Pacific 52, 54
    by Australia 53
    by Britain 48, 49–50, 51n.27,
        53, 55
    by France 48, 53, 54
    by Germany 48, 53
    by Japan 53
    by Netherlands 53
    by New Zealand 51n.26, 53
    by Spain 53
    by United States 53
    see also colonisation
anticolonial movements 7, 96, 123,
    126, 141
anticolonialism 7, 19, 68, 85, 94, 95,
    96, 104, 123, 126, 140, 141, 151,
    156–60, 163, 165, 183, 186
    countering 68, 85, 94, 183
    debates over 141, 151, 165
    and 'Pacific way' 163
    promotion of 183, 186
    see also decolonisation
antinuclear movement 147, 149, 152,
    178–9, 182
    in Australia 147, 149, 152
    church groups 145, 146, 147, 148
    in Europe 178, 179
    framing of Pacific 20, 187–8
    and 'Pacific way' 163
    as participants in regional debate
        141–2

as postcolonial response 126, 147,
148, 165
see also nuclear issues, nuclear
testing
Anzac Pact 62, 67, 69, 70, 96
ANZUS (Australia, New Zealand,
United States) 171, 173, 178,
180, 181, 182
and Cold War regional order 130,
168, 173–4
crisis 167, 169, 177, 178, 179,
180, 183
Apia 112, 135, 255, 261, 264, 300
Aqorau, Dr Transform 289
'arc of crisis' 253, 254
'archipelagic principle' 208–9
Ardern, Jacinda 268, 322
Ariki, Makea Nui Teremoana 83
Ariki, Rongomatane 83
Asia 25, 36, 37, 40, 59, 63, 98, 137,
221, 295
Asia-Pacific 41, 288, 295, 318
Asia-Pacific Economic Cooperation
(APEC) 25
Asian 26, 28, 85, 288
Asian Development Bank (ADB)
130, 233
Asian Financial Crisis 233
Asiatic communism 96, 97, 98
Association of Southeast Asian
Nations 25
Atlantic Charter 65, 67
ATOM, *see* Against Testing on
Mururoa
AusAID 41
Australasia 50, 54, 59–60, 62, 69,
71–2, 129, 251
'Australasian Monroe doctrine' 36,
45, 49–52, 72, 75, 312
Australia 51, 78, 79, 86, 98, 169
antinuclear civil society 147, 149,
152
antinuclear policy 152, 153, 154,
169, 180, 181, 183–4, 187

Anzac Pact 62, 67, 69, 70, 96
'Australasian Monroe doctrine' 45,
50, 51, 72
calls for 'British Pacific' 49, 50–1,
59
climate change policy 271–2, 273,
278, 281–5, 296–7, 301, 302,
313, 320, 322, 323, 325
Cold War framing 98, 126,
129–30, 167–89, 250, 313,
315, 321
colonisation by 48, 53, 56, 57,
58, 137
conflict with Fiji at Pacific Islands
Forum 262, 263, 276, 285,
286–7, 291–3, 296
conflict with global powers 178,
183–4, 188
and creation of South Pacific
Commission 68, 75
criticism of 121–2, 155, 158,
186, 237, 246, 257, 265, 269,
279, 282, 283, 284
decolonisation 127–8, 129
and decolonisation of South
Pacific Commission 117, 118,
121, 135, 309
dominance of South Pacific
Commission 62, 121
and governance breakdown in
Pacific 252, 253, 255, 256,
257, 258–60, 262
inclusion in South Pacific Forum
112, 113, 114, 116, 160, 165,
279
Indigenous 165
intercolonial convention 36, 312
intercolonial cooperation 63, 69
and islander control of
organisations 276, 287–8,
290, 291, 293, 294, 295, 296,
298, 310, 320, 322, 323
and islander political agency 19,
48, 75, 163–4, 166

keeping United Nations at bay
72, 94
labour mobility 245
and 'native welfare' 66, 67, 68,
69, 70, 72, 75
and neoliberalism 189, 217–47,
281, 319
nuclear policy 20, 181, 182, 315
at Pacific Islands Forum 234–6,
237, 246, 278, 280, 282, 291,
294, 297–8, 302
Pacific Security College 272
as part of Pacific 12, 13, 99, 325
policy on China 21, 265, 266–70,
272, 273, 274, 314, 319, 323,
324, 325
policy on waste dumping 154, 155
postwar framing 60, 61–2, 63,
71–2, 82
push for regional cooperation
70–1, 72
push for regional norms 14, 20
and regional crime 249, 250–2,
257, 261
and regional development 70,
173–5, 222, 233, 267–8
as regional hegemon 36, 164,
247, 273, 306, 309, 311–12,
313, 314, 317, 318–19, 320,
322, 323, 324–5
regional security cooperation 252,
253, 257, 272
regional security framing 20, 21,
69–70, 137, 166, 249, 252,
261
regional transport 200, 201, 203
and reinscription of New
Caledonia 159, 183, 188
relations with Nauru 84, 101,
103, 115, 263, 282
relations with Papua New Guinea
88, 89–90, 91, 93, 125, 127,
207, 262, 263, 269, 272, 273,
292

resistance to decolonisation 94,
101, 157
at South Pacific Bureau for
Economic Co-operation 136
at South Pacific Commission 85,
92, 136
at South Pacific Forum 125, 131,
136, 137, 175, 226, 229, 233,
277–8, 321
and Soviet engagement 171, 172,
173, 174–6, 177, 180, 183,
188, 250
'strategic denial' policy 176–8,
180, 187–9, 250, 265, 267,
268, 270, 272, 273, 313–14,
319
support for self-determination 65,
67, 68, 94, 101, 104, 156, 166
thinking about Pacific islanders
85, 93
trade with Pacific 194, 199, 207–8,
215, 222, 231, 241, 242–3,
244, 245–6, 279, 289, 318
as US ally 36, 173, 182, 184, 213,
268
see also Anzac Pact, ANZUS,
Canberra Agreement
Australian Climate Change Authority
283
Australian Climate Commission 284
Australian Federal Police 250, 261
Australian Seasonal Worker Program
245
Ayoob, Mohammed 27, 126n.2, 131,
138

Bainimarama, Frank 261, 262, 285,
286, 291, 292, 324
Baker, Nicola 255, 259
Ball, M. Margaret 114
Banks, Joseph 46
Batley, James 266, 270
Bavadra, Timoci 189
Belade, Michael 84

Belgium 206
Biketawa Declaration 253–57, 258, 259, 260, 261, 262, 263, 264, 273, 313
Biketawa Plus 250, 260, 264, 270, 272, 274
Bikini Atoll 155, 169, 170
Bilney, Gordon 226, 227, 228
Bishop, Julie 265, 267, 268, 291
Bismarck, Otto von 36, 50n.19, 75, 312
'Blue Pacific' ideology xi, 298, 300, 301, 302, 310, 325
Boe Declaration 271, 272, 273, 302, 314, 319, 323
Bouanaoue, Raphael 85
Bougainville 137, 198, 252, 262
Britain 48, 71, 72, 130, 178, 200, 267
    administration policy 49–50, 56
    approach to colonialism 52, 53
    Cold War policy 167, 168, 170, 180, 184, 187, 315
    colonisation by 49, 50n.19, 101, 137
    decline of influence 71, 170, 171
    decolonisation 103, 125, 127, 128, 129, 156
    diplomacy 267–8
    in Fiji 53, 54, 57, 103, 127, 142
    Government 49, 50, 51, 59, 142, 178, 183, 188
    indirect rule 52, 53
    lawlessness of subjects 49, 54
    and neoliberalism 217
    nuclear testing 101, 155, 168, 169, 170, 182, 184, 315
    and Orientalism 32
    protectorates 12, 54, 56, 127
    regional associations 57, 58, 59
    regionalism 59–60, 183, 187, 188
    relations with other powers 55, 63, 69, 71, 72
    settlers 49, 54, 56, 57, 59

    and South Pacific Commission 61, 62, 67, 72, 75, 82, 94, 107, 116, 120, 135, 136
    and sovereignty 49–51, 54
    territories 12, 54–6, 57, 58, 63n.11, 67, 82, 127–8, 170, 171
    waste dumping 154
    see also annexation, of Pacific—by Britain, Australia—calls for 'British Pacific' 49, 50–1, 59
British Colonial Service 94
British Overseas Airways Corporation (BOAC) 200
'British Pacific' 56, 59, 60, 87n.35
British Settlements Act (1887) 56
British Solomon Islands Protectorate 56, 77n.2, 84, 87n.35, 105, 200
    see also Solomon Islands
Brussels 206, 242, 243
Bugotu, Francis 198
Buksh, Mirza Salim 83
Bull, Hedley 27, 126n.2, 131
Burton, Reverend Dr John Wear 65, 79, 85, 92, 94, 95
Bury, Leslie 114
Bush, George H.W. 155

Cairns Compact on Strengthening Development Co-ordination in the Pacific 239, 240
Cairo Conference 71
Cakobau, Ratu Edward 83, 85, 87n.35
Cakobau, Ratu Seru Epenisa 54
Campaign against Foreign Military Activities in New Zealand 147
Campaign for Nuclear Disarmament New Zealand 147
Canada 25, 130, 284
Canberra Agreement 62, 63n.10, 64, 74, 108, 111, 117, 118, 120, 121
Carew-Reid, Jeremy 10

Caribbean 7, 68, 116, 193, 206, 221, 243, 289
  see also African, Caribbean and Pacific group
Caroline Islands 16, 53
Central Medical School 14, 44, 56, 63, 84, 87n.35, 100
Centre d'expérimentation du Pacifique 169
Chamoro 170
Chan, Sir Julius 235
chiefly power 164
chiefs
  American Samoa 83
  Cook Islands 83, 115
  Fiji Council of 53
  Fijian 54, 87n.35, 115
  Melanesian 226
  Nauru 115
  Polynesian 18
  Tongan 53, 87n.35, 115
  treaties with 54
  Western Samoa 115
Chile 13
China 98, 129, 130, 271
  Australian policy on 21, 265, 266–70, 272, 273, 274, 314, 319, 323, 324, 325
  competition with Soviet Union/ Russia 129, 175
  diplomatic links 128, 172
  economic assistance to Pacific 128, 265, 266, 268–9, 274
  engagement with Fiji 129, 273, 287, 288
  engagement with Papua New Guinea 269, 272, 273
  engagement with Samoa 129, 265, 269, 273
  engagement with Tonga 269
  engagement with Vanuatu 266–7, 268, 269, 272, 274
  influence of 265, 267, 274, 312
  interest in Pacific 40, 126, 178

  military presence in Pacific 265, 266, 267, 268–9, 274
  New Zealand policy on 266, 268, 269, 270, 271, 274, 319
  as Pacific actor 71, 129
  Pacific Islands Forum policy on 270, 314
  Pacific islands support for 269, 273, 287, 288, 319, 324
  rise of 315, 321, 323
  as security threat 21, 172, 250, 265, 266, 268, 270
  US policy on 266, 268, 270
Chirac, Jacques 159, 183
Christianity 33, 79n.9, 84, 86, 141, 145, 146
  antinuclear movement 146, 147, 148
  attitudes to 'natives' 47, 48, 75
  in civil society 126, 141, 145, 148, 154, 187
  conversion 53
  evangelism 43, 44, 45, 46, 47, 48
  interchurch organisations 145–6
  Pacific embrace of 53, 126, 141
  and regional development 187, 224
  and regionalism 1, 144, 146
Christmas Island (Kiritimati) 155, 169, 170
Clark, Helen 235, 255, 256, 259, 260
Claxton, Karl 251
climate change 264, 271, 274, 279, 324
  Australian policy on 271–2, 273, 278, 281–5, 296–7, 301, 302, 313, 320, 322, 323, 325
  and Nauru 282
  New Zealand policy on 282–3, 296–7, 320, 322
  Pacific framing of 21, 250, 281–2, 284, 286, 287, 302, 308
  Pacific Islands Forum policy on 270, 279, 280–2, 284, 301, 320

Pacific leadership on 275, 276, 295, 296, 297, 311, 315, 319–20, 323
policy 21, 283, 290, 295, 296, 297, 302, 308, 309, 313, 315–20
as security threat 270, 271, 301, 319
US policy on 301
see also Boe declaration, Copenhagen climate summit, Kyoto climate conference, Paris climate summit, United Nations Framework Convention on Climate Change
Clodumar, Kinza 282
Cold War 19, 39, 101, 323
Australian policy 98, 126, 130, 167, 171, 174, 177, 180, 184, 273, 313, 321
framing of Pacific 130, 150
New Zealand policy 126, 130, 167, 171, 180, 273, 321
rivalry 129, 167, 217
role in regionalism 7, 31, 315, 321
'second' 164, 278
and security management 7, 127, 129, 166, 167–89, 265, 267, 268, 269, 270, 274, 315
thinking 99, 130, 170, 176–9
US policy 126, 130, 180, 184
see also post–Cold War era
colonial
administration 40, 44, 52
boundaries 99, 102
diplomacy 316–17
dominance of organisations 65, 72–3, 101, 115, 116, 122, 137, 166
economies 192, 193, 200, 203, 206, 224
expansion 40

imagining of Pacific 1, 9, 17
institutions 14
intrusion 11, 102, 138
policies 18, 33, 53, 67, 180, 183
press 18
region-building 2, 18, 26, 39, 61–76, 192, 277, 305, 307, 309, 312
regional framing 33
sovereignty 51, 170
structures, control of 19
see also anticolonialism, neocolonial, postcolonial, precolonial
colonial powers 6–7, 40, 103, 126
approaches of 52
challenge to 14, 18, 74, 102, 106–7, 118, 137, 138, 156, 157, 165, 166, 321
cooperation between 58, 59, 60, 61–3
divestment 94, 97, 99, 125, 127, 128, 129
colonialism 6–7, 91, 149, 314, 315
aims of 39
centrality in regionalism 7
criticism of 95
'culture' of 39, 44, 138
engagement with Pacific 8, 316
'fatal impact' of 38, 39
indigenous participation in 68
interruption of indigenous regionalism 15, 16, 138, 140
and maintenance of control 18, 40, 81, 101, 104, 322
and 'native welfare' 65, 97, 192
and nuclear testing 147–8, 187
and Orientalism 32
Pacific as locus of power of 7, 39
perpetual 99
region-building 31, 82
restrictions on mobility 99, 100
see also neocolonial

colonisation 158
  by Australia 48, 53, 56, 57, 58, 137
  of Australia 49, 50–1, 59
  by Britain 49, 50n.19, 101, 137
  European 49, 87, 91
  French approach to 52, 72, 180, 187
  of Melanesia 11
  of Micronesia 52, 55, 103
  of Nauru 55
  of New Caledonia 52, 54, 55, 183–4
  of New Hebrides 51, 55
  by New Zealand 48, 51, 52, 53, 56, 57, 71n.45, 101
  of New Zealand 49, 50–1
  of Pacific 11, 45, 48, 50–1, 141
  of Papua New Guinea 51, 53, 55
  of Samoa 51n.27, 53, 55–6
  and United Nations 65–6, 68
  by United States 17, 52, 53, 55, 68, 101, 104
  see also annexation—of Pacific, decolonisation
Committee of Representatives of Participating Governments (CRPG) 119, 120, 121, 122
Committee on Small Island States 137
Commonwealth 113, 128, 143, 185, 206, 214, 267
'Commonwealth club' 133, 137
Commonwealth Heads of Government Regional Meeting 196
Commonwealth of the Northern Mariana Islands 12
Commonwealth Prime Ministers' Conference 113, 114, 115
Commonwealth Secretariat 195
Commonwealth Secretary-General 196

Congress for International Cooperation and Disarmament of Australia 147
Convention for the Prohibition of Fishing with Long Driftnets in the South Pacific (Wellington Convention) 137, 214
Convention for the Protection of the Natural Resources and Environment of the South Pacific Region 137, 154
Convention on the Law of the Sea 126, 128, 130, 208–9, 210, 213, 318, 321
conventions
  European with Pacific 194, 207, 243
  intercolonial 36, 50, 312
  on nuclear issues 2
  regional 2, 117, 201, 210, 211, 213
  see also Lomé Convention, London Dumping Convention, United Nations Convention Against Illicit Trafficking in Narcotic Drugs and Psychotropic Substances, United Nations Framework Convention on Climate Change, Yaoundé Convention
Cook Islands 55, 57, 69, 134, 192, 269, 286
  associated statehood 12, 104, 123, 131
  and Pacific Islands Producers' Association 110
  politics 115, 228
  self-determination 163
  self-government 103
  at South Pacific Conference 77n.2, 82, 83, 91, 102, 118
  at South Pacific Forum 114, 232
Cook Islands Producers' Association 83

Cook, Captain James 15, 43, 45,
    46, 48
Copenhagen climate summit 282,
    283
Cotton, Robert 172, 235
Council of Regional Organisations in
    the Pacific (CROP) 233, 290
coups 40
    'Bayonet' (Hawai`i) 17
    Fiji (1987) 137, 186, 252, 255,
        257
    Fiji (2000) 262
    Fiji (2006) 261, 262
    'President's' (Vanuatu) 252
    Solomon Islands 254, 255
Crocombe, Ron 10, 144, 198
Customs Heads of Administration
    Regional Meeting 252

Dagabwinare, Jacob 84
Darwinism 31, 40, 44, 48, 315, 321
Davis, Dr Tom 83, 163
de Balboa, Vasco Núñez 62n.1
de Bougainville, Louis Antoine 15,
    43, 45, 46
de Brum, Tony 283
decolonisation 67n.30, 103
    Australian 127, 129
    British 128
    British policy on 103, 127
    and Christianity 141, 145, 146
    and civil society 149, 166
    experience of 18, 104, 138, 141
    indigenous agency over 279, 287,
        290, 302, 307–8, 318
    New Zealand 128, 129
    and nuclear testing 148
    pace of 127, 160
    of Pacific 110, 126, 133, 137,
        143, 171
    Pacific Islands Forum position
        on 12
    of Pacific knowledge 11
    of Pacific studies 41
    and political change 19
    regional networks 100
    regional norms 19, 31, 130
    and self-determination 103, 123,
        138
    of South Pacific Commission 18,
        110, 115, 117–22
    and South Pacific Forum 136,
        137, 279
    support for 14, 146, 156, 157–8,
        165, 166
    and University of the South
        Pacific 143
    see also anticolonialism,
        colonisation, postcolonial,
        United Nations Special
        Committee on Decolonization
Deo, Pandit Vishnu 83
DeRoburt, Hammer 113, 114, 115,
    143
Deutsch, Karl 24
Development Alternatives with
    Women for a New Era (DAWN)
    224
distant water fishing nation (DWFN)
    128, 162, 210, 211, 212, 213,
    214, 215, 315
'doomsday scenario' 41, 221, 227, 228
Dornan, Matthew 246, 266–7, 294
driftnet fishing 130, 137, 213–15,
    310, 315, 318
Dutch 46, 59, 63, 67n.30, 84,
    88n.37
    see also Netherlands

East Asia 25, 141
Easter Island 13
Eastern Europe 7, 153
Elkin, Adolphus Peter 'A.P.' 65
Ellice Islands 53, 77n.2, 83, 88n.37
    see also Gilbert and Ellice Islands
Emberson-Bain, Atu 224, 225
Eminent Persons' Group (EPG) 235,
    236, 237, 238, 262

Enewetak Atoll 155, 169, 170
'Engaging with the Pacific' 263, 285
Engaging with the Pacific Leaders
    (EWTP) 286, 287, 293
Episcopal Conference of the Pacific
    145
Europe 6, 7, 24, 25, 35, 45, 47, 52, 87
    antinuclear movement 178, 179
    conventions with Pacific 194,
        207, 243
    as development model 24, 26, 28
    'idea of' 13, 26, 29, 46
    and Orientalism 32
European
    colonial imperative 47, 48
    colonisation 49, 87, 91
    conceptions of Pacific 1, 9, 15,
        17, 43–8
    economic partnerships with
        Pacific 222, 289, 321
    history 46
    imagination 43, 44, 75, 80
    imperialism 15, 16, 17, 52
    integration 25, 133, 193, 202,
        305, 306–7, 322
    model of power 21, 38
    normative frames 17, 18, 40, 45,
        47–8, 52, 61, 314
    power 15, 47, 99
    racial hierarchy 45, 47, 48, 49,
        56, 86, 93
    regional governance 26, 307, 308
    regionalism 6, 14, 21, 24, 26, 28,
        44, 86, 99, 305, 306–8, 322
    relations with Pacific 8
    society 9
    thinking 1, 9, 17, 38, 46, 47, 93,
        192
    trade with Pacific 194, 207, 231,
        241, 242–6, 247, 318
European Economic Community
    (EEC) 126, 136, 206
European Union (EU) 40, 217, 222,
    231, 233, 241–6, 267, 312, 318,
    321

evangelism, see Christianity—
    evangelism
Evans, Gareth 188, 313
Evatt, Dr Herbert 63, 65, 68, 69, 70,
    71, 94, 96

Fairclough, A.J. 107
Falk, Richard 36, 37
Fangataufa Atoll 104, 126, 129, 155
Far East 32
'fatal impact', see colonialism—'fatal
    impact' of
Federated States of Micronesia 12,
    133, 148, 211
    see also Micronesia
Fiame Mata`afa Faumuina Mulinu`u
    II 143
Fierravanti-Wells, Concetta 265
Fiji 12, 19, 53, 54, 77, 88, 90
    annexation of 53
    'archipelagic principle' 209
    breakdown of governance 252,
        253–4, 261
    British settlers in 57
    centrism 128, 149, 200, 201, 202,
        285, 324
    civil society 145, 146, 147, 148,
        149, 224
    in Committee of Representatives
        of Participating Governments
        120
    conflict with Pacific Islands
        Forum 256, 257, 262
    coup (2000) 254, 262
    coup (2006) 261, 262
    coups (1987) 127, 186, 189, 252,
        254, 255, 257, 262
    and decolonisation of South
        Pacific Commission 102, 105,
        106, 107, 110, 309
    and 'doomsday approach' 228
    economy 192, 199, 206, 319
    engagement with China 129, 273,
        287

engagement with India 287, 288
engagement with Soviet Union/
Russia 128, 129, 171, 287
fishing 209, 210, 211, 215
in G-77 287–8
Government 110, 132, 187, 200,
210, 257, 272, 285
independence 103, 104, 115, 125,
127, 132, 143
Indians in 57, 78, 83, 85, 94, 95,
127
indigenous politics 82
intermarriage in Pacific 16
media 78
medical school 56–7
in Melanesian Spearhead Group
288, 293, 324
nuclear testing policy 113, 147,
152–3
offer of cession 54
and Pacific Islands Development
Forum 286, 287, 291, 293,
298, 324
at Pacific Islands Forum 276, 277,
279, 281, 288, 291, 292, 293
and Pacific Islands Producers'
Association 110
and 'Pacific way' ideology 139,
164
in PACP 289
policy on French decolonisation
157, 159
and Polynesian federation 16, 51
and PSIDS 287, 288
racial conceptions of 88n.37, 89
regional association 113, 165, 205
regional confederation 57, 63
regional criticism of 200, 201,
202, 292
regional institutions 142–3,
200–4, 261, 263, 272
regional relations 87n.35, 114,
139
regional security 69

regionalism 137, 187, 263,
276–7, 285, 286–7, 288,
290–3, 296, 302, 324
relations with Australia 121–2,
276, 279, 291
religion 141, 145, 146
royalty 16, 87n.35
at South Pacific Commission
77n.2, 78, 83, 101, 108, 163
at South Pacific Forum 112, 114,
136, 161–2, 211, 215
and South Pacific Games 74
and Strategic Framework for
Change 285
suspension from Pacific Islands
Forum 256, 261, 263, 264,
277, 285, 287
tensions with Pacific 19, 114,
137, 161, 169, 294–5, 296,
324
trade 192, 199, 207, 244, 245,
289
and United Nations 132, 139,
153, 157, 162, 211, 288
waste dumping policy 154
Fiji Airways 200
Fiji Council of Chiefs 53
Fiji Council of Churches 147
'Fiji Declaration' 147
Fiji Legislative Council 57, 83, 85
Fiji Trades Union Congress 152
Filipo, Vaovasamanaia 157
Firth, Stewart 170, 256
fishing 2, 128–9, 243
exploitation 166, 210
illegal 185, 272
by Japan 209, 213, 310
management 10, 212
Melanesian agency over 162, 211
and Pacific Islands Forum 289
regional cooperation 10, 272
by South Korea 209, 213
and South Pacific Bureau for
Economic Co-operation 136

and South Pacific Commission
work program 74, 80
and South Pacific Forum 210,
307
Soviet deals 180
Soviet–Kiribati deal 176, 187,
212
Soviet–Tonga deal 171–2
Soviet–Vanuatu deal 176, 187
by Taiwan 209, 213
by United States 186, 209, 213,
310, 318
see also distant water fishing
nation, driftnet fishing, Forum
Fisheries Agency
Forsyth, William D. 10, 85, 92, 94,
106, 113, 114
Forum Economic Ministers Meeting
(FEMM) 230, 231, 232, 233,
234, 241, 313
Forum Fisheries Agency (FFA) 135,
136, 162, 211–12, 213, 215, 290,
312
Forum Foreign Ministers Meeting
(FFMM) 255, 259, 264, 313
Forum Island Countries (FICs) 239,
252, 289, 301
Forum Regional Security Committee
(FRSC) 137, 249, 251, 252, 255,
259, 273
France 51, 85, 153, 169, 178, 183,
206
annexation by 48, 53, 54, 55
approach to colonisation 52, 72,
180, 187
and 'Australasian Monroe
doctrine' 50
bombing of Rainbow Warrior 153
Cold War framing 167, 168, 169,
170, 178, 180, 187, 188, 315,
321
colonial imperative 101, 104, 129
constraint on self-determination
103, 156, 157, 170

contest over political agency 75,
160–1, 163, 167, 168
contribution to South Pacific
Commission 62, 109
cooperation with metropolitan
powers 55, 58, 59, 61, 63, 69
decolonisation 128, 137, 156,
157, 158, 159, 183–4
dialogue with South Pacific
Forum 130
exclusion from South Pacific
Commission 116
exertion of influence 167, 168,
312
framing of Pacific 61, 75
Government 152, 153, 159, 160,
183, 184
nuclear testing 111, 113, 126,
129, 130, 133, 146, 152–3,
155, 168–9, 170, 180, 182,
184, 187, 315
and Orientalism 32, 45
Pacific criticism of 118, 158
Pacific territories 12, 55, 127,
128, 160, 165, 170
regional security 178, 182, 187
relations with Australia 178, 180,
183–4, 187
and South Pacific Commission
61, 62, 67, 75, 82, 117, 120,
135, 136, 163
waste dumping 154
see also French Oceania, French
Polynesia
Fraser, Malcolm 174, 176
Fraser, Peter 65, 69
Frater, Reverend M. 65
Freeston, Sir Brian 77, 79, 92
French Oceania 61, 77, 82, 88n.37
French Polynesia 12, 52, 55, 123,
149, 157, 166, 183, 303, 319
nuclear testing in 12, 104, 129,
152, 153, 169, 170

Front de Libération Nationale Kanak et Socialiste (Kanak and Socialist National Liberation Front) (FLNKS) 159, 160, 177

G-77, *see* Group of 77
Gadabu, Raymond 84
Gamble, Andrew 29, 30, 35
Ganilau, Ratu Sir Penaia 201
Gavera, Miria 84
Gavera, Willie 84
George, Dr Nicole 29, 281n.9
Germany 35, 36, 48, 50–1, 52, 53, 54–5, 56, 155–6
Gilbert and Ellice Islands 56, 57, 83, 105, 110, 118, 127, 169, 200
    see also Ellice Islands
Gilbert Islands 53, 77n.2, 84, 88, 206
    see also Gilbert and Ellice Islands, Kiribati
Gina, Reverend Belshazzar 84
Goff, Phil 255
Greenpeace 34, 40, 41, 153, 214
Grenada crisis 167, 179, 185
Grey, George 51n.26
Gribble, Reverend C.F. 86
Group of 77 (G-77) 280, 287–8, 295, 325
Grynberg, Roman 239, 279
Gu'u, Aisa 84
Guadalcanal 254
Guam 12, 55, 123, 129, 157, 166, 169, 170, 214
Gunther, Dr John 89, 93
Gusmão, Xanana 286

Haas, Ernst 24
Hau`ofa, Epeli 3, 10, 11, 15, 16, 33, 144, 300, 309
Havea, Sione 145
Hawai`i 13, 16–17, 46, 123, 135, 142, 148, 149, 155, 157, 165, 169
Hawke, Bob 155, 182

Hawkesworth, John 45, 46, 48
Hayden, Bill 177, 188
Henry, Albert 83, 110, 114, 115, 232
Henry, Sir Geoffrey 228
Herr, Richard 10, 57
Higher Education Mission to the South Pacific 142
Holyoake, Sir Keith 113, 116
Honiara Declaration on Law Enforcement Cooperation 252, 257, 258
Howard, John 201, 234–5, 255, 256, 258–9
Howe, Kerry 9, 10, 39, 46, 47
Huffer, Elise 237, 238
Hughes, Tony 278

Ielemia, Apisai 283
Inder, Stuart 108, 112, 114
Indian Ocean 13, 221
Indo-Fijian 57, 78, 83, 85, 94, 95, 127
Indonesia 13, 40, 63, 64, 67n.30, 76, 84n.23, 98, 111, 157
Institute of Pacific Studies 143
International Court of Justice 153
International Monetary Fund (IMF) 130, 218, 224, 233
Irian Jaya 253

Japan 12, 36, 58, 251, 321–2
    annexation by 52, 53, 56
    engagement with Pacific 40, 126, 128, 130, 172, 178, 179, 184, 187, 312
    fishing 128–9, 130, 209, 213–14, 215, 310
    Government 154
    waste dumping 130, 140, 146, 152, 154, 318
    World War II 69, 83–4
Jinping, Xi 288
Johnston Atoll 152, 155, 156, 169
Jouwe, Nicolaas 84

Kalsakau, John 84, 87n.35
Kanak 159, 177
Kanak and Socialist National
    Liberation Front, see Front de
    Libération Nationale Kanak et
    Socialiste
Kasiepo, Markus 84
Kassi, George 84
Katzenstein, Peter 5, 28, 35, 36
Kavaliku, Dr Langi 235
Keating, Paul 201, 226
Keesing, Felix 85
Kelesi, Mariano 105
Kenilorea, Peter 175
Key, John 292
Kiki, Albert Maori 118, 133–4
King George Tupou I 17
King George Tupou II 83
King Kalākaua 17
King Kamehameha III 17
King Kamehameha IV 17
King Pomare V 17
King Taufa'ahau Tupou I 53
Kiribati 12, 207, 235, 256, 275,
    284, 324
    decolonisation 125, 127, 133
    fishing 176, 187, 211–12, 213
    governance 128
    at South Pacific Forum 133
    Soviet engagement 176, 178, 187,
        212
    trade 206
    and University of the South
        Pacific 204
    waste dumping 154
    see also Gilbert Islands
Kiritimati, see Christmas Island
Koya, Faiyaz 245
Kubuabola, Ratu Inoke 264
Kuranari Doctrine 184
Kwajalein Atoll 169, 170
Kyoto climate conference 281, 282

La Pérouse, Jean-François de 46
'Lae rebellion' 14, 105–9, 110
Lakatani, Sani 257
Lal, Brij 39
Lambert, Dr S. 56
Lameko, Iosefa 83
Langdon, Robert 106
Lange, David 177, 182
Latin America 24, 26, 193
Law of the Sea, see Convention on the
    Law of the Sea
Legge, J.D. 66
Levi, Noel 230–1
Leymang, Father Gerard 158
Libya 176, 177, 186, 188
Lilo, Gordon 289
Lini, Father Walter 158, 177, 187
Lomé Convention 194, 199, 206,
    207, 243, 318
London Dumping Convention 154
London Missionary Society 145
Lotu Pasifika 146
Louisiade Archipelago 53
Loyalty Islands 85

Maastricht Treaty 25
MacIntyre, Duncan 113
Macmillan, Harold 103
McNicoll, David 81, 88, 92, 93
Maiava Iulai Toma 134
Makogai Leper Colony 44, 63n.11
Malaita 254
Malaitan Eagle Force 254
Malekula 44
Malietoa Laupepa 17
Malietoa Tanumafili II 83
Maou Djoel 84
Mara, Ratu Sir Kamisese 113, 115,
    202, 207
    call for 'Pacific voice' 132
    and decolonisation of South Pacific
        Commission 105, 106, 107,
        108, 109, 115, 117, 119, 120
    and Pacific Group Secretariat 206

and Pacific Islands Producers'
Association 110, 115
'Pacific way' 10, 138, 139
reflections on South Pacific
Commission 101–2, 138
and regional identity 14, 16
and regional institutions 201,
202, 204
relations with Papua New Guinea
139, 161
at South Pacific Forum 112, 113,
114, 116, 207, 279
at United Nations 132, 138
Maraj, Dr James 143, 204
Marianas Trench 140, 152
Marquesas 54
Marshall Islands 12, 53, 133, 169,
170, 211, 232, 283
Matignon Accords 160
Matsutaro, Xavier 284
Maude, Harry 73, 74, 86, 94, 97
Melanesia 12, 46, 100, 139, 157
colonisation 11
decolonisation 133, 157, 159
'doomsday scenario' 227
as European construct 8, 49, 51
fishing 162–3
land tenure 226
'Nauru Group' 212
nuclear testing 169, 315
political development 84, 88, 166
racial conceptions of 88, 89, 91, 93
regionalism 18, 74, 78
socialism 175
at South Pacific Forum 133, 139,
159
trade 288
Melanesian
identity 166, 183
–Polynesian divide 81, 87n.35,
88, 89–90, 162, 169
Melanesian Spearhead Group (MSG)
160, 183, 263, 288, 290, 293m
295, 324

Methodist Overseas Mission 65,
79n.9, 86
Meti, Laufo 109
Micronesia 8, 12, 52, 55, 129, 267
colonisation 52, 55, 103
cultural division of 49, 88, 89
decolonisation 133, 149, 166
as European construct 8, 49, 89
governance of 55, 103, 131, 245
'Nauru Group' 211
regional recognition 131
regional relations 74, 78, 295
regionalism 74, 78, 88, 295
at South Pacific Forum 133
United States in 103, 129, 245
see also Federated States of
Micronesia
Micronesian Chief Executives'
Summit 290
Micronesian Presidents' Summit 290
Millennium Development Goals
(MDGs) 233, 234, 239, 240,
241, 247
Misimosa, Afioga 109
Mitterrand, François 153
Modi, Narendra 288
Momis, Father John 163, 198
Morauta, Sir Mekere 227
Morauta Review 240–1, 280, 295,
298, 299
Morgan, Wesley 244, 246
Morrison, Scott 322
Moruroa Atoll 104, 126, 129, 133,
152–3, 155, 169, 184
MSG, see Melanesian Spearhead
Group
Muller, Phillip 215
Munro, Doug 57, 100n.76

Naidu, Vijay 147
Nakasone, Yasuhiro 154
Nandan, S.N. 209
Nasilivata, Livai 121–2
Nasinu conference (1950) 18,
77–100

Nasinu Teachers' Training College 18, 63n.11, 77
Nasonini Declaration on Regional Security 257
Nauru 12, 119, 143, 263, 270, 272, 273, 301
  climate change 282
  colonisation 55
  declaration 210
  decolonisation 103, 104, 127
  and decolonisation of South Pacific Commission 102
  fishing 210, 211–12
  labelling of 88n.37
  phosphate mining 101, 103, 192
  recognition of Taiwan 129
  regional associations 113, 114, 115
  regional transport 200, 203, 204
  at South Pacific Commission 77n.2, 84, 88
  at South Pacific Forum 133, 211, 282
  and United Nations 131
  waste dumping 154
  World War II 84
  see also Parties to the Nauru Agreement (PNA)
'Nauru Group' 211–12, 289
Neemia, Uentabo 10
Nena, Jacob 232
neoclassicism 44, 46, 221, 222
neocolonial 32, 138, 145, 197, 198
  see also colonialism
neofunctionalism 24, 202
neoliberal economics
  ascendancy of 216, 217–47
  failure of 232–3, 242, 245, 247
  and framing of Pacific 40, 189, 218, 220, 231, 234, 247, 255, 315, 321
  free-trade negotiations 194, 245
  globalisation of 26, 31, 35, 37
  imposition of 11, 20, 189, 249, 313

  promotion of 278, 281, 319
  regionalism as response to 6, 31, 37
  resistance to 226, 232–3, 240, 243, 247, 316, 319
neoliberalism 193, 219, 220
Netherlands, the 53, 61, 62, 63, 69, 72, 75, 82, 84, 101
  see also Dutch
Netherlands East Indies 67n.30
Netherlands New Guinea 61, 63, 64, 77, 84, 93, 97, 111
Nettre, M. 111
Neumann, Iver 28, 29
New Britain 53, 55, 69
New Caledonia 12, 58, 129, 146
  Australian support for decolonisation of 159, 166, 180, 183
  colonisation 52, 54, 55, 183–4
  decolonisation 12, 123, 149, 157, 159–60, 166, 183
  Government 95, 183
  links with Libya 177
  at Pacific Islands Forum 303
  regional framing 63, 69
  reinscription of 159–60, 183, 188
  at South Pacific Commission 77n.2, 84–5
  at South Pacific Forum 159, 177
New Hebrides 57, 84, 87n.35
  colonisation 51, 55
  decolonisation 149, 156, 158
  regional associations 69, 77n.2, 84
  see also Vanuatu
New Ireland 53
New Zealand 12, 49, 50, 78, 84, 90, 96, 99, 110, 115
  Aitutaki Declaration 250–3
  Anzac Pact 62, 69, 96
  ANZUS 130, 167, 168, 169, 171, 173, 177–8, 179–80, 181, 182, 183

'Australasian Monroe doctrine' 45, 49–52, 72, 129–30, 186

Biketawa Declaration 253–7, 259, 262, 263, 273

Canberra Agreement 62, 74

civil society 149, 164

climate change policy 282–3, 296–7, 320, 322

Cold War framing 126, 130, 164, 167, 187, 278, 315, 321

colonisation by 48, 51, 52, 53, 56, 57, 71n.45, 101

conflict with Fiji at Pacific Islands Forum 262, 263, 276, 279, 285, 286, 291, 292–3, 296

connection with Pacific 116

decolonisation 66, 67, 78, 96, 103, 127, 128, 129

engagement with China 266, 268, 269, 270, 271, 274, 319

exclusion from Pacific organisations 290, 293, 310, 320

fishing 213, 214–15

Government 66, 152, 153, 181, 182, 255

indigenous population 142, 148–9, 165

intercolonial organisation 61–2, 63, 68

labour mobility 245

and 'native welfare' 67, 68, 72

and neoliberalism 217, 218, 231, 233, 234, 237, 241, 245, 247, 319

nuclear-free movement 147–9, 152, 153, 154, 168–9, 178, 179–80, 181, 182, 187, 315

and Pacific economic development 197, 217, 222, 229, 233, 236, 295

and Pacific Islands Development Forum 287, 291, 296

at Pacific Islands Forum 234, 235, 237, 246, 255, 260, 262, 278, 280, 282, 290, 291–2, 294, 296, 298, 302

and Pacific Plan 236, 237, 238, 239, 260, 280

and Pacific political agency 19, 75, 113, 166, 271, 317, 322–3

regional associations 58, 59, 65, 68, 70, 71, 82, 83, 112, 113, 290

regional framing 13, 20, 45, 51, 60, 61–2, 142, 164, 187, 218, 306, 309, 312

regional hegemony 306, 309, 312–14, 317, 318, 320, 325

regional security framing 20–1, 70, 71, 137, 171, 180, 183, 184, 185, 187, 188, 249, 255, 273, 274, 319

regional transport 200, 203

at South Pacific Commission 62, 67, 72, 74, 75, 135, 136

at South Pacific Forum 114, 116, 125, 131, 136, 137, 160, 165, 186, 277, 278, 279

'strategic denial' policy 174–6, 177, 180, 187, 189, 250, 270, 319

support for self-determination 101, 104, 156, 157–8, 159, 166, 170, 183, 187, 309

territories 12, 63n.11, 101, 103, 123, 127, 131

trade with Pacific 194, 199, 206, 207, 208, 222, 231, 241–7, 279, 289

waste dumping 154

New Zealand Recognised Seasonal Employer Scheme 245

Newton Cain, Tess 294

Niue 12, 137, 161, 162n.22, 203, 210, 211
  decolonisation 103, 104, 123, 127, 133
  and decolonisation of South Pacific Commission 102, 110
  at Pacific Islands Forum 257, 261, 286
  at South Pacific Commission 77n.2, 83
  at South Pacific Forum 131, 133
  trade 110
Non-Aligned Movement 159, 174, 287
Norman, Albert 87, 300
North America 25, 251
  see also Canada, United States
North American Free Trade Agreement 25
Nuclear-Free and Independent Pacific movement 13, 148, 164, 165, 166, 182, 187
nuclear-free movement
  in New Zealand 147–9, 152, 153, 154, 168–9, 178, 179–80, 181, 182, 187, 315
Nuclear-Free Pacific Conference 146, 147, 148, 165
nuclear-free zone 153, 169, 178, 188, 315
  Australian support for 153, 166, 180, 181
  New Zealand support for 153, 166, 180
  push for treaty on 147, 149
  see also antinuclear movement, South Pacific Nuclear Free Zone Treaty (Treaty of Rarotonga)
nuclear issues
  Australian position on 20, 181, 182, 315
  conventions on 2

  and imperialism 170, 321
  Polynesian stance on 169, 315
  and regional security 20, 169, 171, 178, 185, 188
  Samoan stance on 113
  South Pacific Forum stance on 136, 152, 153, 155, 181, 182, 229
  and US bases 129, 169
  Vanuatu stance on 158, 182, 187
  see also antinuclear movement
'nuclear playground' 41, 169–71, 321
nuclear testing 152, 155, 169, 281
  Australian opposition to 152, 153, 154, 169, 180, 181, 183–4, 187
  by Britain 101, 155, 168, 169, 170, 182, 184, 315
  and changing global power 39–40, 170
  collective Pacific response to 10, 12, 102, 104, 113, 133, 140, 152, 166, 182, 315
  and colonialism 147–8, 187
  Fijian response to 113, 147, 152–3
  by France 111, 113, 126, 129, 130, 133, 146, 152–3, 155, 168–9, 170, 180, 182, 184, 187, 315
  in French Polynesia 12, 104, 129, 152, 153, 169, 170
  Melanesian stance on 169, 315
  and Pacific agency 104, 182
  political contest over 168–9
  and South Pacific Commission 111, 133
  by United States 101, 129, 146, 155, 168, 169–70, 178, 181–3, 315
nuclear waste dumping 130, 140, 152, 154, 158, 165, 185

O'Neill, Peter 245, 289, 292, 293, 324
Oceania 23, 49, 50, 55, 59, 87, 129, 189
    French Oceania 61, 75, 77, 82, 88n.37
    as regional frame 1, 13, 15, 16, 31, 40–1, 43, 326
Oceanic
    grouping 17, 208, 209
    identity xi, 16, 300, 302, 309
    societies 40
Oceanic Centre for Arts and Culture 15
Office of the Chief Trade Adviser (OCTA) 279, 289, 290
Ogasawara Islands 154
Ogashiwa, Yoko 10
Olewale, Ebia 120, 121, 157, 158
Orient, the 4, 32, 33
Orientalism 32, 33

'Pacific 2010' 220, 226, 227
Pacific Agreement on Closer Economic Relations (PACER) 244
Pacific Agreement on Closer Economic Relations Plus (PACER Plus) 244, 245, 246, 289, 292, 313, 319, 321
Pacific Churches Research Centre 146
Pacific Community 12, 13, 109, 290, 309
Pacific Concerns Resources Center 148
Pacific Conference of Churches 145, 146, 148, 154, 187
Pacific Council of Churches 147
Pacific Forum Line 135, 137, 203, 204
Pacific Fusion Centre 272
Pacific Group Secretariat 206
Pacific Islands Association of Non-Government Organisations 12

Pacific Islands Development Forum (PIDF) 263, 276, 286, 287, 290, 291, 293, 295, 296, 298, 303, 324
Pacific Islands Development Program 135, 136
Pacific Islands Forum (PIF) 251
    2000 communiqué 257
    2000 meeting 255
    2001 meeting 279
    2002 meeting 257
    2003 meeting 233, 235
    2004 special meeting 235, 236, 261
    2005 meeting 236
    2005 review 278, 310
    2007 meeting 262
    2008 meeting 262
    2009 meeting 282
    2015 meeting 284, 296, 320
    2017 communiqué 241
    2017 meeting 264, 300
    2018 meeting 264, 270, 272, 301
    agenda 290, 297–301
    Australia's role in 13, 234, 237, 278, 279, 291–2, 294, 302, 317
    'Blue Pacific' concept 298, 300, 301, 302, 303
    Cairns compact 239
    challenge to primacy of 288, 296
    and China 270, 314
    and climate change 270, 279, 280–2, 284, 301, 320
    criticism of 237, 239, 246
    EPG review of 235–6, 295
    Fiji Joint Working Group 262
    Fiji's return to 291
    fisheries 289
    Forum Regional Security Committee 249, 251
    frustration with 277, 280, 281, 285–7, 289, 293
    and globalisation 246
    hierarchy within 274, 279

and human development 233, 239, 241, 247
and human security 270
independent states as members 12, 303
and Millennium Development Goals 233, 234, 241
New Zealand's role in 13, 234, 237, 278, 279, 291–2, 294, 302, 317
nomenclature 13, 135
Pacific agency within 277–80, 281, 300–3, 320, 322
and Pacific Islands Development Forum 276, 286, 293, 303
'Pacific Plan' 3n.1, 235, 236, 237, 239, 280, 310
and PACP 289
primacy of 290, 293–4, 298, 302
and PSIDS 287, 288, 295, 296, 302, 310, 322
push to exclude Australia and New Zealand 276, 280, 292, 291–2, 296
RAMSI review 260
region-building 234–5
regional norms 249, 280, 299
and state breakdown 255–7, 259–60, 261–4
suspension of Fiji 261, 256–7, 261–2, 263, 264, 277, 285, 287, 289
and Sustainable Development Goals 241
and transnational crime 261
see also South Pacific Forum (SPF)
Pacific Islands Forum Secretariat (PIFS) 2, 229, 239, 243, 260, 279, 289, 290, 295, 297, 310
Pacific Islands Law Officers Meeting 252
Pacific Islands Monthly 57, 58, 80n.17, 86, 97, 106

Pacific Islands Producers' Association (PIPA) 110, 111, 113, 114, 115, 197, 203
Pacific members of the African, Caribbean and Pacific group (PACP) 289, 290
Pacific Network on Globalisation (PANG) 246
Pacific Ocean 12, 15, 16, 43, 53, 62n.1, 64, 128, 158, 210, 321
'Pacific paradox' 41, 219, 227
Pacific Peoples' Action Front 148
Pacific Plan 3n.1, 225, 234–41, 242, 260, 280, 294, 295, 298, 310
Pacific Regional Seminary 145
Pacific Rim 13
Pacific Small Island Developing States (PSIDS) 263, 286–8, 290, 295, 296, 297, 302, 310, 318–19, 320, 322, 324
Pacific Theological College 145, 147
Pacific Trade Union Forum 187
Pacific Transnational Crime Coordination Centre (PTCCC) 261
'Pacific way' 10, 19, 126, 138, 139, 140, 144–5, 163, 164, 192, 197–9, 215, 225, 279, 286, 309, 319
Pacific Women's Association 149, 187
Pacific Women's Conference 148, 164
Paeniu, Bikenibeu 118, 282
Palau 12, 133, 157, 212, 284, 286, 291, 294
Pan Pacific Education and Communication Experiments by Satellite 143
Papua New Guinea (PNG) 12, 14, 66, 76, 105, 143, 177, 235, 298
in 'arc of crisis' 253–4, 258
Australian economic assistance 267, 272, 273
and Bougainville 252, 262
colonisation 51, 53, 55

conflict over South Pacific Forum 161–2, 211
decolonisation 95, 104, 125, 127, 133, 139
and decolonisation of South Pacific Commission 118, 120, 163
and 'doomsday scenario' 227, 228
economy 192, 245, 319
engagement with China 269, 272, 273
governance breakdown 258, 263
in Melanesian Spearhead Group 288, 294–5
in 'Nauru Group' 212
and nuclear-free zone 153
at Pacific Islands Forum 288, 292, 293–4
in PACP 289
racial conceptions of 88, 89, 91, 93
regional aviation 201
regional framing 12, 53, 69
regional networks 16, 140
regionalism 91, 133–4, 139, 161, 289, 324
at South Pacific Commission 77n.2, 84, 88, 89–91, 93, 95, 164
at South Pacific Forum 133–4, 157, 163
support for French decolonisation 157, 183
support for 'Pacific way' 139, 140
trade 206, 207, 244, 245, 319
and transnational crime 261
World War II 69
see also Bougainville, Netherlands New Guinea, West New Guinea
Papua New Guinea Act (1949) 66
Papua New Guinea–Australia Trade and Commercial Regional Agreement 207

Paris Agreement 271, 301
Paris climate summit 283, 284, 287, 295, 296–7, 319, 320
Partial Test Ban Treaty (1963) 169
Parties to the Nauru Agreement (PNA) 289, 290
Pato, Rimbink 269
Payne, Anthony 26, 29, 30, 35, 220
People's Charter for a Nuclear-Free Pacific 148, 164
Peters, Winston 268
Philippines 12, 64
Phillips, Nicola 220
Phoenix Island 53
Piddington, Ken 197, 277
Pierre, Tamarii 134
PIPA, see Pacific Islands Producers' Association
Pitcairn Islands 12, 157
Pōhiva, `Akilisi 292
Polynesia 110–11, 116, 159, 212
  as category 8, 12, 48–9, 88
  contacts with Melanesia 87n.35, 99–100
  decolonisation 133, 166
  nuclear stance 169, 315
  and 'Pacific way' 139, 164
  regional associations 74, 78, 133, 161, 162
  regionalism 18, 163, 295
Polynesian
  confederation 16–17, 51
  –Melanesian divide 81, 87n.35, 88–90, 162–3, 166, 169, 315
Polynesian Airlines 200
Polynesian Leaders' Group 17, 290
Polynesian Leaders' Meeting 296
Port Moresby Declaration 210, 240, 261, 289, 296, 320
Portugal 46, 69
post–Cold War era 6, 20, 31, 39, 217, 220, 249–74
  see also Cold War

postcolonial 7, 36, 116, 152, 160,
171, 174, 191
    authority 9
    economic integration 25, 193,
        220
    economies 192
    global discourse 39, 125, 150,
        161
    imagining of Pacific 1, 6–7, 10,
        33, 80
    politics 27, 123, 125–50, 167
    region-building 2, 27, 41, 61
    regional framing 33, 116
    regional governance 3, 19, 34,
        128, 138, 151, 165
    regionalism 7, 16, 19, 80, 122–3,
        277
    self-determination 160, 161, 162,
        164, 168
    see also decolonisation
precolonial 8, 16
Prince Tuʻipelehake 82, 83, 110, 111,
115
PSIDS, see Pacific Small Island
    Developing States
Puna, Henry 269

Rainbow Warrior 153
Ramsden, Eric 88
RAMSI, see Regional Assistance
    Mission to Solomon Islands
Ranmuthugala, Douglas 250
Rarotonga 83, 137, 201, 204, 282
    see also South Pacific Nuclear
        Free Zone Treaty (Treaty of
        Rarotonga)
Ratieta, Buren 105
Ravai, Joeli 83
Reagan, Ronald 25, 179, 217
Reganvanu, Ralph 266
Regional Assistance Mission to
    Solomon Islands (RAMSI) 259,
    260, 264, 266, 270

Regional Security Committee,
    see Forum Regional Security
    Committee (FRSC)
Regional Trade Committee 137
religion, see Christianity
Remengesau, Thomas 105
Remengesau, Tommy, jr 291
Rex, Robert 83
Robertson, Max 208
Robinson, Charles 173
Robson, Nancy 79, 80n.17, 89
Robson, Robert W. 57, 58, 59, 60,
    86, 89, 91, 97–8
Rocard, Michel 159
Roko Tui Tailevu 83
Rotuma 53
Rudd, Kevin 240, 283
Russia 40, 287
    see also Soviet Union
Ryan, Yasmine 283

Said, Edward 3, 4, 11, 32, 33, 46
St Julian, Charles 17
Salato, Dr Macu 14, 107
Salin, Aisolf 84
Salwai, Charlot 267
Samoa 12, 57, 63, 69, 115, 131, 143,
    145, 204, 261, 268, 324
    antinuclear issues 113
    colonisation 51n.27, 53, 55–6
    decolonisation 66, 94, 95, 103,
        104, 127
    and decolonisation of South
        Pacific Commission 102, 109,
        112, 134
    economy 110, 192
    engagement with China 129, 265,
        269, 273
    European framing of 69, 88, 89
    and Forum Fisheries Agency 162,
        211
    and Pacific Islands Development
        Forum 286, 292, 293
    at Pacific Islands Forum 286, 300

and Polynesian confederation
16–17, 51, 57
regional relations 16, 114, 286,
292
regional transport 200, 201,
203–4
and reinscription of New
Caledonia 157
at South Pacific Bureau for
Economic Co-operation 136,
206
at South Pacific Commission 63,
77n.2, 78, 82–3, 91, 120
at South Pacific Forum 114, 161
Soviet engagement 128, 129, 171
Samoan Council of State 83
Santa Cruz Island 53
Scott, Henry 57
Secretariat of the Pacific Regional
Environment Programme
(SPREP) 136–7
Seddon, Richard 51n.26
Selyaninov, Oleg 172
Senituli, Lopeti 238
Shaw, Timothy 29
Shibuya, Eric 282
Shultz, George 182
Sikivou, S.K. 132, 139
Slatter, Claire 238, 240
Smith, Adam 193
Smith, Bernard 9, 45, 46, 47, 48
Smith, T.R. 10, 67, 73
Söderbaum, Fredrik 28, 29
Solomon Islands 12, 53, 57, 69, 89,
183, 266, 267, 272
British administration 53, 55, 56
decolonisation 125, 127, 133
governance breakdown 253–4,
255
Government 183
and 'Nauru Group' 212
and PACP 289
political agency in 157, 198, 324
'RAMSI Plus' 264

regional intervention in 234–5,
256, 258–9, 260, 261, 263
regional transport 200, 204
at South Pacific Commission
77n.2, 84, 105
at South Pacific Forum 133, 211
Soviet engagement 175, 176
trade 206
World War II 69, 87n.35
see also British Solomon Islands
Protectorate, Regional
Assistance Mission to
Solomon Islands (RAMSI)
Somare, Sir Michael 134, 139–40,
161, 295
Sopoaga, Enele 284, 324
South Asia 103
South Korea 40, 98, 209, 213
South Pacific
'new' 19, 123, 126, 127, 171, 191
see also South Seas
South Pacific Applied Geoscience
Commission 135, 137
South Pacific Bureau for Economic
Co-operation (SPEC) 25, 111
South Pacific Chiefs of Police
Conference 252
South Pacific Colloquium on the
Special Needs of Small States 185
South Pacific Commission (SPC) 87,
94, 106, 115, 172
boundaries of xv, 63, 102, 123,
125, 136, 140, 149, 160
call for reform of 102, 105–6,
108–10, 112, 116, 117–18
as colonial project 75, 122
decolonisation 115–16, 117–22,
163
end of 121, 122
functions of 64, 68, 72, 74, 97,
110, 118–19, 120, 137, 192–3
governance 102, 107–9
history 10, 14, 18, 61–2, 67, 70,
80n.16, 101, 138, 144

and human development 223,
    233, 234
indigenous agency 72, 74, 101–7,
    164, 166
indigenous involvement 65, 87, 97
limitations of 111–13
membership 62, 85, 120–1, 161
'no politics' rule 64, 111, 116,
    133, 136, 152, 214
regionalism 14, 173, 307
renaming of 12, 290, 309
review of 109, 120
and South Pacific Forum 135,
    136, 163, 165–6
see also Pacific Community
South Pacific Conference 97, 98, 137
of 1950 77–81
of 1959 74
of 1962 105
of 1965 14
of 1966 107
of 1967 112
of 1968 108, 112
of 1969 107, 109, 112
of 1971 109
of 1972 112, 117, 118
of 1974 118, 134
of 1975 119
of 1976 120
of 1978 121, 157, 163, 196
of 1979 158
of 1980 164
of 1989 214
of 1994 226
of 1997 309
and decolonisation 14
and economic development 134,
    196, 226
indigenous agency 74, 164, 309
indigenous involvement 65, 119
metropolitan dominance of 122,
    307
'no politics' rule 64, 111, 116,
    133, 136, 152, 214

regional identity 18, 85
as regional project 68, 93
review of 109, 120
structure of 64, 118–19
South Pacific Forum (SPF) 114
1971 communiqué 152
1971 meeting 115, 116, 125,
    131, 133, 194, 209
1974 meeting 201, 204
1975 meeting 153
1976 meeting 172, 210
1977 meeting 210
1978 meeting 161, 162, 207,
    210–11
1979 meeting 157, 158, 211
1981 meeting 175
1983 meeting 153, 181
1986 meeting 159
1990 meeting 155
1992 meeting 252
1994 meeting 222, 223, 224,
    226–27, 228–9, 232
1996 meeting 230
1997 meeting 232, 253, 282
1998 meeting 232
aims for 132, 197
ANZUS support for 173
Australian support for 166, 172
campaign to strengthen 163, 166
as 'Commonwealth club' 137
and decolonisation 126, 136, 161,
    165
and economic engagement 205–7,
    208, 319
exclusion of Papua New Guinea
    161, 162
Fiji at 161, 162
fishing 162, 208–11, 213–15
formation of 19, 102, 111, 112,
    114, 141, 275, 276, 278, 302,
    307
inclusion of Australia and New
    Zealand 116, 160, 165, 279,
    312

and law enforcement 252
membership of 131, 133, 136,
140, 143, 161–2
metropolitan dialogue with 130
and neoliberalism 222, 223, 224,
225, 227, 228, 231, 233
and New Caledonia 157, 158,
159–60, 183
New Zealand support for 114,
166
and nuclear issues 136, 152, 153,
155, 181, 182
and Pacific agency 19, 102, 139,
197, 275, 277–9, 282, 317,
321–2
and 'Pacific way' 139, 197, 205,
225, 309, 319
regional framing 140
regional norms 130, 218
regional policy 135, 141, 186,
199–204, 225, 229
response to 'no politics' rule 112,
136, 152, 322
rituals of 137
security cooperation 253
and self-determination 115–16,
125, 158, 160, 162
and Soviet engagement 172, 175,
177, 250
and SPARTECA 208
and 'strategic denial' policy 175,
250
and sustainable development 222,
223, 224–5, 227, 229, 232
Tarawa Declaration 213
Wellington Convention 214
women 164, 224
see also Pacific Islands Forum
(PIF)
South Pacific Forum Fisheries Agency,
see Forum Fisheries Agency (FFA)
South Pacific Games 74
South Pacific Nuclear Free Zone
Treaty (Treaty of Rarotonga) 137,
154, 182, 313

South Pacific Organisations
Coordinating Committee 135, 163
South Pacific Regional Environment
Program 135, 163, 229
South Pacific Regional Trade
and Economic Co-operation
Agreement (SPARTECA) 194,
199, 207–8, 243, 318
South Pacific Social Sciences
Association 144
South Seas 1, 9, 13, 43–60, 69, 75, 78
regional commission 62, 69, 71,
85, 96
South Seas Conference 61, 68, 77,
82, 96
South-East Asia 7, 13, 28, 29, 49, 61,
64, 75, 76, 98, 103, 116, 133,
251, 253
Soviet Union 174, 179
aid to Pacific 129, 175–6, 217
competition with China 129, 175
countering influence of 20, 170,
171, 173, 180, 183
engagement with Pacific 128–9,
171–3, 186, 188
and fishing access 128, 171, 176,
187, 209, 212
'strategic denial' of 174, 175,
176–7, 178, 187–8, 269, 273
as threat 176, 180, 184n.29,
184n.32, 250
see also Russia
Spain 46, 52, 53
SPARTECA, see South Pacific
Regional Trade and Economic
Co-operation Agreement
Spate, Oskar 9, 15, 48, 99
SPREP, see Secretariat of the
Pacific Regional Environment
Programme
Stead, Henry 57
Sustainable Development Goal
(SDG) 241, 295, 319
Sutherland, William 208, 229, 230,
232

Suva Declaration on Sustainable Human Development in the Pacific 222, 223, 232, 233, 296, 319

Tahiti 12, 16, 17, 18, 44, 45, 46, 48, 49, 77, 97, 158
Taiwan 40, 126, 129, 130, 172, 209, 213, 214
Talagi, Toke 261
Tanna 44, 84
Tarawa Declaration 213–14
Tarte, Sandra 10, 310
Taureka, Reuben 161
Taylor, Dame Meg 297, 298–9, 301, 302
Tekanene, Tutu 84
Teo, Penitala 83
Thomas, Nicholas 39, 44
Timor 63, 69, 253
Timor-Leste 286, 287
Tinian 170
Tito, Teburoro 235, 256
Tokelau 12, 77n.2, 157
Tong, Anote 275, 284, 324
Tonga 12, 53, 57, 63n.11, 131, 204, 268
    and decolonisation of South Pacific Commission 102, 108, 115
    economy 192
    engagement with China 269
    independence 104, 125, 127
    and neocolonialism 198
    and nuclear issues 113, 182, 315
    at Pacific Islands Forum 211, 235, 292
    as part of Polynesia 88, 89
    Polynesian confederation 16, 51
    recognition of Taiwan 129
    regional relations 16–17, 87, 88, 114
    regional trade 110, 113
    regional transport 200–1, 203, 204
    religion 145
    royalty 16, 17, 53, 82, 83, 87, 115, 143
    and South Pacific Bureau for Economic Co-operation 136, 206
    at South Pacific Conference 77n.2, 78, 82, 83, 91
    Soviet engagement 128, 171–3
    and transnational crime 261
Tongan Community Development Trust 238
Townsville Peace Agreement 259
Treaty of Rarotonga, see South Pacific Nuclear Free Zone Treaty
Trump, Donald 285
Trust Territory of the Pacific Islands 55, 105, 169
Tuamotu Archipelago 152
Tufele 83
Tuiasosopo, Mariota 78, 83
Tuilaepa Sailele 265, 269, 292, 293, 300
Tuilovoni, Setareki 145
Tuitele 83
Tungi, Crown Prince 78, 82, 83, 87n.35
Tupouniua, Sione 145, 198
Tupua Tamasese Lealofi IV 112, 113, 114, 115
Tupua Tamasese Mea`ole 78, 83, 110
Tupuola Efi 134, 161
Turnbull, Malcolm 267, 322
Tuvalu 12, 83n.21, 121, 125, 127, 129, 133, 206, 282, 283, 284, 324

Underhill-Sem, Yvonne 238
United Kingdom, see Britain
United Nations (UN) 6, 7, 62, 284, 311
    Asian group at 288, 295
    charter 65
    colonisation 65–6, 68
    CROP working group 233
    decolonisation 68, 95, 102, 103, 103

framing of Pacific 2, 34, 41
General Assembly 132, 138, 153,
    157, 158, 159, 162, 195, 196,
    211, 214, 318–19
and Law of the Sea 126, 128, 130,
    208–9, 210, 213, 318, 321
Millennium Declaration 232
and nuclear-free zone 153
Pacific members of 131–2, 139,
    214
regionalism 20, 35, 75, 214
reinscription of New Caledonia
    157, 159, 183
resistance to 72, 81, 94
resolutions 214
Seabed Committee 209
Secretary-General 252
Security Council 258
special recognition of island states
    195–6, 263, 286, 287–8, 295,
    324
trusteeships 65, 66, 68, 103
United Nations Conference on
    Environment and Development
    (1992) 229
United Nations Conference on Trade
    and Development (UNCTAD)
    195–6
United Nations Convention Against
    Illicit Trafficking in Narcotic
    Drugs and Psychotropic
    Substances 250
United Nations Declaration on the
    Granting of Independence to
    Colonial Countries and Peoples
    103
United Nations Development
    Programme (UNDP) 41, 130,
    196, 222–3, 233, 234, 237, 247
United Nations Environment
    Programme 130
United Nations Framework
    Convention on Climate Change
    (UNFCCC) 282, 297, 318, 319,
    320, 324

United Nations Global Conference
    on Sustainable Development of
    Small Island States (1994) 229
United Nations Special Committee
    on Decolonization (Committee of
    24) 159, 183, 188, 319
United States (US)
    anti-Soviet stance 173, 175, 178,
        180, 183, 184n.32
    Australia and New Zealand as
        agents of 36, 175, 178, 184,
        312–13
    challenge to 130, 187, 318, 321,
        323
    and climate change 301
    Cold War framing 126, 129, 167,
        178, 180–1, 187–8, 315
    colonisation by 17, 52, 53, 55,
        68, 101, 104
    conflict with Australian policy
        154, 169, 178, 181, 182,
        183–4, 188
    conflict with New Zealand 154,
        180, 181–3, 188
    criticism of 117, 155, 186
    decolonisation 67, 157, 166
    engagement with China 266, 268,
        270
    exclusion from South Pacific
        Commission 116
    fishing 162, 186, 209, 211–14,
        310, 318, 323
    framing of Pacific 20, 75
    Government 36, 68
    House of Representatives 214
    imperial norms 52
    imperium 25–6, 36
    influence in Pacific 72, 173, 175,
        312
    and neoliberalism 6, 35, 217, 242
    nuclear testing 101, 129, 146,
        155, 168, 169–70, 178,
        181–3, 315
    and Orientalism 32

regional cooperation 58, 59, 63, 69
regional security 129, 180, 188, 268, 313
regionalism 35, 36, 71
and self-determination 94, 101, 103, 160–1, 170
and South Pacific Commission 61, 62, 63, 64, 75, 76, 85, 94, 135, 136
and South Pacific Forum 130, 137, 163
and South Seas Conference 68, 82
territories 12, 55, 82, 128, 157, 160–1, 165, 245
waste dumping 152, 154, 155–6
see also ANZUS, North America
University of South Pacific (USP) of 2, 15, 126, 135, 137, 142, 143–5, 147, 198, 200, 202, 203, 204, 246, 290, 301

Vanuatu 12, 44, 133, 155, 183, 204, 268, 295
antinuclear movement 158, 182, 187
Australian assistance to 267, 272
as Australian security concern 175, 267
decolonisation 127, 133, 156, 157, 158, 166
engagement with China 266–7, 268, 269, 272, 274
engagement with Libya 177, 188
nonaligned posture 175, 187
'President's coup' 252
Soviet engagement 175, 176, 187
support for New Caledonia 157, 159
see also New Hebrides
Vietnam 175, 179
Voelcker, Colonel F.W. 90, 96
Vogel, Julius 51n.26
Vunibobo, Berenado 162, 211, 309

Wallis and Futuna Islands 12, 55, 157
Walo, Kamono 84
Ward, Eddie 66
Ward, R.G. 117
Washington Consensus 217, 233
Wellington Convention, see Convention for the Prohibition of Fishing with Long Driftnets in the South Pacific (Wellington Convention)
West New Guinea 63, 67n.30, 76
West Papua 13, 18, 123, 142, 149, 157, 165
Western Europe 24
Western Pacific High Commission 14, 44, 53–4, 56, 63n.11, 77, 200
Western Samoa, see Samoa
Williams, Joe 118
World Bank 7, 41, 130, 218, 219, 220, 221, 223, 224, 227, 233, 237, 255, 298
World Trade Organization (WTO) 231, 243, 244
Wroe, David 266

Yaoundé Convention 206
Young Women's Christian Association (YWCA) 147, 149